Harvard Historical Studies · 137

Published under the auspices of the Department of History
from the income of the Paul Revere Frothingham Bequest
Robert Louis Stroock Fund Henry Warren Torrey Fund

Denazification in Soviet-Occupied Germany

BRANDENBURG, 1945–1948

TIMOTHY R. VOGT

HARVARD UNIVERSITY PRESS

Cambridge, Massachusetts, and London, England   2000

Library of Congress Cataloging-in-Publication Data

Vogt, Timothy R., 1958–
    Denazification in Soviet-Occupied Germany : Brandenburg, 1945–1948 /
Timothy R. Vogt.
        p. cm. — (Harvard historical studies ; 137)
    Includes bibliographical references and index.
    ISBN 0-674-00340-3
    1. Brandenburg (Germany)—Politics and government.   2. Denazification.
3. Germany (East)—Politics and government.   4. Soviet Union—Armed forces—
Germany—Brandenburg.   5. Military government—Germany—Brandenburg—
History—20th century.   I. Title.   II. Harvard historical studies ; v. 137.
DD801.B688 V64 2000
940.53'144'094315—dc21   00-057502

For Katie and Daniel

Contents

Acknowledgments

Many colleagues offered insights and advice during the course of my research. At the University of California, Davis, Daniel Brower, F. Roy Willis, and Ted Margadant offered their comments and assistance. A special thanks goes to my dissertation adviser, William Hagen, whose unwavering support and guidance helped to bring this project to a successful conclusion. I am also grateful to Helga Welsh, who read an early excerpt from my research and offered valuable suggestions. My gratitude also extends to the 1993–94 participants in the Stanford-Berkeley German Dissertation Group and to those at the 1994 Harvard Law and Society in Germany conference who gave criticism and advice at the beginning stages of this research. I owe a similar debt of gratitude to the fellows and advisers at the Berlin Program at the Free University.

I would thank the archivists and staff at the Bundesarchiv in Potsdam and Berlin (SAPMO) for their professionalism and collegiality. Thanks also go to the workers at the district archives in Ostprignitz, Ruppin, and Calau for their help and hospitality. Finally, I extend heartfelt gratitude to the wonderful staff at the Brandenburg Landeshauptarchiv in Potsdam, where most of the research for this project was undertaken. The research for this study was funded in part by a pre-dissertation research grant from the Center for German and European Studies and a History Department Graduate Research Fellowship from the University of California, Davis. I also received generous support through a fellowship granted by the Berlin Program for Advanced German and European Studies of the Social Science Research Council and the Free University of Berlin.

Abbreviations

BDM	Bund Deutscher Mädel (League of German Girls)
CDU	Christlich-Demokratische Union Deutschlands (Christian Democratic Union of Germany)
DFB	Demokratischer Frauenbund Deutschlands (German Women's Union)
DVdI	Deutsche Verwaltung des Innern (German Interior Administration)
FDGB	Freier Deutscher Gerwerkschaftsbund (Free German Federation of Unions)
FDJ	Freie Deutsche Jugend (Free German Youth)
FRG	Federal Republic of Germany
GDR	German Democratic Republic
Gestapo	Geheime Staatspolizei (Secret State Police)
HJ	Hitler Jugend (Hitler Youth)
KPD	Kommunistische Partei Deutschlands (Communist Party of Germany)
LDP	Liberal-Demokratische Partei Deutschlands (Liberal Democratic Party of Germany)
NKFD	Nationalkomitee Freies Deutschland (National Committee for a Free Germany)
NSDAP	Nationalsozialistische Deutsche Arbeiterpartei (National Socialist German Workers' Party, the Nazi Party)
NSF	Nationalsozialistische Frauenschaft (National Socialist Women's Organization)
NSFK	Nationalsozialistische Fliegerkorps (National Socialist Aviation Corps)
NSKK	Nationalsozialistische Kraftfahrerkorps (National Socialist Motorized Corps)

NSV	Nationalsozialistische Volkswohlfahrt (National Socialist People's Welfare Association)
PG	Parteigenosse (Party Comrade in the NSDAP)
SA	Sturmabteilung (Storm Troopers)
SD	Sicherheitsdienst (Security Service of the SS)
SED	Sozialistische Einheitspartei Deutschlands (Socialist Unity Party of Germany)
SMA	Soviet Military Administration
SPD	Sozialdemokratische Partei Deutschlands (Social Democratic Party of Germany)
SS	Schutzstaffeln (Protection Squads of the NSDAP)
VdgB	Vereinigung der gegenseitigen Bauernhilfe (Association for Farmers' Mutual Assistance)
VVN	Vereinigung der Verfolgten des Naziregimes (Union of People Persecuted by the Nazi Regime)

Denazification in Soviet-Occupied Germany

Introduction

In early 1948, Walter Ulbricht, leader of the Socialist Unity Party (SED) and most powerful German politician in the Soviet occupation zone, addressed a conference of interior ministers. In his speech he reviewed recent developments that were pushing Germany toward a division into two separate states. Ulbricht argued that the Truman Doctrine, the Marshall Plan, and the unification of the western occupation zones had revealed two opposing ideological views regarding the future of Germany. Western ideology, spearheaded by the United States, was aggressively imperialist and militarist, seeking to "enslave" Germany in a fight against "democracy in Europe." The opposing ideology, championed by the Soviet Union, was aimed at "the unification of Germany and the securing of a just and democratic peace." In Ulbricht's view, the incompatibility of these opposing ideologies meant that the Soviet occupation zone would increasingly follow its own path of political and economic development. Looking back on the major policies implemented in the Soviet zone since the end of the war—denazification, land reform, and expropriation of industry—Ulbricht declared a successful conclusion to the first phase of development in the Soviet zone. This phase was marked by the elimination of vestiges of the Third Reich and the creation of "the foundations of the democratic order." Thus, "One can truly say that now the period of new construction begins."[1]

Later historians in the German Democratic Republic (GDR)

claimed that policies such as denazification had been an integral part of the creation of "antifascist-democratic" East Germany. On the other side of the Cold War divide, western historians argued that Soviet denazification, along with other occupation policies, had actually paved the way for the establishment of a dictatorship. What was the character of the Soviet denazification, how was it implemented, and what were its results? These are the fundamental questions posed by the present study. In seeking answers to them, I also shed light on topics of wider significance for the postwar period: the nature of the incipient East German state, Stalinism and Soviet control in the GDR, and the thorny problem of Germany's postwar confrontation with its Nazi past.

Denazification was a purge of the German government, economy, and society conducted by the occupation powers. The need for such a purge seemed self-evident at the time, not only to punish those who were responsible for the Third Reich's crimes, but also as a prerequisite for reconstruction and insurance that Germany would never again threaten the peace. The problem was how to conduct this purge. In all the occupation zones, denazification turned into a bureaucratic nightmare that bedeviled occupation authorities, hindered reconstruction, and gained the enmity of the German people. As a result, it was eventually abandoned by all the occupation powers. Denazification, broadly defined as a program designed to purge Germany of Nazi influences, proved impossible to achieve.

To argue, however, that denazification in the Soviet zone proved impossible to achieve begs the question of what the Soviets themselves expected to accomplish. First, there was the goal of a complete removal of former members of National Socialist organizations from the government administration. This did not occur, and by the Brandenburg provincial government's own reckoning, many former members of National Socialist organizations remained in the government's employ after the completion of denazification.

Second, the Soviets wanted to use evidence of a far-reaching denazification in their zone as a lever to force concessions from the western occupation powers. The Soviets attempted, for example, in early 1947 to use the issue of denazification to gain increased reparations from the western zones. This tactic did not succeed.

Third, beginning in August 1947, the Soviets and their German allies in the SED launched a massive propaganda campaign to enlist public support for denazification and, it was hoped, to rally support for the SED and its policies in general. This too failed to materialize: widespread public support for denazification never developed, and the SED was handed a sobering indication of its lack of control over its own cadres and the public's antipathy toward the party and its vision of postwar Germany.

Fourth, denazification was supposed to reintegrate former Nazis into society and thus mark a conclusive coming to terms with the Nazi past in the eastern zone. The problem of reintegrating former Nazis was not solved by denazification, however, simply because only a small percentage of them were affected. The abrupt ending of denazification in March 1948 meant that the majority of former Nazis were never touched.

In a way it could be argued that denazification did represent closure of the Nazi past in that the authorities publicly announced that denazification was a success and this issue had been laid to rest. Thereafter, the SED trumpeted the success of Soviet denazification as evidence of the GDR's "antifascist" national character. Those disinclined to ponder the historical, political, philosophical, and moral ramifications of denazification could be content with the SED party line and consign the Nazi period to the past. More recently, however, the post-reunification debate over the GDR's legacy has brought Soviet denazification back into public view. One can now read analyses that dismiss the GDR's "antifascism" as a myth, or brand the GDR as Germany's second "totalitarian" dictatorship, or see East Germany as a state fatally flawed from birth and suffering from a more or less permanent crisis of legitimacy, both internationally and domestically. This debate is occurring against the backdrop of neo-Nazi activity in the eastern *Länder* that calls into question the extent to which denazification represented an adequate coming to terms with the Nazi past in the east.

Thus, in contrast to East German interpretations, the present study makes the argument that Soviet denazification was a failed experiment. This was due, above all, to the fact that a complete denazification was in itself impossible and nowhere brought to a successful conclusion. Can the Soviet denazification be counted a success by any measure? Approximately 500,000 people were purged between the end of the war and the spring of 1948—about 3 percent of the total population in the Soviet zone.[2] It would be fruitless to debate whether or not this number of people represented an adequate or inadequate denazification. Publicly, the authorities would maintain that this number was adequate, but among themselves there was disappointment, not over the raw number of people dismissed, but because denazification had not met its goals.

This study also calls into question western interpretations of Soviet denazification. The most influential interpretive model used by western historians to analyze the Soviet occupation has been the Stalinization model. The Stalinization model assumes that the Soviet Union's major occupation polices, including denazification, were part of an overall implementation of one-party rule in the east. Much of the evidence that appears here calls into question the usefulness of this model. A close examination of denazification in Brandenburg shows that Soviet policy was not a monolithic plan developed in Moscow and ruthlessly implemented in Germany. Instead, it was marked by confusion and indecisiveness and was much more flexible than the Stalinization model would admit. Compounding this confusion were events on the local level where denazification was actually taking place. The Stalinization model holds its interpretative force only when events are viewed from the "top down." My focus on the local level shows that policy was often formed in reaction to local developments, and that policies handed down from the center were frequently implemented in the towns and villages in ways that were unforeseen by the policy makers.

Allied Approaches to Denazification

In their wartime planning, all the Allies agreed that some sort of denazification, broadly conceived, would have to be part of occupation policy. Understanding what Nazism was and how to eradicate it was a central preoccupation for the occupying powers. The Allies eventually settled on an approach that contained both negative and positive features. The negative aspect, in the sense in which the term is used here, was a purge. On the positive side, there was a hope that denazification could transform German hearts and minds in order to ensure that Nazism would never reappear. Thus, the solution to the "German problem" was seen as both punishing those deemed responsible for the war and the crimes of the Third Reich, and eradicating what were seen as the wellsprings of this criminal behavior: the influence of antidemocratic elites, xenophobia, aggressive nationalism, militarism, and the peculiar German attribute of slavish obedience to authority.

It needs to emphasized that none of the Allies were satisfied with the results of their denazification programs. The main difference among them on this issue was that the western occupation powers—France, Britain, and the United States—publicly acknowledged their disappointment. In contrast, the Soviets publicly claimed satisfaction with their success, while privately they too admitted failure. This insight into the private views expressed on the Soviet side has not been a part of previous studies. To date, historians had no access to East German denazification archives and had to content themselves with official Soviet and East German statistics and studies that detailed the efficacy of denazification in the eastern zone. The result can be seen in postwar historiography; where western denazification programs are held up as self-acknowledged failures while the Soviet program, for better or worse, is accepted as efficacious.

Having accepted the success of the Soviet program, western scholars were left to ponder what the true motivations of Soviet policy were. Here is where the influential Stalinization thesis made its mark. It was argued that Soviet denazification was all too efficacious: that is, the Soviets and their supporters aimed at imposing a Stalinist one-party dictatorship in the eastern zone, and they used denazification as a means to achieve this end. In contrast, the redefinition of Soviet denazification proposed in this study argues that, even though the Soviets and their German supporters may well have wanted to use denazification to effect their broader goals, they failed to achieve this ambition. Soviet denazification stripped of its uniqueness vis-à-vis other Allies' programs should be considered comparatively in the context of general Allied policy during the occupation period.

Let us first consider the negative, or purge, element of denazification. The mechanics of the purge were remarkably similar in all occupation zones. These similarities included German-staffed denazification commissions whose decisions were subject to approval by the occupying power; the use of a questionnaire (*Fragebogen*) filled out by all those called before the commissions; the issuing of decisions based on a determination of "active" or "nominal" involvement in the Nazi Party; and punishments including monetary fines, employment restrictions, and dismissal from one's occupation.[3] There were also developmental similarities with the Allied programs: an initial period of rash dismissals, followed by a reassessment and realization of the need for a more long-term approach, and a subsequent codification of guidelines for a further purge with a prominent role assigned to German denazification commissions. There were also similarities in the results of the purges, which included the summoning of tens of thousands of individuals before commissions and a preponderance of "nominal" over "activist" decisions.

In any comparison of the "positive" aspects of the Allied denazification programs, it is necessary to look at their assumptions regarding the nature of German National Socialism. It is axiomatic that an understanding of how the Allies went about solving the "German problem" has to be based on an understanding of their critiques of Nazism. In general terms, all were agreed that there were deep-rooted elements in the German national character which led to the virulent form of National Socialism that appeared in Germany. How Allied denazification programs developed from their critiques of the "German problem" provides a revealing point of comparison for understanding the challenge of postwar denazification.

Having experienced three wars with Germany since 1870, and defeat and occupation during the Second World War, the French were keen to make sure that they would never again suffer German attack. To this end, the French solution to the "German problem" was dominated by demands that would cripple Germany's future war-making potential.[4] For the French, denazification would serve this goal by combining a purge of individuals with a "reeducation" program designed to wean the Germans from Nazism and simultaneously instill in them a sympathy for France and French culture.[5] French policy makers focused on the role of "Prussianism" in the construction of the German mentality. In this view, Prussianism was the hallmark of Germany's special path of historical development that found its ultimate expression in the Third Reich. This situation was redeemable: the French analysis highlighted the existence of "another Germany," one with democratic and pacific tendencies, which, although overwhelmed in the past by bellicose Prussianism, could still be brought to the fore and made the centerpiece of a new German national character. In this quest, French policy makers thought that they would be aided by what they saw as the Germans' remarkable capacity for hard work and their shared conception of duty. The task would be to harness these tendencies and to point the Germans in the right direction.[6] In the end, the French were faced, as were all the Allies, with the impracticability of combining a far-reaching purge with a program to bring about a transformation of the German mentality. Instead, the French eventually settled for extracting themselves from the purge as quickly as possible and hoping their reeducation policies would bear some fruit in the future. On this point it has been argued that the subsequent development of a democratic West Germany friendly toward France may, in hindsight, be seen in part as a successful result of French policy.[7] Conversely, the failings of the French program and its ultimate unraveling have also been interpreted as allowing the Germans to avoid a meaningful coming to terms with the Nazi past.[8]

Of the four occupation powers, the British have been seen as the least interested in a far-reaching, punitive purge and the most interested in pursuing a transformation of German hearts and minds through reeducation. Like the French, the British analysis of the "German problem" centered on the negative tradition of "Prussian militarism" and its role in making Germany the primary source of aggression in recent European history. It has been argued that British policy makers early on rejected the "witch-hunt" approach championed by the Americans and Soviets, seeking instead "to go for the mind instead of the body."[9] While the British have been credited with developing the most "humane" denazification program, they have also been criticized for an imperial hubris that led them to develop a wholly ineffectual policy based on a "prevailing ignorance about Germany that resulted in historical stereotypes being adopted" at all levels of policy making.[10] In the face of its unpopularity among the Germans, the British eventually abandoned their reeducation approach as ineffectual. British reeducation has been summed up as a "combination of high idealism, arrogant colonialism, and pragmatic improvisation," which failed to "lead to a coherent and carefully coordinated program of implementation and fizzled out as it deserved to."[11]

While the British tended to emphasize reeducation, they did in fact implement a halfhearted purge of some occupation groups. The British, like the other Allies, increasingly relied on German-staffed commissions to implement the purge, and, as was the case in the other zones, they too became increasingly frustrated with the work of the commissions and eventually abandoned the whole denazification scheme, which had come to be seen as a "burdensome commitment."[12] Having emphasized reeducation over a purge, the British ended up with the least successful of all denazification programs. On the one hand, their reeducation program was abandoned as a self-acknowledged failure, while on the other hand, their lack of commitment to a purge meant that many incriminated individuals living in the British zone, who would have faced punishment in other zones, were able to "lie low" and avoid punishment altogether.[13]

The American approach to denazification, perhaps unfairly, has garnered the most negative image in the historical literature.[14] Perhaps as a result of Americans' "characteristically missionary zeal," U.S. policy makers instituted an ambitious denazification program designed to both thoroughly purge incriminated individuals and eliminate the roots of militarism and Nazism through reeducation.[15] The American solution to the "German problem" was similar to the British insofar as it argued that antidemocratic, militarist tendencies had historically triumphed over liberal democratic forces. The result was essentially two Germanys: one Prussian and militaristic which had produced Nazism and the other a redemptive "other Germany" which traditionally championed western-style liberal democracy.[16] The British and the Americans diverged from this shared analysis of fascism when it came to developing occupation policy. Whereas the British tended to downplay the purge and to emphasize the transformative possibilities of reeducation, the Americans tried to do it all: institute both a sweeping purge and an equally far-reaching reeducation program. U.S. denazification was roundly criticized, by both contemporaries and later historians, as an overly complex and unwieldy bureaucratic quagmire in which millions of individuals were forced to complete denazification questionnaires while in the end only a relative few were ever brought to justice. Nevertheless, in light of the subsequent close relationship that developed between the United States (and the west in general) and the West German state—and the latter's stable democracy—U.S. reeducation policies cannot be dismissed as having been completely ineffectual.[17]

To complete this comparison of Allied approaches to denazification, the Soviet approach can be briefly summarized. Although there was a transformative element evident in at least the earliest stages of Soviet denazification policy, the Soviets never developed a reeducation program as such. If there was a redemptive "other Germany" for the

Soviets, it was to be found not in liberal democratic historical trends but rather in the manifestations of class consciousness on the part of the German working class. Germans who had remained ideologically committed to "antifascism" throughout the Third Reich were to form the vanguard for the emergence of a postfascist, peace-loving Germany. While the Germans' need to embrace "democracy" was constantly invoked by the Soviets, their understanding of the concept had little in common with the conception of democracy held by their western counterparts.

The analysis of Nazism that informed policy in the Soviet zone also differed significantly from that in the West. The Soviet critique of Nazism was similar to the western view insofar as the "German problem" was seen as the result of a unique path of historical development in which anachronistic antidemocratic, militarist elites were able to subvert continuously the development of bourgeois democracy. In contrast to the western view, the communist critique did not see the establishment of bourgeois democracy as an end in itself, but saw it rather as a developmental prerequisite to the ultimate building of socialism. The Soviets and their German supporters were also influenced by Lenin's call to seize the administrative apparatus as a first step toward the building of socialism.

The result was an ideological quandary that crippled the formulation of a clear-cut denazification program. On the one hand, historical materialism showed that there were deeply rooted systemic features in Germany that had developed over generations and that were not amenable to short-term solutions. On the other hand, Leninist tactics called for swift action. This contradiction was never resolved, and Soviet denazification eventually came to focus almost exclusively on the purge.

Despite the differences between Soviet and western approaches to the "German problem," the Soviet denazification program was ultimately abandoned for the same reasons as the western programs. The primary causes were an inability to turn ideological assumptions into a workable program, an increasing reliance on German-staffed denazification commissions whose decisions could not be controlled by the policy makers, a ballooning bureaucratic operation that quickly reached unmanageable proportions, and the intractable contradiction between the purge and reconstruction.

Postwar Historians and Denazification

The historical literature on denazification reflects the political and ideological division of Germany. One legacy of Germany's division was the creation of two nearly irreconcilable bodies of historical literature. This can be seen in an analysis of eastern and western historiography and in the reemergence of the topic of denazification in the post-reunification debate regarding Germany's divided past and united future.

Recent works on the legacy of GDR historiography have emphasized the close connection between the historical profession and the state.[18] It is generally agreed that the East German regime instrumentalized the production of historical studies in order to legitimize the SED and its alliance with the Soviet Union.[19] Despite a growing chorus of criticism, East German studies of the occupation period should not be dismissed out of hand. These studies shaped, for better or worse, the contours of our present understanding of the period. In addition, irrespective of the state's appropriation of historical studies, East German historians produced some empirically sound research that retains its usefulness.[20] Finally, by accepting the GDR's instrumentalization of history, East German studies provide insight into how the history of denazification fit into the construction of the GDR's self-image.

Although there were no book-length studies of denazification published in the GDR, the subject loomed large in its historiography. Analysis of denazification centered on a comparison between the "successful" Soviet program and the "failed" western programs. Two major reasons were cited for the Soviet success: a correct understanding of the nature of fascism, which was a prerequisite for a successful purge, and the dynamic leadership of the Soviet occupation authorities, the German communists, and other "antifascists."

The basic outline of this interpretation was clearly laid out in a multivolume history of the German workers' movement produced by an "Authors' Collective" headed by Walter Ulbricht.[21] It was argued that, as early as March 1933, the German Communist Party (KPD) had correctly identified the essential "class character" of German fascism. Fascism was the "answer of the reactionary forces of finance capital in Germany and in the world" to the "general crisis of the capitalist system" signaled by the October Revolution in Russia. The "reactionary" groups that supported the Nazi regime were the "true rulers of Germany . . . monopolists, militarists, and Junkers." [22]

The history of denazification became part of a teleology that reinforced the GDR regime's self-image as an "antifascist-democratic" state. Although denazification was only one of the "Four D's" contained in the Potsdam Agreement (along with demilitarization, decartelization, and democratization), East German historians blurred the lines among these four goals and placed them all in the context of the "antifascist-democratic transformation." [23] Stefan Doernberg, for instance, claimed that denazification was one of the chief means used by the "antifascists" to gain control of the "imperialistic-capitalistic state machine." [24] Denazification was a tool for seizing control of the state machine, which in turn was a prerequisite for a revolutionary transformation of society. [25] This interpretation, which so closely echoed Lenin's argument that the initial task of revolutionaries was to "*break up* at once the old bureaucratic machine and to start immediately the construction of a new one," was not simply indicative of the Marxist-Leninist—or even Stalinist—bent of East German historiography. [26] Rather, the placement of denazification in the context of a broader revolutionary transformation of society was an accurate reflection of how the Soviets and their German supporters conceived of and implemented postwar occupation policy.

A good example of this admixture of goals is the coupling of denazification and land reform. Denazification and land reform fit logically into the communist critique of fascism; nonindustrial sources of economic support for Nazism, imperialism, and militarism were grouped under the rubric of "Junkers." Nazism and the great landowners—and therefore denazification and land reform—were inseparable because, it was argued, the fascist period witnessed the "fusion" of monopoly capital, bank capital, and large land-ownership. [27] It was even argued that denazification not only addressed Germany's fascist past but also destroyed "a state ideology and praxis that, like a nightmare, burdened the German people and other peoples *for centuries*," namely, "the exploitative and rapacious interests of the ruling classes." [28]

The East German analysis also compared what was seen as the successful Soviet program with the failed western attempt at denazification. Capitalism was the root cause of western failure. The western occupation powers found a natural ally in the "German grande bourgeoisie," and together they cooperated in a restoration of the "leadership of monopoly capital" in their zones and later in the West German state.[29] Western capitalism recognized both its class allies and enemies, and the West's obsession with the Cold War led to the steady displacement of antifascism by anticommunism.[30]

Another recurring theme in East German historiography was that the restoration of monopoly capitalism in West Germany led as well to a restoration of fascism.[31] Denazification was central to this development in the west; failure to distinguish between "active" and "nominal" supporters of fascism meant that nominal party members were punished while the truly guilty remained free. This was a result of the complicity between the western powers and fascism.[32] In contrast, Soviet denazification clearly distinguished between nominal party members and the "active supporters of the Nazi regime (with and without party books!)."[33] Thus, Soviet denazification laid the groundwork for the creation of the "antifascist-democratic" GDR, while in the west there was a "continuity" of personnel and institutions between Third Reich and Federal Republic.[34] This failure of western denazification was central to understanding why the "evolving West German Federal Republic was heavily burdened with guilt."[35]

Denazification in Western Historiography

There are two approaches in western historiography to denazification and the occupation period in general: an older, or orthodox, viewpoint based on research done in the 1950s, and a revisionist approach dating from the 1970s.[36] Both of these schools were primarily concerned with the prehistory of the Federal Republic, and Soviet occupation policies were usually examined within a comparative context.

In the older or orthodox view, western denazification was a failure. The western powers, and particularly the United States, implemented a confused and contradictory policy that sought simultaneously to punish and reeducate, purge and rebuild. This "artificial revolution" did not fundamentally transform Germany, failed to distinguish between the truly guilty and merely nominal followers of Nazism, and ultimately earned the enmity of the German people.[37] Both the western orthodox school and East German historians agreed that the failure of western denazification allowed former Nazis to maintain influential positions in West German society.

The most influential revisionist work was Lutz Niethammer's study of denazification in Bavaria. In his view, the orthodox interpretation was oversimplified because it first assumed that the goal was a complete cleansing of Nazi personnel and then concentrated on why this goal was not attained. Niethammer focused instead on what he called the "historical function of denazification."[38] If the U.S. denazification program is placed in the context of its anticommunist goals, then the program actually can be said to have succeeded because it made "the purge of personnel a surrogate for antifascist reform" in the service of a political and economic restructuring of West Germany. The goal of the program was not a thorough purge of fascism but a limited purge that would lead to "the ideological incorporation of the Germans into the Cold War."[39]

Despite his focus on West Germany, Niethammer's work changed the course of all subsequent denazification studies. His approach can be broken down into three main points: (1) an analysis of the occupation authorities' critique of German fascism is a prerequisite for understanding their denazification programs; (2) the growing Cold War tensions between the Allies had a significant effect on the policies the occupation powers implemented in their zones; and (3) denazification cannot be adequately understood without a careful examination of the role played by local denazification commissions.[40]

Niethammer's focus on local commissions also paralleled a growing interest in the methodology of the history of everyday life (*Alltagsgeschichte*). The confluence of denazification studies and *Alltagsgeschichte* can be traced to Niethammer's study of Bavaria, which anticipated the *Alltagsgeschichte* interest in local and regional history. This regional focus, combined with his later position as a leading theorist of *Alltagsgeschichte,* placed Niethammer—and subsequently denazification and occupation studies—within the ongoing *Alltagsgeschichte* debate.[41] Overall, Niethammer's most significant legacy may be the growing body of literature on denazification in the western zones.[42]

Turning to studies of the Soviet zone, one finds it difficult to discern clear-cut schools of thought in western historiography, much less a revisionist trend. A review of the literature does, however, indicate the outlines of a standard view of Soviet denazification. On several points, eastern and western historians are agreed: denazification in the Soviet zone was thorough in comparison to its counterpart in the west, and the purge was an integral part of a far-reaching transformation of politics, society, and the economy. The class analysis that anchored GDR historiography is missing in western interpretations. Instead, Soviet denazification was seen as part of the "Stalinization" of the eastern zone and its eventual incorporation into the Soviet sphere of influence.

Hermann Weber forcefully argued the Stalinization thesis in a long series of books and articles in which all the major Soviet policies during the occupation period were shown to fit into a methodical implementation of one-party rule. In one of his earliest works, Weber dismissed East German and Soviet class analyses as window dressing designed to conceal a naked power grab. In contrast to the East German view, Weber argued that "in reality neither 'the people' nor 'the working class' took over the leading positions, but rather the SED, or more simply put, the SED leadership and its leading corps of functionaries."[43] In the 1991 edition of his survey of GDR history, Weber reiterated his belief in the soundness of the Stalinization model and argued that Soviet denazification was designed to place all positions of power in the hands of communists.[44] The influence of the Stalinization model on western analyses is considerable, and it has appeared consistently from the earliest to the most recent studies.[45]

Another recurring theme in western historiography was the "brutal means" by which the Soviets used denazification in a "fundamental transformation of the social structure in their zone."[46] In the East German view, the uncompromising Soviet denazification was driven by a desire to uproot the social and economic bases of Nazism; in the western interpretation, this goal was "secondary" to the ultimate aim of imposing a "revolutionary restructuring of the economy and society."[47]

Finally, western studies posited continuity between the totalitarian Nazi regime and an equally totalitarian Soviet system. This view is analogous to the East German claim of continuity between the Nazi regime and the West German state. The system of concentration camps in the Soviet zone was frequently cited as evidence of totalitarian continuity.[48] The GDR regime, by arguing so strenuously for the complete and successful eradication of Nazism in the Soviet zone and the unerring nature of Soviet policy, made any discussion of continuity taboo.[49] This and other taboos constitute what western historians labeled the "blank spots" in GDR historiography.[50]

Denazification as a Post-Reunification Problem

The topic of denazification has again become current since the collapse of East Germany. Denazification has entered post-reunification debates in three areas: (1) a reevaluation of the nature of East Germany and, specifically, its self-definition as "antifascist"; (2) an ongoing debate over the legacy of the East German Ministry of State Security (Ministerium der Staatssicherheit, commonly referred to as the Stasi); and (3) a revisiting of the *Vergangenheitsbewältigung* ("coming to terms with the past") debate within the context of Germany's "second dictatorship," the GDR.

Antifascism was central to the East German state's attempt to legitimize its rule, and the purported success of denazification in the Soviet zone was an integral part of this legitimization. Recent commentators have pointed out that the mantra of antifascism—a concept that was "ridden to death" by GDR academics—actually hindered a coming to terms with the Nazi past.[51] In Olaf Groehler's view, the abrupt ending of denazification in the Soviet zone meant that those who were not found guilty of specific acts were able to avoid an "inner moral confrontation" with their own behavior: "millions of citizens of the GDR were in this manner spared from confronting their own individual history in the Nazi regime" and allowed to gain "absolution" by participating in the construction of the new order in the GDR.[52]

Gregor Gysi, a former SED official, argued that the GDR's claim of "antifascism" was actually a "lie from the birth [of the state]" in 1949. In Gysi's view, the SED's self-image was that "we are thoroughly antifascist and that is exactly what the majority of the population want." The problem was that this claim of "antifascism" was not accompanied by an adequate purge: "Thus the majority of the population were also described as antifascist, which they naturally weren't, and absolutely could not have become in such a short time."[53] The debate over "the viability of the GDR's supposedly anti-fascist heritage" is clearly not occurring in a political vacuum: it is also a debate over "who will have the power to define the priorities of the new Germany."[54]

A second field of debate in post-reunification Germany concerns the extent to which post–World War II denazification can provide guidelines for the "destasification" of the former GDR.[55] In an attempt to draw lessons from the past, two historians of postwar denazification, Klaus-Dietmar Henke and Hans Woller, warned against simplistic comparisons of 1945 with 1989–90. Henke and Woller noted that, despite some "totalitarian" similarities, German fascism and the East German system existed in different historical contexts. The main difference is that postwar denazification was integral to reconstruction, whereas a post-*Wende* cleansing of East German society is not an equally pressing issue: "One may or may not deplore the fact, but today there exists a much less burning need for a settlement of accounts and retribution than in 1945." Henke and Woller went on to argue that this means not that "a political cleansing is superfluous," but only that any purge should be part of a "process of social exploration of consciousness" that unfortunately failed to materialize as part of the postwar denazification.[56] The desire to compare 1945 with 1989–90 and the search for parallels between denazification and "destasification" carry the risk of overlooking the significant differences between the Third Reich and the GDR.[57] This is evident, for example, in the prominent role the theory of totalitarianism has assumed in post-reunification debate concerning the East German regime.[58]

Finally, there is the problem of the "second German coming to terms with the past" presented by the fall of the GDR and reunification. Much debate has focused on postwar denazification and the lessons it offers for coming to terms with the legacy of the GDR.[59] Eckhard Jesse posed the problem this way: "Two totalitarian systems have exercised their domination on German soil. This 'double coming to terms with the past' in Germany is a result of the universal question regarding coming to terms with the results of right and left dictatorships."[60] The obvious difference between the postwar and post-reunification periods is that denazification was imposed on the Germans by the victorious Allies, whereas any similar program in the present era will be an all-German affair.[61] "This time," it has been observed, "the Germans have everything in their own hands: no Allied military governor for far and wide to whom the ticklish matter can be turned over."[62]

CHAPTER 1

The Origins of Soviet Denazification Policy

The critique of fascism developed during the 1930s and 1940s by the KPD and the Communist International (Comintern) provided an ideological foundation for the later Soviet denazification. As Niethammer demonstrated in his examination of denazification in the U.S. zone, the Allies' understanding of the origins and nature of the National Socialist state determined how they approached the challenge of denazification.[1] In this chapter I will examine the communist critique of National Socialism, its development before and during the war, and how it shaped wartime planning for the Soviet occupation zone in Germany. As we will see, many of the problems presented by denazification had their roots in this critique.

The Development of the Communist Critique of National Socialism, 1924–1941

Prior to the Seventh Comintern Congress in 1935, the communist critique of fascism was linked to the idea that social democracy was the chief enemy of communism and the working class. Stalin argued in 1924, for example, that there were two "organizations" in fascist movements: one militant and bourgeois, the other moderate and social democratic.

> These organizations do not negate, but supplement each other. They are not antipodes, they are twins. Fascism is an informal political bloc of these two chief organizations; a bloc, which arose in the circumstances

of the post-war crisis of imperialism, and which is intended for combating the proletarian revolution. The bourgeoisie cannot retain power without such a bloc. It would therefore be a mistake to think that "pacifism" signifies the liquidation of fascism. In the present situation, "pacifism" is the strengthening of fascism with its moderate, Social-Democratic wing pushed into the forefront.[2]

At the 1928 Comintern Conference the theory of "social fascism," which tied social democracy to the rise of fascism, was placed within the context of a generalized crisis of capitalism, the "third period" of capitalist development. According to the "social fascism" theory, the "bourgeois-imperialist reaction" utilized fascism's "anticapitalist phraseology" to win over the working class and eliminate the communist movement. Once in power, however, fascism would drop its anticapitalist rhetoric and show "itself increasingly as a terrorist dictatorship of big capital."[3]

The "social fascism" theory was long-lived. In September 1932, just months before Hitler's ascension to power, the Comintern continued to argue that the German Social Democratic Party (SPD), along with the Catholic Center Party, had "paved the way for the fascist dictatorship."[4] Similarly, almost a year after Hitler came to power, and when the SPD had already ceased to exist, the official Comintern line continued to focus on the perceived misdeeds of the Social Democrats. The SPD was criticized for its alleged fight against "the revolutionary unity of the proletariat and likewise against the Soviet Union," which helped keep fascism in power.[5]

The theory of "social fascism" was fundamentally revised at the Seventh Comintern Congress.[6] Hitler's successful takeover in Germany, his banning of both the KPD and SPD, and the ongoing persecution of members of both parties were the primary reasons for this revision. In response to these developments, the Comintern switched from attacking the SPD to promoting cooperation with Social Democrats and trade unionists in a united front against fascism. Although fascism was still seen as a product of finance capital, it was also pictured as a uniquely inhumane and barbaric form of dictatorship.[7] Comintern chief Gregory Dimitrov's speech on the "class character of fascism" summed up the new policy.

Hitler fascism is not only bourgeois nationalism, it is bestial chauvinism ... It is medieval barbarity and bestiality ... The accession to power of fascism is not an *ordinary succession* of one bourgeois government by another, but a *substitution* of one state form of class domination of the bourgeoisie—bourgeois democracy—by another form—open terrorist dictatorship.[8]

The unique form of fascism developed by Hitler's National Socialist German Workers' Party (NSDAP) thus had two components: it remained a product of finance capital, but it also was an inhumane dictatorship based on "medieval barbarity and bestiality." This analysis laid the groundwork for the postwar distinction between active supporters of Nazism (who should be punished) and nominal supporters (who could be rehabilitated). First, since Nazism was a product of capitalism, an individual would not necessarily have to be a formal member of the Nazi Party in order to be an active supporter of the movement. This reasoning became central in Soviet denazification: there were behind-the-scenes supporters of Hitler who saw Nazism as a means to secure the dominance of capital and to destroy the organization of the working class. These supporters of Nazism were to be held just as accountable as Nazi leaders for the deeds of the Third Reich. Second, the redefinition of fascism as a unique form of barbaric dictatorship carried within in it the seeds of later exculpation for many rank-and-file NSDAP members, since the coercion exercised by such a dictatorship called into question the degree to which mere membership in a Nazi organization could be construed as active or voluntary support for the system. The whole concept of the "nominal" supporter of National Socialism, which came to dominate denazification policy, was an outgrowth of the acknowledgment of the "barbaric" nature of Hitler's dictatorship.

Two months after the Seventh Comintern Congress, the KPD convened in Brussels to develop a policy based on Dimitrov's new line. In his report to the KPD conference, Central Committee leader Wilhelm Pieck, while continuing to place most of the blame on the SPD, urged his listeners to acknowledge that the KPD also bore partial responsibility for the victory of National Socialism in Germany. Pieck defended the KPD's goals during the Weimar period, which he listed as "the proletarian revolution, the establishment of a dictatorship of the proletariat, and the creation of a soviet Germany."[9] The party's main mistake had been its incorrect assessment of the fascist threat: "We should have brought our struggle against social democracy into a correct relation with the struggle against advancing fascism. That did not happen and therein lies our worst mistake in the development of our political line."[10] It was now necessary to form a united front with Social Democrats against fascism and to promote communist infiltration of Nazi organizations in Germany in order to win over workers who supported National Socialism.[11] Correctly assuming that the Third Reich would eventually be overthrown, Pieck, with remarkable prescience, touched on what would become the central issue in postwar denazification: distinguishing between active fascists and passive supporters of the regime.

> The hatred against the NSDAP that fills the entire revolutionary working class is a healthy hatred. It should not, however, be directed against the misguided National Socialist worker; rather we must differentiate between the Brown bosses [*braunen Bonzen*] and the masses in the National Socialist movement . . . We must make clear that those truly guilty in the Hitlerist terror and its catastrophic policies will be brought before the law and tried, but that the remaining members of the Hitler party will not be persecuted and there will be no retaliation against them for the unprecedented blood sacrifices [*Blutopfer*] that fascism has exacted from the working masses.[12]

Pieck's analysis was in line with Dimitrov's recent reformulation of the critique of German fascism. Pieck's comments also reflected the KPD leadership's perception that they had lost a portion of the working class to the NSDAP. This element of the working class, which Pieck referred to as "misguided" National Socialist workers, would constitute a large portion of the rank-and-file Nazi Party members who would have to be dealt with after the war. The Comintern's new line on German fascism offered a way out of this dilemma: in the context of a brutal dictatorship, there were those who were "truly guilty" and those who were "misguided." The main challenge, as we will see, would be to differentiate somehow between the two. This would eventually turn into a problem that would cast its shadow over denazification from its inception until its end.

By the next KPD conference, in Bern, Switzerland (30 January–1 February 1939), the party faced an increasingly powerful National Socialist regime and the likelihood of war. In his keynote address, Pieck bemoaned the KPD's powerlessness in the face of the Nazi terror machine. Planned protests against the persecution of Jews and other Nazi policies had failed to materialize. Pieck mused: "I know it is easier said than done and I also do not want to cast blame. But we have to face the fact that we are perhaps facing imminent war and at that point we will not be able to meet again." Pieck called for a redoubling of efforts to show the German people that the KPD stood at the forefront of the "fight against fascism and for the securing of the socialist revolution." Securing a future socialist revolution also entailed countering the anti-Soviet policies of the Nazis since, as Pieck predicted, "there will come a time when the masses will . . . greet the Red Army as an ally in the liberation from fascism and as a helper against hostile intervention by the capitalist states."[13]

The Soviet-German Non-Aggression Pact of August 1939 not only complicated the lives of German exile antifascists in Moscow but also required some adjustments in the KPD's critique of fascism.[14] The Central Committee's declaration on the Non-Aggression Pact emphasized that, unlike the Anti-Comintern Pact signed by Germany, Italy, and Japan, which was "an instrument of war and the imperialist rape of other peoples," the German-Soviet pact was "for the protection of peace between Germany and the Soviet Union." Thus the KPD could call on its followers simultaneously to support the Non-Aggression Pact and oppose Nazism.[15]

The official Soviet view, however, was moving away from criticizing German aggression and toward attacking Britain and France as the primary threats to peace. Soviet Foreign Minister V. M. Molotov derided the idea that the British and French had gone to war to "destroy Hitlerism": "One can either accept or reject the ideology of Hitlerism, just like any other ideological system, that is a question of political views [*Anschauungen*] . . . It follows that it is not only senseless, but also criminal, to lead a war for the 'destruction of Hitlerism,' a war that will be draped with the false flag of a fight for 'democracy.'"[16]

The Moscow-based KPD leadership quickly brought its analysis into line with Molotov's views. Pieck, in a December 1939 article, blamed the war on British and French imperialism, arguing that the aim of the British and French was "the subjugation of the German people and the erection of a 'conservative' regime in Germany, whose goal, one can see, would be to become the gendarme of capitalism against the Soviet Union."[17] Fellow KPD-in-exile leader Walter Ulbricht weighed in two months later, disingenuously arguing that the "working class of Germany has an interest in extensive economic trade with the Soviet Union" because free trade would counter the Nazi claim that the economic problems of Germany lay in a "lack of living space." Moreover, the German working class, "which wants so-cialism," benefited from the Non-Aggression Pact simply because "it strengthens the friendship with the great land of socialism."[18]

The Communist Critique of Fascism during the German-Soviet War

The German invasion of the Soviet Union in June 1941 forced yet an-other revision of the communist critique of fascism. Attacks on British and French imperialism were necessarily dropped in place of a return to the line laid out at the Seventh Comintern Congress in 1935. Once again, the Third Reich was seen as headed by a "criminal band" of "fascist cannibals" driven by "bestial chauvinism" to attack the So-viet Union and other European lands. The fine distinction Molotov had made earlier between ideological versus imperialist war was dis-carded, and Germans were called upon to assist in "the destruction of German fascism."[19] After the ideological gymnastics required during the period of the Non-Aggression Pact, one can imagine the relief with which the KPD leadership returned to vitriolic attacks on Na-tional Socialism.

Soviet wartime planning for the occupation of Germany centered on the KPD exiles and the growing number of German POWs in So-viet captivity. In December 1941, 158 German POWs signed an "Ap-peal to the German People" calling on Germans to resist the Nazi war machine.[20] The surrender of the German army at Stalingrad in Janu-ary 1943 both increased the number of German POWs and acceler-ated Soviet planning for a postwar occupation of Germany. In a Feb-ruary 1943 Radio Moscow broadcast to Germany, Pieck urged the German people toward full-scale resistance: "The day of judgment for those who perpetrated crimes in this war is drawing ever closer . . . Do not allow Hitler to make you fear that your existence is threatened from outside! No one wants to destroy the German people. Only Hit-ler and his criminal bands must and will be destroyed. It lies with our people themselves to bring this act to conclusion."[21]

In July 1943 the National Committee for a Free Germany (NKFD) was founded in the hope of creating an anti-Hitler coalition behind Soviet lines.[22] Composed of German POWs and the leaders of the KPD-in-exile, the Free Germany movement had the twin goals of un-dermining the German war effort and creating a "strong democratic state power" in postwar Germany.[23] In preparation for the formation of the NKFD, the Central Committee of the KPD-in-exile developed a program that called for "punishment of the Hitler clique which bears sole guilt for the war. Punishment for all those responsible for the Nazi crimes committed against the German people and other peoples. Extirpation of fascist racial hatred. Destruction of the roots of the imperialistic rapine policy as well as of Prussian militarism. Elimination of the Hitler party's power apparatus and the Nazi system."[24]

The strident tone of this call to action was eventually dropped from the NKFD's program in order to gain the support of prominent German military leaders in Soviet captivity.[25] The NKFD's Manifesto, released in August 1943, confined itself to an appeal to German officers and soldiers on all fronts to join in the fight against the Nazi regime and a call for the formation of civilian "fighting groups" to oppose the regime on the home front.[26] Officially at least, the KPD leadership did not view this as an abandonment of its role as the leading representative of the German working class; rather, there was a realization that the exigencies of war required the creation of a broad national front encompassing all the "political and religious viewpoints" of the German people.[27]

In early 1944, the KPD-in-exile formed a committee charged with developing an "Action Program" for the creation of a "peaceful future for Germany." This Action Program became the blueprint for building an "antifascist-democratic order" in the Soviet zone after the war.[28] It is a key document in any analysis of postwar denazification because it represents the first confluence of the ideological critique of fascism with the need to develop a concrete program for dealing with National Socialism in the Soviet occupation zone.

Penned by the KPD-in-exile's leading theoretician, Anton Ackermann, the first section of the Action Program focused on domestic policy and political "cleansing." It called for a wide-ranging purge of the Nazi administrative apparatus on all levels, warning that "whoever has not decisively broken with Hitlerism cannot hold a responsible post in a new democratic state." Ackermann returned to the class analysis of fascism, absent from the NKFD Manifesto, and demanded an "uncovering of the threads connecting the NSDAP leadership to armaments and monopoly capital" and the "immediate expropriation of the means of support of those guilty of causing the war, war criminals, and their secret inspirers." Ackermann also called for a far-reaching denazification of the administration through a "thorough cleansing of the state apparatus in the Reich, the provinces, and the communities . . . of all fascist elements."[29]

Commenting on the Action Program in a lecture before a group of KPD members in November 1944, Pieck turned his attention toward future policy in an occupied Germany. Although the details had yet to be worked out, he argued that the occupation would present a "special situation" in which the Action Program could be put into force. This would require, above all, "that a portion of Germany will be occupied by the Red Army, whose regime will be shown to the German people to be a great help in the liberation from the Hitler bands and the reaction, as well as in the democratic transformation of Germany." Pieck went on to observe that the level of German cooperation with the occupation authorities in "securing the peace and making amends [*Wiedergutmachung*] . . . as well as the smashing of the fascist power apparatus" would determine "how quickly the occupation regulations will be relaxed and how long the occupation will last."[30]

In early 1945, as the war drew to a close and the task, in Pieck's words, of "smashing the fascist power apparatus" presented itself, the KPD's critique was transformed into a detailed analysis grounded in Marxist-Leninist historical materialism. Two texts can serve as examples of this attempt to bring together all of the strands of two decades of communist theorizing into a coherent critique of German fascism: Walter Ulbricht's "Theses on the Essence of Hitler Fascism" and Johannes R. Becher's "Regarding the Political-Moral Destruction of Fascism." Taken together, these works offer a clear view of the communist critique of fascism on the eve of the end of the war and bear directly on the denazification policies developed in the Soviet occupation zone.

In Ulbricht's work, the old "social fascism" theory was combined with Dimitrov's 1935 Comintern line. German fascism was a bestial, terrorist dictatorship that grew out of "German monopoly capitalism's period of decay" (that is, the "third period" postulated in the prewar years).[31] The roots of German fascism lie deep in German historical development: "At the decisive turning points in German history—be it the years of the Peasant Wars and the Reformation or the years 1848 and 1918—the forces of reaction were repeatedly able to protect their positions and to inflict defeat on the forces of progress."[32] The year 1918 was a particularly significant one, when a chance arose to "erect a new, truly democratic and socialist order" and to "expropriate the armaments industries, bankers, large landowners, assorted warmongers, and war profiteers." Instead, reactionary forces, aided by Social Democrats (a reprise of "social fascism"), split the working class movement, and Germany missed a chance to alter its trajectory toward the Third Reich.[33] Although Ulbricht resuscitated the old analysis of "social fascism," he overlooked the KPD's self-criticism in the period after the Seventh Comintern Congress. Instead, he only noted vaguely that Nazi terror could have been countered by united action on the part of the working class.[34]

Turning to the nature of the Nazi regime itself, Ulbricht offered a simple analysis: it represented "the direct domination of monopoly capital over the state apparatus": "What Nazi propaganda demogogically attempted to portray as 'German socialism' was nothing more than a form of war economy, the transformation of the state into a concentration camp for workers and a paradise for the armaments plutocrats."[35] The lesson to be learned was likewise simple: "The power of the war criminals, war interests, and other reactionaries will be broken once and for all." This required the "liquidation of the foundations of fascist German imperialism." That would include the following:

Cleansing of the administrative apparatus in the state, local communities, and the economy of all fascist elements.
Expropriation of large landowners and Junkers, because they are the champions of militarism . . .
Expropriation of the big business and bank bosses who belong among those who bear the main responsibility for war and fascism.
Turning over the businesses of Nazi Party members and war profiteers to the provincial and state administrations, thereby ending the possibility of a reincarnation of imperialist politics.
Struggle toward the elimination of fascist ideology in all of its manifestations, as well as struggle against every ideology onto which fascism could latch.
Cleansing of all economic institutes and teaching facilities of Nazi literature and the influence of fascist concepts and teaching methods.[36]

This analysis is in many ways classic Ulbricht. Ever the party functionary, Ulbricht sought to ground his critique in current Marxist orthodoxy, construct an analysis based on a selective interpretation of the past, and conclude with a future policy line that was paradigmatic of Communist Party sloganeering.

Johannes Becher, by contrast, approached his critique of fascism with a more philosophic bent. Formerly the secretary of the KPD writers' organization during the Weimar years, Becher was active in cultural affairs during his exile in Moscow, a co-founder of the NKFD, and later minister for culture in the East German government. Becher grounded his analysis of the political and moral implications of fascism in Lenin's *On Imperialism,* arguing that, since German fascism was fundamentally an imperialist ideology, it could be understood only on those terms. Becher cautioned against "superficial antifascism" that would impede the development of "conscious anti-imperialism." In Becher's view, it was "not enough that one is against Hitler because he lost the war; this position against Hitler as the most brutal exponent of imperialism must become a general aversion to imperialist methods."[37] He therefore called for an ideological struggle on a mass basis to "bind together questions of everyday life with this ideological struggle against fascism and imperialism." This would awaken a "national hatred of the Nazi clique and German imperialism" that would act as "a purifying thunderstorm" preceding national rebirth.[38]

Becher predicted that it would be difficult to make the Germans confront their co-responsibility for Nazi crimes. The concept of the "decent German" would have to be countered with the fact that Hitler's war had resulted in a "moral mass degeneracy."

> Doubtless there will be wide circles in Germany only all too ready to forget everything that has happened. They will say, What has happened, has happened, let's leave it at that. They will assure us, We were of course always against it, we said so right from the beginning—and, with these well-known justifications, they will attempt in the cheapest petty bourgeois manner to swindle their way out of the bloody Hitler affair.[39]

Becher's analysis resembled Ulbricht's in several ways: both held up the Weimar government's failure to punish war criminals and seize the historical opportunity to restructure German society as an example not to be repeated. Both men also adhered to the orthodox communist critique of Nazism as a tool of monopoly capitalism. Unlike Ulbricht's analysis, however, Becher's prescription for coming to terms with the Nazi past focused more on a social and cultural transformation based on historical interpretation. While Ulbricht spoke in terms of "cleansing," expropriation, and struggle, Becher looked for a more long-term transformation.

For Becher, this transformation would be based on a historical analysis that would show the Nazi period in its true colors. This would provide both enlightenment and exculpation. In Becher's view, historical analysis of Nazism should focus on the guilt of "Hitler, the Nazi clique, German imperialists, [and] those who bore primary responsibility" rather than on the "co-responsibility" of the German people.[40] This was an important distinction that echoed Pieck's earlier distinction between the guilty and the misled. Becher was not denying that the German people shared a degree of co-responsibility, but was arguing instead that it made little practical or ideological sense to saddle an entire nation with guilt. Denazification would have to proceed on two tracks: the immediate punishment of those who bore "primary responsibility" and the steady reeducation of those who bore some degree of "co-responsibility."

Reeducation would show the Germans how they had erred in their support of National Socialism. The first step would be a "demythologizing" *(Entlegendisierung)* of Hitler by portraying him as the "war leader of monopoly capitalism" and "the worst enemy of Germany." This should not, however, take the form of a simple "polemical slogan" but should rather be shown to be a "historically derived fact." This task could be accomplished through a historical analysis focused on the imperialist antecedents of Hitler's policies, which would reeducate the people and create "a new independent German ideology in the spirit of a militant humanistic democracy."[41] Concerning the question of who would lead this reeducation effort, Becher came to the unsurprising conclusion that only the KPD had the moral and ideological background necessary to save the German people. To this was added a "historical right" to leadership based on the party's longstanding support for the Soviet Union and resistance against fascism.[42]

Taken together, Ulbricht's and Becher's texts give a clear picture of the communist critique of fascism that shaped denazification in the Soviet zone. On several points, both men were in agreement. First, German fascism was a product of a long process of political, economic, social, and cultural development that culminated in the Third Reich and its collapse. Second, the communist critique of fascism was correct, and its proponents, the German communists and their Soviet supporters, were in a unique position to conduct a denazification. Third, because Nazism was a product of long-term developments in Germany, denazification would have to go beyond simply punishing the truly guilty and aim at a complete social transformation.

Aside from these similarities, Ulbricht and Becher offered fundamentally different approaches to denazification. Ulbricht ultimately looked to state power as the solution to Germany's dilemma. His program consisted of a list of policies, such as expropriation and land reform, which would be implemented by the state. For Ulbricht, the communist critique of fascism provided the justification for the use of state power. This is not to suggest that Ulbricht paid only lip service to ideology: he was calling for revolutionary change, and his use of words such as "liquidation," "elimination," and "struggle" is indicative of the ideological confrontation he expected as a result of these policies.

Becher took a more long-term view of denazification. There would of course be immediate punishment of those who bore primary responsibility, but denazification was essentially a question of reeducation, an ideological offensive aimed at winning hearts and minds and fundamentally transforming the German people. In a sense, Ulbricht and Becher represent two approaches that eventually proved irreconcilable. Throughout denazification, attempts were made to fuse these two approaches: to combine the use of state power with an ideological campaign aimed at eliciting popular support for state policies. The ideological offensive, launched in October 1947, which sought to garner public support for denazification is a prime example of an attempt to fuse these two approaches. Try as they might, however, the SED and the Soviets were unable to create mass support for denazification. The SED was equally unsuccessful in its attempts at bringing its own cadres into line with denazification. In the end, as we will see, the ideological offensive was abandoned in favor of increasingly dictatorial use of state power; Ulbricht's pragmatic approach to revolutionary transformation triumphed over Becher's vision of ideological rebirth.

CHAPTER 2

The Purge Begins

The summer following the end of the war was confused and violent. It was a time of anguish for the followers of National Socialism and a time of hope for those who saw the end of the war as a historic chance to build a new Germany. Denazification began the moment the Red Army entered Brandenburg. In the absence of a functioning state, German "antifascists" organized themselves into ad hoc committees and began the process of purging local Nazis. The story of denazification during the summer of 1945 is one of uncoordinated local initiatives slowly giving way to centralized control imposed by the German political leadership and the Soviet Military Administration (SMA).

In this chapter I investigate the first period of denazification from the end of the war until the end of 1946. Denazification in Brandenburg during this time proceeded in fits and starts and produced mixed results. The major stumbling blocks were that the goals of the purge were poorly defined, the lines of authority within the newly built administration were unclear, and the dismissals that resulted from denazification often complicated reconstruction.

Brandenburg at the End of the War

The modern province of Brandenburg was a product of the post-Napoleonic administrative restructuring in Prussia and comprised the areas known as Kurmark, Neumark, and Niederlausitz. After 1920, the city of Berlin was administratively separated from the province, taking with it almost 2 million inhabitants. After the war, Brandenburg was reduced to the area west of the Oder-Neiße border, about 27,000 square kilometers of territory. Even after this loss, Brandenburg was the largest of the five provinces in the Soviet zone, but also, with only 2.25 million residents, one of the most sparsely populated. The province lost some 640,000 residents east of the Oder, but, by August 1945, approximately 350,000 eastern refugees had flooded into Brandenburg.[1]

Brandenburg's economy was predominantly agricultural and was marked by a system of large landholdings. Prior to the postwar land reform, 1.1 percent of the landowners controlled 31 percent of the agricultural land. The province's only significant industrial activity was centered on the brown coal deposits in the southern Niederlausitz region. The Niederlausitz was also home to textile industries in the cities of Cottbus, Forst, and Guben.[2]

Because of its location between the Soviet front and Berlin, Brandenburg bore the brunt of the fighting in the closing days of the war. The province suffered massive destruction of its industrial, transportation, housing, and agricultural infrastructure. The problems of hunger and disease were compounded by an influx of German refugees from east of the Oder River.[3] Although the overall situation was catastrophic, conditions in individual regions varied according to the level of fighting that had occurred there. The Guben district, which had seen frontline fighting for approximately eight weeks, was particularly hard hit. But while cities such as Potsdam, Frankfurt/Oder, Calau, and Rathenow were severely damaged, the Luckau district had escaped virtually unscathed, and in the city of Kyritz, it was "as if there had never been a war."[4]

The refugee situation also varied. Bernau, for example, was designated as a transfer point for refugees. This designation resulted in waves of people entering the city, where, while the Soviets provided food and shelter for non-Germans, the local administration was responsible for provisioning all German refugees. The refugee problem was compounded by infighting among the districts: the Lübben district, for example, complained that the neighboring districts of Guben and Cottbus were attempting to solve their refugee problems by issuing the refugees passes to travel to Lübben.[5]

The Antifascist Committees

In the wake of the Third Reich's collapse, so-called Antifascist Committees sprang up throughout Germany.[6] Although these committees are usually placed at the forefront of early attempts at German "self-purification" *(Selbstreinigung)*, little is actually known about their membership and actions.[7] It has been estimated that there were approximately five hundred Antifascist Committees spread throughout Germany.[8] East German historians emphasized the leadership of the working class, in particular the role of former KPD and SPD members, in the committees. These individuals were, in Ulbricht's words, the "antifascists—activists of the first hour," who laid the cornerstone for the later development of the GDR.[9] The committees concentrated on everyday needs such as clearing rubble, distributing food, and reestablishing local government.[10] The reestablishment of local administration necessarily included a type of denazification: the replacement of Nazi officials who had either fled or defiantly remained at their posts.

Committees began to appear throughout Brandenburg during the closing weeks of the war. For example, a "resistance group" of thirty-four men was organized in the Niederlausitz town of Waldesruh as the Red Army neared. This group included former KPD and SPD members as well as other "democrats." The resistance group's priorities included hindering the evacuation ordered by the Nazis, protecting the town's dwellings and their contents, and preventing armed resistance against the Red Army by the Volkssturm, the "people's storm," formed in the closing weeks of the war.[11]

Similarly, on "the day of our liberation by the Red Army," a member of the KPD Antifascist Committee in Hohen Neuendorf reported that he and the other members were "at our posts." They opened tank barriers, "showed the Red tanks the way," occupied the town hall, and arrested the mayor and other "leading fascists" and turned them over to the Soviets.[12]

At the beginning of April 1945, the KPD leadership behind Soviet lines released "guidelines for the work of the German Antifascists" in the areas occupied, or about to be occupied, by the Red Army. The guidelines envisioned an orderly reestablishment of governmental systems in the wake of liberation by Soviet troops. After the local Soviet commander appointed a mayor, five to seven local activists would form a communal administration to oversee provisioning, housing, and other necessary tasks. They were instructed to assist in the "exposure and destruction of Nazi criminals, saboteurs, and their helpers and supporters" and the "registration of all members of Nazi organizations as well as members of the Wehrmacht and the Volkssturm."[13] The orderly transfer of power envisioned by these guidelines was the exception rather than the rule. More often the competing interests of local Antifascist Committees, Soviet occupation authorities, and the KPD leadership in Potsdam and Berlin filled the power vacuum.

For their part, the Antifascist Committees placed a high priority on denazifying local administrations that fell under their control. At the first meeting of the Luckenwalde Antifascist Committee, formed by nine KPD and eight SPD members, a KPD member made a strident appeal for a systematic cleansing of the administration.

> In the coming days lists . . . of antifascists will be drawn up. We will then look into the personnel files. Whoever doesn't suit us will be excluded. Perhaps we will also find some people we don't know about, people who remained true to the class struggle but did not belong to a [socialist] party . . . The first Antifa action takes place in the magistracy. Out with the fascists! . . . We must instruct our comrades to concentrate on the fascists. We'll begin at the top and finish at the bottom. Instruct the comrades straightaway to undertake a thorough investigation of the fascists.[14]

Although historians have painted the Antifascist Committees in heroic colors, the committees were uncoordinated local bodies that impeded the imposition of centralized control by Soviet and German authorities. These improvised organizations sprang up in what Christoph Kleßmann has termed a society in general collapse (*Zusammenbruchgesellschaft*). The dislocations of this period of collapse provided an opening for the appearance of the committees. Their role in administration and the purge of Nazis, however, was short-lived: they were ordered to disband in June 1945.[15]

The two forces that combined to end the committees' activities were the SMA and KPD. Ironically, it was exiled German communists, with the support of their Soviet hosts, who had initially encouraged the formation of resistance groups through Radio Moscow broadcasts during the closing months of the war.[16] Writing in 1955, Ulbricht noted that although the committees had performed a valuable service, they necessarily gave way to the more organized power of the "Initiative Groups" made up of Germans who had spent the war years in the Soviet Union.[17] Wolfgang Leonhard, a member of Ulbricht's Initiative Group in Berlin, and later one of his sharpest critics, was sympathetic to the Antifascist Committees. Leonhard recalled that Ulbricht had ordered the dissolution of the committees because, he claimed, Nazis were infiltrating them. Based on his firsthand knowledge of the committees, Leonhard found this claim specious and thought that the primary reason for dissolving the committees was that they were impeding Ulbricht's plans for assuming control over the administration.[18] That these committees were often dominated by KPD members was beside the point; unbeknownst to many KPD members who remained in Germany during the National Socialist period, the party leadership, recently returned from Soviet exile, had shifted its policies away from revolution and toward moderation.[19]

The KPD and Denazification

By June, KPD functionaries were traveling throughout Brandenburg compiling reports on local conditions that were sent to Ulbricht in Berlin. Ulbricht's agent in Brandenburg was Willy Sägebrecht, a long-time KPD member, who was given the task of reestablishing control over the party.[20] Sägebrecht reported that, in a number of small communities, the rebuilding of local government had been "to a large extent incorrectly implemented." Above all, there was a misunderstanding of the current party line. "Our comrades have printed and prepared posters and leaflets with purely communist contents," Sägebrecht noted, adding, however, that the situation in other areas was more hopeful and that in these communities "our work" promised to create local governments rebuilt on "a broader democratic basis."[21]

Many KPD members in Brandenburg were not aware of the party's new line because the postwar KPD's founding Declaration was not published until 13 June.[22] The leaders of the three Initiative Groups, Ulbricht, Anton Ackermann, and Gustav Sobottka, had composed the Declaration in Moscow during a visit in early June.[23] For many—

communists and non-communists alike—the most striking aspect of the Declaration was the KPD's apparent distancing of its political line from that of the Soviets.

> It is our view that the path for Germany is not to be forced into the Soviet system, because this path does not correspond to the present developmental conditions in Germany. We are of the opinion that the most important interests of the German people in the present situation prescribe another path for Germany, and this of course is the path in the direction of an antifascist, democratic regime; a parliamentary-democratic republic with all democratic rights and freedoms for the people.[24]

The KPD Declaration presented a ten-point program for rebuilding Germany. Five of these points dealt with denazification. The Declaration reiterated the main aspects of the communist critique of fascism developed during the war. The influence of Ulbricht and Ackermann is evident in the call for the "complete liquidation of the remnants of the Hitler regime and Hitler party," "total cleansing from all public offices of active Nazis," punishment of war criminals, and the "quickest and most severe measures" against those who persisted in committing "criminal Nazi acts." The Declaration also demanded expropriation of Nazi property and liquidation of large landholdings. The influence of Becher's vision of denazification was reflected in plans for the "creation of democratic rights and freedoms" through a purge of the education system and a "systematic clarification of the barbaric character of Nazi racial theory" and other Nazi ideas. The Declaration concluded with a call for the German people to "acknowledge a duty to make amends [*Wiedergutmachung*] for the damages caused by Hitler's aggression against other peoples."[25]

The KPD followed up on the Declaration by dispatching representatives to explain the new line to the rank and file. Sägebrecht traveled throughout Brandenburg doing the "ideological work" needed to put the new line into practice.[26] He later recalled distributing copies of the Declaration to every party comrade he met.[27] Also active was Gustav Gundelach, a longtime KPD member who had been with Ulbricht in Moscow during the war and later became a key figure in Ulbricht's Initiative Group in Berlin.[28] Gundelach reported from a party conference in Bernau on 14 June that, among a "series of misunderstandings," there was "particularly the question of the struggle against the Nazis."

The comrades do not understand how to differentiate. They proceed completely schematically regarding this question, create completely unnecessary problems, and come into a bad relationship with the [Soviet] commanders. So it has happened that our comrades have taken the ration cards of former Nazis . . . because they are of the opinion that Nazis should work more and eat less than all the others. In Oranienburg, where the administration consists only of communists, family relations of Nazis are generally denied permission to return [to their apartments in the city].

Gundelach noted that these problems were evident in a "series of other places that are administered by our comrades."[29]

The need for "differentiation" between "active" and "nominal" Nazis was clear: it was simply impracticable, particularly in light of the problems of reconstruction, to punish everyone who had been a Nazi. Determining who had been "active" and who could be considered "nominal," however, was the most vexing aspect of denazification. It was easy to say all the guilty should be punished, but how was guilt to be determined? The KPD leadership itself was unclear on this issue and sent out contradictory signals. The party's Declaration is a prime example of this confusion. In answer to the question of who bore the guilt for the "catastrophe," the Declaration stated that it was "Hitler and Göring, Himmler and Goebbels, and the active supporters and helpers of the Nazi Party."

If guilt had been confined to this rather small group, denazification would have been a straightforward matter. The Declaration broadened the scope of guilt, however, by embracing the concept of collective responsibility, arguing that "the German people carry a decisive portion of the guilt and co-responsibility for the war and its results." The circle of guilt did not stop there. The KPD admitted that "we also feel guilty, insofar as, despite the blood sacrifices of our best fighters, as a result of a series of our own mistakes, we were not able to create the antifascist unity of the workers, farmers, and intelligentsia" in the fight against fascism. The SPD also bore a share of guilt for its mistakes during the Weimar period, including allowing the "reaction a free hand," which paved the way for war, the splitting of the working-class movement, and Hitler's accession to power.[30]

The KPD Declaration moved from a specific definition of guilt, which encompassed the political and economic leadership of the Third Reich, to one that included nearly every German. The root of the KPD's confused concept of guilt lay in the party leadership's anger with its own cadres and with the German people. The Declaration enumerated the KPD's warnings to the Germans and the party's attempts to rally the people against Hitler. The Germans failed to rise up or to offer decisive resistance, and the matter was finally settled not by the Germans themselves but by the Allied armies. Despite their own self-criticism, the KPD leadership clearly felt that they had correctly surmised the danger posed by Hitler and that events had proved the correctness of the party's ideological, if not tactical, stance. The problem posed by the Declaration's definition of guilt was obvious: differentiation and collective responsibility were mutually exclusive. It is little wonder that the Declaration raised more questions than it answered for those seeking guidance on how to proceed with denazification.

As a result of their own confusion regarding the question of guilt, the KPD leadership struggled to clarify the party's policies. An article in the first issue of the party newspaper, the *Deutsche Volkszeitung*, for example, reported on an unnamed town where former Nazis were forced to wear swastikas so they could be identified by their neighbors, a marking analogous to the National Socialist requirement that Jews wear the Star of David. The problem with this approach, it was argued, was one of differentiation: only through a "thorough case-by-case examination is it possible to ascertain who was an active Nazi and who remains a Nazi." Although there were former Nazis whose hands were covered with the "blood of hundreds of concentration camp inmates," there were also those who had been repelled by the Nazis' tactics but who never summoned the courage to break with the party. The latter should not be stigmatized but rather should be given the chance to display their "willingness to make restitution" though reconstruction work: "Honest, diligent work—that is how it begins . . . [T]hrough work one shows his true nature."[31]

This article was followed up by an examination of the "often-asked question" of what should be done with the rank-and-file PGs.[32] Punishing all PGs diminished the "large degree of guilt of the Nazi leadership" and simply equated the "uprooting of Nazism" with the "uprooting of members of the NSDAP." This reiteration of the need for differentiation was contradicted, however, as the article went on to note that rank-and-file PGs were in fact "heavily incriminated" by their past support of the NSDAP. To confuse the point completely, it was also claimed that even "the mass of those who stood outside the party became tools in Hitler's hands and carry a definite responsibility and share of the guilt."[33] This article simply reformulated the contradictions contained in the party's Declaration. On the one hand, the KPD had a clear policy of differentiation; this was a pragmatic approach that argued it was senseless to persecute all former PGs, who might otherwise be utilized in reconstruction work. On the other hand, the party leadership had not yet come to terms with its own ambivalence regarding the PGs and the German people in general. The KPD had failed in its struggle against the Nazis, in part owing to tactical blunders such as its failure to drop the "social fascism" line until after Hitler came to power. Beyond this tactical failure, however, the KPD leadership had been let down by the German people, who failed to rise up against Hitler. Although the KPD could put the German people's passivity in the context of Nazi terror, it still harbored a degree of disappointment mixed with hostility toward the German people. As a result, the KPD sent mixed messages regarding denazification and fostered confusion among the party membership. Until party leaders could articulate a clear line on denazification, they would be continually dissatisfied with the results of their policies.

Not surprisingly, Berlin received numerous reports of confusion and misunderstanding during the summer of 1945. In a letter to Sägebrecht, a local KPD leader pleaded for "truly *binding* directions" as to the practical implementation of denazification. The major questions concerned how to proceed with confiscation of property owned by PGs, whether it was permissible to take unspecified "special measures" against former Nazis, which National Socialist organizations one had to belong to in order to be classified as a Nazi, how the wives of former Nazis were to be treated, and who exactly should be considered an "active fascist."[34] Devising answers to practical questions of this sort would occupy policy makers for the next two years.

One impediment to the implementation of the KPD's policy came from rank-and-file communists who clung to the revolutionary tenets of the prewar movement. As Brandenburg SPD leader Friedrich Ebert recalled, among the primary "difficulties" that arose in the summer of 1945 were the "sectarian tendencies in a few of the KPD organizations; many comrades there promoted the dictatorship of the proletariat."[35] Ulbricht, in a speech to a party conference in Berlin, explained that the present conditions in Germany required a democratic rather than a revolutionary policy. "Many workers want to set up socialism straightaway," Ulbricht observed, "but how can that occur in light of the ideological devastation that reaches so deeply into the ranks of the working class?" The working class was not united and did not yet have the requisite class consciousness to create socialism. Rather, the present situation called for "completion of the bourgeois-democratic revolution that began in the year 1848." Only a "democratic order" would allow "complete elimination of Nazism and the growth of progressive forces" while providing the working class with the experience necessary for eventually administering the state.[36]

An example which is indicative of the misunderstanding (or conscious rejection) of the concept of differentiation and the limited reach of the party leadership is provided by the minutes of a 3 August meeting of the "Antifa Committee" of Belzig, the site of the Niemegker concentration camp.

> The age of the concentration camp is past, but it does no harm when known Nazis come into the Niemegker camp and are put to work there . . . Pastor T. made an offer to look after the spiritual needs of the camp inmates, which was universally rejected, because we cannot allow a feeling of sympathy to develop. There is no difference between small and big [Nazi] party members, just as earlier there was similarly no difference between small and big antifascists.[37]

The Belzig Antifascist Committee turned a deaf ear to the KPD's call for "differentiation." It also apparently disregarded Ulbricht's order for the disbanding of Antifascist Committees, since the Belzig committee was still meeting two months after it should have been dissolved. Belzig's exceptionalism may in part be due to the influence of the hard-line local Soviet commander, Kovalov, who warned, "The fascists are continuously disrupting work in the cities and the villages . . . It has been said that the occupation power will remain here for fifty years. It will remain here until the last fascist lies under the earth." This sentiment was seconded by the communist district magistrate *(Landrat)*: "The Nazis will be handled the same way they handled us, that is: hard. We will force the slackers to work and if need be stick them in a camp . . . [B]y next year we want a Germany purged of Nazis [*nazirein*]."[38]

If failure to differentiate between active and passive Nazis was a problem in some areas, in others the Nazi power structure continued to hold sway. Visiting Kyritz in early July, KPD operative Emil Krummel noted his exasperation upon discovering that the "propaganda office" in town was still decorated with a Nazi poster and that former Nazis continued to hold positions in the local administration "while old KPD comrades are occupied with other physical tasks."[39]

The Role of the Soviet Occupation Forces

East German studies lauded the Soviets as the "truest friends and helpers of the German people" and credited the SMA with implementing effective denazification policies.[40] But, while there were some well-intentioned Soviet commanders, many ruled over their military districts as corrupt autocrats who abused both the Germans and the men under their command.[41] As seen in the example from Belzig, the attitude of the local Soviet commander might result in harsh reprisals against former Nazis. Often, however, local Soviet commanders impeded the purge of former Nazis.

One commander, for example, ignored information about the Nazi past of a mayor who had been a Nazi Party member. The mayor was also a schoolteacher who still used Nazi-era schoolbooks and allowed the children to continue to use the "Hitler greeting." In addition, the mayor bore responsibility for burning Nazi membership records and other incriminating materials before the Red Army's arrival. Frustrated locals complained that "although the Soviet commander has known about this for sixteen days, he has continued to allow the mayor to remain in office." In a similar situation, a Soviet commander allowed a Nazi teacher to remain at his post despite his well-known incriminating past. This same commander had failed to institute any denazification measures in the district and permitted soldiers under his command to roam the countryside, where "gardens were plundered, the unripe fruit torn from trees, the houses cleared out, women raped, bicycles taken, etc." The commander was also allegedly in league with the corrupt and "autocratic" town mayor who was "eager to satisfy all the wishes of the Red Army."[42]

The problem of corrupt mayors appointed by Soviet commanders continued to plague communities until after the elections of October 1946, when the power to appoint and dismiss mayors was handed over to communal councils. Many of these corrupt mayors were apparently former concentration camp inmates who had been imprisoned by the Nazis for criminal rather than political offenses. Upon release from the concentration camps, these individuals presented themselves as political enemies of the Nazis and used their prior incarceration as proof of their "antifascist" credentials. Once in power, they used their positions to tyrannize the local population. This apparently occurred frequently in the small communities of Brandenburg.[43]

The exasperation of some Germans with the lack of Soviet support for denazification was exacerbated by a similar unwillingness to control marauding bands of Red Army soldiers and displaced persons.[44] In July 1945 the KPD district headquarters in Forst reported gangs of Poles and Russian soldiers rampaging through the countryside unchecked. The local KPD observed, "We greeted the Red Army as our liberator and are willing to work with them, but this task is greatly complicated when these occurrences continue unchecked. The population is preparing to leave . . . [A]s we watch how the working class becomes increasingly disillusioned, we would probably also just pack up if it weren't for our strong belief in the leadership of the [Communist Party]."[45]

Reporting on the KPD's weakness in the town of Hoppegarten, a local party organizer bemoaned the fact that "the behavior of the Red Army was, in respect to propaganda, a fiasco for us."[46] Another KPD report observed that the Red Army's misdeeds had resulted in a situation in which "the standing refrain is: under the Americans such things would not occur."[47]

The mounting frustration with the lack of Soviet support for the new "antifascist-democratic order" came to a head at the first conference of district magistrates *(Landräte)* and mayors *(Oberbürgermeister)* held in July. Local representatives took up much of the discussion with reports on general conditions in their districts: war damage, rebuilding efforts, understaffing, and housing shortages. One *Landrat* finally broached the sensitive topic of Soviet behavior: "We would probably be further along if our work, in so many cases, was not hindered by the interference of the Red Army . . . [T]hat which we today decree, tomorrow is overturned by another decree or by another commander. We simply cannot make any more plans. We live from one day to the next not knowing if what we have initiated can also be accomplished." The *Landrat* from Niederbarnim, who reported that plundering and rape by Russian soldiers continued unabated, seconded this criticism of the Soviets. He noted that the district commander had attempted to help, but "he can't be everywhere at once."[48]

Taking the podium at the end of the presentations, Ulbricht defended the Soviets. While admitting that plundering remained a problem, but avoiding any mention of rape, Ulbricht offered a rosy assessment of the situation.

> Can one expect, after this criminal war, which German troops waged upon other peoples and directly upon the Soviet Union, that after two and one half months there would already be a free economy in place? No one can expect that. One complains that the Russians took away the bicycles. I say to him who complains about this: naturally we are against it . . . But for soldiers who have come from Stalingrad to Berlin by foot and now say, "We would like to have a bicycle," well, one can also understand that. We should see the big picture and not all of the little things, which will daily diminish step by step.[49]

Ulbricht's reasoning offered little hope that the situation would soon improve. The SPD leadership had formally complained to the Soviet commander, Marshal G. K. Zhukov, in the summer of 1945 regarding "the rapes, the plundering, and the many other encroachments that had terrified the population."[50] KPD members were similarly concerned about the Red Army's lawlessness, but the party leadership's subservience to the Soviets rendered the topic taboo.[51] In October 1945, Ulbricht argued that those who attempted to use the "unacceptable circumstances, which here and there are bound up with the occupation, for political gain" were guilty of "nothing other than support for the fascist forces of subversion."[52] Such denial on the part of the KPD leadership ensured that the situation would continue unabated. In fact, two years later, reports continued to reach the German and Soviet authorities concerning the unchecked lawlessness of Red Army soldiers throughout Brandenburg.[53]

The Provincial Government and Initial Attempts at Denazification

The person ultimately responsible for denazification in Brandenburg was Bernhard Bechler, one of the founders of the postwar provincial government. Bechler, a former German army officer and Nazi Party member, became an active member of the NKFD as a POW in Soviet captivity.[54] Later, as interior minister, Bechler would have a hand in all of the policies—denazification, land reform, expropriations, school and justice reform—that were aimed at "uprooting fascism." Bechler entered Germany in 1945 as an NKFD operative along with the Red Army. Even before the Red Army crossed the Oder River, he had established a "front school" with some sixty men trained to take control of administrative functions in Brandenburg in the wake of the Red Army's advance.[55]

The provincial government was officially established on 4 July 1945, with Karl Steinhoff, SPD member and former deputy *Oberpräsident* in East Prussia (1928–1932), appointed as its first president.[56] Four vice presidents assisted Steinhoff: Bechler, Edwin Hörnle, Fritz Rücker, and Georg Remak.[57] Hörnle and Rücker had been KPD members during the Weimar years and later were compatriots of Bechler in the NKFD. Remak was a non-socialist member of the Prussian government during the Weimar period who had been forced out of office in 1933. Hörnle later became agriculture minister, Rücker assumed the post of education minister, while Remak fled to West Berlin at the end of 1945.[58]

Administratively, Brandenburg was divided into thirty districts, or "circles" *(Kreise)*. A *Landrat* responsible to the provincial government administered rural areas *(Landkreise)*. Each *Landkreis* was divided into districts *(Bezirke),* under which there were the numerous village communes *(Gemeinden),* each with its own mayor and communal council. Urban areas were organized as separate "city circles" *(Stadtkreise)* administered by a mayor *(Oberbürgermeister)* and a city council. The central administration for the province was located in Potsdam.[59]

The purge of former Nazi Party members from the provincial administration was a top priority after the establishment of the government. Bechler outlined the criteria for employment of administrative personnel in a speech before the first meeting of *Oberbürgermeister* and *Landräte* in July. He opened his presentation by observing that "we have got to bring our own house into order."

> It is impossible that a single member of the NSDAP can remain [in the employ of the provincial government] who took part in leading us into this catastrophe. We are therefore giving you instructions from the pro-

vincial government: in the course of this month all the remaining [Nazi] party members will have to be released from service . . . I know that this or that man will say, But I haven't got replacements for this or that employee. This viewpoint would be incorrect. We can find the replacements with the necessary intensity of effort. We have the duty to find the right people among the population . . . It can happen, understandably, that this situation will not immediately go forward in a well-organized manner . . . But it is more important to have a clear political line than a smoothly functioning administration.

Bechler's "clear political line" is striking in its privileging of politics and ideology over the practical implications and problems accompanying a purge of this magnitude. He warned that some would attempt to avoid punishment by claiming that they were "unpolitical." "There is no unpolitical," Bechler stated flatly. "We are not unpolitical, but rather antifascist and have to work as such." Bechler gave the following guidelines for this purge:

Further employment of PGs is allowed only when they have *before* the war risked their lives in the fight against Hitler. It must be made clear that this is the sole exception. It would be a mistake, however, for those who did not belong to the [Nazi] party . . . to hold their heads high and to think that they bear less responsibility for this war. It has nothing to do with more or less guilt. We know that every single one of us shares in the guilt.[60]

Bechler's allusion to the concept of collective guilt reflected the KPD's approach during this period. Accordingly, all Germans shared in the guilt, and yet there were those who bore more guilt than others. These people would have to be expelled from the provincial administration. But this cloudy reasoning simply begged the question that had dogged the denazification process throughout the summer of 1945: How, exactly, were those responsible for the implementation of this policy supposed to differentiate between levels of guilt?

Bechler's plan was doomed to failure: his goal of cleansing the provincial administration in two weeks was unreasonable, given the pressing tasks of clearing rubble, erecting shelters, securing the fall harvest, processing thousands of displaced persons, and combating lawlessness. This goal was doubly unreasonable given that the political and administrative leadership had issued policies that were long on ideology and short on concrete guidelines. Bechler admitted as much in a public announcement of 9 August, in which he noted that although the July conference had set a 1 August deadline for purging the administration, the majority of districts had found it impossible to comply. Bechler's solution was to extend the deadline to 15 August.[61]

An example of the reaction of local administrators to this denazification policy is offered by a letter from *Landrat* Jerx in Neuruppin to Bechler outlining his objections to the 1 August deadline. Jerx noted that he had already dismissed, "without exception," the most incriminated PGs from his administration in the middle of May. The remaining PGs had been only nominal members who "neither in the party nor in its organizations performed a function of any kind." In the *Landrat's* view, firing these employees was not a "political necessity." In order to support his defiance of the provincial government, Jerx had lined up the support of the Soviet district commander.

Above all, Jerx argued that the dismissal of these employees would make it impossible for him to successfully organize the coming harvest to meet demands for agricultural products placed on him by the Soviets and the provincial government itself. He then went on to outline his own denazification program.

It is my intention, in the coming days, to allow a commission to investigate objectively the prior behavior of individual civil servants and salaried employees during the period of their membership in the NSDAP. In this I am counting upon the help of the Propaganda Department of the Russian army. The goal of this investigation is the issuance of a certificate, which will erase any culpability owing to membership in the NSDAP and permit employment in administration positions . . . The only civil servants and employees who will qualify are those whose help is absolutely necessary.[62]

This example from Neuruppin touches on three significant aspects of denazification during this period. First, there is the *Landrat's* understanding of Bechler's policy. In Bechler's view, the benefits of following a clear ideological course outweighed the negative effect of immediately dismissing all PGs. The view from Neuruppin was different. The "active" Nazis had been fired months earlier, and it was not presently "politically necessary" to move against remaining ex-party members. Second, the *Landrat's* position was a product of a much more practical type of politics: he was being pressured by both the provincial government and the district Soviet commander to bring in the harvest and was not about to hobble his ability to perform this task by rashly dismissing employees.[63] Third, there was the role played by the Soviets: Jerx had astutely secured the local commander's support before he confronted the provincial government.

The provincial government apparently did not object to this initiative, and Jerx issued guidelines for implementation of his denazification scheme on 20 August.[64] On 1 September, Neuruppin reported that a list of fifty-seven employees eligible for dismissal had been prepared but had been pared down to fifteen by the Soviet commander in order not to disrupt the administration unduly. The fifteen employees chosen for dismissal were deemed the "most incriminated" of the original fifty-seven.[65]

In contrast to Neuruppin, there were many areas where little was being done to purge former Nazis from local government. This was particularly true in the villages where the fiat of the provincial government had yet to pierce the web of local particularism. In one village, for example, a local KPD member complained that "for the most part nothing has been undertaken against the Nazis, because one farmer protects the other." The mayor, an SPD member, refused to dismiss his deputy mayor, even though it was common knowledge that the deputy mayor had been an active Nazi. The same applied to the local constable, the village schoolteacher, and the woman who ran the post office: "and so it goes from one end of the village to the other."[66] Similarly, the Ostprignitz KPD party secretary reported that "antifascist farmers are only seldom met. The vast majority [of farmers] were members of the NSDAP."[67]

It was difficult to find suitable mayors for the villages. At the beginning of September, Neuruppin reported that although the mayorships of the district's seven towns had been taken over by "antifascists" in May, "in the villages mayors can still presently be found who were followers of the NSDAP." It was promised that these remaining mayors, all of whom had been "non-active" members of the Nazi Party, would nevertheless be replaced as soon as the harvest was over: "The duties of the mayors in the rural communities are unusually great, especially during the harvest, considering the shortage of draft animals, machines, and the like. In many cases it is therefore difficult to find a halfway suitable person for the post of mayor."[68]

In the power vacuum of the summer of 1945—a period when, in provincial president Steinhoff's words, "all administrative work was improvisation"—local authorities had wide latitude to exercise authority.[69] A courier for the provincial government traveling in south-eastern Brandenburg in the first week of August reported that the rebuilding effort in Lübben was proceeding smoothly, mainly because the *Landrat* "does not wait for instructions to be handed to him from above, but rather acts upon his own initiative." This example of individual initiative was compared to the attitude of leaders in Spremberg, Forst, Guben, and Luckau, who felt that "everything must be managed from above and that they themselves are merely the organs that execute the policy. So, for example, a gentleman in Guben expressed his happiness that a provincial government will be formed and then more directives can be expected."[70]

The situation at the local level reflected the disorganization of the provincial administration. In contrast to Brandenburg, the provincial government in Thuringia had instituted a law in July for the "purification of the public administration" which included detailed guidelines for the purge of Nazis.[71] Brandenburg never developed a similarly comprehensive law but rather relied, through the end of 1946, on a series of measures that addressed various aspects of denazification.[72]

At the end of the summer of 1945, the Brandenburg provincial government was still desperately attempting to discern what exactly was going on in the scattered local administrations. A questionnaire sent to all districts in August indicates that Potsdam was still unaware of how many mayors and district committees *(Kreisausschüsse)* there were in the province. By the end of August, nine of the thirty districts had failed to supply this basic information to the provincial government, including *Kreis* Potsdam, where the provincial government was seated.[73] This disorganization was exacerbated by confusion over the separation of powers on the local level. The *Landrat* in Luckau, for example, reported that his district had established a committee, but it was not clear what "functions the members of the committee have and, if the district committee is prepared to meet, in that case, regarding what subjects?"[74]

The KPD and the Politics of Denazification

The fact that the 15 August deadline for purging the administration was effectively ignored on the local level underlines the inability of Potsdam to enforce its will upon the localities. The problem was similar for the KPD leadership in Berlin. Throughout the summer the party had attempted to bring its local cadres into accord with the new political line of the June declaration. The KPD struggled to square its call for the "uprooting" of fascism with the practical need to differentiate between active and passive PGs. Bechler attempted to resolve this issue by arguing that dismissal of all former Nazis from the administration took precedence over the smooth functioning of government. The impracticability of this approach was manifest, and local officials faced with pressing practical tasks such as the fall harvest often ignored Bechler's call for mass dismissals.

For the KPD leadership, denazification was an ideological problem. The practical problems presented by denazification could be addressed only after a clear party line was articulated and communicated to the rank and file.[75] Ulbricht's speech at an October party conference is indicative of the KPD's focus on ideological questions at the expense of developing practical policies. Ulbricht argued that the goals laid out in the KPD's June Declaration were well on their way to being fulfilled. This included "the struggle for the liquidation of fascism and cleansing the state, city, and other public organs of fascists." Despite this apparent progress, Ulbricht felt compelled to address the problem of differentiation.

> The question of the employment of former Nazis has arisen in various districts . . . Often one gains the impression that the big war criminals continue to sit in various directors' offices and that they freely stroll around Berlin, while the main struggle is being directed at the lowly followers [of the Nazi Party]. (Applause) I think we should interest ourselves somewhat more in those who bear the main responsibility and with the active Nazis who assisted them. (Renewed applause) We should, however, help those followers who were not active [in the Nazi Party] to move away from their old beliefs so that we can give them practical rebuilding work. (Very good!) We should be wise enough not to push these people, who were not active Nazis but rather only followers, to the same side as the active Nazis; rather we should bring them into true cooperation in rebuilding. (Lively approval) Now is the time for the former rank-and-file Nazis to recognize the crimes for which they allowed themselves to be misused and to openly renounce, before the entire people, this criminal politics and the false path. (Shout: "But now they are all 'rank-and-file Nazis.'") We have so much trust in you, we are sure that you are wise enough to differentiate between the active and the other Nazis. (Applause)[76]

Ulbricht's insistence that the KPD members were "wise enough" to differentiate between active and passive Nazis and his remark regarding the "trust" the party had in its cadres are evidence of his lack of a concrete policy. This is not to say that the KPD leadership itself was unable to develop a clear policy; in fact, a detailed proposal had actually been completed at the end of July 1945. The main impediment to the implementation of this policy came from the Soviets.

In its June Declaration the KPD had called for the formation of a "bloc of the antifascist, democratic parties" to secure the "solid unity of the democracy for the final liquidation of Nazism and the building of a new democratic Germany."[77] The Soviets gave permission for the creation of "antifascist" political parties on 10 June 1945, and within a month there were four officially sanctioned parties in the zone: the communist KPD, the Social Democratic SPD, the Christian Democratic Union (CDU), and the Liberal Democratic Party (LDP).[78] The "United Front of the Antifascist-Democratic Parties" was formed on 14 July. This body, commonly referred to as the "Antifascist Bloc," was composed of five representatives from each of the four parties who met in Berlin. According to its founding communiqué, the Antifascist Bloc's first priorities were "cooperation in the struggle for the cleansing of Germany of the remains of Hitlerism, the construction of the state on antifascist-democratic principles, and the struggle against the poison of Nazi ideology and all imperialist-militarist thinking."[79]

At the Antifascist Bloc's meeting of 3 August, guidelines for the punishment of Nazi criminals and activists were approved for publication. These guidelines were never published, however, because of objections raised by the SMA.[80] If the guidelines had been put into effect, they would have provided the denazification process with much-needed direction.[81] They defined active and nominal Nazis, specified culpable acts, and called for the establishment of German-run commissions and courts to decide cases. A substantially altered version of these guidelines was finally published three months later.[82] Gone were most of the details included in the original draft, and denazification was left to unspecified judicial action.

The Development of Soviet Policy

The last meeting of the Allied leadership took place in Potsdam and concluded on 2 August 1945. The Allies' Potsdam Agreement included provisions for denazification of the judiciary, educational system, and administrative apparatus, the banning of Nazi organizations, and the punishment of war criminals.[83] The Soviets probably stopped the publication of the Antifascist Bloc's denazification proposal in August because it would have coincided with the release of the Potsdam Agreement.[84] It is reasonable to assume that the Soviets instructed the German political leadership not to outrun the formation of policy by the Allies but rather to bring themselves into line with it.

The question that still remains, however, is why the Soviets would continue to hold up the issuance of concrete guidelines until November. A comparison of the draft proposed by the Antifascist Bloc in August and the scaled-down version issued in November points to possible areas of Soviet objection. The November Declaration did not contain specific guidelines for instituting denazification and made no provision for the establishment of district committees staffed by Germans. In contrast, the Antifascist Bloc's original plan would have established a German-run program with police and judicial powers. This was precisely the type of system that was eventually put into place at the end of 1946. In November 1945, however, the Soviets were not yet willing to sanction a broad granting of power to the Germans. From Naimark's analysis of the Soviet occupation, two likely reasons emerge for the Soviets' actions during this period. First, the SMA itself was seriously understaffed and disorganized, and the Soviets were not yet able to monitor effectively a massive purge implemented by the Germans.[85] Second, the Soviets consistently refused to allow the Germans to run their own affairs "even in the most innocuous of matters."[86] Soviet denazification policy at the end of 1945 was a product of these twin influences: the Soviets refused to allow even German "antifascists" to implement a purge, preferring instead to issue orders that they expected the German authorities to carry out immediately.

The Soviets quashed the Antifascist Bloc's proposal for a German-run purge in August. They then delayed any action on this matter for three months before finally allowing the Germans to issue a vaguely worded declaration at the beginning of November. Two days after the Antifascist Bloc's declaration was published, the Soviets finally acted by issuing a military order that required *all* former Nazi Party members, without distinction between active and nominal membership, to be dismissed from *all* positions in the provincial administrations.[87] The Soviet order gave local administrators two months to dismiss all former Nazis, a far more generous allotment of time than Bechler's two-week deadline handed down in the summer. Nevertheless, just as the summer deadline had proved unworkable, so too would this latest deadline.

An example of the twists and turns involved in putting this Soviet order into force comes from *Kreis* Calau. In a letter of 17 December 1945, *Landrat* Carl Freter notified the provincial government that there were five former Nazi Party members employed in his administration who were irreplaceable: finding substitutes for these men had, "in spite of all efforts, proved impossible and there is no expectation that such replacements can be found." Noting that the city had suffered disproportionately during the last months of the war—60 to 70 percent of the buildings were uninhabitable, administrative buildings lay in ruins, and the administrative records had been destroyed—Freter argued that these men were needed both for their expertise and because replacement workers from outside the community would have to be given lodgings, which were unavailable. Freter, who had been *Landrat* throughout the Weimar period, further testified that he had known these five men for years and considered them "trustworthy and progressive people."[88]

At about the same time, the *Landrat* in Forst submitted a similar request for exemptions, but both requests were eventually turned down.[89] In Calau, the five employees were notified on 30 December that the following day would be their last working for the *Kreis* administration.[90] Freter, however, had not given up on these employees, and he succeeded in persuading provincial president Steinhoff to support the reinstatement of three of the five men. The final decision now lay with the Soviet commander in Calau, Lieutenant Colonel Kolessov. In a letter of 5 January 1946, Freter informed Kolessov that the president of Brandenburg was supporting the reinstatement of three of the men. Kolessov, apparently unmoved, refused to sanction the re-hiring.[91] Nevertheless, it appears that these three were brought back into the Calau administration. In a letter to Kolessov, Freter dissembled, noting that two of the original five had already been dismissed and that the other three workers would remain at their posts only until the SMA made a final decision.[92] Kolessov was not ready to accept this tactic and fired off an angry retort on 30 January: "You have not fulfilled my order regarding the dismissal of the members of the fascist party. I hereby order you to dismiss today, by 20:00 hours, every member of the fascist party."[93]

Undaunted, Freter was eventually able to convince two other Soviet officers that the three men in question were indispensable; whether Kolessov had been replaced or Freter had gone over his head is unclear. The result of this maneuver was the decision by a certain Lieutenant Colonel Sotnikov that "permission from the SMA would no longer be necessary, if these employees were members of a socialist party," that is, the KPD or SPD.[94] By 7 February, Freter could happily report that two of the men were members of the SPD and that the third had "for months" been a candidate for membership in the KPD.[95] Freter had scored a partial victory, and three of the original five employees kept their jobs.

Another example of how local officials dealt with the Soviets' dismissal order comes from Neuruppin. The head of the Water Supply Department notified the *Landrat*'s office that all of his employees who had been in the Nazi Party would be released from their full-time salaried positions *(Angestelltenverhältnis)*. "Since, however, in the fulfillment of my work I am dependent upon the expertise of these PGs, I have reinstated the said workers beginning 1 January 1946 as specialists [*Facharbeiter*] with hourly pay."[96]

This ingenious bureaucratic maneuver was probably replicated throughout Brandenburg. In *Kreis* Ruppin alone, a series of letters from various agencies notified the *Landrat* that former Nazi Party members would remain at their posts past the 31 December deadline because "no replacement workers were available."[97] In the Cottbus district, a report from the beginning of February listed 250 former Nazi Party members who were still in administrative employ.[98]

In a circular letter of 18 January 1946, Bechler angrily placed the blame for the continuing presence of former Nazis in the administration on local mayors and communal superintendents "who have not performed their duty mindful of their responsibility to construct a new democratic state. I receive a vast number of reports that indicate there are a large number of corrupt, criminal, or fascist" mayors and superintendents. Bechler ordered the *Oberlandräte* to investigate the mayors and superintendents thoroughly and to dismiss immediately those found wanting. Bechler suggested that the purge of local leaders be carried out before public assemblies so that the dismissals would be seen as "a decision on the part of the citizens of the community."[99] As a result, approximately 2.5 percent of the mayors in the province were dismissed from their posts by the end of April 1946. In the

Cottbus district, for example, thirty-seven mayors were dismissed: twelve "on political grounds," six for criminal acts, and nineteen because of "professional unfitness."[100]

An example of the politics of denazification during this period was the case of Mayor B. of the town of Bad Saarow. On a Sunday afternoon in late February, about 450 residents crowded into a local restaurant for a public meeting of the Antifascist Bloc. The chairman of the local SPD gave a speech in which he urged that "there must be the quickest possible construction of a central administration in Germany, in which the local communities form the most basic cells. For this reason there must be absolute integrity in the local communities and their administrations." At this point the speaker was interrupted by shouts from the audience: "In Bad Saarow it is otherwise!" and "We demand a new administration!"[101] The "lively and frequent interruptions" from the crowd forced the Antifascist Bloc to drop its original agenda and allow the citizens to express themselves.

A local KPD member in the audience claimed that Mayor B. had been a member of the NSDAP and the SA, and a contributing member *(förderndes Mitglied)* of the SS. After the war's end, Mayor B. joined the SPD, claiming the Nazis had imprisoned him. It turned out that he had indeed been in prison, but for theft, not because of his political beliefs.[102] Another member of the audience then stated that one of the mayor's cronies, a certain Herr G. who was present at the meeting, had been given a completely furnished new apartment even though he already possessed an adequate apartment. When Herr G. rose to defend himself, he was shouted down with cries of "Nazi pig!"[103]

The list of accusations of corruption grew. There was the employee of the communal administration, Herr P., whom the mayor refused to move against even though it was common knowledge that he had been a leading member of the Nazi Party in Berlin. Herr P. had recently opened a store in town, which the mayor had supplied with "a large refrigerator." Herr P. rose to defend himself "even though he was frequently interrupted by indignant shouts from the public."[104] There were tales of confiscated bicycles, furniture, and typewriters, illegal hoards of food, and even of the mayor's brother receiving a piano under questionable circumstances. One speaker claimed that Herr G. had threatened him with arrest by the Soviet secret police if he brought up the subject of corruption at the public meeting.[105] A woman in the audience asked if the citizens had the power to remove the mayor, to which an SPD member of the panel replied that only the Soviet commander or the *Landrat* had such power. The much-maligned Herr G.'s request to address the crowd for two minutes "was answered with an indignant: No!" At this point, the Soviet commander and his interpreter arrived. After being apprised of the issues, the Soviet officer let it be known that the assembled citizens definitely did not have the right to replace the mayor; only the Soviet authorities could take such a step. The commander did, however, permit the citizens to pass a resolution calling for the mayor's ouster; this resolution was drafted and approved with only one nay vote. The records do not indicate if the mayor was dismissed from his post after this incident.[106]

This example shows how denazification could enter into the field of local politics. For the provincial government and the SMA, denazification was to be carried out through the issuance of orders, laws, and deadlines. The unique circumstances in the individual communities, however, transformed the implementation of these policies. Accusations of former Nazi activity quickly merged with charges of corruption and cronyism. The pressing issues of everyday life, such as food and housing shortages, became part of the process and produced a volatile combination of grassroots activism and the politics of the purge. To the multiplicity of voices was added that of the Soviet commander: the Soviet commanders' word was law, and their decisions often determined the course of denazification. As the cited examples demonstrate, factors at the local level could transform the denazification process into something unforeseen by the policy makers in Berlin and Potsdam.

The Unraveling of Denazification

By the end of February 1946, it was becoming clear that a blanket dismissal of former Nazis from the administration was unworkable. The Central Finance Administration for the entire Soviet zone notified the provincial governments that, although "active National Socialists" had been "basically dismissed from the administration," there were, "on special official grounds, activists still employed who are presently also [subject] to immediate dismissal." It was therefore decided, in agreement with the SMA, that "all remaining former National Socialists may be further employed for the present." These former Nazis could not, however, hold "leading positions," and were to be paid as "expert skilled workers." The former Nazis who had already been dismissed were not to be rehired.[107]

In Brandenburg it was decided at the end of June that "all former members of the NSDAP who presently are still active in the administration and who have been approved by the provincial administration may remain at their posts. They are to be verbally informed that they have taken an active part in rebuilding and are therefore rehabilitated."[108] According to the provincial government's own reckoning, 1,945 PGs were working for the administration at the end of April 1946. They were described as "doctors, pharmacists, technicians, and other people whose continuing employment is technically necessary." On the positive side, it was claimed that 10,714 former Nazis had been dismissed from the administration since the purge began.[109]

This inconsistent denazification presented two problems. First, the flurry of contradictory instructions and unattainable deadlines hindered reconstruction and complicated the already difficult tasks of local administrators. Second, denazification was not achieving its goal of "cleansing" the administration. On the contrary, by the summer of 1946, the provincial government was inundated with requests for permission to rehire dismissed Nazis. Although the provincial government maintained a policy of replacing former Nazis with "antifascists" whenever possible, PGs could be rehired "when absolutely necessary" if they obtained permission from the local Antifascist Bloc and the umbrella trade union, the Free German Federation of Unions (FDGB).[110] In August the provincial government decreed that former Nazis in the administration were no longer to be paid wages lower than those paid to other employees but henceforth were to be compensated at the established wage rates for their occupations.[111] A request by the provincial police department to hire former Nazis as policemen was denied, however, since the "PGs do not yet have the trust of the people, which is necessary for the police force and in the interest of the entire population."[112]

The employment of PGs in the administration had always been subject to the proviso that they not hold a "leading position." This stricture was routinely ignored. It was reported, for example, that "very many" of the road construction supervisors *(Strassenmeistern)*—certainly a key group in the reconstruction—had been members of the Nazi Party. Although most of these individuals had been downgraded from salaried to hourly status, they continued to work as supervisors as before.[113]

Denazification of the administration could, however, extend beyond the dismissal of PGs. In the city of Jüterbog, for example, two female employees were dismissed, even though they had never been members of the Nazi Party, because they were married to "active" Nazis. In defending his action, the mayor noted that one woman's husband was the proprietor of a grocery store and that it would not be fair to allow this former Nazi to profit from his wife's income. In the second case, a woman was dismissed because her husband, who was currently a POW, "belonged to the SS and therefore is definitely to be considered an active Nazi." The mayor added, "A marked unrest arose among the population because the wife of a strongly active PG was employed in the service of the municipal administration." In a complaint to the provincial government, one of the dismissed women asked, "What remains of the right of individual freedom of opinion for women? Or should all of the wives of former PGs also be denazified? That would be, exactly as in my case, sheer mockery for women who actually had nothing to do with National Socialism."[114]

Regarding the problems that denazification caused for reconstruction, Franz Dahlem, a leading member of the SED, observed, "There are places and regions where all of the [employees of the] postal service and railroads and all of the teachers and the intellectual occupations [*intellektuelle Berufe*] were forced with unrelenting pressure into Nazi organizations. We will not be so stupid as to push these people away from us and leave [reconstruction] to those who remain."[115]

The results of the administrative purge through the end of 1946 were mixed. While many employees had been dismissed, there were significant variations among the individual departments in the administration, and there was much more work to be done if the goal of complete "cleansing" of the administration was to be met. The Soviets decided in December 1946 that the denazification had not gone far enough and ordered the establishment of district denazification commissions throughout the zone. Perhaps the most remarkable aspect of denazification in Brandenburg through the end of 1946 is the extent to which the Soviet and German policy makers were unable to guarantee the implementation of their orders on the local level. It should be remembered that the Soviets had unequivocally ordered that *all* former Nazi Party members were to be dismissed by 31 December 1945. Yet, by the provincial government's own reckoning, 21 percent of its employees working at the end of 1946 had been Nazi Party members.[116]

In summing up this phase of denazification in Brandenburg, the East German historian Ralf Schäfer pronounced the program a success, noting that the vast majority of the *Landräte, Oberbürgermeister,* and mayors were SED members, which put the "decisive positions for the democratic rebuilding, and thus for the denazification, firmly in the hands of the working class."[117] While this may have been true, it should be remembered that the goal of the provincial leadership and the SMA had originally been to purge all PGs from the administration, not simply to obtain control of the "decisive positions." The failure to accomplish this original goal is indicative of the nature of denazification during this period. No matter how many orders and deadlines the authorities issued, they were continually confronted with the fact that they could not effect the outcomes they desired. Part of the problem lay in the authorities' weak control over their subordinates and over the province in general. In addition, the authorities themselves were of two minds regarding the purge. Although denazification was seen as ideologically imperative, the ideological muddle that arose in the summer of 1945 continued through the end of the following year. The main questions that dogged denazification from its inception—how to differentiate between active and nominal PGs, what should be done after this determination was made, and who should be responsible for making this determination and implementing the decision—all remained unanswered. Added to this confusion was the contradiction between denazification and reconstruction. The overall effect of the experiences of this period finally led to the development of a new type of purge—one that was centrally controlled and based on district denazification commissions.

CHAPTER 3

Expropriation, Land Reform, and the PGs

The present chapter focuses on an often overlooked aspect of denazification: the measures taken against PGs who were not employees of the provincial government. These people constituted most of the former Nazi Party members in Brandenburg. In the period between the end of the war and December 1946, a series of measures was taken to punish the PGs. These measures fell into four categories: (1) the registration of PGs and former German army officers, (2) the organization of forced labor battalions, (3) the expropriation of land and personal belongings, and (4) the denial of voting rights in the 1946 elections.

Examination of these four areas is essential to a redefinition of Soviet denazification. One of the main shortcomings of prior research has been an almost exclusive focus on the administrative and bureaucratic aspects of the purge. This approach is too narrowly construed, however, because it overlooks many measures taken against individuals as a result of their membership in National Socialist organizations. In the present study, the term "denazification" encompasses all the ways in which individuals were called to account for their activities during the Nazi period. The question of what to do with the PGs goes to the heart of Germany's earliest attempts to come to terms with the Nazi past. In addressing the problem of the PGs, society was faced with the most fundamental questions of guilt, retribution, and fairness, and the possibility of constructing a denazified society that had exorcised the demons of the past and could thus rightfully rejoin the community of nations.

Registration

The Allies' call, issued at the Potsdam Conference in August 1945, for the destruction of all organizations that supported Nazism and "militarism" made it necessary to identify individual members of these organizations.[1] On 27 August the Soviets ordered former members of the German army from the rank of lieutenant upward, and former members of the SS, SA, Gestapo, and NSDAP, to register with their local Soviet commander by 25 September 1945. German mayors and *Landräte* were responsible for implementing the registration. Individuals who did not comply or helped others avoid registration were threatened with the "strongest" measures.[2]

In some areas, German administrators had already put registration into force.[3] In other locales, the initiative for registration came from the Soviets. In response to the "unclarified murder or suicide" of a member of the Red Army in the town of Lehnin, the Soviet commander ordered all former members of Nazi organizations to assemble daily at 8 A.M. with their identification papers. These people were either assigned to work details or forced to remain under guard at a local barracks throughout the day. They were allowed to return home in the evening, but were required to remain there under curfew until 7:30 the following morning. Former Nazis caught breaking this curfew were to be shot.[4]

By the end of the summer, there were three registration schemes in Brandenburg: those undertaken on the initiative of the German authorities, those undertaken by local Soviet commanders, and, finally, the official registration ordered by the SMA in August. The consequent overlapping lines of responsibility were indicative of the general state of confusion that reigned during the early occupation period.[5] Another hallmark of this period was the issuance of impossible deadlines, in this case the SMA's 25 September date for completion of registration. A report from the Cottbus district from the middle of October, for example, noted that the registration was not yet complete.[6]

The registration played a role in the later denazification process; the lists were used by denazification commissions to identify former Nazis in the purge that began at the end of 1946. In local communities, registration separated PGs from the general population and marked them for possible future punishment. The police department in the Cottbus district reported that registration produced "resignation" and a "very depressed mood" among PGs: "From the Nazis one hears little, they have become very silent." Among former members of the National Socialist Women's Organization, the NSF, there was reported a mood of "immediate fear because they expect still more oppressive regulations."[7]

Work Battalions

The PGs' fear that registration was the first step toward future punishment was not misplaced. After the collapse of the Third Reich, a pattern of retribution against PGs began to take shape in which registration was the least onerous obligation. The singling out of PGs for special work battalions proceeded in much the same way as the denazification program in general, with a period of improvisation centered on the local level followed by increased central control.

An early example comes from Ruppin a month after the end of the war. On 9 June 1945 the Soviet commander ordered an end to the school year so that all children from age fifteen could be drafted for agricultural work. The order stipulated that former members of National Socialist youth organizations—the Hitler Jugend (HJ) for boys and the Bund Deutscher Mädel (BDM) for girls—were to be organized into a separate work group concentrated in a "controlled area." The *Landrat* suggested that they should occupy themselves with the "hard labor" of clearing rubble from the local airstrip, but insisted that this labor would be "educational" and conducted in a "democratic manner."[8] The attitude of the Soviet commanders could also complicate the work program. At a meeting of district mayors, the Soviet commander in Niederbarnim declared that it was "laughable" to think "the fight against fascism . . . could be conducted in such a petty manner." Unlike his compatriot in Ruppin, the Soviet commander in Niederbarnim ordered that "the Nazis should not be treated in a fundamentally different manner from the remaining population." He prohibited "discriminatory special work [*Sonderarbeit*] as a political measure."[9]

There was a widespread desire to force PGs to do heavy labor. The need to identify former Nazis in order to put them to work was doubtless one of the primary reasons behind the push for registration. The task was simplified in areas where administrative records had not been destroyed during the closing weeks of the war. Local administrators in Angermünde, for example, put together a list of Nazi Party members by utilizing records of the Residential Registration Department that listed, among other things, the names of party members, their membership numbers, and their dates of entrance into the party. This list was turned over to the Employment Office, which then forced these individuals to perform "dirty work, the exhumation of corpses, etc."[10] A similar action was taken against adult PGs by the communist-led Antifascist Committee in Bernau, where "former Nazis were forced to work" and were given reduced rations because it was felt that "the Nazis should work more and eat less than all the others."[11]

The formulation of a general policy of singling out PGs for "special work" began in November 1945. On 1 November the Central Administration for Employment and Social Welfare issued guidelines for "special deployment" of "previously active former members of the NSDAP." The guidelines identified "active" Nazis as those who held leading positions in National Socialist organizations as well as those who joined the Nazi Party before Hitler came to power. In addition, individuals who had denounced people to the Nazi authorities or treated others in a "brutal or base" manner were to be considered activists "whether or not they were in the party." A catchall provision included as activists all persons, irrespective of party membership, who "publicly or in secret, in word or writing, or through substantial monetary contributions, actively supported the goals of the NSDAP."[12]

This was followed by SMA Order 153 of 29 November, which called for former Nazis to do "dirty work" *(Schmutzarbeit)* in the reconstruction. The order required all PGs, men aged twenty-one to sixty-five and women twenty-one to fifty-five, to perform, "above all, especially dirty and unpleasant work serving the public interest and the reconstruction." PGs could be compelled to work on Sundays and holidays and at night. If individuals who fell under this order were already employed doing "nonessential" work, they were liable for up to twelve additional hours of weekly "dirty work." They were to be remunerated as "unskilled laborers," and those who refused this work were subject to arrest and confiscation of ration cards.[13]

As a result of this order, former Nazi Party members were organized into brigades to do agricultural work, remove rubble, and gather firewood for "the aged and ill population."[14] Avoidance of "special employment" by PGs was widespread. The *Landrat* in Cottbus, for example, reported that many employers were giving PGs wide latitude to excuse themselves from work, particularly on Sundays. An investigation discovered that workers were not showing up at assigned workplaces but were still being issued certificates by employers stating that they had performed their assigned tasks.[15]

In some areas, such as Angermünde, the "special brigades" of former Nazis were successfully put to work repairing damaged railroad tracks and digging graves.[16] In other districts, however, utilization of work crews was problematic. Local road maintenance departments, in particular, complained that PGs in their employ were being removed from their jobs to work in special brigades, an action that actually hindered reconstruction.[17] An unforeseen problem arose in Zauch-Belzig when fifty-two PGs sent to work repairing train tracks were rejected by the rail administration because "they want antifascist workers." The director of the Belzig Employment Office argued that since, "aside from invalids," there were no unemployed in the area, he had no choice but to send PGs to the railroad. In addition, he noted, the assignment of PGs to rail repair work was in line with the policy of giving these workers difficult tasks: "We know of no lower form of work." The provincial government's advice was to avoid sending PGs to work for the railroad because it was a "public authority where the demands of the denazification are given top priority."[18]

It is unclear when the forced labor policy came to an end. In July 1946 the Brandenburg Employment Administration decided that PGs were no longer liable to perform special work. Upon receiving word of this decision, however, the SMA in Potsdam overruled it, noting that Order 153 of November 1945 was still in force.[19] That the Employment Department attempted this decision suggests the degree to which special work battalions had probably ceased to exist. In all likelihood, local administrators increasingly abandoned the practice in the face of its unpopularity and limited usefulness in reconstruction. This move away from the forced labor policy in the summer of 1946 was part of a general relaxation of denazification measures during this period. As shown in the previous chapter, the policy of dismissing all former Nazi Party members from the provincial government was also halted in the summer of 1946.

Expropriations, Land Reform, and Denazification

Restructuring of the industrial and agricultural sectors through expropriation and redistribution figured prominently in both the communist critique of fascism and wartime planning. In East German historiography, this was part of the "antifascist-democratic revolution" or upheaval *(Umwälzung)* which took place between 1945 and 1949, and which laid the foundation for the GDR. In this view, expropriation was not so much punishment for past deeds as it was a prerequisite for eradicating the roots of fascism: "It could not suffice to 'punish' individual persons through property confiscation; [the expropriation] had to be aimed at a class that had misused power and would have the economic preconditions of its power expropriated."[20] It was argued that as a result of expropriation "in the Soviet occupation zone, the power bases of imperialism, militarism, and fascism were destroyed. The imperialist German bourgeoisie as a class ceased to exist."[21]

East German historians reached similar conclusions regarding land reform. The agricultural sector was the site of the nexus between the conservative large land-holding class—the "Junkers"—and Prussian militarism, which, along with the industrial bourgeoisie, provided the class support for German fascism. According to Siegfried Thomas, "the fundamental destruction of fascism and militarism in the countryside could only be accomplished through a revolutionary transformation of ownership and property relationships." Thus, "the decisive result of the democratic land reform was the liquidation of the Junkers as a class, the crushing of the bulwark of reaction in the countryside."[22]

In the work of West German historians, expropriation and land reform were often interpreted as two interrelated programs aimed at establishing communist power in the Soviet zone.[23] An alternative interpretation, put forward by Christoph Kleßmann, placed expropriation and land reform within the context of a general denazification and questioned the idea that these reforms were simply "the first step" in the "sovietization of eastern Germany."[24] Kleßmann's approach suggests a new way of contextualizing denazification. Expropriation, land reform, and denazification formed a triad at the center of Soviet occupation policy. Expropriation and land reform can be placed within the broader policy of denazification if we consider these programs in the context of the postwar debate regarding individual Nazi Party members, their degree of culpability for National Socialist crimes, and how they were to be punished.

Expropriation and the PGs

Expropriation took two forms. The first was the seizure of industrial concerns and businesses owned by the state or by Nazi Party members who had supported and/or profited from the policies of the Third Reich. The second was the confiscation of the personal property of individuals as punishment for their role in the Third Reich.

The expropriation process proceeded in a pattern similar to denazification. In the first period, from the end of the war through the summer of 1945, expropriations were localized affairs, often instituted by activists with the support of the mayor or *Landrat*. In the village of Borkwalde, for example, the KPD's plan for "the destruction of fascism" called for "the immediate seizure of administrative records . . . in order to make an exact survey of all PGs."[25] As a member of one local Antifascist Committee observed, "The victims of fascism should be indemnified by the Nazis, because [the Nazis] financed and prolonged the war. The expropriation must encompass them all, since making a distinction [between Nazis] is very difficult."[26]

As we have seen, the Soviet commander in Niederbarnim had derided forced labor and expropriations aimed at the PGs as a "laughable" approach to the "fight against fascism" and had prohibited all such actions. The result of his order was, in the words of one KPD leader from the town of Mühlenbeck, "great strife and unhappiness among the antifascist population, which naturally hold us [the KPD] responsible for this situation." As a result, he pleaded with the KPD leadership for "truly *binding* advice" regarding, among other things, "how we should proceed in regard to the property of the Nazis." This property included both real estate and movable property such as "furniture, vehicles, etc." Advice was also requested regarding the permissibility of seizing the property of Nazis for "public use (for example, books for the establishment of a public library, etc.)." A similar problem surrounded businesses operated by Nazis and whether or not they could be seized. If so, was it necessary to compensate the owner, and was the property then to be considered communal property? Underlying all these questions was the most fundamental problem of this period: "Who can be considered an 'active' fascist?"[27]

Abuse of the expropriation program was widespread in the months following the end of the war. In a circular letter of 16 August 1945, President Steinhoff called a halt to all further confiscation. Steinhoff had received "continuous reports" concerning the seizure of property "in individual cases, up to the taking away of [an individual's] entire possessions."[28] Steinhoff had also received "countless complaints" regarding the confiscation of industrial concerns. Often these seizures were conducted "without any consideration" of whether continued operation of the firms was possible. He warned that such seizures were illegal and could be considered "sabotage" by the SMA.[29] Steinhoff ordered an immediate end to all seizures, with the exception of those that aimed to bring a closed concern back into production.[30]

The promised Soviet guidelines were released at the end of October. SMA Order 124 permitted the seizure of the property of the "National Socialist state and its central and local administrations" and of "officeholders in the National Socialist Party, its leading members, and influential supporters." Also included was the property of National Socialist "societies, clubs, and organizations" and the property of "persons who have been designated by the Soviet Military Command" for expropriation.[31]

Interior Minister Bechler attempted to limit the extent of the confiscations by restricting the definition of individuals liable for expropriation. Bechler ordered that the term "officeholders of the NSDAP" should be construed as meaning those who were "active on a full-time basis and were so paid." "Leading members" of the Nazi Party included "persons from district leader [*Kreisleiter*], district office leader [*Kreisamtleiter*], and Landrat upwards." "Influential supporters" of National Socialism, who were not PGs, were defined as those who had "significantly financed" the party. The goal of these guidelines was to ensure that "small greengrocers or similar businessmen will not be thrown out of their shops and have their property expropriated."[32]

Bechler's clarifications were a response to the widespread misuse of the expropriation process. In the village of Schnackertz, for example, the KPD, in the person of the constable who happened also to be the "political leader" of the KPD in the village, confiscated the furniture from the apartment of the former Nazi *Ortsgruppenleiter*. This furniture later turned up in the offices of the local KPD. The village authorities were incensed at this action and let it be known that the KPD "had no right" to order such a confiscation and that it was "above all a blunder" that the constable had "committed this act by the misuse of his uniform."[33] In the Brandenburg/Havel district, hundreds of people filed petitions claiming wrongful expropriation of property by the Soviets, police, and Antifascist Committees. Many of these petitioners claimed either that they had been merely nominal PGs or that they had never been in a fascist organization. The seized property included everything from automobiles to household items, furniture, and clothing.[34]

The negative effect of such actions soon became evident. The leader of the KPD in Zauch-Belzig reported that the seizures were an "urgent problem" that had led to "the development of a marked unrest that, viewed politically, considerably disrupts our work." Despite these difficulties, he defended the expropriations: "They may at the moment appear hard, but will come to be seen by all antifascists and all democratic parties, as far as I can tell, as having been necessary." Eventually, he predicted, "a feeling of security" would return, "especially among those who have been spared from the expropriations."[35]

Less sanguine was the *Landrat* from Ruppin who reported that Order 124 had resulted in a series of mistakes and transgressions. "The vast majority of the population considers a harsh law directed against the former supporters of the NSDAP to be necessary but is likewise of the opinion that the limits of this law need to be observed by all sides." The *Landrat* feared the rise of "complete lawlessness in which arbitrary acts are perpetrated and the reputation of the antifascist course will be extraordinarily damaged." Particularly troubling was the "series of instances where there without question exists a case of personal enrichment." Another negative result of the expropriations was their effect on economic life. "The initiative of former PGs is beginning to be replaced with passivity. Even the nominal members [of the Nazi Party] give little thought to carrying out economic measures on a large scale. They also have the fear—in the majority of cases completely without grounds—of an expropriation and no longer have the courage to initiate a large undertaking."[36] The *Landrat* blamed the PGs' fear of expropriation on rumors spread by former Nazis who had been recently dismissed from their positions in government service under the administrative denazification program.[37]

As with so many denazification measures, the expropriations hindered reconstruction. The seizure of a Nazi-owned business may well have satisfied a desire for retribution, but it could also prove a brake on economic activity. This situation was similar to the conflict that arose between the contradictory policies of denazification and rebuilding the administrative apparatus. Likewise, punishing PGs by forcing them to perform "dirty work" could in practice remove skilled workers from jobs essential to reconstruction.

Expropriations also exacerbated one of the most serious problems during the period: the flood of refugees that inundated the Soviet zone after the war. Specifically, punishing PGs by seizing their dwellings and turning them over to homeless "antifascists" had the unwanted result of swelling the ranks of refugees with former Nazis forced from their houses.

In the village of Breddin, for example, eleven families were ejected from their homes by the mayor and ordered to leave not just the village but the entire district of Ostprignitz. The families were forcibly transported to the district capital, Kyritz, where the *Landrat* overturned the Breddin mayor's expulsion order and allowed them to remain in the district.[38] One of those who had been expelled complained that "as a small PG, I have nothing to feel guilty about . . . which might legally lead to an expropriation." He reflected that "everywhere, including here, neighbors fish in troubled waters and seek from base convictions to hinder an honest tradesman from making any headway."[39] Another complained that she was expropriated because her husband, who she claimed was missing, had been a Nazi Party member; she herself had not been in the party. This woman ascribed her expropriation to "petty hatred and a desire for revenge."[40] Eventually, in April 1946, the Brandenburg Justice Ministry overturned the Breddin expropriations and ordered the families' property returned.[41]

Cases similar to the Breddin expulsions had led the Brandenburg provincial government to issue guidelines as early as October 1945. It was noted that "in one district refugees were given the apartments of members of the NSDAP and the former apartment owners were expelled, themselves becoming refugees." It was reasoned that it was an "understandable necessity that the living quarters, especially of a member of the NSDAP, could be so reduced that a refugee could be given shelter." There was also "nothing to be said against" giving a former Nazi "other, inferior accommodations." What was forbidden, however, was to expel a PG, "thereby creating again a new refugee."[42]

The expropriation process was eventually transformed in a manner similar to the way in which the denazification of the administration passed from an improvised, localized, and uncontrolled movement to a more centrally organized program. Responding to the continuous stream of expropriation cases that either were "insufficiently grounded" or showed evidence of "formal mistakes," the provincial government issued a set of guidelines in December 1945. A thorough investigation of the grounds for expropriation was to be conducted before the case was forwarded to the provincial government, and a provincial commission was established to review all requests for an expropriation. In order to seize the property of "war criminals, people who denounced others to the Nazis [*Denunzianten*], or particularly brutal fascists," it was necessary to submit "truly concrete evidence with place, date, and those who took part . . . In general, statements such as 'particularly active fascist' [or] 'brutal person' do not suffice for an expropriation."[43]

The expropriation process was brought under zonal control by Soviet Order 97 (29 March 1946), which established a central expropriation commission in Berlin.[44] District expropriation commissions were also established throughout Brandenburg to investigate every expropriation since the end of the war.[45] The district commissions were given the task of drawing up a list of expropriated property that they believed should be returned to the former owners and a list of property that should not be returned.[46]

Some idea of the magnitude of the expropriations can be gleaned from the reports submitted by the commission in Teltow. By summer 1946, the property of 143 individuals had been officially expropriated. This included 49 parcels of real estate, 87 houses, 7 fields, 4 farms, and 20 businesses and factories, including a chemical works and a movie theater. The Teltow records tell only half the story for the district, however, since this was a compilation of properties the commission felt should not be returned to the previous owners. Although it is unclear what became of the majority of these individuals, the records do mention the fate of several: two were reported as deceased; two had committed suicide (one along with his wife and children); three had fled, probably out of the Soviet zone; seven either were under arrest or had been sentenced to prison terms, and four were listed as having been killed by the Red Army.[47]

The thoroughness with which the Teltow commission fulfilled its duty was apparently the exception rather than the rule. In a circular letter of 4 June 1946, the provincial government scolded the commissions for continuing to submit unsubstantiated reports of expropriations; this included the repeated use of the term "activist" as the sole reason for expropriation. Exasperated, the provincial government ordered all commissions to complete an accurate accounting of all prior expropriations in eight days (by 12 June).[48] By August 1946, 1,371 Brandenburg businesses were declared officially expropriated, while 573 were deemed to have been incorrectly expropriated and were returned to their original owners.[49] The businesses, along with all other property expropriated from "active supporters of National Socialism," were subsequently declared the legal property of the provincial government, for which no reimbursement was to be paid.[50] The expropriation process continued for almost two more years until it was finally ended in April 1948.[51]

Although it does not bear directly on the expropriation process in Brandenburg, mention must be made of the "People's Referendum" held in Saxony on 30 June 1946. The Saxon referendum, which was the first exercise of voting rights in the Soviet zone, asked for voters' retroactive approval of the expropriation of "war and Nazi criminals." For the newly formed SED (Socialist Unity Party)—an amalgamation of the KPD and SPD—the referendum was seen as the first test of its ability to mount an electoral campaign. By choosing the "traditionally Red province" of industrialized Saxony, the SED secured a 77.6 percent approval for the referendum over the opposition of the "bourgeois" parties, the Christian Democratic Union (CDU) and the Liberal Democratic Party (LDP).[52] Although, in the view of the Brandenburg SED chairman, Fritz Ebert, the Saxon referendum enjoyed wide support in Brandenburg, no similar vote was held there.[53] Instead, the provincial government contented itself with passing a law that retroactively legalized the expropriations that had occurred in Brandenburg.[54] In the fall 1946 elections, the Brandenburg SED campaigned on a platform that equated a vote for the SED with a vote in favor of a referendum for expropriation.[55]

Land Reform and the PGs

Land reform was a massive restructuring of rural society and the agricultural sector of the economy. The stated objective of land reform was the "liquidation of the feudal Junker large landholding system" which had been a "bastion of reaction and fascism." As with expropriations, land reform targeted individuals seen as culpable for the crimes of the National Socialist state. Under the land reform, all holdings of over one hundred hectares qualified for expropriation. When it came to property held by those deemed to be responsible for the misdeeds of the Third Reich, however, all agricultural property, livestock, machinery, and buildings were to be seized, without compensation, "irrespective of the size of the concern."[56] Exempted from expropriation were "small farmers who were PGs but who cannot be held accountable for any crime."[57] Former PGs, even if they had been only nominal members of the Nazi Party, were not allowed to sit on land reform commissions. This turned out to be a problem in some villages where every farmer had been a member of the Nazi Party. In these cases it was decided that an "antifascist" would have to be imported from the outside to oversee the land reform.[58]

In the land reform program—as in the registration, forced labor, and expropriation programs—former Nazis were separated out from the general population as a class marked for punishment. The communist critique of fascism seemed to give equal weight to the guilt of the "Junkers" and the "active fascists." In the land reform program, however, the harshest punitive measures were reserved for the activists. It was policy, for example, for expropriated large landowners to be allowed to keep "all articles such as clothing, furniture, and household items necessary for running a normal household." The local land reform commissions were also charged with ensuring that these individuals had living quarters so that "such families . . . will not be left homeless with their furniture on the street." It was stressed, however, that these provisions were applicable only to those who had not been "active members of the NSDAP or its organizations."[59]

What was to become of these people is not clear. There is evidence that a few expropriated individuals continued to reside in their home districts and even on rump remainders of their former holdings. An undated document, probably from late 1947, lists seventy-three expropriated people (including children) in all of Brandenburg who continued to reside in their home districts. The majority had been granted exceptions owing to age, illness, destitution, or willing cooperation in the land reform program.[60] These seventy-three individuals represent only a tiny percentage of the overall number of expropriated property owners. In all, 2,357 agricultural holdings were expropriated in Brandenburg, totaling 751,115 hectares, of which 609,000 hectares derived from large estates. This land was subsequently divided among 82,810 village families.[61]

As with the expropriations, land reform initially affected many PGs who were not the intended targets of the program. In a speech before the First Congress of the newly organized Association for Farmers' Mutual Assistance (VdgB), Interior Minister Bechler noted that at the beginning of the land reform program, "the communal land reform committees expropriated a large number of PGs without—as legally stipulated—waiting for permission from the provincial commission." As a result, "a large majority of these expropriated PGs had to be given back their farms." This had to be done, Bechler noted, because "a new mass migration of small farmers who were PGs would have been, in every respect, undesirable for the province."[62]

No doubt many of the overzealous expropriations that took place during the land reform process were driven by a desire to punish the Nazis. At a conference of agricultural workers in Angermünde, for example, a member of a communal land reform commission stated, "to applause," that Nazi village leaders should be expropriated because they were responsible "for forcing us to work on the harvest under Hitler and very often behaved like *Schweinhunde* toward us." A representative from the village of Neuendorf added, "There are also farmers who were not members of the Nazi Party but who denounced antifascists. I believe these people are also ripe for expropriation." Another delegate declared that "very many of those Nazis who formerly handed everyone over to the hangman, who beat their [foreign forced] laborers, and for years profited from the Hitler system now sit unchallenged on their farms. We demand that they also be expropriated."[63]

The problem of the PGs and land reform also arose in the context of the influx of displaced persons. Willy Sägebrecht, Brandenburg's representative at a meeting of the KPD Central Committee in November 1945, brought this matter to the party's attention.

> *Sägebrecht:* A large number of Nazis are arriving from the east whom we do not want to settle, above all not the active Nazis ... [T]hese should remain in a camp for the time being. We do not want to settle the Nazis, because if we do, then the rumors that they spread will only be spread more and the atmosphere they create will only get worse and our work will become more

difficult . . . In this context there is another issue. In Saxony they have come up with the idea of sending expropriated large landowners—the majority of whom are Nazis—to Mecklenburg. In Mecklenburg they have hit upon the idea of sending their 2,000 expropriated National Socialist large landowners to Thuringia. It is obvious that this should not occur. The party must know about this and insist that nothing of this kind take place.

[Anton] Ackermann: Why?

Sägebrecht: The National Socialists in Mecklenburg are known; there they cannot cause any more mischief.

[Wilhelm] Pieck: One can then simply shoot them! (Amusement)

Sägebrecht: Good, then one should shoot them. In Mecklenburg they are known, in Thuringia they are lost.

Ackermann: It cannot be denied that the estate owners can do the greatest harm in their own villages.[64]

Despite Pieck's brutal quip, the solution to the PG problem could not be so easily solved. As Sägebrecht pointed out, given the general goal of denazification, the last thing administrators or local communities needed was an influx of more former Nazis. For the PGs in Brandenburg—both native and newly arrived—the period after the war was one in which they found themselves continually relegated to the position of second-class citizens. They were organized into forced labor battalions, and their land, homes, businesses, and possessions were seized by a new system that held them responsible for the crimes of the Third Reich.

The Elections of 1946

The limited nature of the PGs' citizenship was evident in their exclusion from participation in the series of elections held in 1946. The first elections in the Soviet zone occurred in two phases: an election of representatives to communal assemblies, held in Brandenburg in September 1946, and a second for provincial and district assemblies held throughout the zone in October. Although the Soviets had been first among the occupation powers to permit, in June 1945, the formation of political parties, the first elections were not held until after the amalgamation of the KPD and SPD into the SED in April 1946.[65]

The Brandenburg electoral law was based primarily on statutes devised during the Weimar Republic.[66] These statutes included the concept of active and passive voting rights. Those with active voting rights could run for elective office as well as vote. Passive voters simply held the right to vote but could not run for office. Under Brandenburg's statute, all PGs were denied active voting rights, although nominal PGs could be granted passive voting rights. Those denied even passive voting rights were "war criminals," members of the SS, SD, and Gestapo, and former leaders of the NSF, SA, NSKK (National Socialist Motorized Corps), NSFK (National Socialist Aviation Corps), Hitler Youth, and BDM. Also excluded were "former activists of fascism and war interests whose names will be made available to the communal authorities" by the communal and district level Antifascist Blocs.[67] The exclusion of "active fascists" from the election was, in SED leader Otto Grotewohl's words, an "obvious" necessity, since "there is no place in the politics of Germany for the gravediggers of Germany."[68]

At the local level, the election statutes put the power to grant voting rights in the hands of the Antifascist Blocs. This is significant in the context of the later denazification program. In the three instances discussed in this chapter—expropriation, land reform, and the fall elections—local commissions were organized to render decisions regarding the fate of former Nazis. Each of these commissions produced information on PGs that would be invaluable to the denazification commissions. The *Landrat* of Beeskow-Storkow, for example, forwarded to the Interior Ministry a list of 3,304 individuals denied voting rights.[69] Such lists later formed a basis for calling individuals before denazification commissions. These programs also set the precedent of establishing local commissions to implement policies concerning PGs that was later adopted in the organization of the denazification commissions. Most important, this system permitted the decision-making process to pass through the matrix of shared memory and experience in the local communities.

Consider the reasoning of two voting rights commissions in the Angermünde district. The first case, which came before the commission in the village of Krekow, concerned Herr S., formerly a "Specialist on Farmers [*Bauernreferent*] in the SS." According to his sworn statement, Herr S. had never paid any dues to the SS and thus should not be considered to have been a member. As exculpation for past errors, the commission listed six reasons why Herr S. should be allowed to vote in the upcoming elections. He had planted 50 percent of his fields with root vegetables in keeping with the provincial government's plan to increase the production of these crops (his fields had the largest percentage of root crops in the area).[70] He had been sent five times, under contract with the *Landrat*'s office, to purchase pigs, a task he fulfilled each time "to the full satisfaction of the authorities." He had also been given responsibility over the distribution of seed in the local community for the 1946 planting. In addition, "by the universal wish of the farmers and new settlers in the village," he had been appointed to serve on the local appraisal board. It was also noted with approval that when his sow gave birth, Herr S. had sold the piglets in the community for "normal prices" to the benefit of new settlers and workers in the area. Finally, he was an active member of the local Farmers' Mutual Aid organization. For all of these reasons, none of which had anything to do with Herr S.'s activities before 1945, the commission felt that he had the right to vote in the upcoming elections.[71]

In contrast, there is an example of an individual denied voting rights. The mayor of the town of Britz, along with the four members of the local Antifascist Committee, gave the following grounds "why Herr F. will not be allowed voting rights":

> No antifascist ever felt secure to say a word without running the risk of being denounced by him. F. also struck Russian prisoners of war during the time when he worked at the Britz Steel Works.
>
> Because F. was born in Lods [sic = Lodz] he spoke Russian and understood every conversation the Russians [POWs] had. They were always in danger of being struck by the guards through F.'s denunciations. With the entrance of the Red Army he immediately began to function as an interpreter and wants to appear to have changed his outlook, but we, as longtime residents of Britz, know him well as one who cried "Heil Hitler" up to the very last days.[72]

The reasoning applied in these two cases is indicative of the way in which the denazification process proceeded on the local level. In contrast to the positive assessment of Herr S., which dwelt solely on his postwar activities, Herr F.'s postwar activities could not erase the collective memory of his neighbors. Things were not always as they might appear to the outsider. For the villagers in Krekow, Herr S.'s upstanding position within the community and the positions of trust he dutifully accepted far outweighed any culpability that his former relationship with the SS might have bestowed upon him. As for Herr F. in Britz, by contrast, the fact that he had aided the Red Army as an interpreter after the war did not compensate for his deeds during the Nazi period. Guilt and innocence, within the context of local communities, were relative concepts. This conceptual relativity goes to the heart of the postwar "problem of the PGs." The PGs as a group faced a series of policies and programs aimed at punishing them collectively for their sins during the Third Reich. This theoretical collectivization of guilt ran counter to what many observers felt was the actual situation: that there were varying degrees of culpability, and that the creation of a group of second-class citizens was unjust, harmful to reconstruction efforts, and likely to retard the emergence of a functioning post-Nazi society.

The "Second Class"

In addition to registration, forced labor, expropriation, and denial of voting rights, there were other ways in which the PGs were singled out for retribution and punishment. PGs were forbidden, for example, to own telephones or radios, were prohibited from withdrawing funds from their bank accounts, and were denied welfare and pension benefits. All of these extraordinary measures further contributed to the creation of a large group of individuals who were relegated to second-class status as citizens.[73]

In an early report on the problem of the PGs, a village KPD leader reflected that "it is difficult for us to exhibit the necessary attitude because a fundamental clarity regarding this question has yet to be created." He quoted his *Landrat* as saying in a speech, "If the agitation against the nominal PGs does not let up, we will create a resistance over which we will have no control." Rather than place this "agitation against the fascists at the center of our politics," the KPD leader suggested that the party should attempt to "win them over to our ideas." This did not represent a "compromise" with the fascists but rather reflected the fact that "we are on thin ice and cannot proceed in the manner in which we would like."[74]

A group of KPD and SPD activists in Brück, who saw no reason not to place agitation against the PGs at the center of their program, found themselves stymied by the local Soviet commander. The Brück activists decided to hold a meeting that all PGs in the area would be forced to attend. The theme of the evening was to be "8 Months after the 1000-Year Reich!" After printing posters announcing the event, they requested permission from the Soviet commander to hold the meeting. Much to their chagrin,

> after he read the request the commandant asked what exactly the NSDAP was! His next question was what we wanted to do with the Nazis. The comrades explained the meaning of the presentation, that, among other things, through their vote for Hitler the Nazis had brought about the greatest tragedy. The presentation would show the PGs their task, that they are duty-bound to take part in our reconstruction work. To this, the comrades received the answer that these people bore no guilt and that everybody already knew about these things.

The Brück antifascists were informed by the district KPD leadership that the Soviet commandant had been correct in his rejection of their idea and that "the calling of a meeting with required attendance for former members of the NSDAP is a frivolous return to the methods of the fascists" that would only hinder the solution of the "present political problems."[75]

This cautious approach reflected ambivalence among the general population regarding the PGs. On the forcible closing of businesses owned by PGs, the *Oberlandrat* in Cottbus reported that "opinions are still very far apart. One segment of the population is of the opinion that only active PGs should be encroached upon, while another segment is in favor of making no exceptions even in regard to the so-called nominal members [of the Nazi Party]." For the time being, it was decided to close only the shops of the "active PGs."[76]

The political leadership in Brandenburg echoed this equivocal approach. A local SPD leader, in a speech accompanied by "applause and cries of bravo from the attending Nazis," observed that "many members of the NSDAP, who were members of the SPD before 1933, were good, honest people. They were my friends before 1933 · and they remained my friends and they are also presently my friends, in whom I still have trust . . . We do not want, on the one hand, to liberate the proletariat, and on the other hand to create a new proletariat."[77]

The Brandenburg/Havel KPD noted that there were "strong differences" between themselves and SPD members concerning the problem of the PGs. One local SPD leader was quoted as arguing that "it is not tolerable that we should treat the Nazis as second-class people, if at the same time we also want to win them over for the idea of social-ism. We must now decide if we want to win these people for us or if we want to force them into continuous opposition. There is the dan-ger that, in the latter case, the great majority of the former PGs will build a large opposition bloc against the present state."[78]

Fritz Ebert, co-chair of the Brandenburg SED and former leader of the provincial SPD, echoed this sentiment in a speech before an SED conference in June 1946.

> Twelve million Germans were members of the NSDAP. If we add in wives, children, and various dependents, then we have the fact that ap-proximately 30 million Germans could conceivably be affected by the fate of these 12 million NSDAP members. That is a huge number of peo-ple who have a marked influence upon every political decision we make. The majority of them were only nominal members of the NSDAP. They entered the party and paid their dues in order to secure a more com-fortable life. The question now is, should we, because of this political stupidity, continually banish them and exclude them from society? We must, out of a sense of humanity and out of political considerations, an-swer no.[79]

The zonal political leadership was likewise cognizant of the size of the PG problem and its political implications. As an article in the KPD's newspaper noted, "There are millions of former NSDAP mem-bers. Millions cannot be wiped out."[80] KPD leader Pieck made a ten-tative approach to the PGs in a January 1946 speech calling for coop-eration in the rebuilding efforts: "We call to this struggle all of those willing to rebuild . . . We also call on all the former rank-and-file members of the Nazi Party who are not guilty of any crimes and did not actively support this criminal party. We call on you to join in the great antifascist-democratic fighting front for the advancement of our people."[81]

Pieck's speech apparently occasioned some reassessment within the party, for a clarification of his comments appeared three weeks later. It was noted that

> a definitive solution to this problem is a pressing necessity. It must take place—but how should it be handled?
> Today no one wants to have been a real Nazi. Even the main criminals in Nuremberg and the members of the NSDAP with the lowest party

book numbers have declared that at the bottom of their hearts they were not true National Socialists.

In order to approach the situation fundamentally, we must always separate the wheat from the chaff. The NSDAP was a mass organization. With its countless groups, it encompassed almost half the German people. Some of its organizations were purely obligatory, which members of particular groups . . . and occupations were forced to join . . . We now know that among the members of the NSDAP there were very many who cannot be considered so-called active Nazis. They were members of the NSDAP because they found it advantageous on various grounds or even because they had fear of consequences for themselves, their family, or children if they did not become a member. They did not summon up the inner strength to distance themselves from the Hitler party. The number of these members is in the millions.

It was argued that, nine months after the end of the war, truly nominal party members should have shown "by their acts that they recognize the false teaching of Nazism, have rejected it, and become active helpers in the re-creation of our lives."[82]

The formation of the SED and the upcoming fall elections further focused politicians' minds on the opportunity—and threat—posed by the unsolved problem of the PGs. Grotewohl gave a detailed analysis of the PG problem at a meeting of the party leadership in June 1946, observing that the election law granted nominal PGs passive voting rights and created a large bloc of voters who would have to be taken into consideration. In Grotewohl's view, the SED should strike a "positive note regarding the PGs. They must know and feel that with us they have the possibility . . . to fit into political life, because we cannot leave these forces to the CDU." The PGs "come to meetings together, they appear to have a connection to one another, apparently in order to search for where they can find a political home." Reflecting on the PGs he had met during the campaign for the Saxon referendum, Grotewohl observed that "the majority who came to me gave the impression that they would be made really happy if they were no longer treated with scorn, if they were no longer cursed at as 'Nazi scoundrel' or 'Nazi pig.' They said: We are happily prepared to come over to your side, but no more insults!" In Grotewohl's view, it was not necessary to bring the PGs into the SED, only simply to "declare that we recognize them as equal citizens."[83]

It is certainly no coincidence that the entire panoply of programs directed against the PGs—the denazification of the administration, the work brigades, the expropriations, the land seizures—all came to a standstill in the months before the fall elections. It is likewise significant that the Allied Control Council's Directive 24 of January 1946, which led to the establishment of denazification commissions throughout the Soviet zone, was not put into effect by the Soviets until after the elections of 1946. By the end of that year, Germans in the Soviet zone could reasonably have concluded that denazification was coming to an end. Nothing could have been further from the truth: a month after the elections the SMA ordered a massive purge of PGs from all walks of life. In retrospect, the second half of 1946 was merely the lull before the storm.

CHAPTER 4

The Denazification Experiment

To the end of 1946, denazification was unevenly implemented and lacked uniform procedures and policies. The massive purge which began in December 1946 and ended in March 1948 was different: it was centrally administered and uniformly applied throughout the zone. This new phase in Soviet denazification institutionalized the purge and elevated it to a central position within Soviet occupation policy. In placing denazification at the center of their German policy, the Soviets embarked on an experiment that was to be ultimately abandoned in disappointment and self-acknowledged defeat.

The Soviets' new approach to denazification was essentially an adoption of the model developed in the U.S. occupation zone, a remarkable development in light of the scorn that the Soviets and SED had heaped upon the U.S. program before the end of 1946. The main difference between the U.S. and Soviet programs was the secretive nature of the latter. Plans for the new policy were closely guarded until completion, and district denazification commissions often conducted hearings out of the public eye. There was a fundamental contradiction in this approach: the Soviets instituted a massive purge, which eventually encompassed thousands of Germans, without a public relations campaign to explain the program's goals and to elicit public support. The results were disappointing. Kept in the dark about the goals of the new policy, many Germans came to resent denazification. This resentiment took the form of a reluctance to support investigations of ex-Nazis and to appear as "prosecution" witnesses before the denazification commissions.

In August 1947 the Soviets sought to remedy this situation by introducing a new policy—Order 201—which was accompanied by a propaganda campaign. The propaganda campaign was one of the first tests of the SED's ability to use its party apparatus, mass organizations, press, and growing control over the administration to mobilize public support. By early 1948 it was clear to both the SED and the Soviets that they had failed; they were simply unable to overcome the public's political apathy and deeply held suspicion of the SED and the Soviets.

Despite the failure they acknowledged behind closed doors, it was publicly announced that denazification had been brought to a successful conclusion. The land reform and expropriation commissions were also simultaneously ending their work. Ulbricht supplied the ideological justification for these moves: denazification, land reform, and expropriation had successfully laid the groundwork for "antifascist" control. By spring 1948 the Soviet zone was ready to embark on a new phase of "socialist construction."

The New Purge Begins

The Allied Control Council in Berlin issued denazification guidelines, known as Directive 24, in January 1946. The Soviets could not completely ignore Directive 24, because Four-Power control over Berlin had led to a new approach to denazification in the Soviet sector of the city.[1] This new approach, which was later adopted throughout the Soviet zone, was based on district-level denazification commissions staffed by Germans. This type of commission-based denazification did not exist in Soviet-occupied areas outside of Berlin until the beginning of 1947. After the publication of the text of Directive 24 in the *Tägliche Rundschau*—the official Soviet daily newspaper available throughout the zone—perceptive readers would have realized that the Soviets were conducting two parallel denazification programs.[2] In the Soviet sector of Berlin denazification was in the hands of German-staffed district commissions, while in the five provinces of the Soviet zone denazification was being conducted in a decentralized, ad hoc manner without district commissions.

This situation prompted people in Brandenburg to request denazification under the terms of the Allied Control Council's Directive 24. Fritz Ebert, head of the Brandenburg SED, was questioned in April 1946 regarding the status of Directive 24 and requests for denazification. At a loss for an answer, Ebert improvised and incorrectly stated that a decision regarding this question was expected from the court at the Nuremberg war crimes trial.[3] The Antifascist Bloc in Beeskow-Storkow, meanwhile, regularly notified those seeking denazification in 1946 that Directive 24 was not in force in Brandenburg: "Whether such provisions will come into force for this province . . . is still uncertain. The decision of the SMA in this question must therefore still be awaited."[4] In this instance, the Antifascist Bloc in Beeskow-Storkow was correct; the decision regarding Directive 24 rested solely with the SMA.

People requested denazification because of the double meaning attached to the term during this period. A standard dictionary published in the Soviet zone in 1949 defined denazification as "the exclusion [*Ausschaltung*] of National Socialist influences and persons incriminated by National Socialism."[5] There was also another meaning current at the time: through the process of denazification an individual could become de-Nazified, that is, shorn of responsibility for the crimes of the Third Reich. In this sense, denazification offered the PGs rehabilitation and the possibility of ending their status as second-class citizens.

Throughout 1946 the official line of the *Tägliche Rundschau* and the KPD/SED leadership was that denazification commissions were not needed in the Soviet zone. A series of newspaper articles focused, by way of negative example, on the alleged failures of denazification commissions in the western zones.[6] But since it could not be denied that there were Directive 24 denazification commissions in the Soviet sector of Berlin, newspaper articles gave the impression that the directive applied only to Berlin, not to the entire Soviet zone.[7] In a September 1946 election speech in Cottbus, Pieck summed up the then current SED view of denazification.

> Unfortunately, the reactionaries in the west still have very strong support. The trial of the war criminals in Nuremberg is a noteworthy case. One asks oneself over and over: Why all the expense? The trial in Nuremberg has already lasted nine months, although it is our will to be rid of these bandits in the quickest manner possible.

We must without fail cleanse our factory management and public offices of reactionaries!

We must give the rank-and-file PGs the chance to work with us. However, they must first earn back from us the trust they lost.

What use to us is the time-robbing work of the denazification commissions? We must satisfactorily determine who is a criminal and who committed crimes against humanity. We must denazify the leadership of the factories and public offices. When the reprehensible and well-known Schlange-Schöningen is already back in office in the English zone, we know that reaction is still sitting at the rudder there. If we want to secure the trust of the people, we must completely take away the power of these reactionary circles.[8]

Pieck's comments reflected the SED's 1946 election tactics: dismissal of the threat of a sweeping denazification, an offer of political participation to the PGs, and assurances that an effective denazification was already well under way without the legalistic and "time-robbing" encumbrances of denazification commissions. Pieck's comments also reflected the SED's continuing confusion regarding the question of "differentiation" between active and nominal PGs and the party's inability to develop coherent denazification guidelines.

The Soviets were on the brink of an abrupt about-face in their denazification policy. Ever since the issuance of Directive 24 at the beginning of 1946, the official line had been that denazification was proceeding apace in the Soviet zone and that a new purge based on district commissions and Directive 24 guidelines was unnecessary. Once the fall elections were concluded, however, the bureaucratic wheels began to turn toward the establishment of denazification commissions in the Soviet zone. Directive 24 would form the legal basis for the new policy. Since Directive 24 assumed such a central role in the new Soviet denazification policy, it is important to examine this document in some detail. The directive did not, for example, mandate the use of district denazification commissions but simply called for

the removal from public and semi-public office and from positions of responsibility in important private undertakings of all members of the Nazi Party who have been more than nominal participants in its activities, and all other persons hostile to Allied purposes. Such persons shall be replaced by persons who, by their political and moral qualities, are deemed capable of assisting in developing genuine democratic institutions in Germany.[9]

Although Directive 24 made no provision for denazification commissions, there were several precedents for their use. For example, the land reform and expropriation programs were both implemented by local commissions. In addition, denazification in the Soviet sector of Berlin was based on a commission system.[10] The directive also did not provide for punishment of individuals apart from dismissal from their jobs. They were to be replaced by those "deemed capable of assisting in developing genuine democratic institutions" based on "their political and moral qualities." This formulation was open-ended; how individuals would be "deemed capable" was left unsaid, and the phrase "political and moral qualities" gave wide latitude to the occupation powers.

Three articles of Directive 24 (Articles 10, 11, and 12) catalogued the positions in the Nazi Party, its related organizations, and the economy which were to be purged. These articles formed the legal basis for calling people before denazification commissions. Article 10 listed "compulsory removal" positions. These included leading officials in the NSDAP, in related organizations such as the SS and the NSF, and in what were termed "other Nazified organizations" such as the Labor Service (Reichsarbeitsdienst). Also targeted for compulsory removal were recipients of "Nazi honors" such as the National Socialist Order of the Blood. Article 10 also listed leading civil service positions, military ranks, business officials, organizations in territories occupied by the Third Reich, and members of the judiciary, including lawyers. Article 11 listed individuals who were not subject to compulsory removal but who should be "closely examined." These included career military officers and "persons who represent Prussian Junker tradition." Finally, Article 12 catalogued "discretionary removal and exclusion categories." These included non-conscripted members of the Waffen-SS, recipients of "aryanized" property, "persons who had exceptionally rapid promotions in civil service, education, or the press since 30 January 1933," and those who "through Nazi influence, escaped military service or actual service at the front."[11]

In Brandenburg, planning for the implementation of Directive 24 was almost complete by mid-December 1946, but the program was kept secret until the final details were worked out. A meeting on 12 December of provincial personnel directors was opened by a representative of the Interior Ministry who spoke on "a topic of secretive character that did not appear on the agenda, namely, the complete screening of workers in public and semi-public offices." It was observed that "this screening is to be carefully implemented, since it has become apparent that the implementation of the guidelines of Directive 24 has, to the present, been only laxly followed."[12]

To argue that denazification commissions were necessary because Directive 24 had been only "laxly" implemented was curious, since everyone at the meeting knew that the Soviets had not issued orders for the implementation of the directive. As we have seen, people seeking denazification under Directive 24 in mid-1946 were informed that the directive was not in force in Brandenburg and that the ultimate decision for implementation rested with the SMA. Nevertheless, German authorities were now informed that *their* failure to implement Directive 24 had finally led the Soviets to take matters in hand and order the establishment of commissions. In a letter to the Interior Ministry, the head of the Brandenburg SMA gave the new Soviet line on Directive 24.

> From the material sent by the provincial administration during 1946, it is apparent that Directive 24 . . . has been only weakly implemented. A large number of National Socialists and militarists who fall under Directive 24 have not yet been dismissed . . . Formerly, the establishing of denazification commissions . . . was not allowed by the military commanders. For the purpose of improving the cleansing of offices and businesses of National Socialists and militarists, the Minister President of the province of Brandenburg, at our direction, has ordered . . . new denazification commissions to be established in all *Stadt-* and *Landkreise*.[13]

The Soviets' new line ignored their year-long refusal to implement the directive. On the contrary, they acted as though Directive 24 had been in force since its issuance and that it was the Germans who had failed to implement the policy. Faced with this German "failure," the Soviets had no recourse but to order the establishment of denazification commissions to force the Germans into action.

The Brandenburg Interior Ministry could not publicly deny the veracity of the Soviets' version of events, but in a report sent to the SMA, the Interior Ministry gave its own interpretation. The report noted that, since denazification of the provincial administration had been largely completed by the end of 1945, there had been no reason "to establish special commissions for the dismissal of former Nazis and militarists from public and semi-public offices." Nevertheless, after the issuance of Directive 24, the Interior Ministry claimed it had "repeatedly requested instructions from the SMA regarding whether or not Directive 24 would also be brought into force." Yet "the implementation of Directive 24 was strictly forbidden by the SMA with the observation that no sort of commissions were necessary since all of the former Nazis had already been dismissed from public offices."[14]

Although the Soviets' version of events was at odds with what actually happened, the German authorities quickly adapted themselves to this new Soviet policy. Writing in early 1947, Bernhard Bechler noted that, since the end of the war, the provincial government, along with "all antifascist organizations," had considered "the complete dismissal of National Socialists and militarists from public and non-public positions" as its "highest task." Nevertheless, despite this "great success . . . there still are positions in which one believes anti-democrats have provided themselves a hiding place." For this reason it was necessary to implement Directive 24 and establish district denazification commissions. Concerning the popular perception that denazification erased individual responsibility, Bechler wrote: "In contrast to certain occurrences in the western zones, I emphatically declare that the permission for a person who falls under Directive 24 to continue employment in any position does not nullify his former membership in the NSDAP, its organizations or bands."[15] Thus the Interior Ministry's reminder to a local official that

> there are no denazification commissions in Brandenburg, but rather, commissions for the implementation of Directive 24 [*Ausschüsse zur Durchführung der Direktive 24*] . . . have been organized that will, solely and exclusively, render decisions regarding further employment in public and semi-public service. The decision of the concerned *Stadt* and *Kreis* commissions does not equal nullification [*Aufhebung*] of membership in the former NSDAP, its organizations, or related groups.[16]

For the PGs, this meant that appearing before a commission would not lead to a final reckoning with the past: instead, it would reinforce their status as second-class citizens. There was still the possibility that PGs would face further punishments and administrative measures in the future. As the program progressed, the rehabilitative aspect of denazification slowly came to be accepted. At the beginning, however, the authorities were unwilling to accept the idea that denazification was both a purge and a means for reintegrating nominal PGs into society.

The provincial government wanted to keep the approaching denazification program secret until the details were completed. In at least one instance, however, news of the pending purge was leaked to the public. Fritz Lange, the *Oberbürgermeister* of Brandenburg/Havel who was to prove an ardent supporter of denazification, informed the pastor of a local church of the impending purge. Lange had unsuccessfully attempted to force the dismissal of a PG from a position in the diocese. This individual, a certain Herr J., openly declared to police investigators, "Well so I am one of the Nazi pigs, but there won't be anything without us!" This comment, along with the church's refusal to dismiss Herr J. from his post, incensed Lange. In a letter to the rector dated 18 December 1946—just six days after the Interior Ministry requested the program be kept secret—Lange announced that victory would soon be his.

> In the next days an official commission, under my direction, will be established on order of the military authorities with the task of a complete denazification of all local public, semi-public, and private concerns as defined by Directive 24. Based on my knowledge of the case, you can rest assured that the Nazi J. will be among those persons who fall under the provisions of Directive 24. I am informing you of this as a precaution so that the diocese might spare itself any unpleasantness.[17]

In any event, the program did not remain secret for long. The provincial denazification commission held its first organizational meeting on 23 December 1946. Bechler chaired the meeting and emphasized that the commission's work was a "great responsibility." He also cautioned that decisions should be reached with care, "and it should never be forgotten that it concerns the fate of individuals."[18]

The Establishment of the Denazification Commissions

The legal basis for the implementation of Directive 24 in Brandenburg was a circular letter of 9 December 1946, signed by President Steinhoff. A Provincial Commission was established in Potsdam, and local commissions were set up in every *Landkreis* and *Stadtkreis*, making a total of thirty-one commissions in the province. Bechler or another Interior Ministry official chaired the Provincial Commission; in the *Landkreise*, the *Landrat* headed the commission; in the *Stadtkreise*, commissions were led by the *Oberbürgermeister*. The local commissions were permitted to call employees from all public and semi-public positions and from private businesses located in the district. The following organizations, however, fell under the sole control of the Provincial Commission: justice and police; post and communications; railroads; the four *Oberlandrat* offices; offices financed by the provincial government; banks and savings institutions; chambers of commerce and industry; and the provincial insurance system. It was stressed that the commissions' decisions concerned only employment status and that final decisions rested with the Provincial Commission and the Brandenburg SMA. All previous decisions regarding the employment of PGs were nullified. As a result, the entire denazification that preceded Directive 24 was overturned, and the door was open to a reinvestigation of everyone who fell under the terms of the directive.[19]

The provincial guidelines were unclear regarding the directive's "dismissal categories." Those who fell under Article 10 (compulsory dismissal) were to be dismissed from their jobs as of 1 January 1947, although how this mass dismissal would occur was unspecified. In actuality, those who fell under Article 10 usually remained at their posts until they were called before a commission, and many of them were subsequently allowed to continue in their employment. People who fell under Articles 11 and 12 (discretionary dismissal) were automatically placed in an "employment status subject to daily approval" until a commission could hear their case.[20] This was simply a bureaucratic maneuver, for a large percentage of these people were also eventually allowed to keep their jobs.

The local branches of the SED, CDU, LDP, and FDGB nominated the members of the commissions. Three commission members, including the chair, constituted a quorum. Each commission member had a single vote. A simple majority was required to render a decision, and in case of a tie, the chairman's vote was decisive. The commissions were to adjust the frequency of their meetings to their caseloads, but "as a rule" they were to meet "not more than once a week."[21] This final recommendation was quickly revised. After the first week of the program, Bechler informed the commissions that "Directive 24 must be implemented faster. In the future there must be more than one sitting per week."[22]

Thus, from the very beginning a pattern was set whereby increasing pressure was placed on the commissions to produce results quickly. This pressure included the setting of unreachable deadlines. Just two weeks into the new program, it was decided that the original deadline of June 1947 would have to be revised. Now, owing to "special circumstances," a deadline of 28 February was imposed.[23] This new deadline reflected the Soviets' desire to process as many cases as possible before the March foreign ministers' conference in Moscow.

This pressure was backed up with invocations of the historical and political significance of denazification and reminders of ever-present Soviet supervision. In mid-January, Bechler observed, "much to my regret, that the political necessity of the assigned task has not always been sufficiently realized." Particularly troubling was the "indifference" displayed by some officials toward implementation of Directive 24. In addition, in spite of clear guidelines to the contrary, in some districts more than one denazification commission had been established. Not surprisingly, a major problem had also arisen concerning those who fell under Article 10 of Directive 24. These people were supposed to be immediately dismissed, not simply reclassified as "hourly employees" and allowed to remain at their posts. Bechler turned up the heat on the commissions by revising the deadline; he now ordered that all government offices should be completely "cleansed" of "militarists and Nazis" by 31 January 1947 (within eleven days). A deadline of 28 February 1947 was set for the "cleansing" of nongovernmental positions. Bechler soared to rhetorical heights in his exhortation to redoubled effort: "It is a holy duty to replace all fascists with antifascist employees and to make no allowance for those individuals who one may believe are 'irreplaceable,' but who will then be able to fish in troubled waters. Every true antifascist is responsible to the innumerable dead and to the other victims, who established a lasting legacy in the fight against fascism and in the struggle for the creation of democracy."[24]

As if this furious pace were not sufficient, Bechler further expanded the denazification program in the first week of February. Since the purge of all administrative organs was scheduled to conclude on 28 February, he ordered the commissions to direct their efforts toward the industrial and trade sectors of the economy.[25] Although denazification of businesses was sanctioned by Directive 24, the purge of this sector differed significantly from denazification of government employees. Government employees could be easily dismissed since their employer, the provincial government, was also in charge of denazification. Those in the private sector could not, however, be summarily dismissed on order of the provincial government. The power the provincial government held over the private sector lay in its control of the licensing of all business and trade. Therefore, denazification of the private sector was carried out by revocation of the business licenses of those judged "activists" under the terms of Directive 24.

The power to revoke business licenses was given to the *Landräte* and the *Oberbürgermeister.* A revoked license could not be transferred to a family member of the license holder, even if that individual did not fall under the terms of the directive. At their discretion, local authorities could transfer the license to an "antifascist worker." Individuals whose licenses were revoked had the right to appeal within two weeks of the decision. Excluded from this order were licensees who worked as manual laborers in their businesses, even if they fell under the directive. Also excluded were those involved in essential businesses, such as agricultural repair shops and food industries, if a "special disadvantage to the community" would accompany the immediate revocation of the license. In these cases, a "suitable replacement" for the licensee was to be found "in the near future."

There were specific guidelines for the disposal of closed businesses. The owner immediately lost all legal control over the business and its goods, which were expropriated and placed under the control of the local administration. The owner was to be indemnified after local officials determined the property's value. Local administrators were given two options for disposal of the business: either to sell the firm and turn the proceeds over the former owner as indemnification, or to rent the business and transfer the rent payments to the former owner. In the latter case, the local authorities were to determine the rental conditions.

The Moderation of Denazification

The result of this the flurry of orders, deadlines, and invocations of the "holy duty" was chaos. Local officials, accustomed to a more leisurely pace and the ability to ignore or stall implementation of government orders, were often slow to grasp the new policy's significance. One *Landrat,* for example, criticized his mayors for "not correctly understanding" the new emphasis placed on denazification and its "political necessity." The mayors were ordered to give their full attention to the program in light of the "extraordinary urgency of this action." Three weeks later the *Landrat* reiterated his demands, noting that "not all mayors have fully grasped the political meaning of the Directive 24 cleansing. As of yet, several communities have not submitted a single report."[26]

In contrast to the recalcitrance of some authorities, some local SED activists were quick to grasp the "political meaning" of the new denazification program. The Ruppin SED, for example, observed that denazification offered a chance for "a one hundred percent democratization through cleansing of the district administration."[27] The Cottbus SED saw denazification as a chance to replace Nazis with SED members.

> It is clear that in this case the provincial administration's policy is more progressive than the view held by many of our comrades in the employment offices. We must energetically tell our comrades they must revise their views.
>
> Up to this point, we always complained about insufficient and often incomprehensible instructions from the provincial government. In this case, however, the situation has been completely turned around and we must utilize this opportunity . . . [A]n opportune means has been provided to eliminate the PGs and to install our comrades.
>
> We therefore urgently request the immediate use of these instructions to rectify previous injustices wherever administrative dismissals are carried out.[28]

The attempt by some SED members to use denazification as a jobs program was not always limited to replacing ex-Nazis with "antifascists." In a case that reached the highest level of Brandenburg politics, three policemen were dismissed because of their police service during the Third Reich. All three, who had also been former SPD members, were replaced with former KPD members. Although the amalgamation of KPD and SPD had ostensibly ended a long-standing rivalry, old habits died hard.[29] The case became a major issue when Fritz Ebert—head of the provincial SED, son of the Weimar Republic's first *Reichspräsident,* and himself a lifelong SPD official—interceded on behalf of the dismissed policemen. Ebert wrote Bechler observing that he could see no reason why the three had been dismissed. And since they had been replaced with KPD men, Ebert cautioned, this could give the impression that there was a system of "personnel politics, the goal of which is the expulsion of members of the former SPD from the police force."[30] After an investigation, Bechler informed Ebert that in the case of at least one of the policemen, who had voluntarily quit the force in 1934, there appeared to be insufficient grounds for dismissal. Bechler went on to remind Ebert that "more than a few comrades from the former KPD were also dismissed on the same grounds." Nevertheless, Bechler assured Ebert that he would act "with all available means" to combat the impression that denazification was being used to replace SPD men with KPD men.[31]

These two approaches to denazification—the lackadaisical attitude of many local authorities and the activism of some in the SED—assured the uneven implementation of the purge. It was quickly apparent that initial goals would have to be revised. Bechler's deadline of 28 February proved unfeasible. One *Landrat,* for example, informed Bechler that the deadline was "practically impossible" since only about one hundred cases had been settled and a backlog of approximately two thousand remained: "Therefore the set deadline can in no way be met."[32]

Rapid denazification also stalled reconstruction. Local authorities complained that denazification was robbing them of irreplaceable experts needed for reconstruction and the smooth operation of administrations.[33] In response to this growing problem, a Brandenburg SED official countered the oft-mentioned "political necessity" of denazification by arguing that "it would be a political mistake, and would damage our reconstruction, if one proceeded too inflexibly in the implementation of this directive."[34]

The clearest sign that denazification would take a back seat to economic development came in the *Tägliche Rundschau*'s lead editorial on 13 February. In response to western press stories alleging a lax Soviet denazification, the author criticized the western programs, particularly the U.S. program, on the grounds that "millions of people were deemed responsible independent of whether or not they were criminals, and denazification commissions have to investigate tons of formal questionnaires." The Soviets rejected this approach, opting instead for a program aimed at "the quickest reconstruction of a peacetime economy and peaceful life in Germany." This meant that "former nominal PGs, above all from the working class," should assist in reconstruction.[35]

That this article represented a shift in policy was apparent four days later when the Antifascist Bloc in Berlin released a call for a moderation of denazification. The Antifascist Bloc specifically cited the

Tägliche Rundschau article and observed that "a schematic implementation of this directive, as it has been observed in many cases, would have the result of eliminating many workers and specialists in the economy and administration. This situation fills the [Antifascist Bloc] with sincere concern for the continuation of economic progress in the eastern zone."[36] The SED quickly brought itself into line with the new Soviet policy in an article penned by Pieck. Pieck analyzed what he called "the meaning of denazification" and cited the *Tägliche Rundschau* article as the basis of a Soviet program that the SED, of course, wholeheartedly supported.[37]

The possibilities offered by this shift in Soviet policy were not lost on local administrators and officials. Citing both the *Tägliche Rundschau* article and Antifascist Bloc letter, a hospital director in Eberswalde requested permission to rehire nine dismissed employees. In his view the new policy represented a "moderation" of denazification that should allow his employees to remain on the job in light of the importance of maintaining adequate heath care.[38] The Interior Ministry fired off an angry reply, noting that of thirty-nine hospital employees who fell under Directive 24, only thirteen had been dismissed. "The Provincial Commission," it was warned, "is not about to allow hospitals to become a safe haven for fascist reaction."[39]

Nevertheless, there was widespread perception that the Soviets had moderated the program. As one mayor observed in a speech:

> You are all aware, and I am therefore not saying anything new, that the majority of all those here who were once in the party of National Socialism were nothing more than small and harmless fellow travelers and one can say that this is a sort of ground for excuse. Basically speaking, they have not turned with the wheel of history. As a result, we want to make it as easy as possible for these normal [sic] PGs to find a way into the newly constructed society, to bring them closer to us and not to make some kind of profit out of all this. As mayor, I could not approve of such a thing, and whoever reads the article in the *Tägliche Rundschau* regarding the question of the rank-and-file PGs will be of the same opinion as I am . . . Again and again the question is raised: Will I lose my business, will I be expropriated, because I was a Nazi? When one is truly guilty, that's another question than when one was only a fellow traveler. Should I expropriate these people or not? I mean, we must also make these people into good antifascists. A second point is that we are speaking about a [process of] democratization.[40]

In response to this change in policy, Bechler revised his guidelines for denazification of the private sector. A month after he ordered a sweeping purge, new guidelines were issued that limited the scope of the policy. Instead of all businesses, now only those that employed more than fifty people were to be denazified. The focus was further narrowed since "only the leading personnel" of businesses employing over fifty people were subject to denazification. The order did, however, give local authorities, "in individual exceptional cases," power to investigate smaller firms "in the event it becomes known that an active PG can be found there."[41]

While many welcomed this moderation, others viewed Bechler's latest guidelines as an unwarranted concession to former Nazis. One denazification commission, for example, reported a "noticeable unrest . . . [A]bove all, the working class is embittered because in the business community there are former supporters of the NSDAP who once again have their position as owners to thank for their ability to attain a better standard of living for themselves."[42] Similar complaints were voiced regarding the PGs' ability to keep their businesses open. Among the complaints "repeated daily" was: "These Nazis managed to juggle their way through the war without sacrifice and now they live on the basis of their business connections better than we small folk."[43]

The reappearance in the SED press of the debate over the "problem of the PGs" was indicative of growing resentment. Newspaper articles observed that, although it was "foolish to throw all of the millions of former members of Hitler's party in the same pot," "antifascists" naturally had "doubts and mistrust" regarding the PGs, and the latter could hardly expect "to be straightaway welcomed with open arms."[44]

For administrators and commission members, the moderation of policy had the welcome effect of decreasing the absolute number of possible cases. In mid-April, Bechler confidently predicted that denazification would be completed by the end of May. The month of June would be reserved for correcting any "mistakes or incorrect decisions" the commissions might have made. Imagining that the end of the program was at hand, Bechler allowed himself to muse about the problem of the PGs in a post-denazification era: "There is an incorrect conception regarding the implementation of Directive 24 among our population. It does not concern denazification of all former PGs and militarists in the sense that these people will then no longer be treated as PGs; it concerns only a final cleansing of all public and semi-public offices and large private concerns." This begged the question of "what will happen to the 273,000 former PGs in our province" after denazification ended. Bechler offered a "practical solution" to this problem. After the completion of denazification, PGs would appear before yet-to-be-established tribunals that would pass final judgment upon them. Those who cleared this last hurdle would then be free to assist in the "securing of our democratization." Apparently unaffected by the delays that had plagued denazification to date, Bechler blithely predicted that "these measures could, without difficulties, be completed by the end of this year."[45]

In this instance Bechler was far off the mark: his newest deadline was just as untenable as his previous ones, and his idea for handling the PGs after denazification never came to pass.[46] It was not the interior minister of Brandenburg who set general denazification policy but rather the Soviets, and their policy was in the process of being redirected in a way unforeseen by Bechler.

The Transformation of Soviet Policy

In mid-1947 there was yet another transformation of Soviet policy that led to a reorganization of the district commissions and an increase in cases. Three developments during the first half of the year combined to bring this transformation about. First, there was the deterioration of Allied unity and the beginning of the antagonism that would mark the Cold War. Second, the results of denazification were judged to be unsatisfactory: commissions were difficult to control, processing of cases was too slow in the face of an ever-mounting backlog of work, and there were negative economic effects and administrative difficulties. Finally, there was the "problem of the PGs" that had dogged every denazification scheme since the end of the war: this was a political, legal, and social problem that had to be solved before Germany could return to normalcy.

The March 1947 Council of Foreign Ministers meeting in Moscow was a turning point in the relationship among the Allies. The conference has been judged a "fiasco" in which the Allies were unable to agree on key issues such as the structure of a future German government, reparations, and the German economy.[47] General Lucius Clay, commander of the U.S. occupation zone, later recalled that Soviet Foreign Minister Molotov had attempted to make an issue out of denazification at the conference: "Each paper presented by representatives of the Western Powers drew new charges from Molotov. In this conference, which had as its great purpose the establishment of a common policy for Germany, he charged the British with failure to denazify Germany, citing as examples some obscure names of persons alleged to be playing 'a significant role.'"[48]

In his presentation, Molotov compared the shortcomings of western denazification, many of which had been acknowledged by the western powers, with Soviet successes. He derided the U.S. program that required millions of Germans to fill out questionnaires, sarcastically observing that "denazification has been not infrequently replaced by a formal census of practically the entire German adult population."[49] As for the Soviet zone, he stated:

> Here the military administration in carrying out denazification concentrated its main attention on removing active fascists and persons who held leading positions under Hitler's regime from public and semi-public offices and replacing them with persons recommended by democratic organizations. In the course of this work, enterprises sequestered by organs of the Soviet military administration, as well as the landed estates of Nazi leaders and war criminals, were turned over to German democratic administrative organs . . . I would call attention to the data published in the report regarding the number of former Nazi officials dismissed and barred from responsible positions. It can be seen from these data that the figure for the Soviet zone is 390,478 persons, which is more than in any other zone. Perusal of the report of the Control Council will show that the Soviet military administration has furnished full information concerning the progress of denazification in the Soviet zone.[50]

The main question debated at the Moscow conference was not denazification, however, but the Soviet demand for more reparations. The rush to process as many denazification cases as possible before the conference was intended to give the Soviets another point on which the western powers could be accused of failing to live up to the Potsdam accords. This was the same approach Molotov used in accusing western powers of not fulfilling reparations agreements.[51] Curiously, the "moderation" of Soviet denazification actually began in mid-February rather than, as one might expect, after the foreign ministers' conference in March. One reason for this may be that, by mid-February, the Soviets already felt that they had evidence of a denazification more thorough than the others'. Having processed more cases than any other occupation power by mid-February may have led the Soviets to give the green light for a "moderation," owing to the economic damage that had accompanied the purge.

The role of denazification in Soviet foreign policy through the Moscow conference can be briefly summarized. From the end of the war through mid-1946, denazification was a low priority. Only half-hearted attempts were made to remove active Nazis from the administration, no centralized control was placed over the program, and deadlines were routinely allowed to lapse without serious repercussions. During this period the main policy goal was economic revitalization, for both repatriations and reconstruction, and this required a functioning administration, not a continuous purge. There was also a policy of securing political power for pro-Soviet Germans, which was accomplished by the creation of the SED in April 1946 and the fall elections. These economic and political goals effectively suspended denazification by summer 1946.

After the fall elections, the Soviets turned their attention to the benefits that might be gained by full-scale denazification. The go-ahead was given for a purge at the end of 1946, and pressure was applied to process as many cases as possible before the Moscow conference. The result of the conference was not, however, an acknowledgment of the superiority of the Soviets' denazification program, their overall commitment to the fulfillment of the Potsdam accords, or an agreement on increased reparations deliveries, but rather a growing realization that the German problem would not be settled by unified Allied action.

For the political leadership in the Soviet zone, one result of the Moscow conference was a redirection of denazification policy. Speaking before the SED leadership in May, Pieck observed that there would not be Allied agreement on a unified denazification program. Instead, the occupation powers would pursue their own programs. Pieck hinted that "in a short time we can expect in our zone" instructions for the completion of denazification.[52]

A week later Ulbricht intimated that a new Soviet policy was in the offing: "We have, by and large, completed denazification of the administration. But we should not use the phrase 'it is completed' at least during the course of the next year." Ulbricht was candid regarding the opportunities provided by continuing denazification: "In class terms, we have an interest not only in seeing active Nazis driven out but also, wherever one lays hands on them, in using the opportunity to expropriate them." Ulbricht argued that if it were not possible to "lay hands on" Nazi "activists" through denazification, they could be expropriated "as profiteers and black marketers because their productive capacity is utilized not for construction by rather for the black market."[53]

The expected guidelines were released on 17 August 1947 as SMA Military Order 201. The text began with a recounting of the "great progress" that had been made since the end of the war in the Soviet zone in the "cleansing of public offices, of state and private undertakings of former active fascists, militarists, and war criminals, and towards the replacement of these persons by men and women able to help in the democratic reform of Germany in the interests of the German people." Yet, although "the basis of fascism, militarism, and reaction" had been "seriously shaken," there was still more work to be done. The final act of denazification would entail separating the "genuinely guilty" from "nominal, non-active fascists who are really able to break with the fascist ideology and to participate with the democratic strata of the German people in the general endeavor to re-create a peaceful, democratic Germany." In calling for differentiation between nominal and active PGs, the Soviets rejected a "general legal prosecution" that would only "retard the democratic reconstruction" and "strengthen the remnants of fascist and militarist reaction."[54]

Order 201 represents the point at which denazification was recognized as both a purge and a means for rehabilitating nominal PGs. The order provided a solution to the problem of the PGs by ending their second-class status, repealing all "decrees, regulations, and instructions issued by German administrative bodies or by the offices of the Soviet Military Administration of the Soviet Zone of Occupation limiting political and civil rights." In addition to offering a solution to the problem of the PGs, Order 201 also aimed to bring denazification to a rapid conclusion. No denazification policy was complete without an unrealistic deadline, and Order 201 was no exception: the entire program was to end in three months. In Brandenburg a deadline was set for 15 November 1947, although the commissions were admonished that "an earlier completion is to be striven for."[55]

The full effect of Order 201 came in a series of "implementation decrees" that followed the order's release. The most important was the Second Implementation Decree, which reorganized the commissions and fundamentally altered the process. Until Order 201, denazification commissions were composed of representatives of the three political parties (SED, CDU, and LDP) and the FDGB. Under this system, the SED had only a tentative hold over the proceedings. The FDGB representative was usually an SED member, but if either the SED or FDGB representative did not attend a hearing, or if the chair was not an SED member, then the decision was in the hands of non-socialists. Order 201 rectified this lapse through the addition of three members: a representative of the German Women's Union (DFB), another from the Free German Youth (FDJ), and one from the farmers' organization (VdgB).[56] In addition, the organization established for "victims of fascism," the Union of People Persecuted by the Nazi Regime (Vereinigung der Verfolgten des Naziregimes, or VVN), could also appoint a representative.[57] Since the representatives from these organizations were almost always SED members, the reorganization secured SED control of the commissions. Yet, officially at least, commission members were instructed to reach decisions "to the best of their knowledge and belief, in a nonpartisan and impartial manner."[58]

The introduction of denazification under Directive 24 was treated as a secret. Although news must have spread as an increasing number of people were called before commissions, the program was not accompanied by a campaign to win over a skeptical public. In contrast, Order 201 was coupled with a massive propaganda effort to mobilize public support.

The need for a more public approach was summed up in a report following the publication of Order 201. The public mood was described as a "wait-and-see attitude." This was because, "on the one hand, the publication of Order 201 was a surprise and, on the other hand, because a discussion of the broadest implications [of the order] has not yet taken place." There was a widespread feeling that "it is high time that one ceased oppressing the rank and file [PGs] since, in many cases, the big PGs have come away with very lenient judgments and are once again recognized as equal citizens." In contrast, the attitude of local SED activists was described as divided, with many still viewing nominal PGs as responsible for the mass support enjoyed by the Nazis. For many in the SED, the PGs had "made very few amends under the current democratic regime for their active support of the

Hitler regime." Overall, the general attitude was described thus: "It is correct that the masses of nominal PGs should not perpetually be given the cold shoulder but rather that they should be brought into shared responsibility for work—with equal rights, but also with equal duties." The report concluded that, for the SED, Order 201 had a twofold meaning: it was an "act of trust in the power of the antifascist parties" as well as a solution to the problem of the PGs. This dual character would have to be emphasized if denazification were to succeed.[59]

Bechler's right-hand man in the Interior Ministry for denazification issues, Paul Hentschel, echoed this view at a meeting called to discuss Order 201.[60] He argued that Order 201 gave "equal citizenship rights to the nominal PGs" but was not to be construed as a "carte blanche for the PGs." The order was a "vote of confidence in the just power of our people and thereby has a great significance." In admonishing his listeners to weigh the evidence carefully in denazification cases, Hentschel opined that "nothing could be worse than if unrest developed among the population owing to an incorrect interpretation of Order 201."[61]

Order 201 presented a major challenge to the SED leadership in Berlin: "a great task, above all of an organizational nature" for "all democratic German organs." The "bourgeois" parties, the CDU and LDP, had already stated that they would use the occasion to begin recruiting members from the ranks of PGs. Although the SED wanted "as far as possible to win the nominal PGs for us," the party was not yet ready to admit former Nazis as members. Instead, the party laid primary weight on "recruitment of these Nazis in mass organizations, trade unions, and women's and youth organizations. The party will make a decision regarding admission of those who have proved themselves first in these organizations."[62]

Although Order 201 presented the SED with political and organizational challenges, initial press reports emphasized that the order was a solution to the "problem of the PGs." *Neues Deutschland* published the text of Order 201 under the headline "Passive Voting Rights Also for Nominal PGs."[63] In Brandenburg, the SED press lauded Order 201 as a policy that "definitively opens to all non-active members of the former Nazi Party the path toward equal citizenship and gives them, by and large, the possibility now also to take an active part in new political life."[64]

The emphasis placed on Order 201 as a solution to the problem of the PGs gave rise to a widespread misinterpretation. Many thought that Order 201 would lead to rehiring of dismissed PGs. This misunderstanding stemmed from a *Tägliche Rundschau* editorial that extolled the "historical significance" of Order 201, claiming that the order "makes possible a far-reaching enlistment of the former non-active members of the Nazi Party and its organizations in the service of the reconstruction; this is in line with the desires of the progressive democratic public in the Soviet zone."[65] A short time later an SED report observed:

> There are comrades who have not always correctly understood Order 201. These comrades are apparently of the opinion that the order is to be so understood as though all former decisions regarding denazification are to be once again investigated and dismissed Nazis once again are to be hired. We cannot go in the direction of placing dismissed Nazis back in their positions. That would mean pushing aside the democratic element in our administration and reinstating the Nazi element. It is clear that this should in no way occur. Individual people can be reinstated after they have proved themselves in other work and have been investigated.[66]

This view was reiterated at a meeting of the SMA and leaders of the judiciary in Berlin at the end of August: "In no way should Order 201 lead to the introduction of Nazis into the administration . . . The article in the *Tägliche Rundschau* . . . has been repeatedly misunderstood. Order 201 creates only the *possibility* of bringing former PGs back into the administration."[67]

In Brandenburg, Bechler attempted to counter this misinterpretation in a front-page interview in the *Märkische Volksstimme*. In answer to the question whether Order 201 was a "campaign to place all former nominal PGs in their old employment relationships or to bring them back into all public and semi-public offices," Bechler emphatically responded, "This view is fundamentally wrong!" He observed that "no nominal PG has a right to his old employment situation." Nevertheless, Bechler could not dismiss the order's ending of the PGs' second-class status, and he conceded that the main goal was to "clear the path of incorporation into the community of our population for all former nominal PGs."[68]

In a move indicative of the provincial government's new interest in the public perception of Order 201, mayors were requested to submit reports on the reaction to Bechler's statements in the 28 August article. One mayor reported that "Order 201 had resulted in universal satisfaction among the population" because most felt that the "certain percentage of former PGs" yet to be called before a commission would now be "quickly and correctly investigated." Yet the mayor noted that there was also support for giving nominal PGs the "possibility to take part in reconstruction. Each should be employed to the best of his ability and be brought into cooperative work."[69] Nevertheless, evidence of how far the provincial government had to go in its propaganda campaign came from another mayor who noted that reaction to Bechler's interview could not be weighed since the latest edition of the *Märkische Volksstimme* had not been delivered to the village.[70] Similarly, another mayor reported that "the *Märkische Volksstimme* is read very seldom or almost not at all in our village. Observations in the community regarding Order 201 are not known."[71]

The fact that denazification was not eliciting a storm of public interest reflected a general apathy toward politics during this period. An August 1947 police report explained that the public remained uninterested in politics because "there prevails as before a marked unhappiness among the population resulting from the food shortage and lack of available clothing."[72] In another report, a general mood of "uninterest" in politics was evidenced by "poor attendance at public meetings." The opinions of a fifty-two-year-old male worker and SED member were cited as representative.

> Owing to the food shortages the mood at the factory has sunk to the nadir . . . In the newspaper we always read that they are hungry in the [western occupation zones]. Are we also not hungry? Admittedly, subsistence has been secured at a quantitative level, but the quality of food available in the shops is so poor that a considerable portion of food is actually unavailable. When I come home after eight hours of work at the factory I collapse with exhaustion and can no longer even put one foot in front of the other.[73]

In the absence of scientific polling data, public opinion from this period can be gauged only on the basis of anecdotal evidence. Local authorities periodically forwarded so-called opinion reports to the Interior Ministry that provide some indication of public opinion. A review of these reports shows that, in some districts, the public was aware of and interested in the denazification program. In Ruppin, a September report noted that Order 201 was "much discussed" and that "the majority of the population" was supportive of the new policy.[74] This support did not translate into active participation; a Ruppin report from November noted that "the participation of the population in the completion of Order 201 is negligible because of fear that later one will be punished as a denunciator."[75] In the village of Ströbitz, interest was so low that a public meeting on the topic of Order 201 had to be canceled "owing to a lack of participation."[76] In a neighboring community, a public meeting on the theme "Regarding the Guilt and Atonement of the former PGs" was successful, but it was noted "that it could be seen on the faces of the 'formers' that they were not in complete agreement."[77]

In response to an SMA request for information on public attitudes toward Order 201, the Brandenburg Interior Ministry forwarded a selection of opinions culled from the reports, but the ministry made sure that the majority of reported opinions were favorable. For example, "Housewife P." reportedly stated, "We are thankful to Marshal Sokolovsky that he gives the nominal PGs the possibility to partake 100% in the creation of our democratic Germany."[78] In general, respondents identified as PGs expressed relief that Order 201 would allow them to get on with their lives. A female PG was quoted as saying, "I was truly surprised when I realized that denazification will finally be completed. Marshal Sokolovsky's proclamation entered my life like a beam of light." More concretely, another observed, "I am in fact not aware of any guilt on my part but, owing to various rumors, I had thought of going to the western zones. I am now so glad that I did not do it and I will never forget the Russians for this." In contrast to the PGs' positive responses, those identified as SED members expressed misgivings. One woman stated flatly, "I am not in agreement with Order 201. First all former PGs and Nazis should be pushed out of their businesses and positions and forced to break rocks." Similarly, another SED member observed, "I am thoroughly upset, I think the present time is much too soon. In a few years we will see how it works out when the Nazis will all be back in their positions and we will be on the outside again."

Order 201's solution to the problem of the PGs presented policy makers with a formidable public relations task. For the PGs, Order 201 held out the possibility that their status as second-class citizens would end and they would be integrated into society. For "antifas-cists," Order 201 posed a twofold threat: the possibility that PGs would escape punishment and the fear that integration of PGs would lead to displacement of "antifascist" workers. Hentschel touched on these issues at a meeting of personnel directors in September. In his opinion, "it is part of the nature of our people not to assess events in a correct and logical manner. So it is also with Order 201." Hent-schel described the attitude among former Nazis as "now every door is opened to us! . . . They understand 'equal citizenship rights' as meaning privileges for themselves at the cost of the people." On the other side were some SED members, whom Hentschel derided as "Radikalinskis," who claimed that Order 201 was "based on an in-correct policy" and "now antifascists will be dismissed from positions in the democratic administration to make way for former PGs on the grounds of technical qualifications." According to Hentschel, both of these views were wrong. He outlined an interpretation of Order 201 to guide future policy, arguing that the order reflected the "actual situ-ation and is based on an absolutely correct policy," that it was not "carte blanche" for the PGs but a "vote of confidence in the real strength of our people," who were duty-bound to assist in its imple-mentation. He concluded that a "successful implementation" of the order would allow Germans "to win back the trust we lost" during the Nazi period.[79]

A propaganda campaign to mobilize public support was launched at the beginning of October. In a published appeal, Bechler called on "all parties and organizations as well as the entire population of our province" to assist in the completion of denazification. The public's "special task and duty" was to report all information concerning Nazi activists.[80] The provincial government distributed copies of this article to local authorities as an example for mobilizing the popula-tion. It was suggested that this article might be printed on posters, al-though local authorities were free to write their own text. In addition, the public was to be invited to denazification hearings, and local au-thorities were to make sure that a sufficiently large meeting place was available.[81]

The process was now opened to public participation. In Ruppin, for example, upcoming hearings and a list of those who were to ap-pear were regularly announced, along with an "urgent appeal" for all information regarding the accused.[82] In Angermünde the public was invited to hearings by posters that also listed the names and addresses of the accused.[83] The chairman of the Luckau commission publicly appealed to a desire for revenge in his call for citizens to report former Nazis.

> It makes a mockery of the principles of democratic development when you must receive your ration cards from a former official of the Nazi Party who actually bears co-responsibility for the fact that there is presently rationing, or when your former [National Socialist] farmers' leader [Ortsbauernführer], who sent your sons to the front if they did not bow down to the Nazi dictatorship, still holds power over all things in your community.[84]

Ulbricht stressed the importance of a press campaign at an interior ministers' meeting in mid-October. His main concern was political; he feared that the "bourgeois" parties would capitalize on public distaste for denazification and "bring a portion of the population into a movement against us." To counter this, he suggested that "articles and reports regarding the activities of denazification commissions appear in the press clearly stating that Order 201 is a measure for the protection of the democratic order."[85]

Shortly afterward, the central German Interior Administration in Berlin (DVdI) instructed the provincial interior ministers to maintain "the closest personal relationship to the editors of the daily newspapers" and to supply "materials for editorial articles" to ensure press coverage of Order 201. Ideally, press stories would create "active cooperation" and a "lively interest" in denazification."[86] The Brandenburg Interior Ministry also published guidelines for using the press "to involve the population, more fully than has heretofore been the case, in the punishment of active PGs."[87]

Bechler's 28 August interview in the Märkische Volksstimme signaled the beginning of the press campaign in Brandenburg. Future articles stressed that Order 201 was a solution to the problem of the PGs.[88] The press campaign was short-lived, however, and by mid-December, Bechler was complaining about the lack of attention being paid to Order 201 in the press, newsreels, and radio.[89] A month later, the Interior Ministry again criticized the "very paltry" attention given by the press to Order 201.[90]

An attempt was also made to mobilize SED-led mass organizations. The DFB, for example, issued a statement in support of Order 201 at the end of August.[91] The Brandenburg Antifascist Bloc also issued a proclamation in support of Order 201 signed by representatives of the four political parties, as well as by representatives of the "antifascist-democratic organizations."[92]

The campaign was taken directly to the population in the form of a series of public meetings planned for every district under the auspices of the Information Office. The theme of these meetings was "Guilt and Atonement," and copies of a speech to be made at meetings were distributed to the district administrations. The speech summarized the communist critique of fascism and explained the role of Order 201 in the transformation of society. Denazification in the western zones was criticized as a failure, a "comedy" that played into the hands of the "reaction." The Soviets, unlike the western Allies, realized that it was impracticable to purge all former Nazis. It was now people's duty to assist the authorities in dismissing the remaining "activists" so that the process could finally be concluded, bringing the "separate status of the nominal PGs" to an end.[93]

The attempt to enlist public support for Order 201 was ultimately unsuccessful. In many areas, political apathy simply could not be overcome. As I noted earlier, in at least one case a public meeting on the topic of Order 201 was canceled for "lack of participation."[94] In Spremberg, the *Landrat* refused to participate in the mobilization, citing the harvest and winter planting as "much more important" than Order 201.[95] In Rathenow, an attempt by the *Oberbürgermeister* to issue a proclamation calling for public support of Order 201 was blocked by the local Soviet commander on the grounds that he had received no instructions from his superiors concerning such an action.[96] The failure of local officials to follow Interior Ministry directives for the mobilization of public support forced Bechler to reiterate his policy at the end of October.[97]

Even some SED members seemed unable to grasp the importance of Order 201, and this led to growing frustration among the political leadership. An SED report issued at the end of October noted that Order 201 was too often handled by the authorities "as a secret operation." Order 201 was not just a matter for the "mass organizations and the police, but rather a matter for the entire population."[98] At a 30 October meeting in Berlin, the head of the DVdI, Erich Mielke, vented his fury over the fact that the whole program had ground to a "standstill."[99] "It has even come to the point," Mielke complained, "that representatives of our party have appeared at police stations and offered money in order to free this or that accused [Nazi]." He noted sarcastically that there were SED members who were "racking their brains" trying to find ways to keep former Nazis in responsible positions. Mielke minced no words in discussing the significance of denazification for the SED.

> Order 201 is of course a part of the further securing of our power. Only at first glance does this order appear to be a theoretical document. We are talking about a peaceful way of liquidating fascism and militarism. This general proposition must be once and for all clearly explained or the order will not be implemented in the manner in which it must be implemented. It is not simply a question of trust, but first and foremost a test of the degree to which we are in a position to follow through with this order. This means that the order is a barometer for the party to measure whether the population has correctly understood [the order] . . . [and] whether the population has broken with fascist ideology. If the directives of the Interior Ministry are acted upon by the people, then that indicates they want to put an end to fascism and militarism. Unfortunately, this proposition has not yet been made clear enough to each and every party comrade [of the SED].

The bluntness of Mielke's comments reflected a shift in policy. Oblique references to the "political importance" of denazification had failed to rouse the party. Now the *Realpolitik* behind the program was bluntly stated: denazification was a tool to make the SED the predominant political power in the Soviet zone. The task at hand was first and foremost organizational; the cadres had to realize how high the stakes were. With a proper dose of "self-criticism," Mielke cited the failure of the FDGB to join the Order 201 campaign. "The weaknesses are the fault of the party itself. For example: the FDGB. Have any of you seen the FDGB proclamation sent to the factory representatives informing them of Order 201? I know of no such document and you probably do not know of one either. How is that possible? The FDGB is a mass organization and the party is its leader. This is a weakness of our party." Mielke's solution was the unleashing of a "mass campaign" by the party and provincial administrations to explain "what Order 201 means." He cited the mobilization campaigns in Brandenburg and Saxony as positive examples for other provinces.[100]

Despite Mielke's positive assessment of Brandenburg's propaganda campaign, its results were lackluster. At the beginning of November, a DVdI report traced most of the problems in the province to the non-cooperation of the populace.[101] The performance of the "mass organizations" was likewise disappointing; a December report from the Brandenburg Interior Ministry criticized the organizations for their "completely passive attitude" toward Order 201. This failure was seen as the reason why the "population has also taken very little part in denazification."[102]

At a 22 December meeting of representatives of the provincial interior ministries, DVdI, and SMA in Berlin, it was obvious that denazification would continue for some time. Brandenburg representative Hentschel confided that the public's attitude toward denazification continued to be one of "lethargy." This disappointment did not stop Hentschel from optimistically predicting that the program could be ended by 10 January 1948.[103] In a remarkable about-face, Mielke now played down the importance of strictly adhering to deadlines and dismissed Hentschel's obsession with ending the program in January as too "formal." In a fundamental reformulation, Mielke observed that "we have ended a period of preparation and now stand in a period of serious work that makes necessary the introduction of a strict organization." In Mielke's view, if it had been possible to complete the program by the original deadline of 15 December, that would have been optimal, but there was no objection to simply extending the deadline. He noted ominously that a "deadline in this form was never set for the investigatory organs." The new approach had two components: denazification commissions would complete their public investigation of cases and then be dissolved, while the police and judiciary would continue arresting and prosecuting Nazis and "militarists" for an indefinite period of time. In a reflection of this new long-term view, provincial representatives were instructed to make sure that money for the continued implementation of Order 201 was allocated in their 1948 budgets.[104]

The End of Order 201

The new approach was immediately communicated to the commissions in Brandenburg. In a circular letter of 12 January 1948, Bechler disingenuously claimed that previous deadlines "applied only to the most important positions in the administration, economy, trade, and industry." Most of this work had already been completed and now there were only "a few critical gaps to close." The list of these few "gaps" was, however, quite extensive. Commissions were instructed to focus on individuals who *currently* held minor positions as nonsalaried workers, but who had *formerly* held important positions during the Third Reich. It was reasoned that these people might have escaped attention because they no longer held positions of responsibility. Commissions were instructed to pay particular attention to those who held jobs before 1945 as teachers, bureaucrats, judges, lawyers, foresters, and police officers. They were also directed to turn their attention to farmers and workers who might have been Nazi activists.[105]

This new policy ensured that denazification would continue for an unspecified period of time. At the end of January, the commission in Forst claimed that the new policy would result in approximately six hundred new cases. Although by Interior Ministry reckoning approximately 70 percent of the commissions in Brandenburg had finished their work by January 1948, they were now required to continue investigating new cases. Hentschel admitted that the result of this new policy was that "a deadline for the ending of Order 201 cannot be determined."[106]

At a January meeting of commission representatives, Hentschel displayed the new candor with which the SED was approaching denazification. He argued that "the class character of Order 201" was being ignored. The "standard for measuring" the success of Order 201 should be the degree to which it was used as "a political weapon in the struggle for the vanquishing of political opponents." In addition, there was the "inactivity" of the SED: "The party must and will be the motor, the mainspring in the application and completion of Order 201."[107]

Despite these exhortations, the SED was never able to gain control over the program or satisfactorily influence its outcome. In an SED postmortem on Order 201 only one province, Saxony, was singled out as a success story. In the other provinces, Brandenburg included, the "great political meaning of Order 201" was never sufficiently grasped.

> The provincial and district leadership of our party viewed Order 201 as a task for the administration and never created enough clarity within the

party regarding the meaning of Order 201: if they had there would have been a marked change in the denazification commissions. The party did not succeed in establishing real control over the implementation of Order 201, but rather, almost without exception, turned it over to the administrative organs, which only paid attention to technical problems and, for the most part, disregarded the political significance [of Order 201].[108]

The SED's inability to control denazification led to its demise. The SED and the Soviets ultimately abandoned their failed attempt to mobilize the party's rank and file and the population at large. This was made abundantly clear by Ulbricht in a speech before an interior ministers' conference at the beginning of 1948. Ulbricht's discussion of the "current situation" focused on American plans for splitting Germany and the "enslavement" of the western zones through the Truman Doctrine and the Marshall Plan. In light of these developments, and in order to "secure the foundations of the democratic order in the Soviet zone," denazification would have to be finished "as quickly as possible." Ulbricht posited a periodization of developments in the Soviet zone: the first period, which was just ending, had witnessed social, economic, and political transformations that laid the groundwork for the new "democratic" order. The second period, which was now beginning, would focus on economic development to secure the new order.

> One can truly say that now the period of new construction begins. As long as we sequester, expropriate, and denazify, the result will be nervousness in the economy. We are therefore interested, on political grounds, in essentially ending these projects . . . [T]he denazification under Order 201 (not including the judicial processes and the work of the investigatory organs, but rather the work of the denazification commissions) will be ended.[109]

Ulbricht's parenthetical reference to denazification echoed Mielke's prior redefinition of the program. In Ulbricht's opinion, the public purge was contributing to "nervousness" in the economy, and, he might have added, disquiet and uncertainty among the general populace. The denazification process would have to be jettisoned before public attention could be turned toward the task of socialist construction. The propaganda campaign and the attempt to mobilize mass support had failed. This did not mean, however, that denazification would be abandoned as a means of securing power for the SED.

Denazification as a public policy would be ended but the purge would be continued, out of public view, by the courts and police. Ulbricht was frank about this.

> Now, regarding the question of Order 201. Politically, the problem for us is similar [to the expropriation program]. Recently, in the period since the last interior ministers' conference, we have corrected various measures taken in the implementation of Order 201. We do not have any illusions, however, that these measures have produced very strong results: it is simply not good enough. We must proceed from the proposition that we punish the war criminals and the truly activist [Nazis] and leave all the others alone. Why? Because at present we have so much to do with saboteurs and criminals that we cannot allow ourselves to be set back by ancient history. We have a large number of people who were not formally Nazis but who strive with all means to sabotage our democratic order, and with these gentlemen we currently have much more concern. Therefore we recommend . . . that the [denazification] commissions concentrate on the most concrete cases and on cases that concern people in responsible positions. The denazification commissions must deal with these cases and conclude the work as quickly as possible. That does not mean that the judicial process will be ended at the same time. That does not mean that the criminal police will stop their work. The state organs continue their work as before. When, however, the denazification commissions end their work, that means that the cases of the nominal Nazis are dealt with. The state organs, the criminal police, etc. will continue working for years. The criminal police turn their cases over to the courts, this remains and continues in its own way, but the denazification commissions must bring their work to an end.[110]

Ulbricht was equally frank concerning the negative effect of denazification on economic development.

> Why is this politically necessary? When in the next months the question of reconstruction comes to the foreground, when we declare that the foundations of our democratic order have been created and now it is time for construction, then we cannot at the same time keep conducting denazification. Because we must appeal to the entire mass of the working class, including nominal Nazis and to the masses with technical know-how who were Nazis. We will no longer speak in terms of "now is your chance to truly work together with us." Our viewpoint will no longer proceed from the standpoint "nominal or not nominal," but rather, it will be a test through work in the reconstruction. When someone performs poor work, he will be held accountable because he is a saboteur, not because he was a Nazi.[111]

In the six weeks following this conference, the Brandenburg commissions worked at a feverish pace.[112] This period also witnessed the steady transfer of the means to continue the purge from the commissions to the police. The police gathered lists of those who had appeared before commissions, of people who had been denied voting rights, of PGs who were allowed to continue working because they were "specialists," and of "activists" who had fled to the western zones. In addition, the Interior Ministry set up an archive of cases handled before the release of Order 201.[113] All denazification records were transferred to the Interior Ministry after the dissolution of the commissions.[114] At the same time, the expropriation commissions were also bringing their work to a close and transferring all of their records to the Interior Ministry.[115]

The SMA made the dissolution of the denazification commissions official with Order 35 of 26 February 1948, which set a deadline of 10 March.[116] For once in the denazification program, a deadline was finally met in Brandenburg. An unintended result of this decision was that Germans POWs who returned to the Soviet zone after the end of the program were able avoid the purge even though they were "often more incriminated than the other PGs."[117]

From the point of view of the policy makers in Berlin and Potsdam, the Directive 24–Order 201 denazification must be counted as a failed experiment. From January to August 1947, denazification was kept out of the public eye. The initial plan was to conduct a quick and massive purge to aid the Soviets in their war of words with the Allies. Another advantage of the purge would of course be the further removal of Nazis and their replacement with loyal "antifascists." The results were disappointing; too few cases were processed, and the Soviets gained little in the way of public relations, either with the Allies or with the population in their zone.

The solution to this problem offered by Order 201 was novel: a propaganda campaign aimed at mobilizing broad public support would ensure a thorough purge and elicit public gratitude for the Soviets' solution of the problem of the PGs. To ensure a favorable outcome and expedite the processing of cases, the SED was given control over the commissions. This approach also failed. The public wavered between apathy and antagonism toward denazification. Most disappointing of all was the SED's inability to mobilize its own cadres and mass organizations in support of the program.

The end of denazification in March 1948 marked a turn toward the type of non-public purge under the control of the police which the Soviets and their SED allies found more to their liking. The commission system had not been without effect: many "activists" were removed from positions both great and small. This cannot, however, be touted as a success of the program; there is no doubt that German and Soviet police forces could have done a much more thorough job in a shorter amount of time without the encumbrances of public participation. This is, of course, precisely the approach that was taken after the dissolution of the commissions.

Why did the Soviets bother to stage this public purge? The commissions did not, it should be recalled, have to conduct business in public, and at first, many hearings were held behind closed doors, frequently without the defendants present. The summer of 1947 was the turning point. Faced with disappointing results after half a year, the Soviets could either dissolve the commission system and hand the job over to the police and courts or restructure the system and try to gain public support. They chose the latter option, and when it too failed, they decided to remove the program from the public sphere.

Why the Soviets believed that they could successfully enlist public support is a more complex question. Much of the explanation lies in the ideological and organizational hubris of the Soviets and their German allies. Ideologically, they were convinced of the correctness of their critique of fascism; if this were clearly explained to the public, support would follow. Thus, beginning in the fall of 1947, policy makers in Berlin and Potsdam instituted a series of measures aimed at mobilizing public support through the SED and its affiliated organizations, the press, and public meetings. All of these measures failed to shake the public's deep-seated apathy and distrust. The cumulative effect of Soviet occupation—the lawlessness of the soldiers, expropriations, dismantling, reparations, and the Soviet-backed SED's control of political life—combined with dire shortages that made everyday life so difficult, created an insurmountable barrier to a successful propaganda campaign. In a development that must have severely shaken the political leadership, the SED was even unable to mobilize adequately the support of its own rank and file.[118]

By early 1948 it was obvious that there would not be a unified Germany in the near future: the Soviet zone would have to go its own way. In private meetings of the German leadership, the view that denazification was a means to defeat the "class enemies" of the SED and to solidify the party's power was increasingly expressed in unequivocal terms. The transformation of denazification from a public process to a behind-the-scenes police operation was part of a general development during this period. By mid-1948 other avenues of public participation, such as expropriation commissions, land reform commissions, and the system of democratically elected factory representatives, had also been eliminated. Ulbricht's claim that the Soviet zone was entering a phase of "construction" based on the new "democratic order" was not mere idle talk. The dissolution of the denazification commissions was part of a fundamental shift toward the creation of the East German state.

CHAPTER 5

The Denazification Commissions and the Purge

In the present chapter, and the remainder of this study, I closely examine the district denazification commissions, the people who appeared before them, and the process by which decisions were reached in individual cases. Historical research into denazification in the western occupation zones has shown the insights that can be gained through detailed investigation of district denazification commissions and their activities. The value of this type of approach is self-evident given the central role the commissions played in the purge. In contrast to the work that has been done on western denazification commissions, we know very little about the commissions in the Soviet zone. The remaining chapters of this book represent an initial attempt to bring the study of Soviet denazification into line with the methodologies and source materials that have been so successfully utilized by historians of western denazification programs.

The importance of the district denazification commissions in the purge cannot be overemphasized. If we confine our investigation to policy formation and its results, we are telling only half of the denazification story. The policy makers determined the structure, guidelines, and scope of the purge. But, having done this, the site of the purge's implementation became the district commission hearings. In short, the district commissions are where denazification happened, and a clear understanding of the process has to take their role into account.

The present chapter begins this investigation by offering an overview of the district denazification commissions in Brandenburg. This overview includes the political affiliations of the commissioners, their socioeconomic and political backgrounds, the results of their hearings, and the central authorities' attempts to control the commissions' work. In subsequent chapters we will consider the age, gender, and occupations of those called before the commissions and the complex set of inculpating and exculpating factors that shaped the decision-making process. The methodologies and categories employed in this analysis are in no way exhaustive, and some of these finding will be modified by future research. What this and the remaining chapters offer, then, is an initial attempt at understanding the denazification process in the Soviet zone and its effect on those who took part in it.

Commission Membership and the Politics of the Purge

The denazification commission system was a unique experiment, and, despite the machinations of the SMA and SED, it was a remarkably open process. The thirty district commissions in Brandenburg had some of the attributes of democratic bodies: they were time-consuming, difficult to control, and unpredictable. We have already seen how both the Soviets and the SED leadership eventually came to view the denazification experiment as a failure. The commission system was at the heart of this experiment, and it was the commission system's failings that eventually doomed the program. The commission system represented the Soviets' last great attempt to solve the postwar problem of denazification. The contradictions inherent in their conception of denazification began to appear at the very beginning of the Soviet occupation. Chief among these was the contradiction between the purge and reconstruction, the twin desires to punish and rehabilitate the PGs, and the intractable problem of how to differentiate between nominal and active Nazis. The legacy of these long-standing problems was handed down to denazification commissions, whose task was to provide heretofore elusive solutions to the denazification conundrum. In hindsight, this was perhaps too great a burden to place on the commissions, which were charged with finding solutions to seemingly intractable problems. For the commissioners themselves, service on the commissions was a difficult and thankless task. On one side, they faced a public that wavered between apathy and hostility, while on the other, they were under continuous pressure to settle cases as quickly as possible while simultaneously producing the desired results.

During the first, "Directive 24" phase (January–September 1947), there were five members on district commissions: the *Landrat* or *Oberbürgermeister* as chair, plus representatives from the SED, CDU, LDP, and FDGB. In the second, "Order 201" phase (October 1947–March 1948), representatives from the mass organizations, DFB, FDJ, VdgB, and VVN, were added. The Order 201 expansion of membership placed decisions in the SED's hands. As we saw in the previous chapter, however, the SED was often unable to use its political dominance to accomplish its goals.

The political arithmetic was simple: commissioners each had one vote, and in case of a tie, the chair's vote was decisive. During the Directive 24 phase, local commissions had five members: the chairman, usually an SED member; a representative from the SED itself; another from the FDGB, also usually an SED member; and one from each of the non-socialist parties, the CDU and LDP. Ideally, this gave the SED a 3 to 2 majority. In practice, however, commissioners did not attend all sessions, which meant that if one or more of the SED members were absent, the decision could be in the hands of non-socialist commissioners.

For the SED leadership this was a political process, and there was an assumption that SED members, regardless of their background and the evidence presented in individual cases, would vote together based on their understanding of the oft-mentioned "political importance" of denazification. An SED report on Order 201 noted that the party's "main task" was to ensure a "correct composition" of the commissions.[1] In order to accomplish this task, the commissions were expanded to include members of SED-directed organizations: the DFB, FDJ, and VdgB.[2] At the end of August 1947, another SED-dominated organization, the VVN, was also permitted to send a representative.[3] It was suggested that a district commission should have seven or eight members, including the chairman.[4] Ideally for the SED, all of the representatives of the mass organizations would be SED members, so an eight-member commission would have six SED votes against two for the CDU and LDP. As a result of this restructuring, the SED had a majority on all but four of the thirty district commissions. The stacking of the commissions in favor of the SED did not, however, produce uniform results.

One way to gauge the work of the commissions is to look at the number of petitioners whose petitions were approved, that is, those whose National Socialist pasts were judged to have been "nominal" by the denazification commissions. There were three possible decisions commissions could make in judging petitions: approval, which meant that the individual could continue, without reservation, in his or her present employment; conditional approval, which stipulated that the petitioner could continue in his or her present position but could never assume a supervisory position; and rejection, which led to immediate dismissal. Table 5.1 correlates the percentage of approved petitions with the commissions' political composition.

The commissions in Table 5.1 are ranked from the lowest percentage of cases declared nominal to the highest. The percentage of PGs declared nominal swung wildly, from the hard-line Brandenburg/ Havel commission, which found only 24.2 percent of all petitioners nominal, to the extremely lenient Eberswalde commission, which approved a generous 91.5 percent. Despite the SED's attempt to control the process, there is little evidence that the political composition of the commissions correlated with their decisions. Granted, three of the four commissions with weak SED representation (Niederbarnim, Angermünde, and Forst) were among the most lenient. Nevertheless, the one commission where the SED was weakest, the Ostprignitz commission, chaired by a CDU *Landrat,* had an approval rate below the mean.[5]

The same data used to produce Table 5.1 can also be used to take a "snapshot" of the commission membership at the outset of Order 201. Table 5.2 gives a breakdown of the district commission members by gender and average age. As can be seen, middle-aged men dominated the commissions. Of the political parties, the CDU sent the most female representatives, while the lack of female SED representatives reflects that party's difficulties in attracting female members. Indeed, had it not been for the inclusion of DFB representatives, most of the commissions would not have had any female representatives. Table 5.2 also shows the level of representation for each of the organizations. Every commission but one had representatives from the three political parties, the FDGB, and the DFB. The FDJ, VVN, and VdgB, however, had a limited presence; the VdgB was the most poorly represented, with membership on only sixteen of the thirty commissions.

In order to give some insight into the socioeconomic status of the

Table 5.1 Party affiliations and decisions of Brandenburg denazification commissions, October 1947–March 1948

Commission	Party affiliations				Total cases	Nominal cases
Brandenburg/Havel	6SED	1CDU	1LDP		66	16 (24.2%)
Stk. Guben	5SED	1CDU	2LDP		237	76 (32.0%)
Ruppin	6SED	1CDU	1LDP		986	331 (33.5%)
Luckenwalde	5SED	1CDU	1LDP	1NP	496	171 (34.4%)
Beeskow	5SED	1CDU	1LDP	1NP	324	119 (36.7%)
Stk. Cottbus	5SED	1CDU	1LDP	1NP	174	70 (40.2%)
Lübben	6SED	1CDU	1LDP		199	85 (42.7%)
Westhavelland	6SED	1CDU	1LDP		514	249 (48.4%)
Calau	6SED	1CDU	1LDP		1,695	855 (50.4%)
Templin	6SED	1CDU	1LDP		345	180 (52.1%)
Luckau	6SED	1CDU	1LDP		766	412 (53.7%)
Ostprignitz	4SED	2CDU	1LDP	1NP	452	247 (54.6%)
Frankfurt/Oder	5SED	1CDU	1LDP	1NP	915	504 (55.0%)
Wittenberge	5SED	1CDU	1LDP	1NP	675	390 (57.7%)
Spremberg	6SED	1CDU	1LDP		483	280 (57.9%)
Osthavelland	6SED	1CDU	1LDP		636	380 (59.7%)
Prenzlau	5SED	1LDP	1NP		412	250 (60.6%)
Lebus	5SED	1CDU	1LDP	1NP	792	509 (64.2%)
Rathenow	5SED	1CDU	1LDP	1NP	109	71 (65.1%)
Westprignitz	6SED	1CDU	1LDP		522	356 (68.1%)
Lk. Guben	6SED	1CDU	1LDP		220	160 (72.7%)
Potsdam	6SED	1CDU	1LDP		737	543 (73.6%)
Teltow	5SED	2CDU	1LDP		411	307 (74.6%)
Oberbarnim	5SED	2CDU	1LDP		257	193 (75.0%)
Zauch-Belzig	6SED	1CDU	1LDP		420	322 (76.6%)
Lk. Cottbus	5SED	2CDU	1LDP		645	521 (80.7%)
Niederbarnim	4SED	1CDU	1LDP	2NP	569	468 (82.2%)
Angermünde	4SED	1CDU	1LDP	2NP	204	177 (86.7%)
Forst	4SED	1CDU	1LDP	2NP	170	149 (87.6%)
Eberswalde	5SED	1CDU	1LDP	1NP	307	281 (91.5%)
Total	168SED	33CDU	31LDP	16NP	14,738	8,672 (58.8%)

Sources: BLHA, Rep. 203, Entnazifizierung, 645, Bl. 110–145; BLHA, Rep. 203, Entnazifizierung, 8, Bl. 24, 10 March 1948.
Notes: NP = no party affiliation.

Table 5.2 Gender and average age of district denazification commission members in Brandenburg, October 1947

Commissioner	Total number	Men	Women	Average age
Chairman	30	30	0	50
SED	30	29	1	48
CDU	29	26	3	51
LDP	30	30	0	57
FDGB	30	29	1	43
DFB	30	0	30	44
FDJ	24	21	3	24
VVN	19	18	1	49
VdgB	16	16	0	49
Total	238	199 (83.6%)	39 (16.4%)	46

Source: BLHA, Rep. 203, Entnazifizierung, 645, Bl. 110–145. No information beyond gender is given for the VVN representative in Luckenwalde.

commissioners, Table 5.3 shows the occupations of those chosen to serve on the district commissions. As the data indicate, skilled laborers and salaried white-collar workers dominated, accounting for nearly half of all commissioners. Unskilled laborers and farmers, by contrast, had little voice in the proceedings. It is also apparent that the SED and the FDGB, which both claimed to represent the working class, did not provide an avenue for participation for unskilled workers in the denazification process.

The Order 201 reorganization of the commissions established SED control over the purge. Of the 237 district commissioners appointed in October 1947, 67 percent (158) were members of the SED. The SED had firm control over the chairmanships of the commissions: twenty-eight of the thirty chairmen were in the party, while two were members of the CDU. In addition, only one of the thirty FDGB representatives was not a member of the SED. The expansion of commission membership to include representatives of the "antifascist" mass organizations further strengthened SED control of the proceedings: 74 percent of the representatives from the women's organization, the DFB, were SED members; 83 percent of the representatives of the youth organization, the FDJ, were in the SED; 73 percent of the representatives of the farmers' organization, the VdgB, were in the party;

Table 5.3 Occupations of district denazification commissioners correlated to party affiliation (as of October 1947) (percent)

Occupation	Chair	SED	CDU	LDP	FDGB	DFB	FDJ	VVN	VdgB	Total
Skilled labor	22%	30%	24%	23%	44%	10%	21%	21%	0	24%
Salaried	32	13	24	16	20	33	25	26	7	23
Party official	0	23	10	10	23	7	13	26	7	13
Professional	32	7	21	37	0	0	0	5	7	13
Unskilled	0	10	7	0	10	3	4	11	65	9
Civil servant	14	10	14	7	3	0	0	11	7	7
No occupation	0	7	0	7	0	20	8	0	0	5
Student	0	0	0	0	0	0	29	0	7	3
Housewife	0	0	0	0	0	27	0	0	0	3

Source: BLHA, Rep. 203, Entnazifizierung, 645, Bl. 110–145.

Notes: Total number of commissioners = 237. "Party official" includes officials from mass organizations. "Unskilled" includes agricultural workers. Not included: chairman Westprignitz, chairman Zauch-Belzig, and VVN Luckenwalde.

and all but one of the representatives of the organization for the victims of fascism, the VVN, were likewise SED members.

Looking back to the political affiliations of the commissioners during the pre-1933 Weimar period, we find a strong presence of individuals with long-term ties to socialist politics. Nearly half (48 percent) of the commissioners had been affiliated with a socialist party (KPD or SPD) before 1933, whereas a paltry 7 percent had been active in a non-socialist party during the Weimar years. Significantly, 45 percent of the commissioners had no party affiliation during the Weimar period and were thus newcomers to party politics. This lack of pre-1933 party affiliation was in part due to the large number of FDJ representatives who had no previous affiliation (92 percent) owing to their young age, and the female representatives of the DFB (57 percent) who had not played an active role in Weimar party politics. More surprisingly, the majority of the middle-aged male CDU (72 percent) and LDP (67 percent) representatives had also abstained from party politics during the Weimar years. For many of the FDJ, DFB, CDU, and LDP representatives, the postwar period presented their first experience with organized political activity, and their appointment to the commissions was likely their first experience with public political life. The same cannot be said for the chairmen and the SED, FDGB, and VVN representatives. The majority of these predominantly male (only three were female) commissioners had been members of one of the socialist parties during the Weimar years. Thus, to the extent that pre-1933 party activity would have prepared commissioners for their task, it can be said that they were relatively well prepared to take a leading role in the decision-making process.

To sum up these data, several generalizations can be made regarding the district denazification commissioners in Brandenburg. Chairmen on the average were middle-aged men, white-collar professionals or self-employed, former members of a socialist party, and currently in the SED. SED representatives had a similar profile, except that they were more likely to be skilled workers or party officials. The CDU and LDP commissioners were largely middle-aged men, skilled laborers or white-collar workers or self-employed, with no previous political affiliations. The FDGB representatives were relatively younger men (average age forty-three), mostly skilled laborers, former members of a socialist party and currently in the SED. The women from the DFB were also relatively young (average age forty-four), either had no occupation or were housewives, had no previous political experience, and were currently in the SED. FDJ representatives were young men with no political experience, generally working as skilled laborers or white-collar workers, and belonged to the SED. The VVN representatives were middle-aged men, skilled laborers or white-collar workers, and political officials who belonged to a socialist party before 1933 and to the SED after the war. Finally, VdgB representatives were middle-aged male farmers who belonged to a socialist party during the Weimar years and later joined the SED.

On paper at least, the SED dominated the commissions throughout the Soviet zone.[6] Despite its dominance, the party remained skeptical of the intentions of the non-socialist commissioners. The Brandenburg SED warned that "reactionary" CDU and LDP members were disrupting the commissions' work and "must be hindered from assuming responsible positions in the work of the denazification."[7] In the SED's view, the CDU and LDP withheld incriminating evidence about former PGs (who were presumably currently members of one of the non-socialist parties) from the police and commissions.[8] An October 1947 investigation of the commissions reported that in Forst, "almost all" of the commission's decisions against former Nazis were made over CDU and LDP objections. It was further noted that the local LDP contained "a large percentage" of former Nazi Party members.[9] The SED observed that "in commissions in which progressive elements do not predominate, or in which the chairman is a member of a bourgeois party, or when a member of the workers' organizations is not present, there were, in a conspicuous manner, fewer punishments handed out." It was noted that decisions by commissions with a "politically strong" chairman usually corresponded to the chairman's "political outlook."[10] The Justice Ministry in Berlin seconded this observation.

> An investigation of the lists of commission members shows that progressive elements have for the most part a majority on the commissions. After a closer look, however, it is clear that only a few had an organizational connection with the working class before 1933. Perhaps this is the reason for the large number of incorrect decisions. The influence of the bourgeois representatives on the [denazification commissions] in these incorrect decisions is plainly evident.[11]

For their part, the CDU and LDP also had complaints. According to a complaint lodged by the CDU, the *Landrat* in Beeskow-Storkow

was so "uncomfortable" with the CDU's representative on the commission that he appointed another CDU representative who had not
been nominated by the party. Thereafter, the *Landrat* refused to seat
the CDU's chosen representative or allow him to attend hearings.[12] In
Guben, the non-socialist parties complained that the SED chairman
had withheld information about upcoming cases and obstructed their
participation in hearings. It was also alleged that, when LDP and
CDU representatives appeared for a scheduled hearing in March
1947, the chairman told them the hearing had been postponed: they
later learned that the hearing took place after they left.[13] In Niederbarnim, the CDU and LDP complained that the SED chairman refused them access to the evidence against SED members who were
scheduled to appear before the commission. It was claimed that the
chairman was attempting "to catch the commission members un-
awares by rushing the proceedings and other similar methods" in order to assure the approval of petitions from SED members.[14]

Although denazification was supposed to be conducted in a nonpartisan manner, the Interior Ministry and commission chairmen
worked to ensure SED control of the proceedings. Nevertheless, the
SED was continually frustrated in its attempts to secure a "correct"
implementation of the purge. The example of the politics of the denazification commissions serves as a useful reminder of the limited
nature of SED control during the occupation period and the need to
separate the party's stated intentions from the results of its policies.

The Commissions at Work

The use of a questionnaire *(Fragebogen)* was part of the purge in all
four occupation zones. The questionnaires used in Brandenburg elic-
ited detailed information regarding an individual's past. In addition to
basic information such as name, address, and employment history, the
respondent was asked not only for his or her National Socialist affiliations, but also for similar affiliations of spouse, children, parents, and
siblings. Information was also requested regarding political and trade
union affiliations before 1933. Ex-soldiers were queried on their rank,
years of service, foreign postings, date and place of demobilization,
and medals or decorations received. Respondents were also given a
chance to list any "antifascist activity" that they might have taken
part in and "antifascist organizations," if any, to which they currently
belonged. In addition to filling out the questionnaire, respondents

were instructed to include a short handwritten autobiography (*Lebenslauf*).[15]

Individuals were usually informed by their employer or local mayor that they were under investigation by a denazification commission. They then forwarded a completed questionnaire, an autobiography, and, if possible, statements of support from local officials or, at the very least, from neighbors and friends. Also included was a petition addressed to the commission requesting permission to continue in their present employment. At this point, an individual became the "petitioner" in the process. After a period of time, usually between one and five months, the petitioner was assigned a date for an appearance before a commission. During the Directive 24 phase, petitioners were often informed of the commission's decision in writing, whereas after the Order 201 reorganization, decisions were only transmitted orally. District commissions forwarded decisions to the provincial government for approval, and the SMA had final say in every case, although there is little evidence that the Soviets systematically reviewed individual cases.

The investigation of petitioners was usually completed before they were called before a commission. Information was culled from a variety of sources, including the 1945 registration lists, land reform, expropriation, and voting rights commissions records, reports submitted by local officials, testimony from witnesses, and anonymous tips. The Interior Ministry advised that "it is necessary to make particularly sure that the petition is carefully and seriously investigated before [petitioners] are invited before the commission." Careful investigation before a public hearing would give the process a certain predictability, focus the commissions' attention on possible "activists," and, in keeping with the policy of gaining public support during the Order 201 phase, help assure the population that denazification was not a reckless witch-hunt. The Interior Ministry observed that it was "necessary under all circumstances to hinder the outbreak of a general anxiety psychosis. Nothing could be worse than if unrest developed among the population owing to an incorrect interpretation of Order 201."[16]

Commissions conducted investigations with the assistance of their own staffs and the police. In a search for incriminating evidence, for example, one commission ordered citizens to turn over all newspapers, magazines, and brochures published between 1930 and 1945.

The commission noted that "equally interesting are illustrated reports and photos of assemblies of every kind from this period."[17] Another commission availed itself of a handy catalogue of Nazi Party members and their contributions contained in the party's "Golden Book of the Winter Relief Fund."[18] Commissions were also assisted by police "investigatory organs," particularly the notorious "Fifth Department" of the criminal police, known as K5, which was the genesis of the East German secret police.[19]

A statistical analysis of PGs was completed sometime in early 1947. The figure of 273,371 PGs was frequently cited by the Interior Ministry in the context of denazification. Table 5.4 gives a breakdown of PGs by National Socialist organization and shows the formidable task facing the commissions. Although the commissions were instructed to concentrate only on "activists," theoretically at least, all 273,371 individuals would have to be investigated in order to determine who had actually been an activist. Despite the daunting nature of this task, there is no evidence that the Interior Ministry, at least at the begin-

Table 5.4 Former members of national socialist organizations in Brandenburg, 1947 (total population: 2,197,341)

Organization	Number of members	Percentage of total population
NSDAP	121,795	5.54
NSF	66,770	3.03
BDM	36,303	1.65
HJ	28,490	1.29
SA	14,103	0.64
SS	2,622	0.12
NSKK	2,180	0.099
NSFK	1,051	0.047
FMdSS	43	0.0019
Gestapo	14	0.0006
Total	273,371	12.4

Source: BLHA, Rep. 203, 8, Bl. 199.

Notes: The National Socialist Motorized Corps (NS-Kraftfahrerkorps, NSKK) and the National Socialist Aviation Corps (NS-Fliegerkorps, NSFK) were paramilitary organizations. Contributing members of the SS (Fördernes Mitglied der SS, FMdSS) were not members of the SS but those who gave supporting contributions to the organization.

ning, expected anything less than a thorough investigation of each
and every one of these people.

The 273,371 PGs actually represented only a portion of those who
fell under Directive 24, since the directive called for both denazification and demilitarization. Demilitarization required investigation of
those who represented the Prussian "militarist tradition," as well as
former members of nationalist organizations, the Harzburg Front,
German National People's Party (Deutschnationale Volkspartei),
Stahlhelm, and Kyffhäuser-Bund.[20] In the absence of statistical information regarding these individuals, it is difficult to estimate how
many people in Brandenburg fell under this aspect of the directive. At
the beginning of the purge, it was estimated that there were 12,051
people in public and semi-public positions who fell under Directive
24, but this figure did not include employees of the post office, railroads, or coal mining industry or those in private employ.[21]

The commissions' success in handling this task can be measured by
an examination of the monthly reports compiled by the Interior Ministry. Table 5.5 shows the number of cases completed by the commissions, along with rates of approval and denial. The data from Table
5.5 can also be presented in graphic form to give a picture of the work
of the commissions over time (Figure 5.1). Several observations can
be made regarding the data in Table 5.5 and Figure 5.1. If we accept
the Interior Ministry's figure of 273,371 PGs at the beginning of
1947, then the 28,901 individuals who appeared before the commissions represented 10.6 percent of all possible cases. The real percentage of PGs is actually lower, since a considerable number of petitioners were not PGs. The sharp increase in the number of cases during
the first months reflects the frantic pace initially set as commissions
were pushed to process as many cases as possible before the March
foreign ministers' conference in Moscow. The period of moderation
following the conference is also clearly evident in a sharp decrease in
cases beginning in April; this steady decrease, aside from a slight up-
turn in June, continued until the new commissions began their work
in October. The effect of Order 201 can be seen in the dramatic increase in cases in November. By January 1948, approximately 70 percent of the commissions in Brandenburg had completed their work,
and this is reflected in the decreased number of cases in this period.
The final upsurge in cases in February and March 1948 evidences the
effect of the Interior Ministry's January 1948 order calling on all com-

Table 5.5 Approval and denial of denazification petitions in Brandenburg, January 1947–March 1948

Month	Approved	Denied	Total
Jan. 1947	676 (78.4%)	186 (21.6%)	862
Feb. 1947	1,899 (69.5%)	831 (30.5%)	2,730
March 1947	1,919 (68.0%)	899 (32.0%)	2,818
April 1947	1,575 (80.6%)	379 (19.4%)	1,954
May 1947	1,257 (77.9%)	355 (22.1%)	1,612
June 1947	1,422 (78.6%)	388 (21.4%)	1,810
July 1947	667 (76.2%)	208 (23.8%)	875
Aug. 1947	460 (71.7%)	181 (28.3%)	641
Sept. 1947	289 (80.2%)	71 (19.8%)	360
Oct. 1947	657 (71.2%)	266 (28.8%)	923
Nov. 1947	3,194 (71.4%)	1,276 (28.6%)	4,470
Dec. 1947	2,259 (67.4%)	1,092 (32.6%)	3,351
Jan. 1948	643 (61.6%)	401 (38.4%)	1,044
Feb. 1948	924 (41.0%)	1,330 (59.0%)	2,254
March 1948	1,180 (36.9%)	2,017 (63.1%)	3,197
Total	19,021 (65.8%)	9,880 (34.2%)	28,901

Sources: BLHA, Rep. 203, Entnazifizierung, 8, Bl. 192–198 (January 1947); Bl. 182–188 (February 1947); Bl. 161–168 (March 1947); Bl. 152–157 (April 1947); Bl. 143–149 (May 1947); Bl. 135–141 (June 1947); Bl. 119–125 (July 1947); Bl. 111–116 (August 1947); Bl. 97–100 (September 1947); BLHA, Rep. 203, 529 (October 1947–March 1948).

missions to continue their work and to focus on PGs who might have been overlooked.[22]

Turning to a comparison of the approval and denial rates, we find that between 70 and 80 percent of petitioners were declared nominal during most of the process. This percentage dropped dramatically in the final two months, when the number of approved petitions fell below the number denied for the first and only time. One can only speculate on the reasons for this sudden drop in the number of nominal cases. District commissions came under increasing pressure to expedite cases quickly in order to meet the 15 March 1948 deadline for ending the purge, and this increased tempo of work correlates with the sudden drop in nominal cases. At the same time, the Interior Ministry lifted its ban on calling laborers before the commissions. This ban (discussed in Chapter 6) exempted manual laborers from denazification regardless of their political history. The lifting of the ban in January 1948 may have increased the number of incriminated labor-

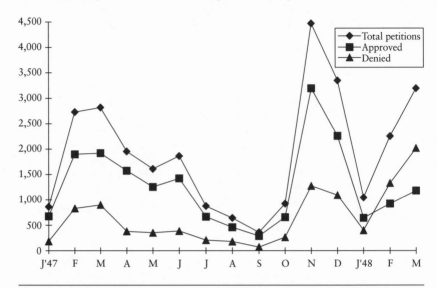

Figure 5.1. Brandenburg denazification petitions with rates of approval and denial, January 1947–March 1948. *Sources:* BLHA, Rep. 203, Entnazifizierung, 8, Bl. 192–198 (January 1947); Bl. 182–188 (February 1947); Bl. 161–168 (March 1947); Bl. 152–157 (April 1947); Bl. 143–149 (May 1947); Bl. 135–141 (June 1947); Bl. 119–125 (July 1947); Bl. 111–116 (August 1947); Bl. 97–100 (September 1947); BLHA, Rep. 203, 529 (October 1947–March 1948).

ers called before commissions, although there are no Interior Ministry statistics that would shed light on this possibility. A final reason for the drop in nominal cases may be that, following the Interior Ministry's order that commissions concentrate only on previously over-looked "activists," the commissions actually did uncover a higher percentage of incriminated individuals than was previously the case.[23]

Oversight of the Commissions

The central authorities fought an unsuccessful battle with the district commissions aimed at ensuring consistent application of the purge. This was a bureaucratic and a political problem that lay at the heart of the program and assured its ultimate failure. In short, the decentralized commission system proved impervious to centralized control. This was not for want of effort by the authorities: they complained, cajoled, pleaded, and threatened the district commissions to make them abide by the guidelines for implementing the purge. The provincial interior ministries occupied the most unenviable position in this situation. The Soviets issued the general policy, but it was the German authorities—specifically the Interior Ministries—who were held accountable for its successful implementation.

One of the Brandenburg Interior Ministry's primary concerns was the lackadaisical approach some commissions took toward their task. Two months after the beginning of the purge, for example, the Westhavelland commission was singled out for criticism because it had held only one hearing and decided a paltry eleven cases.[24] It is noteworthy that the Ostprignitz commission, chaired by a CDU *Landrat*, was credited with an exemplary implementation of denazification guidelines, and its record keeping was held up as a model for others.[25] Conversely, the Oberbarnim commission was severely criticized for unacceptable record keeping that made it impossible for the Interior Ministry to gain "a clear picture" of its proceedings.[26] As a result of this unevenness, after less than two months of the program, the Provincial Commission in Potsdam was bogged down with reexamining approximately 50 percent of district commission cases. This reexamination was seen as one of the main reasons why the initial deadline for completion of denazification (set for 28 February 1947) was not met.[27]

Accurate record keeping was essential for ensuring that decisions were enforced. There were reports of dismissed public employees who found their way back into the administrations in other districts: this was usually accomplished by individuals' changing residence and lying about their past. Likewise, individuals ordered to continue work in a non-supervisory position often resumed their supervisory roles "after a few months."[28] A full year after the denazification commissions began their work, there were still "numerous reports . . . from Interior Ministry representatives, showing that many of the decisions of the denazification commissions are not being realized. People who were ordered to be dismissed three or even five months ago are still working in their old positions." The situation could be remedied, it was argued, by careful record keeping: the commissions were ordered to review their past work to make sure they had correctly recorded all of their decisions.[29]

The need to keep detailed and orderly records was not simply a matter of bureaucratic pedantry. A DVdI report noted that the lack of accurate statistics made it impossible to gauge the successes and failures of the program. Accurate statistics were seen as especially important in light of the effect of denazification on the economy.[30] Anton Plenikowski, head of the SED's provincial affairs department (Abteilung Landespolitik), took up the call for accurate statistics in a memo to the SED leadership at the end of May.[31] The SED was slow in following through on this suggestion: an August report sent to Ulbricht complained that only two provinces, Brandenburg and Saxony, had forwarded "exact statistical results."[32] In Brandenburg, a plan to bring order to the commissions' records was developed at the end of June 1947. The Interior Ministry issued guidelines for the protocols of the hearings and established a weekly meeting of officials to review the records and clarify "all mistakes and deficiencies." The Interior Ministry acknowledged it was a "mistake" that it was only just addressing these problems six months into the program.[33]

The central authorities increased their oversight during the Order 201 phase. Berlin instructed each province to establish a central control commission composed of representatives of the DVdI and provincial interior and justice ministries.[34] Personal information on every individual appearing before the commissions was to be forwarded to the provincial Interior Ministry and to the DVdI in Berlin.[35] A complex reporting system was devised that led to the collection of personal data by the K5, its judicial counterpart the P5, and the DVdI: information forwarded to the DVdI in Berlin was to be personally addressed to Vice President Mielke.[36] In Brandenburg, the central office in charge of collecting data and coordinating the work of the commissions was renamed Office 201, and commission members who telephoned were instructed to use the password "Order 201" when they called.[37] At an interior ministers' conference in October 1947, Mielke suggested that a special department for Order 201 should be set up at DVdI headquarters and that a central registry be established to collect denazification data from throughout the zone.[38] In November, Mielke ordered that registration cards for all persons who appeared before a commission were to be sent to the DVdI in Berlin.[39] A month later, however, the DVdI complained that the registration cards were not being sent to Berlin: "According to the last weekly report, in every province there were several thousand cases reported as decided. The number of registration cards and accompanying archival material reaching us here is in no way equal to the above-mentioned number of cases."[40]

The DVdI remained dissatisfied with the district commissions' record keeping. The continuing "weakness" of the district commissions in this task made it difficult for the DVdI to produce an "accurate assessment" of the progress of the purge and issue directives to correct mistakes. As a remedy the DVdI suggested that the provincial interior ministries set up evening courses for the members of the district commissions in order to instruct them in accurate record keeping.[41]

Another problem was the mounting backlog of cases. In November 1947, Bechler complained that the new Order 201 commissions were not working diligently enough and that some commissions were deciding between 8 and 10 cases a week although they had backlogs of 150 to 180 cases. In Bechler's view, this was a political shortcoming on the part of commissioners who lacked the appropriate "antifascist consciousness."[42] One commission explained its slow progress by noting that "it was not always simple to reach a decision. The handling of single cases lasted up to one hour."[43] At the beginning of 1948, commissions were still being upbraided for not grasping the "urgency and political meaning of Order 201" since they continued to hold "only one hearing a week or often not even a single hearing [per week]."[44]

During the Order 201 phase, the Brandenburg Interior Ministry began a series of inspections of district commissions. The October inspection revealed a series of deficiencies: in Teltow there was "a marked lack of interest" on the part of the local authorities; in Wittenberge "active fascists" were receiving "positive decisions"; in Westprignitz none of the hearing transcripts were properly composed; in Ostprignitz the commission was so lenient that the Provincial Commission was forced to rehear their cases; in Guben one of the commission members had not been approved by the provincial government so that all of the cases in which this commissioner had voted had to be reheard; and, in Spremberg the LDP commissioner was forced to resign after it was discovered that he had been a Nazi Party member for three months in 1931–32.[45] Similar problems occurred throughout the Soviet zone, leading one SMA representative to remark in January 1948 that it was "completely inconceivable, after four months of operation under Order 201, that again and again unclear reports were being submitted" by district commissions.[46]

The full effect of the commissions' haphazard record keeping finally came to light after they ended their work and forwarded their records to the provincial government, which had to try to bring some order to the "many mistake-ridden and incomplete" records. The poorest-kept records dated from the period before Order 201, when the majority of registration cards contained only the name and incriminating evidence for each case without any further information. Five months after the end of the purge, it was reported that the protocols of the district hearings were still in complete disarray.[47]

From the point of view of a researcher using German archives to investigate denazification in the Soviet zone, the Soviets appear to have had little direct influence over the day-to-day operation of the purge. This view is contradicted, however, by Naimark's recent work based on extensive use of Soviet archives. Naimark paints a picture of Soviet authorities who obsessively micro-managed affairs and distrusted their SED allies and the German population in general. For its part, the SED often bridled at the overweening Soviet presence.[48] This was evident in Ulbricht's remarks at an interior ministers' conference in June 1947. Regarding the German tendency to clear denazification problems with local Soviet commanders, Ulbricht argued that "we should not always make this an issue for the military authorities . . . If the military authorities make the decisions, then we are hindered in the political education of our own organs. These things should not be clarified *through* the military authorities. *With* yes, but not *through* . . . We must not give the impression that we are reacting nervously."[49] Nevertheless, German authorities continued to clear policy decisions with the Soviets. For example, a DVdI circular letter of 21 February 1948 regarding Order 201 was, on Mielke's orders, translated and sent to the SMA for approval before it was released.[50]

There is some evidence in the German archives of Soviet oversight. Throughout the purge, the Interior Ministry sent reports detailing the progress of the program and the successes and difficulties encountered by the district commissions.[51] District officials also sent reports on the denazification program to the SMA.[52] There is also one file in Potsdam indicating that the SMA reviewed Provincial Commission decisions in appeals cases during 1947: of the 568 cases in this file, the SMA agreed with the decisions in 475 cases and, in the remaining 93 cases, overturned the Provincial Commission's approval of petitions and ordered the immediate dismissal of the employees.[53]

Overall, though, remarkably little information on the Soviet role can be gleaned from the German archives. The fact that the German authorities regularly kept the Soviets apprised indicates that the Soviets were monitoring the program, although from the vantage point of the German archives, the written communication appears one-sided.

In part the lack of a paper trail may be due to the Soviet propensity for issuing verbal orders, the most noteworthy case being the verbal order that initially started the formal denazification at the end of 1946. Still, there must have been a good deal of written communication from the Soviet side, and it can only be assumed that a conscious effort was made to eliminate this evidence from the archives. In light of the wealth of evidence uncovered by Naimark in the Soviet archives, it is reasonable to assume that there is much to be learned about the denazification program through research in Russia.

Trouble in Calau

To conclude this chapter, we turn to the extraordinary case of the Provincial Commission's investigation of the district commission in Calau. The Calau commission was singled out by the Interior Ministry in April 1947 as a major problem because of its large number of approved cases and a general misapplication of denazification guidelines. The perceived weaknesses of the Calau commission led to the Provincial Commission's decision to travel to Calau to rehear some previously decided cases.[54]

The available biographical information on the Calau commission gives no indication that this was a group of untrustworthy men. Indeed, on paper at least, they would seem to be just the sort of people who could be counted on to assist in the effort to rebuild a new "democratic" Germany. All eight of the men who served on the commission had been members of a left-wing political party in the Weimar years: six had been in the SPD and two in the KPD.[55]

Although *Landrat* Freter, a former SPD member, was commission chair, he appeared only at the first session; thereafter, Deputy *Landrat* Fritz Wollny chaired meetings. Freter was sixty-nine years old in 1947 and had served as *Landrat* for nearly the entire Weimar period, from 1919 to 1932. He had also been a representative in the Prussian State Assembly. In July 1932, Chancellor Franz von Papen dismissed him as *Landrat.* During the Nazi period he was arrested six times, the last in the aftermath of the failed attempt on Hitler's life in July 1944.[56] The SED leadership had reservations about Freter's "weaknesses," which were attributed to his advanced age, but they permitted him to continue as *Landrat,* probably because of his standing in the community.[57]

Fritz Wollny, the deputy *Landrat,* was fifty-six years old in 1947.

Wollny chaired the denazification commission and dealt with its day-to-day operation. A former SPD member, he was mayor of the mining town of Brieske-Gruba Marga from 1919 until his arrest in 1933. His eighty-year-old mother petitioned the then-president, Paul von Hindenburg, who released Wollny from custody five months before his sentence was completed: after Hindenburg's death in 1934, however, Wollny was re-arrested and forced to serve his remaining sentence. He was reappointed mayor by the Soviets on 28 April 1945 and continued to served in that position in addition to his duties as deputy *Landrat*.[58]

Two men, Robert Harnau and Heinrich Schapp, shared the SED slot on the commission. Harnau boasted solid antifascist credentials. A native of Klettwitz in *Kreis* Calau, he was born in 1908, the son of a master tailor. Harnau worked in the region's glass industry and joined the SPD in 1929. After Hitler came to power, Harnau spent from June to December 1933 in "protective custody" at a concentration camp. Upon release, he engaged in underground activity with other ex-SPD members until his re-arrest in 1935. After serving four years in prison, he was transferred to the Sachsenhausen concentration camp. Three weeks before the end of the war, Harnau and a group of prisoners were evacuated from Sachsenhausen on a forced march that was overtaken by the Red Army on 2 May 1945. After joining the postwar KPD, Harnau eventually became the secretary of the SED in Senftenberg.[59]

Heinrich Schapp, the other SED representative, was also a native of *Kreis* Calau. Son of a miner, Schapp, like Harnau, eventually found employment in a glass factory. A former KPD member, he was "nonpolitical" during the Nazi period. After the war he immediately rejoined the KPD, eventually becoming a representative of the SED and the FDGB in Senftenberg.[60]

Karl Krause, the CDU representative on the commission, was the only member who attended all twelve sittings of the commission during the Directive 24 phase. The oldest commission member, Krause was born in 1878 in Calau. A cigar maker by trade, he took over his father's tobacco concern in 1904. During the Weimar period he served as an elected member of the district assembly running on the Democratic Party ticket. He also served for many years as a town councilor. Krause's activities during the twelve years of National Socialism are not mentioned in his *Fragebogen*, apart from the fact that he never joined the Nazi Party. After the war, he resumed his political life by joining the SPD. In April 1946, the same month the SPD and KPD merged into the SED, Krause quit the party and joined the newly formed CDU, rising to become a party official.[61]

The other non-SED commission member was Johannes Roblick, representative of the LDP. Sixth child of a shoemaker, Roblick joined the SPD in 1926. He served in the Wehrmacht during the war and was in Russian captivity as a POW from May to July 1945. Although Roblick never joined the Nazi Party, he was in the NSKOV (National-sozialistische Kriegsopferversorgung) from 1933, served as a block warden between 1937 and 1939, and as section leader in the Reichs-bund der Kinderreichen (RdK) for one year.[62] After release from Russian captivity, he returned to his hometown to become the founding member of the LDP.[63] Less information is available for the two FDGB representatives, Max Figura and Bernard Gonschorowski. Figura was an SPD member before 1933 and Gonschorowski was in the KPD; by 1947, both were in the SED and officials of the FDGB.[64]

Despite these "antifascist" backgrounds and the SED's predominance, the commission distinguished itself by its leniency. The commission held only 12 hearings during the Directive 24 phase and made decisions in 217 cases. The vast majority of these were approved: 186 petitions equaling 85.7 percent of the total. When the petitions receiving conditional approval are included, the approval rate increases to 89 percent. The commission denied only 24 petitions.[65]

The Calau commission's high approval rate caught the attention of the Provincial Commission, which was particularly alarmed by the large number of cases approved "despite concrete evidence" of Nazi activity. In response, the Provincial Commission, chaired by Paul Hentschel, decided to travel to Calau to reexamine some of the cases.[66] The commission's arrival in Calau was seen as a rebuke by local commissioners.

This extraordinary hearing was attended by the Calau commission members, *Landrat* Freter, the chairman of the Calau *Betriebsrat*, and a representative of the *Betriebsgruppe* of the district SED. Hentschel opened the session by noting that this was the first time the Provincial Commission had conducted a hearing outside Potsdam, but that there were certain "peculiarities, which are present here in Calau, to be reexamined." Laying down the ground rules, Hentschel stated that, although the *Kreis* commission members could make recommendations, "in these special cases they possess no voting rights."

Taking the floor, Wollny acknowledged that the Soviet district commander had found fault with his commission, an act that apparently initially drew the Interior Ministry's attention to Calau. Despite this Soviet action, Wollny stated, "I would like to declare here in the name of the individual members that we have never handled a single case in a superficial manner, but rather have directed ourselves to the instructions of the provisional government and have consistently and exhaustively examined the available evidence."

Faced with Wollny's defensive attitude, Hentschel temporized, noting that he had no cause to criticize the Calau commission's work. He also commiserated with their task, one that was "often impeded because the population does not play a sufficient part" and was quick to criticize the commission's decisions. Far from coming to criticize, Hentschel claimed, the Provincial Commission had traveled to Calau only because there were certain cases that needed to be settled "here and now." "This is also not a criticism of the Soviet commandant," Hentschel diplomatically added. The Soviet commander had simply brought to the Provincial Commission's attention that "here in the district of Calau there are still various people employed, who[,] . . . in light of their militarist careers, should not be in public service." What was required was a joint examination of these cases so the Soviet commander could see that "we as Germans clear up this matter."

Of the fifteen cases examined at this extraordinary hearing, the Calau commissioners vigorously defended their prior decisions in three instances. All three cases had initially been heard by the Calau commission during its first sitting in January, all three petitions had been summarily approved, all three petitioners were acquaintances of the commission members, and in all three cases the visiting Provincial Commission overturned the prior approval of the petitions. A close look at these cases uncovers the differences between the provincial leadership's conception of denazification and the manner in which the Calau commissioners interpreted their task.

The first case is that of Herr H., former leader of the Calau Volkssturm, who had gained the gratitude of the commission members and other residents of Calau by halting his work as Volkssturm leader just prior to the Russian advance into Calau. Instead of organizing resistance to the Red Army, Herr H. allegedly sent the men under his command back to their houses.[67] Three months after he received a clean bill of political health, Herr H. found himself once again standing before a denazification commission, this time with his allies from the

Calau commission shunted off to the side as spectators. In his defense, Herr H. recounted his activities on 19 April 1945, the day the Red Army entered Calau.[68] He recalled that, before the Russians entered the town, he had decided that the men under his command would not fight. He led them through the city to the outskirts of town, where, around ten o'clock in the evening, he disbanded the unit and "sent them home to their families." *Landrat* Freter substantiated this version of events, noting that he had been a member of the Volkssturm unit.

A further witness was the Catholic pastor of Calau parish, who claimed that on the day of the Russian advance, Herr H. had spoken to him on the way to the Volkssturm gathering and had stated that "he wanted no shot fired and no operation to go forward." The record notes, however, that during the course of the hearing it became clear that the pastor did not speak to Herr H. regarding the actions of the Volkssturm unit until after the Russian entry into Calau. The pastor was also of little help when pressed regarding the movement of the Volkssturm unit that day. According to Herr H., the route he used to march his troops through Calau would have taken the group past the pastor's door; the priest, however, could not remember this having happened, claiming that he was probably occupied tending to the "care of a Soviet officer." A Soviet officer? When had the Soviet army entered Calau on 19 April? The priest recalled that it was around noon, further confounding the story, since Herr H. claimed that he had disbanded his unit at ten o'clock in the evening.[69]

Herr H.'s final witness was the chairman of the Calau *Betriebsrat*, who declared that Herr H. was now a member of the SED and "in every way eager to make amends for his past failures." This was apparently too much for Schönborn, the SED representative on the Provincial Commission, to accept. Schönborn interrupted "energetically and decisively" and "gave expression to his great astonishment that here in the local SED organization in Calau people would be accepted as members who in no way exhibit an assurance of an antifascist-democratic attitude." The record notes that Schönborn then "confiscated the [SED] party book of Herr H." on the spot. Needless to say, the Provincial Commission declared Herr H. unfit for public office and ordered him immediately dismissed.

The second case concerned a director in the district Department of Trade and Public Assistance. When Herr T. initially appeared before the Calau commission, his petition was approved because of his energetic efforts to keep the region furnished with meat and other supplies and because he had been only a nominal member of the Nazi party from 1942 to 1945. The Calau commission concluded that it was "not necessary to hear any witnesses for his petition."[70]

The Provincial Commissioners felt differently. Herr T. claimed that his local Nazi cell leader *(Zellenleiter)* had pressured him into joining the party in 1942. He recalled that this pressure had increased just prior to his joining the party when a rumor began to circulate that he was going to be pressed into working for the Sicherheitsdienst (SD). Although he apparently never worked for the SD, he argued that entry into the SD "should be understood as a punishment." SED representative Schönborn disagreed, arguing that service in the SD was actually "a special position of trust."[71] Chairman Hentschel wanted to know why Herr T., in his position as an "independent agent" working for the *Kreis* administration, felt that he had to succumb to pressure to join the NSDAP and, in the same year (1942), to join the National Socialist livestock trade organization, the Viehwirtschaftsverband. To this query Herr T. gave no answer. He was then asked why he did not serve in the war. He claimed that it was because he had sustained a hand injury and been wounded in a gas attack in the First World War. In the commission's view, "this statement does not seem to be consistent with the facts; rather it is entirely because of his activity as a district official in the Viehwirtschaftsverband and his membership in the NSDAP that Herr T. was not called up by the Wehrmacht, when in the course of total mobilization, as everyone knows, even the one-armed were drafted." The direction of the Provincial Commission accusations was now clear: Herr T., as an independent livestock trader working for the district government during the war, had joined the NSDAP and the traders' association to protect his business arrangement with the local government and to avoid the draft. This point was driven home when the Provincial Commission leveled the further charge that Herr T. "in the interest of his personal advantage as a profiteer had even, in October 1945, made an application for membership in an antifascist party." In summing up the case against Herr T., it was noted that no exculpating factors had been presented.

The Calau leadership rose to Herr T.'s defense. The charge was led by *Landrat* Freter, who reported that Herr T. had helped to disentangle a completely disorganized meat distribution system at the end of the war. Wollny opined that Herr T. was simply a man "who lived for his work" and that his success in supplying the region with meat had had "a great effect on the attitude of the population." The *Betreibsrat* chairman added that Herr T. could in no way be considered more than a nominal party member, to which the *Landrat* added that, since the Department of Trade and Public Assistance was currently under the control of a proven antifascist, Herr T. could not conceivably pose any real threat. Hentschel rejected these arguments.

> Considering that the Department of Trade and Public Assistance here in the district administration is under the control of politically aware people, one could take the risk of continuing to employ Herr T., if he would give the assurance that he stood upon the ground of antifascism. That he, however, was not merely a nominal member of the NSDAP is evidenced by his entrance into the Viehwirtschaftsverband, because of which he was not drafted. It is under all circumstances necessary, here in the district administration [and] in such an important position, to employ people whom one can trust, and this assurance has not been provided to the Provincial Commission by Herr T.

In light of these considerations, the Calau commission's approval of Herr T.'s petition was overturned and he was ordered immediately dismissed from his post.

In the third case, the Calau leadership brought all the pressure they could muster to prevent the Provincial Commission from overturning one of their previous decisions. Herr P., a caseworker in the district Department of Youth, was a longtime resident of the region who had been acquainted with the Calau commissioners before the Nazi period. At his initial hearing in January, Herr P. was identified as a nominal Nazi Party member whose service in the Jugendamt was highly esteemed by the commissioners. The Calau commission approved his petition, noting that there was no need to call any witnesses in such a clear-cut case.[72]

Appearing before the Provincial Commission three months later, Herr P., a man who had been "80 percent incapacitated" by wounds received in the First World War, claimed that he had come under extraordinary pressure beginning in 1933 to join the Nazi Party. As a former SPD member, Herr P. had initially been dismissed from his post in the Jugendamt after the Nazi seizure of power. He was, however, quickly reinstated, apparently because of his service in the First World War. Under continuing pressure for all civil servants to join the

NSDAP, Herr P. finally relented and joined in May 1937. Despite his party membership, he claimed he had never changed his antifascist convictions.

Unfortunately for Herr P., an article under his name had appeared in the *Calauer-Jahreskalender* in 1937 which displayed "strong Nazi tendencies." This article, apparently overlooked by the Calau commission, was, in the eyes of the Provincial Commissioners, very inculpating. The hearing transcript notes that the 1937 article "bursts the soap bubble of his 'antifascist' attitude." In his defense, Herr P. claimed that he had actually penned an article free of fascist overtones, but that his article was then rewritten by the former Nazi *Landrat* and published under P.'s name. Chairman Hentschel then asked, if Herr P. was such a committed antifascist, why was he married to a woman who had been a member of the NSF? This was explained away by the claim that his wife had joined the NSF because she thought the organization was "purely socialist" in character.

Becoming more defensive, Herr P. went on to argue that he had had to consider what would happen to his wife and four children if he lost his job because of a refusal to join the Nazi Party. Hentschel rejected this argument, observing that "this could hardly be the case since Herr P. had not been dismissed owing to his extreme war injuries." To this observation, Herr P. gave no answer.

Landrat Freter initiated the defense, arguing that his long acquaintance with Herr P. had led him to esteem their friendship, and P.'s extraordinary work in the Jugendamt had made him indispensable. Upon questioning, Freter denied any knowledge of the 1937 article allegedly authored by Herr P. Wollny seconded Freter's testimony, noting that he had been friendly with P. since before 1933 and had always, despite his NSDAP membership, found him to be an antifascist. All these arguments were dismissed by the Provincial Commission, which ordered P.'s immediate removal from office.

After hearing seven more cases, and with a session begun at 9:30 in the morning approaching eight o'clock in the evening, Hentschel attempted to bring the hearing to a close by noting that, "despite the differences in opinion" that had arisen during the day, "a clear judgment and decision in the preceding cases was reached." At this point, the *Betriebsrat* chairman interjected that he would like to say a few words about the case of Herr P. He went on record as strongly supporting the reinstatement of P. in light of his nominal party membership. Hentschel countered by observing that the incriminating evidence against P. was simply too great and that P. had given no good reason for his joining the NSDAP. Furthermore, Hentschel argued, it was "intolerable" for the district administration to employ in "the present democracy" someone who had written a strongly fascist article. Acknowledging that the *Betriebsrat* chairman had a right to his "sincere" attempt to revise the decision, Hentschel then reiterated his observation that the day's proceedings had been a positive experience and reminded the Calau leadership that the strongest measures had to be taken against former Nazis, that they should "never forget that the district administration represents the highest democratic body in the district and all decisions should be arrived at with this in mind." *Landrat* Freter then took the floor to close the proceedings by agreeing with Hentschel that a "stronger standard" should be applied in cases with "special circumstances" and stating that he supported the principle of reexamining troubling cases. "On the other hand," Freter continued, "I would like, however, to support the opinion of the chairman of the *Betriebsrat,* that despite all necessary severity here in the case of Herr P., my conviction is that we here are thoroughly acquainted with the situation, and in particular with the personality of Herr P., and must look upon this decision as incorrect." Having said one last word in Herr P.'s favor, Freter concluded by assuring the Provincial Commission that "it is naturally without question that this decision will be carried out."

The extraordinary hearing in Calau brings together many of the themes presented in this chapter. First, there is the political predicament the SED faced under the commission system. Despite all of the authorities' admonitions, the "antifascists" in Calau did not comprehend the political importance attached to denazification. Even worse, when shown how they had erred, the Calau commissioners became outspoken in their disagreement with the provincial authorities. Although they submitted in the end, the Calau commissioners clearly did not agree with the Provincial Commission's findings. The Calau case also highlights an essential contradiction in the commission system: by giving decision-making power to local commissions staffed by longtime local residents and by encouraging these commissions to work in a bipartisan manner, the central authorities had created a system impervious to central control. This is the dynamic that no "top-down" approach to studying denazification could uncover. *Landrat*

Freter touched upon this issue in his final defense of Herr P.: "My conviction is that we here are thoroughly acquainted with the situation, and in particular with the personality of Herr P." No directives from the central authorities could alter what the Calau commissioners considered common sense: they lived in Calau, they knew what the "situation" there was, and, most important, they knew Herr P. and had knowledge of his "personality," to which the outsiders from Potsdam were not, and could never be, privy.

In conclusion, this review points to one of the main reasons why the denazification commissions were eventually disbanded. The commission system was laborious and difficult to control, and produced widely varying and unpredictable results. An example of the chronic problems that plagued the system comes from an SED report of February 1948. The number of petitions declared nominal was cited as too high, the large number of district commission decisions overturned by the provincial commissions on appeal was seen as "a serious indication" of problems with the district commissions, and it was noted that the number of petitions given conditional approval varied widely among the individual provinces. The appeals process was producing particularly troubling results: a comparison of decisions from the five provinces produced "very divergent" results, and the difference between the number of district decisions overturned by the individual provincial commissions was cited as "enormous." Brandenburg and Saxony were judged to be the only two provinces that were successfully implementing policy, while in the other three provinces of the Soviet zone there were "very serious weaknesses."[73] A later SED report singled out Saxony alone as a success story and found that Brandenburg, along with the other provinces, showed "lesser or greater degrees of weakness" in the implementation of denazification.[74]

CHAPTER 6

The Demographics of Denazification

Who were the 28,901 individuals who appeared before denazification commissions in Brandenburg? The three measures on which I focus in this chapter are the petitioners' age, gender, and occupation. Two types of data were used to construct this demographic analysis. First, there are the official statistics compiled by the Interior Ministry. Second, for this study I compiled a detailed sample of 2,740 individuals from the records of four selected commissions. This is referred to as the data sample, and an explanation of how it was compiled may be found in the Data Sample Appendix at the end of this book.

The three measures of age, gender, and occupation are certainly not exhaustive. They are offered in an attempt to formulate at least a partial group biography of the targets of the purge. Dividing the group by age reveals the extraordinary leniency shown to young people by the commissions and the concerns that surrounded the question of the denazification of youth. A gender analysis shows significant differences between the commissions' decisions regarding men and women and also touches on gender relations in the Third Reich and the roles of men and women in the family structure. The final analytical category—the occupations of those called before the commissions—calls into question previous historical interpretations of the nature of Soviet denazification policy.

The Denazification of Former Hitler Youth Members

The Hitler Jugend (HJ) organization for young men and the parallel organization for young women, the Bund Deutscher Mädel (BDM), brought millions of Germans into a National Socialist organization that fell under Directive 24. Former members of Nazi youth organizations were open to definition as "more than nominal participants in party activities," since they were "active" in one of the party's "subordinate organizations" that furthered "militarist doctrines." HJ and BDM members could also be classified as "avowed believers in Nazism or racial and militarist creeds." "Officers and NCOs" of the HJ were subject to "compulsory removal" under Article 10 of Directive 24, and all members who joined before 25 March 1939 fell under Article 12, which listed "discretionary removal and exclusion categories."[1]

The question of what was to be done with HJ and BDM members arose during the earliest phase of the denazification process. In December 1945, Bechler ordered that HJ and BDM members, with the exception of "paid functionaries," were not to be denied public or private employment opportunities based on their membership in the youth organizations. In addition, those born after 1 January 1920 who became members of the NSDAP or one of its organizations "through a collective transfer [*Sammelüberweisung*]" were "no longer to be considered members of the NSDAP."[2]

The advent of Directive 24 brought the problem of HJ and BDM members into public debate. The Provincial Assembly took up the question of exempting Hitler Youth from denazification at the beginning of February 1947.[3] In introducing legislation to exempt those born after 1 January 1919, SED representative Otto Meier argued that it was an "injustice" that Directive 24 made no provision for young people. "Our youth were brought up in a thoroughly poisoned atmosphere. That was not their fault. The young people are truly not responsible for Hitler coming to power and for the propagandizing of National Socialist ideas that brought about the war . . . They cannot be held accountable for this."[4] CDU representative Peter Bloch warmly supported this legislation and observed that these young people, who were currently twenty to twenty-eight years old, still had many "National Socialist tendencies," but that this could not be remedied "by turning our backs on them." "We will not change anything," Bloch continued, "if we make them second-class citizens, but only if we bring them into cooperative work on the basis of equal citizenship rights."[5]

The law as finally passed guaranteed "equal citizenship rights" to all former members of Nazi organizations born after 1 January 1919, so long as they had been only "nominal members."[6] The law did not specifically mention denazification, nor did the Interior Ministry's guidelines regarding its application.[7] The Interior Ministry, however, had already moved toward exempting young people. Two weeks after the beginning of the Directive 24 phase, commissions were instructed not to hear petitions from those who had joined the HJ or BDM when they were between ten and fourteen years of age.[8] The *Landrat* in Lübben similarly ordered that young people should be treated leniently because "Directive 24 is above all directed against the dark powers of reaction, not against the youth."[9] Nevertheless, the new law, which was widely referred to as an "amnesty" for young people, caused confusion among district commissions. At first the Interior Ministry advised commissions that the amnesty law had no effect on Directive 24.[10] By the end of February, however, commissions were informed that all former HJ and BDM members below the rank of *Scharführer* "no longer fall under Directive 24."[11]

There are 160 former BDM members in the data sample. The commissions judged these women leniently: 133 petitions (83.1 percent) were approved, 12 (7.5 percent) were given conditional approval, and a mere 15 (9.4 percent) were rejected. Of these 160 women, 83 had been in the BDM only, while the remainder (77) had moved from the BDM into the NSDAP, NSF, or NS-Frauenwerk.

One of the primary reasons given for approval of BDM members' petitions was the women's age when they first entered the organization. In a typical example, the Provincial Commission approved the petition of a woman who had joined the BDM in 1936 by noting, "[She] is young and at the age of 14 was automatically enrolled in the BDM."[12]

The commissions also judged these women in the context of their family's Nazi affiliations. One young woman had been in the BDM from 1933 to 1938 and thereafter in the NSF. In addition, her father was a PG, and her brother had been in the HJ and SA. In defense of her brother (and herself since his activities were inculpating), "Fraulein D. reported that her brother had been in the Hitler Youth and was transferred to the SA." The SED commissioner went on record as "doubting this automatic transfer from the HJ to the SA," and the petition was denied.[13] Also denied was a woman who had entered the BDM in 1938 and later joined the NSDAP, but had failed to join an "antifascist" organization after the war. The SED representative on the Provincial Commission "gave his astonished impression that [she] had been sufficiently interested in politics to be politically active for eleven years. Yet today she is not politically organized." In light of this, and because she "unquestionably received a Nazi upbringing" from her National Socialist parents, the petition was rejected, since "her attitude even today cannot be considered democratic."[14] Another former BDM and NSDAP member was incriminated by her father's membership in the Nazi Party from 1933, her sister's membership in the BDM, and her mother's membership in the NSF. All of these factors combined to create "surroundings" that were judged to have been "strongly Nazi."[15] A final example is a woman who joined the BDM in 1932 at the age of ten. The Ruppin commission acknowledged that a ten-year-old girl would have been "under the influence of her parents," but still felt compelled to reject the petition since "one cannot say that there was any pressure [to join] in 1932," that is, a year before Hitler came to power.[16]

Family members with Nazi affiliations were not, however, always a cause for rejection. One woman who had been in both the BDM and NSDAP and was heavily incriminated by her family's Nazi past had her petition approved. It was noted that "the attitude of her parents offers no assurance for a positive attitude toward a new democratic Germany." Nevertheless, this petition was approved because she performed "no function in the party, is young, and as a stenotypist holds a minor position."[17]

Family members' political affiliations cut both ways: having socialist family members could lead to approval. One BDM member was approved because "her father was politically organized before 1933 and is currently a member of the SED." This was enough to convince the commissioners that she had "an absolutely positive attitude toward the democratic state."[18] Another was excused on the grounds of her youth, her membership in the FDGB, and her husband's membership in the LDP.[19]

In addition to BDM members' age and their families' political affiliations, some of these petitions were approved because the women had experienced "compulsory transfer" *(zwangweise Überweisung)* from the BDM to the NSDAP and were therefore judged not culpable for their party membership.[20] Of the twenty BDM members in the data sample who claimed forced transfer to the NSDAP, all but two were excused. Both denied petitioners were daughters of Nazi functionaries, and this status apparently overrode any exculpation owing to their transfer to the NSDAP.[21]

A final example of how the commissioners handled BDM members' cases comes from the records of the Ruppin commission. At its 16 January 1947 meeting the commission heard petitions from two office workers at the city hall in Teschendorf. The two women had almost identical political backgrounds. Frau R. was born in 1925, joined the Jungmädel in 1936, BDM in 1940, and NSDAP in 1943. Frau S. was also born in 1925, joined the Jungmädel in 1935, BDM in 1939, and NSDAP in 1943. The LDP commissioner observed that there was evidence of an "ever stronger connection with National Socialism" in both cases. The FDGB representative countered that this succession of organizations "was a natural development" during the Nazi period. The *Landrat* and the SED representative were in favor of dismissing both women because "workers in the communal offices should have undoubted antifascist attitudes." The FDGB and CDU representatives disagreed, arguing that dismissal of both women would be too drastic "because in both cases it concerns youngsters." After "a small debate," the Ruppin commission compromised: Frau R. was dismissed because she had been a *Führerin* in the BDM, but Frau S., who had held no comparable leadership position, was allowed to keep her job.[22]

There are no discernible differences between the handling of HJ and BDM cases. As with their female counterparts, the majority (82.6 percent) of the one hundred HJ members in the data sample had their petitions approved. This percentage increases to 90 percent if petitions requiring restricted working conditions are included. Similar numbers for the BDM group are 83.1 percent approved, 90.6 percent including restricted occupations. Both groups were often excused because of age. Likewise, former HJ members were also often judged in light of their family's past political affiliations and whether or not they or members of their family currently belonged to an "antifascist" organization. One HJ member, for example, was excused because he "entered the Communist Party in August 1945. Since the father-in-law of Herr C. is a communist functionary, Herr C. through conversations and instruction was able to form opinions about politics and today stands firmly on the foundation of democracy."[23] Another was excused because of his youth, because his father had not been a PG, and because "today both the father and Herr W. are SED."[24] Membership in an "antifascist" party was not, however, always enough to overcome a Nazi past. One young man's model National Socialist upbringing (Deutsches Jungvolk, 1933–1936; HJ, 1936–1939; NSDAP, 1939–1945) and his father's history as an NSDAP *Blockwart* (block warden), led to rejection despite his youth and the fact that he was "presently in an antifascist party."[25]

The only difference between the handling of BDM and HJ members was that the commissions also examined HJ members' wartime activity. Beginning in 1936, a close relationship developed between the HJ and SS, and the war accentuated the HJ's military role. In wartime Germany, HJ leaders were poised to assume elite positions when they reached draft age.[26] The commissions rejected petitioners who appeared to have used their HJ membership as a springboard for a successful adult career in the military. In one example, a former HJ *Scharführer* (troop leader) was rejected because of his "swift advancement in the Wehrmacht." In this case the commission was particularly troubled because he had been in an SPD youth organization before 1933 and "his father as an SPD man" had been against his HJ membership.[27] The negative implications of careerism in the army were compounded in the case of another petitioner who had failed to join a postwar "antifascist" party. This former HJ and NSDAP member was berated by Provincial Commission chair Hentschel, who noted that for "fourteen years he was voluntarily politically organized, but even today as an adult has still not made the decision for one of the antifascist parties."[28]

In sum, both BDM and HJ members generally received lenient treatment. The primary exculpating factor was that they were children when they joined a National Socialist organization. Owing to their age, young women and men were often judged in the context of the political influence wielded by their parents. The commissions had little real recourse but to approve the vast majority of these petitions; it would have served neither the cause of justice nor that of the reconstruction effort to punish these young people by depriving them of their livelihood. Most of these young people already held subordinate positions, and those who were dismissed from their jobs would have to be found other work. The commissioners' and policy makers' hopes for the eventual reconstruction of German social, political, and economic life rested, in the final analysis, with the next generation. This was the reasoning behind both the high approval rate of these petitions and the passage of the youth amnesty law.

The Denazification of Adults

The handling of adults differed significantly from the treatment received by the younger generation. First of all, adults did not have recourse to their age as exculpation. Since membership in National Socialist organizations was considered prima facie complicity in the Nazi system, adults needed to give concrete evidence to mitigate their pasts. The vast majority of adults (those born before 1919) in the data sample were men: 1,851 (89.5 percent) to 218 women (10.5 percent). Figure 6.1 gives a breakdown of these adults by gender and age. The majority of men in the data sample were between forty and sixty years

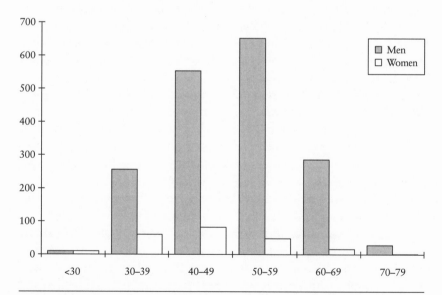

Figure 6.1. Gender and age of individuals appearing before four Brandenburg denazification commissions, January 1947–March 1948 (N = 2,069). *Source:* data sample (see Appendix).

of age. These men would have been between twenty-six and forty-six years old when Hitler came to power in 1933 and between thirty-two and fifty-two at the outbreak of war in 1939. It is not surprising that the majority of petitioners belonged to this cohort: they were too old to have been in the HJ, were past prime draft age during the war, but were young enough to survive the war years. These men were in the prime of their economic and political lives during the Nazi period and thus most likely to have joined a National Socialist organization. The decrease in the number of men over sixty years of age reflects a normal life expectancy rate. The sharp drop in the number of men who were less than forty years of age in 1947 correlates to the mortality rate of draft-age men during the war; there is a much less dramatic drop in the number of women in this age group.

A comparison of approval and denial rates shows that 24 percent of the men were dismissed from their jobs, while 11 percent of the women suffered a similar fate. The rate of approval for petitions from men was 54 percent, from women 76 percent. If we add individuals whose petitions were conditionally approved, the total rate of approval for men becomes 76 percent, for women 89 percent. Men were dismissed more often than women because they were more likely to have held responsible positions in Nazi organizations and thus to have a greater degree of culpability.[29] Men were also more likely than women to hold positions in the public and private sectors targeted by the denazification.[30]

As with BDM and HJ members, commissions also took the family life of adults into consideration. To the male dominance of German political and economic life was added a paternalistic family structure in which women were seen as less than autonomous actors while men were held to a high degree of accountability not just for their own actions but for those of their wives and children as well.[31] It was assumed that a woman's political beliefs would reflect those of her husband. As one commissioner noted in the case of an NSF member who claimed that she never joined the NSDAP even though her husband was a Nazi propaganda leader, "Since your husband was a propaganda leader, I would assume that he brought you into the party too."[32] Some women were excused because their Nazi affiliations were seen as the product of pressure from their husbands. An office worker from Neustadt (Kreis Ruppin) was incriminated because her deceased husband had been a Nazi activist; she herself never joined the party though she was an NSF member. *Landrat* Diedrich opined that "the whole family is very incriminated and was known as openly supporting the NSDAP." The FDGB commissioner successfully countered that she "probably only joined because of her husband since she was only a nominal member" of the NSF.[33] A heavily incriminated shopkeeper who joined the Nazi Party in 1933 and served as an NSF leader testified that her husband had joined the NSDAP in 1931 and that she had become involved because of "persuasion" on his part. The commission accepted this as exculpation and noted, in order to support her contention that her husband was a Nazi activist, that he had been imprisoned (apparently by the Soviets) since the end of the war.[34]

Men, by contrast, were held accountable for the Nazi affiliations of their wives and children. One PG, who had been an SPD member before 1933, claimed that he had been pressured to join the NSDAP because of his political background and that he finally relented in 1939 "in order to have peace." A commissioner retorted, "You joined in order to have some peace, but there is no reason why your wife and daughter had to join the Frauenwerk! How can you explain that?"[35] Of a former member of the SA and NSDAP, the Provincial Commission noted that "he is furthermore strongly incriminated because his wife was also a former member of the NSDAP and in addition was active as a leader in the NSF."[36] Another example is the case of a painter from Senftenberg who joined the NSDAP in 1933 and served as a *Blockwalter* (block warden). The painter was incriminated not only by his own past but also because his wife was a PG and an NSF leader.

> *Petitioner:* My wife was in the Frauenschaft. She was enrolled in the party through no effort of her own. I even tried to forbid her from serving as the Frauenschaft leader.
> *Chairman:* In general, doesn't one assume that the husband has a marked influence over the wife?
> *Answer:* With us that was not the case.[37]

In a variation on this connection between husbands and wives, one hapless petitioner was undone by evidence supplied by his ex-wife.

> *VVN:* Well, Herr W., you claim you were never an active National Socialist, what do you say about the letters you wrote to your wife?

> *Answer:* I was a soldier at that time and our orders were to help to keep the home front calm.
>
> *VVN:* But there are letters from soldiers that have completely different contents; they couldn't force any soldier to write about the things you wrote about. Every neutral letter got through. You directly glorified National Socialism and openly attacked bolshevism.
>
> *Answer:* Our leave [from the front] depended on it.
>
> *VVN:* They could force someone in a prison or concentration camp to write this kind of letter, but they didn't force soldiers. You even accused your own wife of listening to enemy broadcasts.
>
> *Answer:* That's not true, I never did that. I never denounced anyone, not even my ex-wife.
>
> *VVN:* The main reason you divorced your wife, as this document makes clear, is because of her antifascist attitude and her remarks against Hitler.
>
> *Answer:* That is not true. That woman squandered everything I owned: we had personal conflicts with each other.[38]

Men were also held accountable for their children's political affiliations. The Ostprignitz commission touched on the responsibility of a father for his children's political affiliations in questioning a chimney sweep who had joined the NSDAP in 1935.

> *VVN:* Were you already interested in the party before 1935?
>
> *Answer:* No.
>
> *VVN:* Well, then, how did it come about that your son joined the party in 1925?
>
> *Answer:* I was relocated to Rathenow by that time and my son was still in Strassburg. He entered the party on his own volition. We never saw eye to eye politically, and for that reason there was a lot of tension in the family.
>
> *SED:* But you were responsible for your son at that time?
>
> *Answer:* He wasn't part of the family any longer at that time.

In this case the petitioner was approved on the grounds that "he has not had contact with his son for years, so the culpability of the father in this instance cannot be inferred."[39] In another case, a man was even confronted with the political reputation of his father-in-law, who was

known as a "true-blue reactionary," to which he replied, with justification, "I am not responsible for my father-in-law."[40]

Having a family that was not enrolled in National Socialist organizations could work to the advantage of male petitioners. As the Ostprignitz commission noted in approving one man's petition, "He was
never active in the party, and none of the members of his family were
members of the NSDAP."[41] This type of family connection could not
always save a petitioner, however. In rejecting a petitioner who had
belonged to five National Socialist organizations and whose wife was
in the NSF, the Provincial Commission noted that "all that can be said
regarding exculpation for Herr K. is that his children did not belong
to the Hitler Youth."[42]

In rare cases the "antifascist" credentials of a family member could
result in the approval of a case for the head of the family. A worker in
Calau who joined the NSDAP in 1933 had little to show in his defense
except that his son was an active member of the FDJ (Freie Deutsche
Jugend). This activity of the son secured approval of the father's petition. The FDJ commissioner stated that he knew "the son of Herr M.
and [the son] is a good antifascist and is active in the work of the
FDJ." As further exculpation, it was noted that the SED had submitted an affidavit attesting to the son's active role in the FDJ.[43] In another example, the Ostprignitz commission gave conditional approval
to a petitioner who joined the NSDAP in 1934 on the grounds that
"his wife was a KPD functionary who was incarcerated for over one
year in 1933–1934."[44]

Denazification by Occupation

In the Stalinization model of developments in the Soviet zone, the ultimate goal of denazification was simple: to remove Nazis and other
"reactionaries" from leading positions in the government and economy and to replace them with "antifascists" who supported Soviet
plans for Germany's future. There is no doubt that the Soviets and the
SED wanted to use denazification to replace PGs with "antifascists."
But the objectives and the results of denazification were not always in
harmony, and the purge was in part abandoned precisely because policy makers could not control the results.

With the opening of the East German archives, we can now gain
greater insight into the connection between denazification and an in-

dividual's occupation. An analysis based on this new source material leads to the following conclusions: (1) certain occupational groups were targeted, but a petitioner's occupation was not always the primary consideration in the decision; (2) there are instances in which the occupation of the petitioner was the primary consideration, but this was as likely to result in approval as in denial of the petition; (3) the use of the proviso that petitioners could continue their present employment status but could never assume a supervisory position was widespread and often meant that petitioners remained at their posts without any change in their employment status; (4) equally widespread was the reclassification of workers or the imposition of limitations that may have affected future employment possibilities but did not alter petitioners' present occupations. In sum, the correlation between the petitioners' occupations and the decisions of the commissions is not as strong as previously assumed: for some occupations the correlation is strong, but for others it is weak.

There are three important pieces of information not included in the following analysis that would be required to draw a comprehensive picture of the connection between denazification and individuals' occupations. First, there is no evidence here on those who were hired to replace dismissed workers. It may be impossible to discern the political backgrounds of the thousands of replacement workers, although a future study may be able to shed some light on this problem through an investigation of the records of the Employment Offices and the personnel records of the individual government departments and private concerns. This complex undertaking is beyond the scope of the present study.

A second piece of information not included here is what became of those who were dismissed from their jobs. Individuals released from their jobs were required to report to their local Employment Office for reemployment. Beginning in October 1947, the Interior Ministry ordered that the general population should be informed of the details of a dismissed individual's Nazi past through the posting of this information in the communities where the PG lived and, in cases of reemployment, in the new workplace.[45] Despite these safeguards, it is possible that an individual who was dismissed by a commission in one locale could have been hired in another. Attempts were made to keep track of dismissed workers, but given the fluid movement of people within the Soviet zone and among the four occupation zones during this period, it would have been impossible to know the political background of every individual.[46] There is also the possibility that individuals, having been dismissed in one locale, would be able to change their identity, move to another place, and be hired in a new position.

Finally, an analysis of denazified individuals would ideally have to be extended at least into the 1950s. Because a person was dismissed in 1947 or 1948, it cannot be assumed that years later he or she was not hired under different circumstances. The East Germans claimed that those dismissed by denazification commissions in the Soviet zone eventually made their way to the western zones, where their political past was not a liability. The Interior Ministry reported in February 1948 that a "relatively high" percentage of those who had been declared Nazi activists by the commissions were leaving for the west, although the sole example given in this report was that 1,023 "activists" from the Cottbus district had recently moved west.[47] This must have been the case in many instances, but it is unlikely that all of the dismissed people packed their bags for the west.

Let us begin this analysis of denazification and employment by reviewing the general guidelines under which the commissions worked. During the first, Directive 24 phase of denazification, from January 1947 until Order 201 came into effect in October 1947, the guidelines were loosely structured. The commissions were simply charged with determining under which article of Directive 24 the petitioner fell and then either denying or approving the request to continue working.[48] Although there were no provisions for a decision allowing petitioners to continue working with the qualification that they could not hold a supervisory position, in practice this type of decision was routinely made from the beginning. The Provincial Commission, for example, began to make this type of decision at its second hearing in January 1947: in the case of a master printer who worked for the provincial government, the commission decided to remove him from his position as a master but to allow him to continue to work "only as a printer."[49] This decision probably resulted in decreased income for the printer and a limitation on his ability to advance in his occupation in the future. This was clearly a form of punishment, but since the printer remained in the employ of the government, this petition was counted as approved by the commission. Table 6.1 gives the Interior Ministry's statistics for the occupations of those who appeared before the district commissions from January to the end of August 1947. The occupa-

Table 6.1 Brandenburg district denazification commission decisions by occupation, January–August 1947

Occupation	Total	Approved	Dismissed
Health/social services	2,296	83.6%	16.4%
Industry	252	81.0	19.0
Finance	73	80.8	19.2
Business/skilled trades	2,954	79.4	20.6
Agriculture	527	75.7	24.3
Transportation	374	70.2	29.8
Public Offices	4,855	69.3	30.7
Education	188	17.5	82.5
Total	11,519	74.4	25.6

Source: BLHA, Rep. 203, Entnazifizierung, 8, 29 August 1947.

Notes: Does not include 35 individuals who worked for press and information services. "Public offices" includes communal offices, police, and the judiciary.

tional groups in Table 6.1 are ranked from the highest to the lowest approval rates. As mentioned earlier, during this phase of denazification, petitions approved with the proviso that the individual could continue working only in a non-supervisory position were counted as approved.

The guidelines for decision making were more detailed under Order 201. Paragraph 7 of the Second Implementation Decree for Order 201 laid out the commissions' fundamental task: "Denazification commissions are to investigate formerly active fascists, militarists, beneficiaries of Nazi rule, and industrialists who spiritually or materially promoted or were enriched by the war," as well as "members of the fascist party or its organizations, against whom there are personal accusations of criminal conduct." The commissions were empowered to remove these individuals from their jobs or deny them the right to practice their occupations or any other occupations "which the denazification commissions decide are important."[50]

This was a fundamental reformulation: commissions were no longer instructed to determine under which article of Directive 24 petitioners fell, but rather were to determine whether or not petitioners fell under Paragraph 7 of the Second Implementation Decree. Although it was claimed that Paragraph 7 was based on Directive 24, Order 201 had precedence over Directive 24.[51] As Hentschel noted in reviewing a case, under Directive 24 the petitioner "formally belonged to those persons who must be dismissed, but under Order 201 he is not to be considered a Nazi activist." In Hentschel's view, "Order 201 clearly differentiates between Nazi activists and militarists and the large number of only nominal former Nazis. That means that one should not apply Directive 24 . . . schematically and formally in every case."[52]

Under Order 201 commissions were given two options: to decide that the petitioner did not fall under Paragraph 7 and therefore would not be subject to any "limitations," or to decide that the individual did fall under Paragraph 7. In the latter case, commissions could either decide on immediate dismissal or grant permission to continue in a lesser position. This lesser position could entail restrictions on future employment or reassignment from a supervisory role.[53] Commissions were not allowed to levy monetary fines, order arrests, or impose any other form of punishment not prescribed in the guidelines.[54]

The Interior Ministry compiled statistics for the Order 201 phase which break down the purge by occupational groups. Table 6.2 shows the total from each occupation group, the number of cases declared nominal (approved), the number given approval to continue work in a lesser capacity (conditional approval), and the number dismissed from their jobs. The occupation groups in Table 6.2 are ranked from

Table 6.2 Brandenburg district denazification commission decisions by occupation, October 1947–March 1948

Occupation	Total	Approved	Conditional	Dismissed
Health/social services	633	76.2%	13.1%	10.7%
Education	1,539	70.7	19.9	9.4
Transportation	3,713	67.0	26.3	6.7
Public offices	2,582	62.4	23.0	14.6
Banking and trade	876	59.7	24.7	15.6
Industry	2,244	49.1	41.4	9.5
Agriculture	863	42.6	49.6	7.8
Total	12,450	61.5	28.4	10.1

Source: BLHA, Rep. 203, Entnazifizierung, 8, Bl. 22.

Notes: Does not include 6 cases from the press and information services, 347 cases from church employees, and 2,666 cases listed as "other." "Public offices" includes communal operations, police, fire, the judiciary, and communication; "banking and trade" includes finance.

the highest to the lowest approval rates. This ranking shows that people employed in heath and social services occupations had the greatest chance of retaining their positions. If, however, petitions approved conditionally are counted as also approved, then those working in transportation were treated with the most leniency, closely followed by those in agriculture.

We can now take a closer look at how different occupations were handled. The following analysis focuses on those in health care, education, public offices, skilled trades, and private business, white- and blue-collar workers, and agricultural workers.

Health Care

The leniency shown to health care workers is an example of practical considerations of public well-being outweighing the mandate to denazify. Health care workers were employed in both the public and private sectors. Workers in public hospitals, sanitariums, and community health clinics were public employees who could be dismissed from their positions by the commissions. Workers in the private sector, such as doctors, dentists, apothecaries, and midwives, held licenses issued by the provincial government, and a negative finding resulted in revocation of the license. Some doctors worked in both the private and public sectors, simultaneously holding a license for private practice and a position in a public hospital.

There are 287 health care workers in the data sample: only 26 (9 percent) of these individuals were found to be "activists," while 247 (86 percent) were declared nominal, and the remaining 14 were given conditional approval. These people were highly trained and thus practically irreplaceable, particularly in light of the high rate of infectious disease that marked the occupation period.[55] It was estimated in 1946 that the province of Brandenburg lacked 25–50 percent of its required health workers and suffered in particular from a shortage of doctors and nurses.[56] In light of this situation, commissions were reluctant to dismiss any health workers. Thus, the Ostprignitz commission approved the petition of a doctor who joined the NSDAP in 1933 simply by noting that "he has worked at the Breddin typhus station, where many caregivers have met their deaths, since the summer of 1945."[57]

Of all health care workers, doctors were treated with an extraordinary degree of leniency. With the release of the March 1947 guidelines for purging the private sector, the question immediately arose as to whether doctors in private practice were to be exempted. The provincial government decided that the primary consideration in the cases of doctors in private practice should not be their political past but rather the principle that "the population should suffer no damage to its health care."[58] In a report to the SMA, the Interior Ministry admitted that the health care sector had a "particularly high" number of former Nazis but that "most of the Nazis in the health care services had to be left in their positions because there are almost no politically unincriminated doctors and because they just could not be replaced as easily as, for example, administrative employees."[59]

In order to rectify the need for health care workers, especially doctors, with the desire to denazify, a balanced approach was eventually adopted. It was suggested that incriminated doctors with private practices could be punished through revocation of their license to practice privately, but could still be utilized by assigning them to work at public hospitals and clinics.[60] This reassignment of doctors became a standard procedure.[61] It was further decided that the degree to which doctors had "proven themselves through practical work in the democratic construction since 1945" should be carefully considered by commissions.[62]

In an attempt to ameliorate the purge's effect, the Central Administration for Heath Care in Berlin tried to gain special treatment for health workers. The Health Administration suggested that a doctor could serve on a denazification commission when the case of another doctor was being decided. This was seen as necessary because, "owing to the composition of the denazification commissions in the districts, they are often not qualified to judge the conduct of a doctor and the character of his duties." It was further suggested that, in those "exceptional cases" when a truly nominal worker was incorrectly dismissed, there should be a special appeals process so that the decision could be overturned and the worker reinstated.[63] The request for the addition of a doctor to the district commissions was eventually turned down.[64] An extraordinary appeals process was established, however, for "specialists" such as doctors and other health care workers. It was decided that the Provincial Commission would hear the appeal and that a representative of the ministry concerned would be able to attend the hearing.[65]

A review of health care workers from the data sample indicates that extraordinary measures were not necessary to assure approval. As noted earlier, commissions were reluctant to reach a decision that would deprive the population of scarce health care workers. The Ostprignitz commission, for example, quickly approved a surgeon's petition by noting that he had played only a "passive role" in the NSDAP (although he joined in 1933) and, more important, that there were several severely ill patients currently awaiting his care at the hospital: "The commission recommends an immediate approval of the services of Dr. H. in order to assure that there will be no loss of life."[66] Similarly, a dentist from Meyenburg who claimed that he had joined the NSDAP in 1934 in order to gain access to customers with national health insurance was approved because he was "never active" in the party and "in light of the dental needs of the population . . . since Meyenburg is particularly poorly cared for."[67]

Education

The purge of the educational establishment, and particularly of elementary school teachers, was a high priority for the policy makers in Potsdam and Berlin and a constant source of worry for local administrators. Teachers were a key element in the elimination of National Socialist influences and the rebuilding of a new "democratic" Germany.[68] As an SMA representative observed in March 1946:

> We have determined that there are thousands of teachers who are former PGs and who maintain that they want to educate the children in the new democratic direction. But one has to admit that it is quite improbable and unbelievable that former PGs can actually educate children in the new democratic direction. In the first place, the teachers themselves have never had a democratic education, and second, they remain under the influence of their own fascist upbringing and they pass this along to their students . . . [A]fter twelve years of fascism, the population and the children have become much too accustomed to this situation. They have never heard of democracy and they do not know what democracy actually means.[69]

Although the SMA released an order in August 1945 calling for "complete elimination" of fascist and militarist influences in the school system, a purge of the teaching corps was slow to develop.[70] At the beginning of 1946, the Brandenburg SMA complained that a large number of PGs were still employed as teachers, that schools continued to use Nazi era books, and that classrooms were still decorated with Nazi posters.[71] In March 1946 there were 2,336 former members of Nazi organizations working as teachers in Brandenburg.[72] By the beginning of the 1946 school year, the situation had improved somewhat, with the figures reduced to 1,253 PGs (14.4 percent of the total) teaching in elementary schools and 115 (8.3 percent) in the high schools. An examination of individual districts, however, shows regional variations in the employment of PGs. In Potsdam only 3 percent of elementary school teachers were PGs, while in Spremberg the figure was 28.3 percent. The situation in the high schools shows more variation: five districts no longer had any PGs working as teachers, while in Prenzlau 35.7 percent of the high school teachers were PGs, and Angermünde reported a figure of 40 percent.[73] In response to this unevenness, the provincial education ministries were directed at the end of 1946 to establish a Commission for School Questions staffed by representatives from the "democratic organizations" and provincial government. These commissions, which were set up at the same time that district denazification commissions were being established, actually functioned as denazification commissions, even though they ostensibly had only an "advisory function" regarding employment of PGs as teachers.[74]

The main problem with dismissing teachers was the need to find qualified replacements rapidly. The Interior Ministry admitted that teachers were similar to health care workers insofar as they could not be easily replaced, and that this was delaying the purge.[75] Although the Education Ministry scrambled to train thousands of new teachers quickly, there were serious shortages in some areas.[76] A month into the purge, one local school superintendent complained that the "suddenly decreed dismissals [of teachers] have led to a marked unrest among the mayors, the parents, and the [local branches of] the SED."[77]

The Soviets closely monitored the purge of teachers and applied significant pressure on the Education Ministry to replace PGs. In February 1947 it was estimated that there were about 800 teachers who should be dismissed under Directive 24, but that they would have to be kept on for the near future "or the schools will come to a standstill [since] we cannot train replacements quickly enough." In *Kreis* Teltow, for example, there were 600 teachers, 100 of whom were PGs. Despite these staffing problems, the Soviets decreed that no more than 10 percent of the teachers in any district could be PGs.[78] Some local

Soviet commanders attempted to ameliorate the effect of dismissals by ordering district commissions to forward all negative decisions for final approval.[79] The Soviets persisted, however, in setting quotas for the number of former Nazis who could work as teachers. In August it was estimated that there were still 650 PG teachers, and the Soviets decreed that it would be permissible to allow 300 to 400 of these teachers to remain at their posts since this would equal only 3 percent of the entire teaching force. The Soviets also agreed that the approximately 340 teachers who were not denazified because of the youth amnesty could continue working.[80]

Teachers were apparently the only occupation group on which the Soviets imposed an arbitrary quota. The effect of the quotas can be seen in the Ostprignitz commission's handling of the cases of four teachers from Wittstock. The Wittstock school superintendent appeared as a witness for all four teachers and secured approval of their petitions by reporting that he had "received instructions from the government that allow us to retain about 10% [of these teachers]."[81] Despite these quotas, the denazification of teachers proceeded slowly. Brandenburg was criticized in a DVdI report of November 1947 because there were still 120 teachers whose cases had yet to be judged.[82]

Although denazification commissions were ostensibly in charge of purging teachers, the Education Ministry controlled the process. The ministry forwarded lists of employees to district commissions. Only those who appeared on these lists were examined and all others were allowed to remain at their posts.[83] In practice, this meant that few teachers ever appeared before district denazification commissions. *Oberbürgermeister* Lange in Brandenburg/Havel complained that a list of teachers had not been forwarded to his commission, and that "through intrigues among the teachers, the poor work of the former superintendent of schools, and the careless handling of personnel matters by the former director of the Education Ministry, a number of teachers were allowed to remain in employ although they fall under Directive 24." "I was completely prepared," Lange concluded, "to take up cleansing the schools of activist Nazi elements through the present denazification commission," but the Education Ministry's intervention meant that "a number of these teachers, whose dismissals are necessary, will remain in the schools. I am afraid that the situation in the other cities and districts will be similar, in fact probably even worse."[84]

Unlike other occupational groups, teachers were, to a large extent, denazified outside the district commission system. It is noteworthy, for example, that the Central Administration for Education's guidelines for implementation of Directive 24 contained no mention of denazification commissions.[85] In the data sample prepared for this study, there are only 20 cases of teachers appearing before a commission out of a total of 2,740 petitions. According to Interior Ministry statistics, commissions dismissed only 300 Education Ministry employees during the entire period of denazification (Tables 6.1 and 6.2). Since there were numerous non-teaching jobs under the Education Ministry's control, it cannot be assumed that all of these 300 people were teachers. Nevertheless, thousands of teachers were dismissed because of their political background. Local school superintendents and the Education Ministry in Potsdam apparently carried out most of these dismissals. As one former teacher described his dismissal, "I was called to appear before School Superintendent M., who said to me: 'I know you and I respect you but you must go, Zhukov's order.'"[86]

Public Offices

From the beginning of the occupation, the "cleansing" of public offices was seen as a prerequisite for the construction of an "antifascist" Germany. Despite a series of purges, there were still many incriminated individuals in public employ at the beginning of 1947. Public employees appeared before denazification commissions more often than any other occupational group: 31 percent of all petitioners were public employees (Tables 6.1 and 6.2). Because of the importance attached to public offices, it was widely believed that public employees should be held to a higher degree of accountability than other workers. Thus, the SED representative on the Provincial Commission argued that all white-collar workers in public employ who had been members of a Nazi organization, "even if they only [held] subordinate positions, represent a danger for democratic Germany."[87]

In addition to a purge of PGs, equal weight was given to replacement of dismissed workers with "antifascists." The Interior Ministry advised district commissions that "it will not do that active Nazis remain in the administration . . . while thousands of class-conscious workers do not have steady employment and move from one occupation to another."[88] Thus, for example, an employee of the Forestry Service who had joined the NSDAP in 1933 was dismissed "because he as a white-collar worker . . . can definitely be replaced by an anti-fascist worker."[89]

Although there was a policy of replacing PGs with "antifascists," finding qualified replacements was a constant problem. The mayor of Beeskow, for example, wrote to the district denazification commission complaining that they had crippled his ability to run the city by depriving him of irreplaceable workers.[90] The problem of dismissed workers was particularly acute in villages and communal governments with few employees. In these cases, the incompatibility of the need to maintain the day-to-day operation of the local administration with a political purge was clearly evident. Since communal governments had only small numbers of employees, the loss of a few could prove devastating. Yet, precisely because the number of employees was so small, there was a desire to ensure that none were politically incriminated. As one *Landrat* observed, "Communal offices should be completely cleansed of former NSDAP members, because office workers have political and economic influence . . . [O]nly antifascist workers guarantee an irreproachable conduct of business. In large concerns, employment of someone who joined the party in 1937 is justifiable, but in small communal offices there is not enough supervision."[91] Still, the size of communal administrations led commissions to moderate the hard-line approach to PGs in public service. The Ruppin commission, for example, heard two cases from the mayor's office in Manker: both men were white-collar employees, one of whom had joined the NSDAP in 1935, the other in 1943. The commission decided, "in order not to dismiss both workers from the communal office," that the man who joined the party in 1935 would be immediately dismissed and the second remain employed until the mayor could find a replacement.[92] Similarly, the Ruppin commission decided to approve the petition of an office worker in the Plänitz communal office solely because they had already ordered the dismissal of another worker from the office.[93]

The high standard to which public employees were held meant that petitioners with incriminated pasts stood a far better chance of keeping their jobs if they worked in the private sector. Among public employees, those who worked in offices with a large number of workers were more likely to retain their positions than similar workers in small communal offices. The differences between the handling of public and private workers reflected the policy makers' concern with seizing control of the state administration, a goal dating back to the communist critique of fascism developed during the war.

The focus on public offices did not, however, lead to a complete purge of every incriminated employee. During the first, Directive 24 phase of denazification (Table 6.1), 69.3 percent of public employees called before a commission were permitted to keep their jobs. During the second, Order 201 phase, those permitted to keep their jobs (approval and conditional approval, Table 6.2) was even higher: 85.4 percent. This meant that approximately three quarters of all incriminated public employees remained in public service after the purge was completed.

In light of all the effort put into the purge of the public sector, the number of incriminated employees who remained at their posts seems large. There are several possible explanations for this. First, the leading appointed positions, such as the heads of the provincial ministries, had long been in the hands of "antifascists." Second, after the 1946 elections the SED had secured control of the majority of elected positions, and most of the remaining elected posts were held by unincriminated non-socialists. This did not mean that all of these positions were held by unincriminated people: the SED *Landrat* in Ruppin, for example, was a former member of the HJ and NSDAP, and in perhaps the greatest irony, the head of the purge, Interior Minister Bechler, was a former German army officer and a former member of the NSDAP.[94] Both of these men compensated for their past by going over to the Soviet side during the war: the *Landrat* deserted to the Russians in the closing weeks of the war, while Bechler was active in the NKFD as a POW in the Soviet Union.

There was at least a presumption that public offices should be thoroughly "cleansed" of all incriminated workers: one has only to recall that the SMA originally issued an order calling for the dismissal of *all* PGs from public service by 31 November 1945. This, of course, never occurred. The idea of a thorough purge of public service was finally abandoned: not only was it impractical to dismiss all of these employees, but also, and more to the point, it was not necessary. The PGs' response to SED and Soviet polices was not, for the most part, active opposition but rather resignation and apathy. Most PGs in administrative employ were not sabotaging reconstruction but rather were simply happy to keep their jobs. In addition, despite the desire to replace PGs with "antifascists," in practice the pool of qualified "antifascists" was small. In the final analysis, the need for a competent work force outweighed ideological demands for a "cleansed" administration.

Skilled Trades and Private Business

The commissions were instructed to focus on the private sector in February 1947.[95] The private sector was regulated by the issuance of licenses by the provincial government. There were three possible decisions commissions could make in these cases. A nominal finding meant that petitioners could unconditionally continue in their occupations. A negative decision resulted in revocation of the business license, and, in theory at least, reemployment in another line of work. Conditional approval for license holders usually restricted their conduct of business in some way; a master skilled tradesman, for example, could have his master's license revoked but be allowed to continue in the same line of work under another licensee.[96]

Decisions in the cases of licensees could be complex. In the case of one master locksmith, for example, the decision reads, "Not permitted for public or semi-public service, in civilian occupations only in non-supervisory positions, the license is to be revoked."[97] This decision meant, in the first place, that the locksmith lost his master's license and his ability to run his own business and train apprentices. In addition, the locksmith could not work for any public or semi-public concerns in the future, but was free to work, even as a locksmith, in a private concern run by another license holder.

The commissions were sensitive to the plight of skilled tradesmen during the Nazi period. In approving the petition of one master craftsman, the Ostprignitz commission noted that the petitioner had been forced by his employer to join the NSDAP as a condition for taking his master's examination. As exculpation it was observed that "the commission is aware that masters . . . who trained apprentices were forced to join the party, because the party was concerned that all training personnel in industrial concerns . . . must be in line with National Socialism."[98]

Skilled workers could also receive special treatment if they were seen as irreplaceable or important to reconstruction. The Calau commission, for example, approved the petition of a skilled machinist at a glass factory by noting that his special knowledge of machinery "could hardly be replaced."[99] Aside from health care workers, almost all of the petitioners in the data sample who were approved because of their occupations were masters in trades essential for reconstruction, such as masons, machinists, and electricians. In a few cases, commissions attempted to reconcile denazification and reconstruction by denying a petition while simultaneously allowing the petitioner to continue working for a specified length of time. A bridge-building specialist, for example, had his date of dismissal extended for three months because "at the moment he cannot be replaced." [100] Similarly, a civil engineer was ordered dismissed from his public position in February 1947 but allowed to remain until May because his help would be needed with the impending spring flooding of the Oder River. [101] Whether or not this rather meager extension was enough to induce these petitioners to continue at their posts is unknown, but it is easy to imagine that they might have approached their work with a lack of enthusiasm after learning of their imminent dismissal.

There are 230 skilled workers in the data sample encompassing 52 different occupations: 69 percent of these petitions were approved. Although a few of these occupations, such as furriers, photographers, and dance teachers, can be seen as superfluous to reconstruction, most of these occupations would have been considered essential, and yet 31 percent of these petitioners lost their licenses. It should be kept in mind that just because a skilled worker, say, a master electrician, lost his license, it did not mean that he could not continue to work as an electrician, only that he could no longer be self-employed: revocation of the license did not mean that the economy "lost" an electrician (unless he decided to move to the west). The most logical explanation for the treatment of skilled workers is that commissions tended to judge petitions based on a complex set of considerations that included occupation but also encompassed a wide range of other types of evidence.

In addition to skilled craftsmen, the other license holders who appeared before the commissions were engaged in trade or business. The majority of these petitioners in the data sample were shopkeepers or owners of bars, restaurants, or hotels *(Gastwirte)*. There are more *Gastwirte* in the data sample than any other trade or business group: 36 out of a total of 156 cases. *Gastwirte* also had the highest denial rate of any group of private business owners: 21 of these petitions were denied, 15 approved. The commissions seemed to feel that Nazi *Gastwirte* were incriminated because their businesses could have been used as regular meeting places for local party members. The *Landrat* in Ruppin, for example, declared at a hearing in July 1947 that all *Gastwirte* who joined the party before 1933 should have their licenses revoked.[102]

Although some occupation groups, such as *Gastwirte,* were singled out, the results of the denazification of tradespeople and business owners are similar to those for skilled workers. Of 156 petitions from tradespeople and business owners in the data sample, 60 percent were approved. In contrast to a skilled worker with specialized training, a shopkeeper or bar owner played a lesser role in the reconstruction and could be more easily replaced by an "antifascist" licensee. The Interior Ministry's guidelines for denazification of the private sector specifically suggested that revoked business licenses should be reissued to "antifascists."[103] That there was no wholesale revocation of the business licenses of former PGs is further evidence that district commissions decided petitions on a case-by-case basis.

Labor

Although laborers can be analyzed as a single group, distinctions need to be made between those employed in the public and private sectors. At the beginning of denazification, commissions were instructed to purge all incriminated workers thoroughly from public employ, but "persons in obviously subordinate positions in industrial concerns" were to be allowed to keep their jobs.[104] Bechler's February 1947 order for a purge of the private sector also drew a contrast between public offices and private concerns by noting that individuals who fell under Directive 24 but who were employed as manual laborers *(Handarbeiter)* in private concerns should not be called before denazification commissions.[105] Brandenburg was apparently the only province in the Soviet zone to have an exemption for manual laborers. At a December interior ministers' conference, Mielke sharply criticized this exception for laborers, observing that "all persons, regardless of their occupations, are to be investigated if they had been active fascists."[106] Bechler quickly moved to end this exception in an order of January 1948. Businesses were instructed to forward lists of manual laborers who might have been activists to the district denazification commission.[107]

Despite the claim that denazification did not differentiate among occupations, some occupations were treated differently than others.

We have already seen, for example, the extraordinary treatment given to health care workers. The commissions also singled out some skilled and unskilled workers for extraordinary treatment. Workers in print shops, for example, were carefully examined. Although I have been unable to find evidence that print shop workers who were PGs used their skills to produce fascist propaganda, there was a fear among the commissions that this might occur. In dismissing five employees from a private printing firm in Neuruppin, the *Landrat* observed that the print shop was an "important business, in which gross misconduct might be carried out." The FDGB commissioner seconded this opinion: "In the print works we must have trustworthy workers because there is the danger that illegal work could be carried out there." So great was the Ruppin commission's concern, they even ordered the dismissal of the watchman from the print shop because he had joined the NSDAP in 1933.[108]

Most workers, however, were treated leniently simply because they already held unimportant jobs. Theoretically, all dismissed workers would have to be found new work by the Employment Offices, so there was little reason to dismiss workers from one menial task just to shift them to another. Take the street sweepers of Neuruppin. The cases of these eighteen men were decided in absentia by the Ruppin commission in January 1947. The mayor of the city forwarded a list of the workers along with a request that they all be allowed to keep their jobs since the matter concerned "the [type of] lowly work which it has been agreed former members of the NSDAP should perform." The *Landrat* disagreed, observing that "there are still a number of refugees who do not have regular work, and the Employment Office is also currently sending workers to build dikes along the Oder River, to which there is always a degree of resistance. This often includes politically unincriminated people, the sons of antifascists, and likewise activists in the FDJ, who are required to do this work [at the river]." In the end, the commission decided that three of the street sweepers who joined the party or SA before 1933 and one who had been in the SS should be fired. The remainder were allowed to keep their jobs, but the mayor was advised that they should be replaced in the future if "politically unincriminated people apply for these jobs."[109]

Three large groups of workers were virtually untouched by denazification until the advent of Order 201 in October 1947. During the first phase of denazification, the postal service (Oberpostdirektion), railroads (Reichsbahndirektion), and the coal mining industry (Zentralverwaltung der Brennstoffindustrie) were given control over the purge of their own employees through the establishment of extraordinary denazification commissions that were independent of the district commissions. Order 201 dissolved these extraordinary commissions and charged the newly built district commissions to investigate workers in these sectors of the economy.[110]

The dissolution of the extraordinary commissions seriously disrupted the work of the district commissions. The root of the problem was that Order 201 mandated that the extraordinary commissions end their work and turn over all of their outstanding cases to the district commissions. At the same time, Order 201 also called for the standing district commissions to be replaced by the new, enlarged Order 201 district commissions. In what proved to be a major bureaucratic snafu, the extraordinary commissions disbanded and turned their cases over to the district commissions, and this sudden flood of cases made it impossible for the district commissions themselves to end their work by the prescribed deadline of 15 November.[111] The Luckau commission reported that the influx of petitions from rail workers meant that they would not be able to turn their work over to the new Order 201 commission by the November deadline.[112] In Calau, the heart of the brown coal industry, the commission was suddenly swamped with approximately 750 petitions from coal industry workers, which made the completion of the commission's work in November also impossible.[113] The *Landrat* in Teltow, with a hint of irritation, informed Bechler (two months after Order 201 was supposed to begin) that he would not be able to attend the upcoming People's Congress since he was spending almost every day chairing the district denazification commission in an attempt to finish the backlog of cases and start the new Order 201 system.[114] In order to speed the conclusion of the Directive 24 commissions' work, the Interior Ministry decided in November that Reichsbahn laborers should no longer be examined by the commissions.[115] Eventually, Mielke ordered the Directive 24 commissions simply to stop their examination of cases and turn material regarding pending cases over to the new Order 201 commissions.[116] At the end of January 1948, the Interior Ministry reported that these three sectors had a large number of workers who had been ordered dismissed but who were still at their old jobs and supervisors given conditional approval who were still in management positions.[117]

As in other sectors of the economy, the dismissal of laborers hindered reconstruction efforts. The managers of the district railroad in Prenzlau complained, for example, that it made no sense to dismiss laborers who could not be replaced. The local Employment Office had informed the rail district that there were no replacement workers available and that none could be brought in from other districts owing to a severe housing shortage.[118] Gustav Sobottka, the head of the Zentralverwaltung der Brennstoffindustrie, bridled at Order 201's dissolution of the extraordinary denazification commission that had been under his control and requested that future dismissals be cleared with him and that dismissed employees be given the chance to be reemployed in other positions.[119]

In the case of workers, reconstruction took precedence over denazification. There were both practical and ideological reasons for this. As Ulbricht observed in October 1947, "The reconstruction of the state and economy has shown that there are indeed enough workers, but that they cannot all be fully utilized because they are still not good democrats. On the other hand, we definitely have good antifascists, but they must first be trained in order to be useful workers."[120] This was wishful thinking. The pressing need for reconstruction had to be met immediately, not in some distant future when a sufficient number of "antifascist" workers could be "trained." A few short months after Ulbricht made this observation, he turned his back on the entire denazification program and argued that reconstruction was of such paramount importance that there was no need to get bogged down in the "ancient history" of the Nazi backgrounds of workers.[121] This privileging of reconstruction over denazification was evident in Brandenburg's exemption for manual laborers and the policy of allowing the post, rail, and mining sectors to denazify their own workers. In the case of unskilled workers, a further practical consideration was that these individuals already held menial jobs and their reassignment made little sense. As we saw in the example of the Neuruppin street sweepers, there was the possibility that these PGs could be given even more distasteful work, but there probably was not a large group of "antifascists" clamoring for the chance to be street sweepers.

There was also an ideological and political aspect to the treatment of workers. The SED, after all, claimed to be the party representing the working class. As was seen in the previous discussion of the communist critique of fascism, the perception that the KPD had "lost" a portion of the working class to the Nazis became a postwar problem.

Nazi workers may have suffered from insufficient class consciousness, but they were still workers. If the SED's ideology was worth anything at all, then the party should be able to win over the working class. This could not be accomplished if workers who were PGs felt that they were being punished by the party that was simultaneously attempting to win their allegiance.

Agriculture

The denazification of farmers was a challenge for Brandenburg. Since agriculture was the foundation of the provincial economy as well as the source of the population's sustenance, the purge of this sector directly affected the reconstruction. Given the large number of people in Brandenburg's agricultural sector, the purge of farmers got off to a slow start and never encompassed all who may have fallen under the denazification guidelines. As Tables 6.1 and 6.2 show, only 1,390 individuals from the agricultural sector were examined. An SED report from the end of August 1947 noted that although there were few Nazi *Kreisbauernführer* (district farmers' leaders) left in the villages of the Soviet zone, there were still quite a few *Ortsbauernführer* (local farmers' leaders) and a considerable number of "activists" in the rural areas. Brandenburg, along with Thuringia and Mecklenburg, was sharply criticized in this report for "especially poor denazification of agriculture."[122]

The denazification of agriculture was a complex problem. On the one hand, rural areas, such as *Kreis* Ostprignitz, were seen as hotbeds of reaction and "strongly fascist tendencies."[123] On the other hand, the commissions were limited in the measures they could take against farmers who were found to have been active Nazis. The commissions could not, for example, take away a farmer's land. The primary result of declaring farmers activists was to ensure that they lost voting rights and that they would not, at some future date, hold an important position in the administration or economy.[124]

Some agricultural laborers were actually employees of the provincial government if they worked on expropriated estates *(landeseigene Güter)*. These agricultural workers fell under Brandenburg's exemption from denazification for manual laborers.[125] The Provincial Commission, for example, overturned a negative decision by the Ruppin commission in the case of one agricultural worker *(Landarbeiter)* because, according to the guidelines, all manual laborers *(Handarbeiter)* were excluded from denazification.[126] As we have seen, however,

Brandenburg's exemption for manual laborers was rejected by Mielke at the end of 1947, and the Interior Ministry revised its guidelines in January 1948 and ordered the commissions to investigate all possible "activists" regardless of their occupation. This reversal also meant that agricultural laborers were no longer exempt from the purge.[127]

The number of farmers in the data sample is surprisingly small, given that two of these districts, Ostprignitz and Ruppin, had agricultural economic bases. In all, only 89 farmers appear in the data sample: 1 of the petitions was denied, 17 were approved, and the remaining 71 were approved on the condition that the petitioner could never work in the public sector. This high level of conditional approval is the key to understanding the denazification of agriculture. The commissions' two main goals—to ensure that politically incriminated farmers could not find their way into public employment in the future and to deny voting rights to "activist" farmers—were met through conditional approval.

The Ruppin commission examined the majority of farmers in the data sample. The approach taken by this commission toward farmers was superficial at best. Typically, a petitioner was asked how he had treated his foreign laborers during the war, and the inevitable answer was along the lines of "We all ate at the same table" or "Just like my other workers."[128] In one case the chairman posed a single question to a farmer who had joined the party in 1938, served as *Ortsbauern-führer*, and as mayor of his village from 1930 to 1945: "What are you guilty of? [*Was haben Sie ausgefressen?*]," to which the farmer answered, "Me? Nothing." Apparently satisfied with this response, the commission ruled that the farmer could continue in his line of work, and even work in a public or semi-public position in the future, so long as it was not a supervisory position.[129] That the commissioners asked such questions indicates that they had not done much prior investigating of the cases and did not place much weight on the outcome. Indeed, the halfhearted denazification of agriculture seems somewhat pointless: none of the farmers would voluntarily admit to any culpable past activity; most probably they had no intention of ever holding a "leading position" in public employ; and, given the evolving SED control of politics and the state, a loss of voting rights was a minor form of punishment. Of all occupational groups, the denazification program had the most negligible effect on agricultural workers.

* * *

The categories of age, gender, and occupation reveal much about the denazification process in Brandenburg. Both age and gender prove to be highly predictive of the outcome of denazification cases. As a general rule, young people were treated with greater leniency than adults, and adult women were treated with greater leniency than adult males. Age and gender also seem to be exclusive categories insofar as there is no significant difference between the handling of female and male youths. Based on this study's data sample, gender is a significant variable only for adults.

Among adults, the gender variable points to significant differences in the way the commissions judged women and men. Not surprisingly, the patriarchal social structure of pre-1945 Germany persisted into the immediate postwar period. Likewise, the dominance of men in the Nazi organizational hierarchy was reflected in the fact that the overwhelming majority of adults targeted by the commissions were men.

As for occupational groups, perhaps the most significant finding of this study is that occupation alone has limited predictive value. The relationship between the denazification process and occupational category was complex, and our understanding of this relationship will evolve with future research. The results of the analysis presented in this chapter indicate that while the petitioners' occupations were taken into consideration by the commissions, there was also a variety of other factors that influenced the final decision in individual cases. The remainder of this study is an examination of some of the most significant factors that influenced the decision-making process.

CHAPTER 7

The Varieties of Guilt and Innocence

There was an ever-present gap between the intentions of the policy makers and the implementation of their policies and between the stated goals of the program and its results. As far as public pronouncements were concerned, this gap did not present a serious problem: all major policies of this period—denazification, expropriation, and land reform—were preordained to be successful. Thus, at the conclusion, each program was duly trumpeted as meeting or exceeding expectations. To judge from the case study of Brandenburg, however, Soviet denazification cannot be counted a success. We have already seen how the authorities struggled for three years after the end of the war with the thorny problems presented by denazification. The district commissions were intended to solve the unresolved: once and for all to pass judgment, impose punishments, grant absolutions, reintegrate the PGs into society, and finally put the legacy of National Socialism to rest. The result, to borrow Ulbricht's terminology, would be an end to the period of "antifascist-democratic" restructuring and the beginning of the construction of a new socialist Germany. Through the process of denazification, Germans in the east could turn their collective gaze away from the dark past and toward a brighter future.

Why did denazification fail to meet expectations? The answer lies in the work of the district denazification commissions. We have already seen how the Soviets and the SED manipulated the process: the Order 201 reorganization of commission membership was a clear example. And yet, try as they might, the authorities were unable to force the commissions to produce the desired results. In her study of local purge trials in the Soviet Union under Stalin, Sheila Fitzpatrick argued that the authorities' concept of the purge was fundamentally altered when it was put into practice at the local level. In Fitzpatrick's words, a "master plot" for a purge trial was developed by the central authorities, "but its application in any specific circumstance was the work of local hands."[1] The Stalinist purge trials and the denazification in Brandenburg occurred in markedly different social, cultural, and historical contexts, and yet something similar developed in both cases: the policy makers' intentions—the "master plot"—had unintended consequences when interpreted by local actors.

In this chapter I take an in-depth look at the varieties of evidence considered by the district commissions in their decision making. The picture that emerges is one of flux and unpredictability, not one of local denazification commissions marching in lockstep to orders handed down by the central authorities. The Soviet and German leadership may well have had plans to use denazification as a means to "communize" or "Stalinize" eastern Germany, but, as they were to discover, putting decision-making power in the hands of local commissions was an ineffectual means of achieving their goals.

Personal Impressions and Witnesses

Creating a clear picture of how denazification commissions reached decisions in individual cases is a complex task. Every case presented a unique set of variables in which a person's past and present became incriminating or exculpating circumstances. The commissioners' duty was to weigh this evidence and decide if the person before them had been an "active" or a "nominal" participant in the Third Reich's crimes. Commissioners handled this task in various ways. In the face of unrealistic deadlines and an ever-mounting backlog of cases, decisions were often perfunctory. At other times, however, the commissions paused to investigate the details of a case in a fair-minded and thoughtful manner. Often, commissioners wearily followed what could be termed a denazification "script," asking a series of questions the answers to which they seemed to know already. Sometimes, however, commissioners went beyond the script, lashing out at unsuspecting petitioners with anger or sarcasm, or, alternatively, communicating sympathy and understanding.

Owing to the brevity of the commissions' records, the petitioners are often invisible and voiceless. In instances when their answers, justifications, arguments, and opinions do appear, it is possible to glimpse fragments of their attitudes and personalities. Some petitioners, weighed down by Germany's destruction and the hardship of daily life in the rubble of 1947, seem passive and resigned to their fate. Others were rueful and repentant as they sought absolution, or, conversely, obdurate and argumentative in defending their past beliefs and actions. There are also those who seem confused and genuinely unaware of what was at stake in the denazification process.

An understanding of how all of these factors came together can be reached through a close examination of the hearing transcripts. It should be stressed that the hearings were not true judicial procedures, although the results were legally binding. Decisions were based not on a body of law, but solely on the provisions of Directive 24, Order 201, and the policies developed by the SMA and German authorities. The commission members were chosen not because of their judicial acumen but rather because of their political affiliations. A permanent staff, in addition to the evidence-gathering powers of the police and the Interior Ministry, assisted each commission. In contrast, the petitioners' ability to mount a defense was meager. Since the hearings were not viewed as judicial procedures, they did not have the right to the assistance of a lawyer. They could do three things to bolster their defense: make favorable impressions on the commission, present written evidence and statements of support, and call witnesses.

Personal Impressions

The personal impression petitioners made on the commissions must have played an important role in the decision-making process. Usually no mention of these impressions was made in the records. Among the four commissions in the data sample, only the Provincial Commission regularly noted personal reactions to petitioners. The Provincial Commission specifically noted the impression *(Eindruck)* made by petitioners in 110 cases in the data sample: of these 72 were positive and 38 negative.[2]

Typical of the positive impressions is the observation that the petitioner seemed "honest" or "sincere." An example is the comment made about a PG who joined the Nazi Party in 1937: "His claims were believed owing to his sincere and honest manner, and the commission came to the decision that [he], in his present position, poses no danger to the democracy."[3] Similar positive assessments note that a petitioner "left behind a personally good impression" or made "a believable impression."[4] More neutral, but still essentially positive, are comments such as "he makes a harmless impression" and "he makes a completely unpolitical personal impression."[5] In one instance a petitioner's claim that he had felt compelled to join the NSDAP in 1937 was believable because "he gives the impression of being a fearful person."[6] Another PG, who belonged to the NSDAP for ten years, claimed that he had never actively supported the party; the commission found this believable on the grounds that he "gives the impression of being a follower [*Mitläufer*]."[7]

Some district commissions, particularly during the Directive 24 phase, decided cases in absentia, thereby depriving petitioners of the possibility of making a positive impression. The importance of giving petitioners their "day in court" is underscored by a case originally decided in absentia by the Lübben district commission. The commission revoked a furniture dealer's business license on the grounds that he had been an "active" party member. The dealer appealed to the Provincial Commission and, on the basis of the "believable" impression he made, successfully argued for overturning the revocation.[8] But sometimes making a good impression was not enough. In rejecting the petition of a lawyer who joined the NSDAP in 1933, the Provincial Commission noted that "the sole exculpating factor" was that he made an "honest impression."[9]

While a good impression may not always have secured a favorable finding, those who made a poor impression were assured denial. Negative impressions ranged from "not particularly favorable" to "absolutely terrible."[10] Of a former Hitler Youth who served twelve years in the army it was noted, with obvious distaste, "The personal impression he makes upon the commission is unmistakably that of a sergeant."[11] Also rejected was a veterinarian in Potsdam; a Stahlhelm member since 1933 (though never a member of the NSDAP), "in his entire behavior and outlook he embodies militarism and reaction to such an extent it will be impossible to employ him as a district veterinarian in a democratic state."[12] Another petitioner apparently offended the commissioners' class sensibilities: "He gives the impression of a typical petty bourgeois who never thinks for himself and simply follows in the direction where he believes he sees the best conditions for his business."[13]

Defense and Prosecution Witnesses

A key element in a successful defense was the assembling of witnesses. Under the system established at the beginning of the Directive 24 phase, a petitioner was permitted to name defense witnesses, but they appeared only after being invited in writing by the commission. As a rule, cases were rescheduled when invited witnesses failed to appear. Witnesses could not be persons who themselves fell under Directive 24 and could not be related to the petitioner. At first, no more than five defense witnesses could be called, but this limit was dropped during the Order 201 phase.[14]

Prosecution witnesses were harder to come by. The authorities were continually frustrated by the public's apathy toward denazification. In the case of prosecution witnesses, this apathy was combined with a reluctance to open oneself to later charges of being a "denunciator."[15] This reluctance to provide incriminating evidence was viewed by the authorities as indicative of an abiding passive, if not active, support for fascist ideology. An example is the hearings held by the Provincial Commission at the huge synthetics factory at Schwarzheide (*Kreis* Calau) on 30–31 October 1947. Of the forty-five supervisors examined at these hearings, eighteen were dismissed, and the remainder were allowed to continue working in non-supervisory positions. Posters listing the time and date of the hearings and the individuals scheduled to appear were put up in the factory a few days earlier.[16]

> About 100 people visited the hearing. It is noteworthy that almost no prosecution witnesses appeared, but rather only defense witnesses. What is more, a member of the personnel department publicly appeared as a defense witness for an active fascist. The strange passivity of the factory workers during the hearing leads to the conclusion that the fascist ideology has yet to be completely removed [from the factory]. Even though Chairman Hentschel presented damning incriminating evidence (crimes against humanity, etc.), only five prosecution witnesses stepped forward during the entire process. Since there are approximately 5,000 employees at the Schwarzheide synthetics factory and, to the present, only 45 have been named [as active fascists], it is reasonable to suspect

that there are still active fascists in supervisory positions who have committed crimes against humanity.[17]

After this disappointing experience, the Interior Ministry decided that future hearings would not be held in the factory. It was reasoned that there might be some workers who were hesitant to give incriminating evidence in front of an audience of their fellow workers.[18]

The SED's frustration with its own party members' reluctance to appear as prosecution witnesses was compounded by the large number of SED members who appeared as defense witnesses. A report from the Justice Ministry bemoaned the fact that "defense witnesses who are members of the democratic parties, in particular members of the SED, continue to appear before the denazification commissions. Likewise, a large number of statements of good character from the SED and even from the VVN continue to appear in the protocols. In contrast, the number of people appearing as prosecution witnesses is very limited."[19]

A report sent to Ulbricht at the beginning of 1948 noted continuing reports of SED members providing evidence for "incriminated PGs." (Ulbricht's marginalia, alongside an anecdote about two SED members who signed a statement of support for a former SS member, consisted of a series of large exclamation marks.)[20] The frustration regarding this situation was equally pronounced on the provincial level. In a speech before denazification commission representatives, Hentschel complained that members of "antifascist parties and organizations appear before denazification commissions as *defense* witnesses" while prosecution witnesses "hardly ever appear." Hentschel demanded an end to the "political nonsense" of SED members providing exculpatory statements or appearing as defense witnesses. Although Hentschel admitted that individual SED members had the civil right to act as witnesses, he felt that they should not use their party membership to "legitimize" their testimony.[21]

The abundance of defense witnesses and dearth of prosecution witnesses endured until the commissions were dissolved. In a postmortem on denazification, the *Kreisrat* from Guben reported that there had always been "enough defense witnesses but only a few prosecution witnesses." "In most cases," he noted, the denazification commission worked without the support of the citizenry and had to "search for incriminating evidence by itself."[22]

Because of the often incomplete state of the hearing records, it is difficult to determine the effect of witnesses and evidence presented by the petitioners. Often the records indicate only that the decision was based on "material" in the commission's possession, without any mention of the source of this material. In the majority of cases in the data sample, it appears that no witnesses or evidence were used at all; instead the commissioners quickly reviewed the information on the petitioner's *Fragebogen*, perhaps asked a few perfunctory questions (if the petitioner was present), and then made a decision. It is possible, however, to identify 393 cases from the data sample in which petitioners presented some sort of evidence. As a rule, the burden of proof lay with the petitioner. Astute petitioners realized that their appearance before a commission was their one and only chance to stage a defense, which would be strengthened by the presentation of concrete evidence. The payoff was great for those who bothered to present evidence; of 393 petitioners who presented evidence, 347 were exonerated. Incriminating evidence, beyond what was contained in the petitioners' *Fragebogen*, was rare: there are only 76 cases from the data sample in which incriminating evidence was presented. In contrast to defense evidence, which was usually helpful to petitioners, incriminating evidence did not always lead to denial of petitions: 27 of these cases were approved despite the presentation of incriminating evidence.

Even though the burden of proof lay with petitioners, it would not be entirely accurate to speak of the hearings in terms of "defense" and "prosecution." Some petitioners did indeed defend themselves, but this was undertaken without the aid of counsel. Likewise, commissioners sometimes led the questioning in a manner that could be termed prosecutorial. The policy guidelines did not, however, specifically set a role for a prosecutor, and, more often than not, commissions functioned more as deliberative bodies in which all members had equal opportunities to ask questions and air opinions.

MAYORS AS WITNESSES

Mayors frequently gave exculpatory testimony on behalf of petitioners but only rarely supplied incriminating evidence. Although mayors commonly provided written statements of support, they sometimes appeared in person to give evidence. The testimony of Mayor Voigt of Pritzwalk (*Kreis* Ostprignitz) is an example of how mayors could lobby the commissions on behalf of their constituents. Voigt attended a hearing and gave testimony in several cases, which resulted in rulings in favor of the petitioners. In the case of a local businessman who had been a Nazi Party member since 1938, the mayor testified that Herr G. was "one of the best employers" in the city, who consistently offered his services, without pay, in the difficult months following the end of the war. Herr G. did this, the mayor noted, "even though his house was occupied by the Russians."[23] Mayor Voigt, an "antifascist" of working-class background, also successfully lobbied for a local pharmacist, Herr W., who was heavily incriminated by his past: membership in the SA since 1933 and in the Nazi Party since 1937. Voigt recalled that, after seeing Herr W. in Nazi uniform at a rally in 1944, he confronted him with the words: "Oh, man, I don't understand you. Do you have to be hit over the head to realize what is going on here?" "He could have turned me in for my words," Voigt continued, "but he didn't do it. We workers always got our medicine from W. . . . [H]e always helped us, which is something one cannot say about the other pharmacists." In this case the pharmacist was simply too incriminated to be completely exonerated; the commission revoked his license as a self-employed pharmacist but, in deference to the mayor's wishes, ruled that he could continue in his occupation as a salaried employee under another licensee.[24]

Mayors were not always helpful to their fellow citizens. The corrupt mayor of Lehnitz, for example, gave damaging testimony before the Niederbarnim commission against a self-employed electrician in the town. On the basis of the mayor's testimony, the commission revoked the electrician's license. Four months later the Provincial Commission overturned this revocation and noted that "the decision of the district commission was based on the testimony of the former mayor [who] has recently been arrested and his incriminatory statements against [the electrician] have been shown to be untrue and unfounded and to have arisen from purely personal motives."[25]

ANTIFASCIST COMMITTEES AS WITNESSES

When first organized in the summer of 1945, Antifascist Committees were the officially sanctioned replacements for the spontaneously organized committees disbanded in June 1945. The new Antifascist Committees, sometimes referred to as Antifascist Blocs or United Fronts, were composed of local representatives of the Soviet-approved political parties.[26] Antifascist Committees performed many governmental functions in the period before the 1946 elections. This was also the period before the implementation of Directive 24, and Antifascist Committees often functioned as unofficial denazification commissions. In this role they issued documents verifying the "nominal" status of PGs. Given the unwieldy name of "certificates of unobjectionability" *(Unbedenklichkeitsbescheinigungen),* these certificates were eagerly sought by PGs hoping to ameliorate their status as second-class citizens.[27]

Certificates of unobjectionability were part of almost every bureaucratic transaction during the occupation period, such as receiving a driver's license, taking a master's examination in a trade, applying for an interzonal pass, gaining admittance to a university, and filing for pension benefits.[28] With the implementation of Directive 24, many people thought that they could also secure these certificates from denazification commissions. One denazification commission reported being flooded by a "large number of verbal and written requests for certificates of unobjectionability . . . from former NSDAP members who allegedly had not been active. These people make these requests because the authorities demand [certificates] for work and professional transactions, pensions, disability, social services, etc." The commission also reported that many of these requests came from former residents who lived in western zones and needed proof of their "nominal" status because they had been called before a western denazification commission.[29] After the 1946 elections many of the Antifascist Committees' governmental tasks ended, and they were relegated to an advisory role in the new political system.[30]

Denazification commissions often relied on the Antifascist Committees' opinions. The Calau commission, in particular, relied heavily on the judgment of Antifascist Committees, often giving tentative approval to petitions by noting "approved on the condition that the yet-to-arrive certificate from the local Antifascist Committee proves favorable."[31] Several examples of the relationship between denazification commissions and Antifascist Committees can be found in the records of the Neustadt Antifascist Committee (*Kreis* Ostprignitz). Herr A., a fifty-year-old worker on a local farm, wrote the committee in May 1947: "I am urgently requesting a political certificate of unobjectionability for use in the implementation of Directive 24. I was a member of the NSDAP from August 1937 to May 1945 and I declare under oath that I never had a function or office [in the party]. I have in addition never acted in a fascist manner." The Neustadt committee dutifully issued the following document:

Certificate
Herr A., resident of Neustadt/Dosse, was not an officer or civil servant in military offices and also not a member of the SA, SS, or Gestapo.

According to his sworn statement and our own investigations, he belonged to the NSDAP from August 1937 to 1945. He performed no function. According to our determination, he is to be considered only nominal.

This certificate serves as an [evidentiary] submission before the Provincial Commission for the implementation of Directive 24 in Potsdam.[32]

A fellow employee at the farm, Herr B., first attempted to get a certificate in August 1946. Writing four months before a denazification process was in place, he requested a certificate "for the purpose of my denazification." Since Directive 24 was yet to be implemented in the Soviet zone, the Neustadt Committee replied that a certificate could not be issued until Herr B. gave "indication of the grounds for which you feel this certificate is necessary." A year later, in October 1947, the provincial government supplied Herr B. with the grounds by calling him to appear before the denazification commission in Potsdam. He renewed his request, and the Neustadt committee complied with a document attesting that he was to be considered a nominal member of the Nazi Party.[33]

As will be seen later, in some cases commissioners personally knew petitioners and formed opinions based on their own experience. In most instances, however, commissioners relied on local Antifascist Committee members, who spoke, as it were, for the communities in which the petitioners lived and worked. This was similar to the role of mayors, who, like Antifascist Committees, could give evidence based on firsthand experience. The denazification commissions' reasoning was straightforward: if the local "antifascist" leadership had no objection to a petitioner's continued role in the community, then the commission had little ground for objection. This line of reasoning underscores the pivotal role local authorities played in the denazification process.

This reliance on Antifascist Committees and mayors meant that local squabbles and rivalries could be transferred to the denazification proceedings. A shopkeeper in Woltersdorf, who joined the Nazi Party in 1933, had both the mayor and the Antifascist Committee against him. After the district commission revoked his business license, he appealed to the Provincial Commission, and his case was heard on 30 September 1947.

> *Chairman:* When was your business license revoked?
> *Answer:* In June 1947.
> *Chairman:* So you don't have a business any longer?
> *Answer:* I have a partner. At the moment I am taking legal action against him.
> *Chairman:* Who put this partner in place?
> *Answer:* He rented my business while I was under arrest.
> *Chairman:* So when were you arrested?
> *Answer:* In 1945, right after the entrance of the Russians . . .
> *Chairman:* Did Hitler once personally receive you?
> *Answer:* That was absolutely never the case, this is all just agitation against me.
> *Chairman:* But how do explain the fact that the entire Antifascist Committee is against you?
> *Answer:* My partner was a member of the Antifascist Committee.
> *Chairman:* What can you say toward your exculpation?
> *Answer:* I can only state that I was never politically active.
> *Chairman:* Have you lived in Woltersdorf a long time?
> *Answer:* Yes, for twenty-five years.
> *Chairman:* And yet every person of authority in Woltersdorf has come out against you.
> *Answer:* I can only swear that I was never politically active.[34]

That the Provincial Commission denied this petition despite the questionable dealings surrounding the case is indicative of the value placed on the testimony of local "antifascist" authorities. In fact, commissions denied only four petitioners in the data sample who had strong "antifascist" support. An example is Herr L., who joined the Nazi Party in 1933. In addition to his party membership, L. was incriminated by his rapid advancement to the rank of captain in the army. In his defense he claimed that he had been expelled from the party in 1939 and later demoted in rank, claims which, however, he could not substantiate. Nevertheless, he was able to present impeccable references from the district SED and "confirmation of an un-

doubted antifascist attitude from individual persons who knew him."
The hearing transcript records the following exchange:

> The commission considered the evidence and came to the decision to ask
> Herr L. once again if he could say something further regarding his exon-
> eration. [Commission chairman] Herr Hentschel asked: "You led a bat-
> talion as captain, can you give us some evidence that, at risk to your
> own person, you and your men engaged in antifascist work?" To this
> question, Herr L. declared once again that he was in a regiment where
> all the men were antifascists. Herr Hentschel questioned further that,
> since [Herr L.] was still in service in 1945, didn't he, in the position of
> commander, have any occasion to engage in antifascist activity? To this
> Herr L. answered: "I fought as a solider for my fatherland. My father-
> land was in danger so there was nothing for my men and me to do but to
> fight."

Herr L.'s evocation of one's duty to fight for the fatherland, combined
with his military rank, was enough for the commission to conclude, in
spite of his references, that here was a case of an undoubted militarist.
Herr L. was immediately dismissed from his job in the provincial administration.[35]

WORKS COUNCILS AS WITNESSES

The Works Councils *(Betriebsräte)* were another frequent source of
evidence. The election of Works Councils began during the Weimar
Republic and was ended by the Nazis in 1934.[36] In April 1946 the
Allied Control Council permitted the reestablishment of elected
Works Councils. Works Councils were to serve in an intermediary position between workers at individual firms and unions. In addition,
Works Councils were charged with "cooperation with the authorities
in . . . denazification of public and private enterprises."[37] At the beginning of the Order 201 phase, the SED leadership specifically instructed the FDGB to make sure that Works Council representatives
took an active role in "investigating whether there are still active fascists and militarists in the management of their firms."[38] In practice,
this led to Works Council representatives appearing as witnesses.

Of the four commissions in the data sample, the Ruppin commission relied most on the testimony of Works Council representatives.
During the Directive 24 phase, the Ruppin commission implemented
a unique method of denazifying local firms, in which cases from individual firms were heard at the same sitting. Petitioners were not in-

vited to the hearings; instead, the commission reviewed cases with the assistance of a Works Council representative. At its 30 January 1947 hearing, for example, the Ruppin commission heard fifteen petitions from a chemical factory with the aid of the Works Council chairman. The chairman testified to the nominal status of all fifteen workers, and the commission approved all the petitions.[39]

At the same hearing, the commission heard nine petitions from a Printers' Cooperative with the help of a Works Council representative. The commission turned down only one of these petitions, that of the plant supervisor, a PG since 1938, on the grounds that he had an "influential position in the firm."[40] Fearing that the print shop could be utilized to spread fascist propaganda, two commission members (SED and FDGB) also felt that the cooperative's skilled machinist, a PG since 1937, should be dismissed because of the danger that he might "engage in illegal work." Seeking a compromise, the commission chair asked if there were a worker of "completely good political character" who could supervise the machinist's work. The Works Council representative clinched approval of the petition by assuring there was a suitable "antifascist" on hand and that the machinist could be reclassified as an hourly worker.[41]

Works Councils could also assure the rejection of petitions. In deciding cases of workers at an electric power station in Lauta, the Calau commission relied on the combined testimony of the local SED organization and the plant's Works Council. The commission heard eight petitions from the plant at its 26 February 1947 hearing and rejected six on the basis of the "attached certificates from the SED *Ortsgruppe* Lauta and the Works Council."[42]

COMMISSION MEMBERS AS WITNESSES

In a surprising number of cases, petitioners received assistance from an unlikely source: commission members themselves. There are sixty-three instances in the data sample of petitions approved on the grounds that one or more commission members could vouch for the petitioner and three petitions denied on the basis of incriminating evidence supplied by a commissioner.

The district commissions heard most of these cases. In contrast to district commissions, the Provincial Commission heard thousands of cases from throughout Brandenburg, and the odds were slight that the commissioners would personally know petitioners. In the data sample there are only two instances of a petitioner personally known by a provincial commissioner. In both cases Interior Minister Bechler knew petitioners as fellow POWs who had been active in the National Committee for a Free Germany. A citizen of Brandenburg could not wish for a better character reference than Bechler, and both men had their petitions approved on his recommendation.[43]

Among the three district commissions in the data sample, the Calau commission recorded the highest number of cases in which the commissioners personally knew petitioners: forty-seven cases, and in forty-five of these cases this relationship led to approval of the petition. In a few instances, the petitioners' activities in the community had brought them into contact with commission members. The former leader of the Calau Volkssturm, a Nazi Party member since 1937 and an official in the district Agriculture and Forestry Department, had been personally "known for a long time" by all the commissioners. In his position as Volkssturm leader he had won the commissioners' gratitude, and probably that of many of the other men in the town, by disbanding the Volkssturm and "sending all the men home" just before the Red Army entered Calau.[44]

The Calau commissioners also made the acquaintance of petitioners in the workplace. In one example, SED representative Harnau, who worked in the district's brown coal and glass industries throughout the Weimar period, was familiar with the H. Heye Glasfabrik in the town of Annahütte. Harnau reported that one Heye employee was an NSDAP *Ortsgruppenleiter* who had pressured fellow employees to join National Socialist organizations. Harnau knew four Heye employees who appeared at a hearing in March 1947. In three cases he testified to the nominal party membership of the petitioners.[45] In the fourth case, Harnau was able to turn his knowledge of the Heye works against a former Stahlhelm and party member by noting the man's activist past.[46]

In addition to public and workplace acquaintances, commissioners also considered petitions from people they knew through private friendships. One man appeared with a damming Nazi past: a PG since 1933, he was also in the National Socialist lawyers' organization (NS Rechtswahrenbund) and the NSV.[47] This man was fortunate, however, to have a friend on the commission. The CDU representative interceded, noting that he had known "Herr D. for many years and, on the occasion of casual conversations during the Nazi period with Herr

D., I gained the impression that D. did not champion the Nazi ideology."[48] *Landrat* Freter could also prove to be a useful friend, as exhibited in the case of Dr. K., a Nazi Party member since 1933. At Dr. K.'s hearing, acting commission chair Wollny stated that Freter had spoken with him, and "Freter lives, like Dr. K., in Groß-Räschen and has given K.'s petition the warmest approval."[49]

The commission also used its powers to repay personal favors rendered during the Nazi period. A doctor from Senftenberg, incriminated by her membership in the Nazi Party and the NSKK (National Socialist Motorized Corps), also enlisted the support of *Landrat* Freter. Freter testified that the doctor had provided him with a certificate allowing him to avoid military service, a favor she also provided for others in the town. In addition, Freter stated that the doctor had spoken out against political arrests in Senftenberg, and "furthermore, upon the appearance of Rosenberg's book *Mythos des 20. Jahrhunderts,* Dr. S. expressed a very unfavorable opinion of the book and noted, from a scientific point of view, that it was a lot of nonsense."[50]

FRIENDS AND ACQUAINTANCES AS WITNESSES

Personal relationships between the commissioners and the petitioners were not, of course, the norm. Most petitioners who presented exculpating evidence had to rely on representatives of political parties, mayors, Antifascist Committees, and Works Councils. There was an alternative to "official" support: verbal or written statements from acquaintances attesting to either nominal Nazi membership or resistance activity. One needs to keep in mind that the hearing records are often characterized by a maddening lack of detail. The primary deficiency is precise information regarding the type and source of evidence. Typical are notations such as "statements of support submitted that demonstrate her antifascist attitude" or "numerous witnesses regarding opposition to Nazism."[51]

The testimony of witnesses and the presentation of concrete evidence often determined commissions' final decisions. In some cases, however, petitions were rejected even though the accused presented witnesses and/or written statements of support. Testimony could be rejected out of hand if the witnesses themselves fell under the provisions of Directive 24.[52] Witnesses' statements concerning the petitioners' "nominal" status in the Nazi Party could be contradicted by evidence of the petitioners' apparently deep involvement with the party.

Thus the testimony of witnesses regarding the "non-active" status of a teacher from Spremberg could not outweigh the fact that she had been a member of the NSF since 1935, the NSDAP since 1937, the National Socialist Teachers' Organization (NSLB), and the NSV.[53] In a similar example, a lawyer presented affidavits of support from his local mayor and Antifascist Committee and the Justice Ministry, as well as "further statements of good character." This impressive array of support did not erase the fact that he had joined the NSDAP in 1933 and also belonged to three other Nazi organizations; the commission concluded, "He is not suitable to be a lawyer and notary in the present democratic state."[54] Witnesses were also of no use if they could not offer evidence of a petitioner's "nominal" status. The petition of a chimney sweep who appeared before the Calau commission was rejected on the grounds that "the statements of the two witnesses do not suffice because both maintain that they never engaged in a political discussion with him."[55]

Petitioners who presented ineffectual evidence should at least be given credit for having attempted to stage a defense; some petitioners simply tried to claim "antifascist" activity without presenting any concrete evidence. The petition of a provincial employee who claimed to have taken part in the 20 July 1944 conspiracy to assassinate Hitler was rejected because "he cannot supply any witnesses or any evidence for his actions" on that date."[56] Petitioners who claimed that they either were dismissed from the Nazi Party or left of their own volition were likewise disappointed if they could not present supporting evidence.[57]

Denunciations and the Denazification Process

Political denunciations were an integral part of the Nazi system of social control. By the end of the war, the Germans had had twelve years' experience of a system based on denunciations, unannounced visits from the secret police, and the disappearances of family, friends, and neighbors into concentration camps. The Soviet version of this system must have been all too familiar to those living in the eastern zone; former Nazi prisons and concentration camps continued to function, and thousands of Germans were "disappearing" after visits from Soviet security forces.[58] As in the Nazi period, denunciations continued to play a prominent role in the arrest of suspected political enemies during the Soviet occupation.[59]

This tradition of denunciation, with all of its flaws, was kept alive by the denazification program. As we have seen, Interior Minister Bechler, in an effort to elicit public participation, argued that it was the "special task and duty" of citizens to report information regarding "the guilty" in their communities.[60] Some people did not need encouragement in order to realize the utility of denunciation. A day after Bechler's appeal was published, the mayor of Treuenbrietzen sent a letter to the interior minister complaining that "Order 201 and the subsequent commentary regarding it have had the result that former members of the NSDAP, whose nominal status is completely clear, have been denounced in the worst possible manner. This is definitely not done on political grounds but rather because of personal squabbles." The mayor cautioned that this situation could damage the SED because of the party's close association with the denazification program: "It will naturally all be blamed on us . . . [T]he result will be that no one will believe us anymore, not even our own comrades."[61] The fear of a political backlash was shared by others in the Brandenburg SED who complained that Order 201 was creating a "new culture of denunciation."[62]

It would not be correct to assume that all denunciations stemmed from personal motives. There were, needless to say, many crimes committed during the Nazi period and many people who deserved to be brought to justice. It is nearly impossible to determine what motivated many to denounce others; in some cases it must have been an altruistic desire to see the guilty punished; in other cases people were unjustly denounced by rivals seeking revenge or personal gain. In still other cases there may have been a mixture of these two motives: denouncing those who were in fact incriminated by their past actions could have the added benefit of settling a personal grudge or enhancing the economic status of the denouncer. It is particularly difficult to discern motives in cases of anonymous denunciations. The following is a rare example of a surviving anonymous denunciation, a letter without a return address received by the denazification commission in Guben.

> At a holiday party on Sunday evening the 24th in Schlagsdorf there was a Listener who heard a conversation between Schlagsdorf residents in which former Nazis were discussed. It was said that N. was beaten by the SA, that in addition W. was taken away and that K. also received a beating . . .
>
> During the conversation, the following names were often repeated:

[the names of six men], who, according to the conversation, were all in the SA. It was further mentioned that the SA was following the orders of certain persons, the names mentioned were: [the names of five men]. These [men] were apparently even worse than the SA.

It would be proper if these matters were clarified and such elements were brought to justice.

[signed] The Listener from a Neighboring Village[63]

It is impossible to know what motivated the Listener to send this anonymous letter—perhaps a sense of justice, or personal motives, or maybe a combination of both. There are several cases in the data sample of denunciations that turned out to be false.[64]

Although it is difficult to determine the sources of evidence presented in the hearings, it does not appear that anonymous denunciations played a role in a significant number of cases. Public denunciations, however, occurred more frequently. As we have seen, denazification was hindered by a widespread reluctance on the part of people to appear as prosecution witnesses. This problem was compounded by the fact that, when prosecution witnesses did come forward, it was often for less than altruistic reasons. Although some people used denazification as a means to further their interests or settle personal scores from the past, sometimes the accusations were actually true, despite the fact that they were colored by the accuser's self-interest. In other instances, the accusations proved to be unfounded and based solely on personal animosities. The commissions' task was to untangle this web of contradiction and half-truths in an attempt to construct a more or less clear picture of what actually happened.

Sometimes this process of discovery was relatively straightforward. An office worker in the Forestry Department, who joined the NSDAP in 1935 and served as an *Ortsgruppenleiter* for the party, was confronted with accusations that he had beaten foreign laborers. The petitioner denied this and claimed, to the contrary, that he had always cared for the foreign workers. The chairman countered, "But a whole group of your fellow citizens have come out against you and have made accusations against you." To which the accused replied, "Well, gentlemen, who doesn't have any enemies? One just can't please everybody." Unable to reach a decision without further investigation, the commission held the case over until its next session. In later approving the petition, they noted that there was no evidence of the peti-

tioner's mistreatment of foreign workers, and his claim that he provided workers with food had been substantiated. Because of his Nazi
past, he had been removed from a supervisory position in December
1945, and his replacement was discovered to be the source of accusations against him. The motive behind these accusations was put down
to a "game of intrigue since his successor is uncomfortable with [the
petitioner's] technical knowledge and his irreproachable behavior."[65]

Denunciations, even when accurate, did not always lead to rejection of a petition. A female refugee from the Oder-Neisse territories
who managed to find herself a job in 1944 as a municipal employee
was brought before a commission when it was discovered that she
had been a PG since 1933.

> *Chairman:* You did not register under Directive 24?
> *Answer:* No, I did not admit that I was in the party.
> *Chairman:* Why didn't you say anything?
> *Answer:* Out of fear, I could have lost my job. I was denounced. If
> it had not been for that [the fact] still would not have come out.

The commission, perhaps impressed by this woman's disarming forth-
rightness, decided that she could remain in her present position with
the qualification that she could never assume a supervisory position in
the future.[66]

The complexity of the hearing process and the role of denunciations can be seen in a particularly detailed case heard by the Ruppin
commission. The case involved Herr W., a teacher and director of an
elementary school in Neustadt. One set of accusations against Herr
W. involved his role in the community as a teacher during the Nazi period.

> *Chairman:* Did you have children in the school whom you stuffed
> with racial theories?
> *Answer:* Oh, for God's sake.
> *Chairman:* Were there schoolchildren who passed you on the street
> and failed to greet you, whom you called back and forced to
> repeat "Heil Hitler" three times?
> *Answer:* That is absolutely not true . . .
> *Chairman:* What is the story about the Hitler pictures? You
> painted them yourself and hung them in the school and in the
> local party office?

Answer: At that time, the school superintendent ordered that a picture of Hitler must be hung in every school. I was supposed to purchase one, but they cost more than 100RM. There wasn't enough money for that. So I painted one myself and bought school materials for the children with the money saved.

Chairman: You painted Hitler pictures galore [*in rauhen Mengen*]?

Answer: That's just not so.

Another charge against the teacher was that he denounced a school superintendent to the Gestapo. The superintendent appeared as a prosecution witness and stated that he had given a lecture in 1937 in which he had said, "These are terrible times [*es ist böse Zeit*]." The accused teacher W., according to the superintendent, denounced him to the Gestapo for saying, "Politically these are terrible times." Although the teacher denied reporting this to the Gestapo, the superintendent stood by his claim, saying, "I don't have any interest in denouncing anyone but only to let the truth be known."

Yet another charge concerned the teacher's pro-Nazi convictions. The difficulty in making this charge stick was that the teacher had in fact never been a member of the Nazi Party or any other National Socialist organization. To the contrary, he had been a member of the SPD from 1927 to 1933. A neighbor who testified against the teacher was asked a loaded question by the chairman: "Was he like a 150% PG?" To which she answered, "Much worse, his wife was like that too." Herr K., the deputy mayor of Neustadt, echoed this sentiment: "He wasn't a PG but he was an activist in support of the Nazis." The deputy mayor then went on to tell an anecdote to support his claim.

Two days before the arrival of the Red Army, I met Herr W. and asked: "Herr W., now do you believe that the thing is finally lost?" He replied, "No, I'll tell you a parable: there were two rats that fell into a container of milk; one gave up the fight and drowned, the other kept the faith and continued to swim until finally the milk turned into butter and [the rat] stood victorious upon the butter. That's exactly what we have in this case. Whoever believes up to the last will triumph."

The deputy mayor also claimed that W. had painted the picture of Hitler that hung in the local Nazi Party headquarters, although he had to admit that W. never went into the headquarters.

The veracity of this circumstantial evidence was lessened by the testimony of Frau B., who appeared as a defense witness. She claimed that W. "never said anything in support" of Nazism; "I know he is a decent person, although he is somewhat inept . . . He did perhaps make himself a bit unpopular." To hear Frau B. tell it, the root of W.'s problems was the scheming Deputy Mayor K. The trouble actually began, she testified, after the war, when the teacher requested the deputy mayor's help in securing firewood to heat the school. The deputy mayor, according to Frau B., was unsympathetic and dismissed the request, saying, "It's not my problem." The teacher's anger over this refusal increased with the arrival of winter, when "there were no warm rooms for the children" at the school. The teacher then allegedly went directly to the local Soviet commander to request aid, a move that incensed the deputy mayor because he was then upbraided by the Soviet commander. From this point on, Frau B. testified, "there was just hatred and hatred. I put it mostly down to the vindictiveness of [Deputy Mayor] K." Asked if she thought the deputy mayor's testimony was "believable," Frau B. simply replied that the deputy mayor was "very unpopular." Asked her opinion of the prosecution witness who testified that the teacher had been a "150%" Nazi, Frau B. stated, "This I will say, I can only shake my head over her character. She stole a wardrobe from a refugee." The chairman then asked if Frau B. thought that the superintendent, who testified that the teacher had denounced him, was "trustworthy." Her opinion of the superintendent was equally negative: "He has the manners of a public prosecutor." As for the young woman who claimed the teacher had forced her to say "Heil Hitler" three times as punishment, Frau B. was dismissive: "That girl is a little gadabout."

Unfortunately, the Ruppin commission did not conclude this story. Faced with a tangle of contradictory evidence, the commission decided to turn the case over to the police (K5) for further investigation. The commission listed two reasons for washing their hands of this case: first, since the teacher had not been a member of any Nazi organization, he did not fall under the provisions of the denazification. This excuse was unfounded, since, as the Ruppin commissioners well knew, the denazification guidelines allowed for cases of suspected "activists" regardless of formal membership in Nazi organizations. The second reason was that this confusing case arose five days before the deadline for ending the denazification program: the record concludes, "Because of a lack of time, the commission is not able to hear the remaining defense witnesses, since the district commission has been ordered to end its activities on 10 March 1948."[67]

The case of the teacher from Neustadt offers a window into the way personal animosities and denunciations became intertwined with the denazification process. What is striking about this example is how little it actually had to do with the goals of denazification. Granted, if the teacher had been shown to have been a "150% PG," that would have been grounds for dismissal. The evidence presented to support the teacher's "activism," however, was circumstantial. The teacher denied instructing his students in racial theory and forcing them to say "Heil Hitler" as punishment. He also offered a reasonable explanation for painting a picture of Hitler, and the "parable" of the rats and the butter was a weak indication of active support for Nazism. The fact that the case did not come before a commission until March 1948 suggests that he was probably not an active supporter of Nazism: it would have been very unusual for a known activist to continue as the head of an elementary school for nearly three years after the war. Instead, the picture painted by the defense witness is probably closer to the truth: the deputy mayor refused to help the teacher secure firewood for the school, the teacher complained to the Soviet commander, who scolded the deputy mayor, and the deputy mayor then attempted to use the denazification process to exact his revenge. At the outset, the chairman of the Ruppin commission must have thought that a long-hidden active fascist had been uncovered. His initial questioning of the teacher was aggressive and prosecutorial in one. When interviewing prosecution witnesses, the chairman changed his tone and asked leading questions designed to elicit incriminating evidence. With the testimony of the defense witness, however, the case against the teacher began to unravel, and as the contradictions and evidence of personal animosity mounted, the commission realized that it was faced with something more than just a denazification petition. It was probably with a collective sigh of relief that the commission voted to turn the Neustadt intrigues over to the police.

At the beginning of this chapter I mentioned Fitzpatrick's observations concerning the "master plot" of Soviet purge trials and the role of local actors in the reinterpretation of this "plot." The case of the teacher from Neustadt is an example of how Fitzpatrick's approach can be adapted for an analysis of postwar denazification in Germany.

Even if we accept the idea that the "master plot" behind Soviet denazification policy was part of a plan to "Stalinize" the eastern zone, we can also acknowledge that this plot was transformed in unforeseen ways in the hands of local actors. It is all the more telling that the Neustadt case arose not at the beginning of the denazification process but rather in its closing weeks. The Soviet denazification experiment was eventually abandoned because the authorities had lost control of their own "master plot."

CHAPTER 8

Responses to the Nazi Period and the PGs in the New Germany

So far we have looked at the sources of evidence considered by the de-nazification commissions. The testimony of witnesses was not, how-ever, the only type of evidence that played a role in the process. The commissions also often noted the mitigating circumstances *(Entlast-ungsmomente)* and incriminating circumstances *(Belastungsmo-mente)* in individual cases. These circumstances concerned not only individuals' past actions but also their postwar activities and their fu-ture role in the "new democratic Germany." There were two broad areas the commissions considered when judging petitioners' pasts: ev-idence of "antifascist" activity and the question whether they should be considered "active" or "nominal" participants in the National So-cialist system. The assessment of an individual's role in Germany's fu-ture was primarily a political question: To what extent was a peti-tioner prepared to partake in the construction of a new "democratic" and "antifascist" state?

Resistance and "Antifascist Activity"

The question of active and passive resistance during the Nazi period has been subject to debate among historians. Well-known public acts such as the conspiracy to assassinate Hitler in July 1944 can un-problematically be seen as active resistance; these were, in Peter Hoff-mann's words, actions "aimed at the overthrow of Hitler's Nazi dictatorship." Resistance did not, however, always have the overthrow of the regime as its purpose. As Hoffmann noted:

> The phenomenon of a determined but largely ineffective resistance was made up of a variety of forms of behaviour, from semipublic gestures to direct antigovernment activity at the highest level. Something took place that could be termed "popular resistance," but it was not "popular" in quantitative terms. Opposition behaviour could consist in a refusal to offer the "German greeting" ("Heil Hitler"). Many paid with their lives for such a refusal, or for remarks to the effect that the war was not going well.[1]

Nonconformist behavior, which was overlooked by historians for many years, is now seen as part of the story of German opposition to the Third Reich.[2] Detlev Peukert's study of everyday life in the Third Reich broadened the concept of opposition to include the telling of jokes and the nonconformist behavior of the "Swing Youth."[3] In Klemens von Klemperer's view, the German word *Widerstand* should be rendered, interchangeably, as either "opposition" or "resistance": "In the context of total rule there is, unlike in open societies, clearly no place for legal or loyal opposition. Any opposition therefore becomes, in effect, resistance."[4]

The Brandenburg denazification commissions drew no distinctions between active resistance and passive opposition. Instead, they looked for evidence of "antifascist activity" encompassing the whole spectrum of opposition, from membership in an underground organization to private speech. Often commissioners would specifically ask for evidence of "antifascist activity," and those who could produce it were usually exonerated. Such evidence included: (1) incarceration or other forms of punishment for political crimes or membership in a resistance organization, (2) persecution or threats by Nazi officials, (3) voluntary resignation from the party or one of its organizations, (4) giving aid to Jews, foreign forced laborers, or "known antifascists," (5) sabotage of the Nazi war effort or aiding the Red Army during the war, (6) listening to or reading anti-Nazi propaganda, and (7) private speech critical of the Nazi system.

Evidence of incarceration for political crimes during the Third Reich was extremely rare in the data sample: I found only three instances, and all three petitions were approved.[5] Membership in resistance organizations was also rare: only fourteen petitioners in the

data sample substantiated membership in such organizations.⁶ Three
of these were former POWs who had been incarcerated in the Soviet
Union and either belonged to the NKFD or attended an "Antifascist
School" while in captivity; another belonged to a "resistance group"
in Czechoslovakia, and a fifth to the "underground" in Holland.⁷ One
petitioner, who claimed to have belonged to resistance group in Germany, was confronted by a commissioner concerning the duty of an
"antifascist."

> *VVN:* When things were coming to an end in 1945 and you were
> in the Volkssturm, why didn't you have the opportunity to either
> disarm or shoot some of the fascist criminals who were on hand,
> such as the commander of the Volkssturm?
> *Answer:* He never put up any resistance. His name was W. and he
> was a teacher by profession and leader of the Volkssturm. I
> advised him to leave the city in order to allow it to be liberated.
> *VVN:* But what might have happened is that they would have shot
> you. You should have taken him into custody. To be an
> antifascist means not simply to avoid taking action, but rather to
> take action in order to break the [Nazi] resistance, in order to
> alleviate the suffering of the people.
> *Answer:* That's what one says now. That's not what I did. The
> moment the *Volkssturmführer* was gone, there was peace and
> quiet in the town.⁸

Four petitioners who claimed membership in an illegal organization had been members of the Confessing Church (Bekennende
Kirche), founded by a group of Protestant ministers in reaction to
Nazi attempts to control the church through the so-called German
Christian Movement. At first grudgingly tolerated, the Confessing
Church was suppressed in 1938. Two of these petitions were approved on the grounds that membership in this group constituted re-
sistance.⁹ In one case, however, membership in the Confessing Church
actually worked against a petitioner. This tradesman had been a member of the German National People's Party (DNVP) and the Stähl-
helm. In 1934 he joined the Nazi Party and the SA, where he served as
a *Truppenführer*. The Provincial Commission, after listing this incriminating string of organizations, noted, "In addition he belonged to the
fellowship of the Confessing Church, but he never acted accordingly
and he did not leave the SA or the NSDAP . . . [T]here are no mitigat-

ing circumstances . . . [H]e can only be considered an activist and a reactionary."[10]

Evidence of persecution or threats of punishment, usually by a local party official, always resulted in approval of petitions (seventeen cases). Persecution could stem from what was vaguely described as "standing differences" or an "unpleasant relationship" with local Nazi officials.[11] Others were persecuted owing to their membership in the SPD or KPD before 1933, despite the fact that they later joined the Nazi Party.[12] Evidence of a standing conflict with the local Nazi leadership could even mitigate a particularly incriminating past: one petitioner, who joined the Nazi Party in 1932 and held the position of *Blockleiter,* was exonerated owing to the fact that "he was disliked by the district leadership of the NSDAP and was frequently threatened with the revocation of his business license."[13]

Persecution and threats of punishment also arose from public acts of dissent. In one example, a bank employee "made remarks against the NSDAP in 1934 and was therefore pilloried in a public assembly."[14] Others were singled out for symbolic acts of dissent, as happened to the owner of a dairy, who was criticized in a district newspaper for refusing to fly the Nazi flag at his business. This same businessman also claimed that his sole reason for joining the Nazi Party in 1933 was that two of his former employees, both SA members, were committing acts of "sabotage" at the plant, and the only way he could dismiss them was by being a party member.[15]

Another form of dissent, voluntary resignation from Nazi organizations, occurred in fifty-one instances and invariably led to approval of the petition. Typical is the Provincial Commission's approval of the petition of a former member of the NSF: "Fraulein H.'s exoneration is that she was not politically prominent and left the Women's Organization in 1943."[16] Resignation was both an act of dissent and an exoneration of past party membership: as the Calau commission noted in the case of worker who belonged to the party from 1933 to 1943, "The resignation compensates for his incrimination."[17]

Society during the Third Reich was highly politicized, and few individuals could avoid becoming a member of at least one of the plethora of National Socialist organizations. The politicized nature of Nazi society sometimes blurred the lines between the public/political and the private; as a result, some took the public step of declaring resignation for private reasons. One petitioner, for example, served from 1932 to

1939 as an *Obertruppführer* in the Reich Labor Service (Reichsar-beitsdienst, or RAD). He claimed that he had resigned from the RAD because he wanted to marry the daughter of a former KPD leader whom the Nazis had murdered. Whether he resigned out of deference to his future wife's loss or because this betrothal led to his own "anti-fascism" is unclear. Regardless, in the eyes of the commission his res-ignation (and probably also his wife's political pedigree) constituted an act of dissent, and his petition was approved.[18]

The outbreak of war turned many Germans away from their initial enthusiasm for National Socialism.[19] In instances in which resignation from Nazi organizations was tied to the war, this disenchantment be-came dissent. One young woman joined the BDM in 1934, over her father's objections, "because it was the normal thing to do." She later resigned, in 1939, after her father "convinced her the Nazis were re-sponsible for the outbreak of the war."[20] Another petitioner declared his resignation after an air raid: "When he saw that the people af-fected [by the raid] were not cared for and only political circles [re-ceived aid], he complained and declared his resignation from the party. He was ordered to appear before a party tribunal, but this never came to pass."[21]

In petitions where evidence of voluntary resignation existed, this was usually cited as the primary mitigating circumstance. Sometimes, however, resignation was only one of several mitigating circum-stances. The case of a doctor from Finsterwalde is an example of the multiple layers of evidence that commissions often had to sort through. The doctor was heavily incriminated by membership in "militarist" and "nationalist" organizations, including one of the elite Students' Corps, the honorary Old Students' Association, an organi-zation for former officers, and the paramilitary Stahlhelm, which he joined in 1923. In addition, the doctor belonged to the SA from 1934 to 1935, and joined the Nazi Party in the latter year. Four reasons were cited for approving his petition: his voluntary resignation from the SA in 1935, evidence that he had been pressured into joining the Nazi Party, statements from witnesses attesting that he had never been "politically active," and, finally, the fact that, since the end of the war, "he has been committed to caring for the health of the population."[22]

Another type of "antifascist activity" included extending aid to the ideological and "biological" enemies of the Nazi "people's community" *(Volksgemeinschaft).*[23] These "enemies" were so defined by a "racial state" in which racial ideology permeated daily life. Draconian punishments were levied against those who assisted the regime's racial enemies.[24]

In light of the harsh penalties imposed on those who continued their relationships with Jews or aided them in avoiding deportation, denazification commissions considered this activity as strong mitigation.[25] A small number of petitioners in the data sample (twenty-three cases) presented evidence of dissent relating to Jews, and twenty-two of these petitions were approved. This form of exculpation extended to those who had maintained friendships with Jews and even, in one case, a continuing friendship with a minister "in spite of [his] Jewish wife."[26] Others took the more daring risk of protecting Jews either by hiding them or by helping them flee to avoid arrest and deportation.[27] Relationships with Jews arose from public as well as private circumstances. Examples of public relationships include protecting a Jewish employee or defying boycotts of Jewish businesses.[28] One petitioner claimed that he had joined the SA for the sole purpose of protecting the pharmacy of his Jewish employer from being boycotted.[29] There were also private relationships with Jews that extended from spouses to in-laws.[30] Having a family relationship with Jews did not automatically lead to complete exoneration, however. Of a petitioner dismissed from the Nazi Party in 1935 because of the "non-Aryan ancestry" of his wife, it was noted that this fact alone "does not, however, prove that he had a negative attitude toward fascism."[31]

Like Jews, foreign laborers were subject to discriminatory treatment within the racial state.[32] While Jews ultimately faced deportation from Germany, foreign workers had been transferred to Germany to alleviate wartime labor shortages. Foreign laborers, designated by the Nazis as *Untermenschen,* received substandard clothing, food, and shelter.[33] Germans who gave compassionate aid to foreign workers were threatened with draconian punishments.[34] As in the case of aid to Jews, there were very few petitioners who had helped foreign laborers: twenty cases in the data sample, of which nineteen were approved.[35] In a few cases, petitioners took daring risks to aid foreign laborers. A truck driver for the postal service, who joined the Nazi Party in 1933, presented affidavits from former forced laborers attesting that he had helped them escape from Germany. This petitioner, who had been dismissed from his job with the postal service because of his Nazi past, was ordered reinstated by the Provincial Commission because of this resistance activity.[36]

In most cases, Germans aided foreign workers in a less risky manner. Employers, for instance, presented evidence that they had simply treated foreign laborers humanely; that this would be considered an act of dissent is indicative of the cruelty fostered by Nazi racial policy.[37] Even small acts of kindness could be seen as dissent and resistance. A power station worker reportedly championed the welfare of the Russian laborers at the plant by frequently buying cigarettes in large amounts to distribute to them. On more than one occasion he was nearly apprehended by the Gestapo in the course of this activity.[38] A nurse illegally gave medicine to sick foreign workers.[39] Others gave vegetables and milk to underfed foreigners.[40]

Political opponents of the Third Reich constituted another persecuted group. Petitioners who aided "known antifascists" ran the risk of punishment, and proof of this activity was usually a compelling exculpation. The number of petitioners who presented evidence of aiding antifascists, as in the case of those who had aided Jews and foreign laborers, was small. In the data sample there are only nineteen instances, all but two of which were approved. Usually the aid given to "antifascists" was simply humanitarian. This included sending packages to concentration camp inmates, supporting the families of incarcerated dissidents, or in other ways helping individuals who had been persecuted by the Nazis for their political beliefs.[41]

That so many petitioners with long-standing membership in Nazi organizations were exonerated because of such activities underscores the seriousness with which many commissioners took their instructions to weigh all evidence. Consider the examples of two men who both joined the Nazi Party in 1933 and who both, at considerable risk, actively supported opponents of the Nazis. The first is a dentist who, in addition to regularly lending aid to antifascists, had also publicly complained when four concentration camp inmates were paraded through town in shackles. Despite this evidence, the dentist was called before the Ostprignitz commission because the mayor had accused him of being a Nazi activist. The commission, however, noted that the mayor "has to the present time been unable to supply witnesses to support this claim." In the commission's view, the mayor was acting as a stooge for a "reactionary clique" that sought to use the denazification process as way to exact revenge for the dentist's outspoken dissent. The dentist's petition was approved, the transcript noting that the commission "will make decisions case by case regarding the extent to which [each instance] concerns nominal or active PGs."[42] In the second example, a man who regularly aided "antifascists" and their families had used his connection to his brother, who was the commandant of a concentration camp, to secure the release of a camp inmate. He had engaged in this dissident activity even though he was a *Blockleiter,* having joined the Nazi Party in 1933.[43]

A rarely encountered type of active resistance was contributing to the military defeat of the Third Reich. This included sabotaging the Nazi war effort or directly aiding the Red Army. Only nine petitioners in the data sample presented evidence of sabotaging the war effort, and all but one of these were approved. Several had had the opportunity for sabotage while serving in the Volkssturm. Given Germany's increasingly hopeless military situation, conscription into the Volkssturm (begun in the fall of 1944) was unpopular. It presented an opportunity to carry out resistance activity to those who were unwilling to take part in what one historian called a last-ditch attempt to "substitute élan and fanaticism for military skill and equipment."[44] Two petitioners were exonerated for having committed acts of sabotage while serving in the Volkssturm and another for preventing an act of sabotage: the destruction of three bridges in Rheinsberg ordered by the Nazis as the Red Army approached the town.[45]

Instances of petitioners' directly assisting the Red Army were extremely rare; there are only two cases in the data sample. One of these concerned the *Landrat* from Ruppin. This man was appointed mayor of Neuruppin by the SMA immediately after the war and later became *Landrat.* During the Nazi period, he served in the Hitler Youth as a Leader of Physical Training, entered the NSDAP in 1938, and finally joined the German army. In 1945, in what proved to be a wise move, he deserted to the Red Army. Since the end of the war, he reportedly had devoted "his entire energy" to his job and had quickly "earned the trust of the antifascist parties." Not satisfied with this litany of positive attributes, the CDU representative on the Provincial Commission argued forcefully against approval of the *Landrat's* petition on the grounds that he was "to be considered a militarist and through his function as squad leader [*Hauptfähnleinführer* in the HJ] he had a fundamental influence over the education of youngsters." Furthermore, the CDU representative smelled a careerist and received the impression that the *Landrat* "only entered the party in 1938 in order to retain his position and also, by deserting to the Russians, only sought his personal advantage." These objections failed to carry the day: four commissioners voted in favor of his continuing as *Landrat*.[46]

Private Resistance: Foreign Radio, Contraband Literature, and Private Speech

The varieties of opposition we have considered so far consist of public acts witnessed by others. There were also private forms of opposition less likely to be witnessed. While it was difficult for Nazi authorities to catch people in the act of listening to radio broadcasts, reading forbidden publications, or having private conversation critical of the system, there were harsh penalties for those who were apprehended.

Several petitioners claimed, usually without success, that they had listened to foreign radio broadcasts. There are nine such claims in the data sample, but only two carried any weight with the commissioners. There were two problems with such claims. First, unless combined with other mitigating circumstances, this activity had little exculpatory force. In rejecting a petitioner who had joined the NSDAP in 1937, the commission noted that "as evidence of his antifascist attitude [he] could only claim that during the war he listened to foreign broadcasts." This sole mitigating circumstance, in light of the "terrible personal impression" he made on the commission, assured rejection.[47] A second problem for those making such claims was that some of the commissioners, themselves "antifascists" during the Nazi period, were familiar with these broadcasts and could easily catch unwary petitioners in a lie. The following exchange was recorded in the case of an employee of the postal service.

> *VVN:* You were a wireless specialist with the postal service. Tell us something about the call signs of the individual stations, for example, London Radio. Did you listen to this station?
> *Answer:* Yes, but I can't describe the call sign.
> *VVN:* But you've already spoken about listening to enemy stations, therefore you must also have some idea about the call signs they used. Did you listen to Moscow Radio? How did they sign on?

Answer: [fails to answer].

VVN: So, regrettably, you can't tell us anything about this.

Chairman: Can you remember a specific program? Did you
perhaps hear the "Internationale" on a Moscow broadcast?

Answer: Yes, it must have been in 1944.

Chairman: So you claim to have listened to Moscow. Did you hear
the "Internationale" at the end of the broadcast?

Answer: Yes.

Chairman: See how you lie. In 1943 or 1944, when you claim to
have listened, the "Internationale" wasn't played anymore.
Don't try to pull a fast one on us.[48]

In contrast, one petitioner who was exonerated because he had listened to radio broadcasts did not need to prove he knew the stations'
call signs: instead he produced evidence that he had received two rep-
rimands and spent a day in the custody of the Gestapo for tuning in to
forbidden radio stations.[49]

A petitioner who claimed to have seen communist newspapers was
subjected to the same close questioning as the radio listeners.

Chairman: Can you give any evidence of antifascist activity?

Answer: No. I would only just quickly say that I knew that, at the
shop of a certain barber, communist newspapers were circulated
after 1933, which was forbidden.

Chairman: Which newspapers were these?

Answer: That I can no longer remember.

Chairman: Can you remember the size of these newspapers?

Answer: Yes, they were the same size as all the others.

Chairman: That isn't correct; the [communist] newspapers weren't
the same size. You never saw such a newspaper.[50]

While few petitioners were exonerated on claims of listening to radio broadcasts or reading forbidden literature, evidence of private
speech critical of the Nazi regime was a form of opposition often helpful to petitioners. Since this speech was a private act, testimony from
witnesses was essential. Typical examples are a petitioner who supplied evidence from acquaintances confirming that he had expressed
"a completely oppositional attitude" toward fascism, and another
whose friends testified that in conversation he "revealed himself as a
champion of the democratic worldview."[51] Witnesses to private

speech also came from the workplace, as in the case of a bank employee "who was known among the personnel of the [bank] as an opponent of the Nazi regime," and, in another case, a fellow worker who testified that a petitioner "in every private conversation was always unfavorably disposed toward the party."[52]

Defining the Nominal PG: Inner Migration, Unpoliticals, and *Mitläufer*

So far we have examined how the commissions considered concrete evidence. It is indicative of the complex nature of the denazification process that there was yet another set of incriminating and exculpating circumstances that played a role in the decision making. Many petitioners could not present evidence of "antifascist activity" and instead pleaded that they had retreated to an "inner migration" as a silent form of opposition. Others simply claimed that they had conducted themselves in an "unpolitical" manner that should be construed as exculpation.

Petitioners who claimed "inner migration" had to rely solely on their ability to convince the commissioners of their sincerity. Usually a claim of "inner migration" involved persons who realized, after joining the party, that they did not "agree with the goals of the NSDAP" but that they simultaneously "did not have the courage to declare their resignation" from the party.[53] A defense based solely on "inner migration" rarely succeeded, a fact the Ostprignitz commission acknowledged in approving a petition: "What is presented here is one of the rare instances in which it can really be determined that [the petitioner] had no inner ties to the NSDAP, a fact that will surely be proven [by his future actions]."[54]

Recourse to "inner migration" could usually succeed only when it was coupled with other mitigating factors. An example is the case of a doctor who, as a former Danish citizen, joined the party in 1933 (as well as the SA and later the NSV) because he feared that his non-German ancestry might damage his career and because all of his colleagues were already party members. Witnesses testified, however, that the doctor "in later years was spiritually liberated from the ideology of Nazism, which he also openly confirmed." In addition, the doctor had aided foreign workers and assisted in postwar reconstruction.[55] This plea held little water, however, for a petitioner who had joined the Nazi Party in 1933 but argued that "already in 1934 he had noted that National Socialism was not what it had promised to be." The Provincial Commission rejected this claim with the observation that he "remained nevertheless a member of the NSDAP . . . [T]his provides no exculpation for him."[56]

Claims of "inner migration" often shaded off into references to a general "unpolitical" attitude. It was usually difficult to gain exoneration with this type of defense since, in short, it required petitioners to argue that after joining the Nazi Party they became appalled by its policies but, in response, took no action. They simply retreated into an "unpolitical" attitude that they felt effectively distanced them from the crimes of the Third Reich. A heavily incriminated petitioner who had joined the NSDAP in 1933 and later an SS motorized division appeared before a commission and argued that his attitude toward the Nazi state had soured owing to the persecution of the Jews and the outbreak of war. The SED commissioner queried him as to why he did not take action and resign from the Nazi organizations.

> *Answer:* At the time that wasn't grounds for resigning, it was out of the question.
> *SED:* But many did leave the party.
> *Answer:* Perhaps I didn't act energetically enough. I'm sorry. I can't change it now. I wasn't politically oriented, I was never interested in politics.

On account of his membership in the SS, the commission felt that it had no alternative but to deny his petition, even though the transcript noted, "There is no doubt about the truthfulness of his testimony; one can see that [he] was not a bad person."[57]

It is questionable whether unpoliticals can even be considered to have been the most passive of dissenters. Denazification commissions, however, definitely considered an unpolitical background to be a mitigating factor. The question of unpoliticals is part of the *Mitläufer* phenomenon examined by Niethammer in his study of denazification in the U.S. zone. As Niethammer shows, the appellation *Mitläufer* (followers or fellow travelers) indicated political passivity during the Nazi period and resulted in exoneration.[58] There was a key difference, however, between the U.S. and Soviet denazification programs regarding this concept. The U.S. system officially categorized individuals into groups according to the degree of incrimination in each case. The

Fragebogen used in the U.S. zone actually gave PGs the opportunity to state which category they thought they belonged to: in Nietham-mer's study, 61 percent of the respondents answered that they consid-ered themselves merely *Mitläufer*. In the Soviet zone, by contrast, the concept of *Mitläufer* was not officially incorporated into either the *Fragebogen* or the commissions' guidelines. Commissions were in-structed simply to determine "nominal" or "active" status based on the evidence. The term *Mitläufer* is rarely used (seven cases) in the data sample, and then usually in a manner synonymous with being a "nominal" member of the Nazi Party. A representative quote comes from the case of a petitioner who had been in the NSDAP from 1934 to 1944: "He gave no support in any way to the NSDAP. Herr M. gives the impression of a *Mitläufer* . . . [and] represents no danger to the democratic state."[59] In contrast, the petition of a PG who joined the party in 1930 was denied on the grounds that the case "does not concern a *Mitläufer* or nominal membership" in the NSDAP.[60]

Perhaps the clearest articulation of the characteristics of the *Mit-läufer* within the Soviet denazification process was given at a meeting of denazification commission members at the inception of Order 201.

> The members of the NSDAP who lived as decent people [*als Mensch gelebt haben*], who in no form are guilty of a crime against humanity and who have worked with all their strength for the democratic con-struction, will be given the possibility to enjoy all citizenship rights. This provision clearly shows the great political and historical meaning of Or-der 201.[61]

Many, maybe the majority, of the members of Nazi organizations never even performed a subfunction within the party: they were truly nominal members who gained little or nothing from membership, only to be faced with accusations of co-responsibility during denazi-fication.[62] The primary reasons given for joining a National Socialist organization by those who appeared before denazification commis-sions were workplace pressure, automatic enrollment, economic pres-sure, and communal pressure.

Commissions accepted claims of feeling pressured to join a Nazi or-ganization as a generally acknowledged aspect of life in the Third Reich. As one commission reported, "The fundamental tendency in the hearings was that the majority [of petitioners] were forced by their supervisor or employer to join the party. Only a few people claimed to have entered the party out of conviction or belief in Hitler's cause."[63] Claims of pressure at the workplace were indeed common: in the data sample there are 170 instances of workplace pressure, and 157 of these cases were approved. Most of these claims were simply that a supervisor had pressured employees to join an organization and threatened those who refused with dismissal. Representative notations in the hearing records include, "The reason for his entrance into the NSDAP was his position at the Deutsche Bank" and "Forced by his boss to join the NSDAP." One petitioner successfully claimed that he had been forced to join the Nazi Party in *1931* by his activist boss, who threatened to fire him if he refused.[64]

The pressure to join Nazi organizations often did not stop after an individual relented; once in an organization, people could then be pressured to assume a function in the organization, with the constant threat of dismissal awaiting those who refused.[65] Thus a member of the Hitler Youth was forced to assume the post of senior squad leader in order to keep his job with the police.[66] The owner of a cartwright firm was pressured to take on the task of *Blockwart* because he could use his apprentices to collect party dues in the neighborhood, and another petitioner was forced to become *Blockwart* by default since "in all the other families in his *Block* the men had been drafted."[67]

Some occupations were especially targeted by the Nazis for recruitment. Nurses were often pressured to join the National Socialist women's organization, the NSF.[68] Gas station owners and auto repair specialists were pressured to join the paramilitary NSKK.[69] In addition, chimney sweeps and foresters seem to have been under extraordinary pressure to join the NSDAP.[70] The NSDAP also forced masters in trades who trained apprentices to join the party.[71] A train engineer claimed that, on 1 April 1939, a sign was posted at work ordering all employees who were not yet members of the party to sign up. This practice was apparently widespread in the rail service.[72] Germans who held administrative positions in the so-called Eastern Territories *(Ostgebieten)* were also particularly pressured to join party organizations.[73]

Commissions were especially sympathetic to the plight of fathers who were responsible for large families. In approving the petition of a train engineer who succumbed to workplace pressure and joined the party in 1939, it was noted, "He had seven children . . . and in consideration of this large number of children and the financial difficulties that would follow, he finally decided to make this step" and join the party. A fellow rail employee, who had been an SPD member before 1933, succumbed to the pressure to join the NSDAP in 1941, "with a heavy heart," because he had five children.[74]

Some petitioners were not even subjected to pressure to join a National Socialist organization but simply found themselves "automatically enrolled" or "forcibly transferred" to the membership rolls without their consent. A farmer reported that when the local Nazi *Ortsbauernführer* died in 1942, he was chosen to fill the post. When he informed the local party leadership that he could not accept the post because he was not a party member, he was told, "Well, what isn't yet can still be." Shortly afterward he was informed that he had been made a candidate member of the NSDAP without his consent.[75]

In most cases, individuals were not automatically enrolled in their first National Socialist organization but rather were transferred from one of the party's ancillary organizations into the party itself. In the hearing transcripts this is usually referred to as a compulsory transfer (*zwangsweise Überweisung* or *Übernahme*) from one organization into the party, and, as with automatic membership, the commissions saw such transfers as mitigating circumstances. The most common transfer was of Hitler Youth into the NSDAP. Young women were particularly apt to be transferred from the BDM to the NSDAP, and in all but two cases in the data sample these women were exonerated. Some SA members also claimed to have been automatically enrolled in the NSDAP.[76]

The date when an individual joined a National Socialist organization was another significant piece of evidence considered by the commissions. Entrance before 1933 was particularly incriminating as it evidenced active support for National Socialism before Hitler assumed the chancellorship. Entrance between 1933 and 1937 was less incriminating. PGs who entered in 1933 could often convincingly claim that they had joined in the general rush of excitement following Hitler's assumption of power but later turned against the party as domestic terror increased, and that, like so many unpoliticals and nominal PGs, they did not have the courage to break publicly with the party despite their disenchantment. Those who joined the party from 1937 onward were the least incriminated; 1937 was a key year because that was when the NSDAP began to compel individuals to join.[77]

Figure 8.1 shows rates of approval and denial of petitions correlated with date of entrance into the NSDAP. The sharp spikes in overall membership in 1933 and 1937 are clearly displayed in the figure. A comparison of approval and denial rates shown in Table 8.1 underscores the relative incriminatory weight placed on entrance dates by the commissions. There is a clear pattern in the commissions' decisions in these cases. On the simplest level, the longer a person belonged to the NSDAP, the greater the chance the petition would be de-

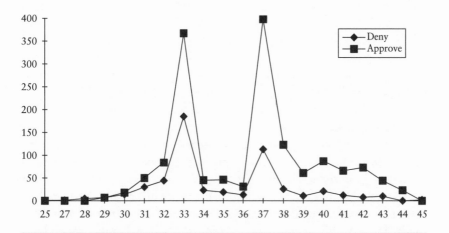

Figure 8.1. Rates of approval and denial of denazification petitions in Brandenburg correlated with year of entry into NSDAP. The approval rate is a combination of petitions approved without reservation and those approved with the condition that the petitioner could not work in a supervisory position. Based on 2,041 former NSDAP members in the data sample (see Appendix).

Table 8.1 Denial and approval of denazification petitions in Brandenburg from NSDAP members for selected years of party entrance

Date joined	Denied	Approved	Total
Before 1933	102 (43.6%)	132 (56.4%)	234
1933	185 (33.5%)	367 (66.5%)	552
1934–1936	55 (31.1%)	122 (68.9%)	177
1937	113 (22.1%)	398 (77.9%)	511
1938–1945	90 (15.9%)	477 (84.1%)	567

Source: 2,041 petitions from the data sample (see Appendix).

nied. That petitions were denied, however, no matter how brief the membership in the party, indicates that the number of years in the party was only one of the factors commissions considered. It is noteworthy, for example, that there are only two individuals in the data sample who joined the NSDAP in 1945, and both of these petitions were denied because of other factors.[78] Nevertheless, it is safe to say that the date of entrance into the party was an important piece of evidence.

A good example comes from the Ruppin commission's handling of members of the Neuruppin city orchestra. Over the course of two hearings, they considered nineteen petitions from the musicians. All of these cases were decided in absentia, and the transcript includes only the barest minimum of facts about each petitioner. In this instance, the commission clearly based its decisions solely on the date of entry: all petitioners who entered Nazi organizations in 1933 or after were approved (thirteen petitions), and all who joined before 1933 (six petitions) were denied.[79]

Even though there is a strong correlation between the year of entry into a Nazi organization and the fate of petitioners, commissions also considered purely economic justifications for joining. One petitioner, for example, stated that he had joined the SA in 1933 because he had been unemployed for the previous six years and felt that membership might increase his chances of securing a job.[80] A similar claim by a former communist worker evoked sharp questioning.

> *Chairman:* Why did you join the KPD in 1932?
> *Answer:* We had to do something against the Nazis.
> *Chairman:* But that didn't work out so you turned straight around and joined the NSDAP [in 1933]?
> *Answer:* I was unemployed and I had four children.[81]

In the face of the Nazi *Gleichschaltung* (coordination) of the German economy, some people found membership in a National Socialist organization necessary to continue making a living. Dentists, for example, discovered that they were banned from treating people with public health insurance unless they belonged to a party organization.[82] A self-employed locksmith convincingly argued that he had had to join the NSDAP in 1932 "or else none of the farmers would buy from him or give him work."[83] An apparel dealer likewise claimed that the sole reason he had joined the SA in 1935 was that "he wanted to sell SA uniforms in his shop."[84]

Commissioners had to consider such economic justifications carefully since "people who have received financial favoritism from the Nazis" were subject to discretionary removal under Directive 24.[85] Those who appeared to have joined a Nazi organization solely for personal gain and who could present no further exculpating evidence were usually dismissed. Many of these individuals were doubly incriminated because they had joined a National Socialist organization before 1933 in response to economic conditions in the final years of the Weimar Republic.[86] Others had used their membership to increase the profitability of their businesses after the Nazis were in power.[87] A master barber, for example, had his license revoked because it appeared that he had been named head of the Barbers' Guild owing to his membership in the party and the SA, even though there were "older colleagues who had worked in the town for decades" who should have been given the position.[88]

Another claim which was usually effective was of having joined a Nazi organization because of pressure from local Nazi leaders. Given the power of Nazi officials in local communities, commissions were sympathetic to claims of pressure from a *Landrat,* an *Ortsgruppenleiter,* or, in rural areas, a *Bauernführer.*[89] The Ostprignitz commission noted in its approval of a petition from the village of Triglitz, "Considering the fact that Triglitz was very well organized by the Nazis and *Kreisbauernführer* K. was quite energetic in support of the goals of the NSDAP, it is to [the petitioner's] credit that he was able to maintain only a nominal membership [in the NSDAP]."[90]

People also claimed with noteworthy success that they had felt a more diffuse type of communal pressure to conform. Communal pressure was particularly strong in small towns and villages. A village midwife joined the NSF in 1933 because she did not want to be "the only one out of step after all the other women of the village had joined."[91] As a bar owner explained, he had joined the party in 1932 because "80% of the population [of the village] was already in the party, [and] I didn't want to be left out."[92]

For the self-employed, communal pressure could combine with economic motives. The Ostprignitz commission noted in approving the petition of a baker who joined the party in 1935 that "he followed the trend of the times. Because many businesspeople were in the party, he went along with them."[93] The combination of communal norms and business concerns is also evident in the case of an electrician from the village of Lindenberg.

Chairman: What convinced you to join the NSDAP in 1933?

Answer: We had an assembly in 1932. The trade situation had sunk very low and it was suggested that we join the party.

Chairman: And you hoped to gain an advantage through your membership?

Answer: Yes. And after 1933 the economic situation was somewhat better.

Chairman: So, you were of the opinion that your business actually improved and that the Hitler system was the right way for you?

Answer: Oh, well, you know, in the village it was the normal thing back then.

Chairman: So you stood by the ideology and openly declared that the Hitler system had brought advantage to your trade. You remained true to the Führer because he, so to speak, laid a protecting hand on your trade.

Answer: But I never was politically active.

Chairman: But you took part in assemblies and were excited about the fascist ideology?

Answer: When the war broke out I was of a completely different opinion.

Chairman: So then what was your position? Did you keep playing along or did you make a declaration of your change of heart there and then?

Answer: We couldn't do that yet back then.

Despite this rough questioning, the commission approved this petition with the notation "Only a *Mitläufer*."[94]

The village barber, who followed the electrician, seconded this view from Lindenberg.

Chairman: So did everything the Führer promised really come to pass?

Answer: Well, until 1939 our economy did actually get better.

Chairman: Oh, are you really incapable of making any other observation?

Answer: Well, in the village one doesn't have much of an opportunity to closely follow the political developments.

Chairman: But you did hear about quite a few events like the Jewish question etc.?

Answer: The persecution of the Jews was completely against my beliefs, but it seemed as if it was only a passing state of affairs. About the existence of the concentration camps etc., we, even the whole country, had absolutely no idea.

Chairman: Did you have faith right up until the end that Hitler could bring better times?

Answer: Yes, I believed in the beginning, but not up until the end. But as a good German one shouldn't stab the government in the back during bad times.

The barber, like his neighbor the electrician, had his petition approved, despite the fact that he had joined the NSDAP in 1930.[95]

In approving these two petitions from Lindenberg, the commissioners revealed their particular understanding of village life. If these two men had been, say, salaried employees of the *Kreis* administration, there would have been little chance, in the absence of overwhelming exculpating evidence, that their petitions would have been approved. The hearing transcript notes no mitigating circumstances in either case: these two men—focused on the economic situation of the village, unconcerned with politics and ideology, and willing to go along with what everyone else seemed to be doing—were in many ways archetypes of the nominal PG in rural Brandenburg. There is evidence of a generally accepted view among commissioners that the villages were places where politics did not happen—certainly not the kind of politics that denazification was designed to root out. As the Calau commission remarked in approving the petition of a shepherd from the village of Ogrosen, "It is to be noted that in this small village there was hardly any political life."[96]

People living in towns also were not immune to communal pressure. The following was recorded in the case of a master chimney sweep from Lübbenau.

Chairman: What was your attitude toward the persecution of the Jews?

Answer: For a time I lived in Lübbenau at the home of a Jew by the name of L. I eventually moved, but when the persecution of the Jews started, my former landlord often came to our house to speak with me. He then left for England. I thought the persecution of the Jews was horrible.

Chairman: Nevertheless, you joined the NSDAP [in 1937] and became assistant block leader in 1940?

> *Answer:* I had no choice, I don't know, it wasn't my good
> naturedness, perhaps it was really partially weakness.
> *Chairman:* But in Lübbenau it wasn't so bad really, you wouldn't
> have been too harshly judged.
> *Answer:* Oh, to the contrary, it was so. How often it would happen
> that, if I used the old greeting, "Good morning," it was
> answered with, "Don't you know the official greeting?" It
> wasn't so simple.[97]

The Calau commission accepted this argument and approved the petition. The chairman of the commission, in this case *Landrat* Freter, had a preconceived notion of the situation in Lübbenau; his impression was that pressure to conform was "not so bad" in the town. Freter, who did not live in Lübbenau, may have been stating a generally accepted opinion about the lax atmosphere in Lübbenau. For a resident of the town, however, the situation was anything but lax: the chimney sweep's recollection was of an ever-present communal pressure to conform. His telling comment, "It wasn't so simple," probably rang true with the commissioners; they all had lived through the Nazi period and knew how communal pressure could subtly work its way into even the most innocuous aspects of everyday life. Outward conformity to the Nazi system was the path of least resistance for many people who, like the chimney sweep, may not have been lacking in "good nature" but who also were too "weak" to resist. A factory worker who had been in the SPD before 1933 succinctly explained his entrance into the NSDAP in 1939: he had finally relented to the pressure "in order to have some peace."[98]

The PGs in the "New Democratic Germany"

A final set of considerations included the petitioners' postwar activities and their probable future role in the "new democratic Germany." Although difficult to quantify, the concepts of guilt and atonement were central to denazification. In appeals for public support, denazification was described as a measure of the degree to which Germans had accepted responsibility for the crimes of the Third Reich. Admitting guilt or some degree of co-responsibility was only the first step and would need to be followed by acts of atonement. Getting PGs to admit co-responsibility was a difficult task. In part, this can explained as the result of an aversion to the concept of collective guilt: it was difficult for many to accept that mere membership in an organization implied criminal culpability.

In attempting to elicit statements of remorse, commissioners were trying to evaluate petitioners' future roles in post-fascist Germany. This differed from evaluation of past activities. In evaluating a person's past, the goal was to categorize the individual as either a "nominal" or an "active" participant in the Nazi system. In regard to the future, the question became whether or not the petitioner was opposed to the new "democracy." The term "democracy" was frequently invoked during the Soviet occupation period, but its meaning would have been foreign to citizens of western democratic states. In the denazification hearings, the term "democracy" was used as the antonym for "fascism"; thus, people judged "enemies of democracy" had failed—through words or deeds—to renounce Nazism and exhibit remorse. Conversely, those who presented "no danger" to "democratic Germany" had shown remorse for their past political affiliations and a willingness to cooperate in reconstruction.

Commissioners often gave petitioners an opportunity to make a public declaration of regret. Given the chance, however, few petitioners were willing to admit to any wrongdoing. This may simply have been out of fear of prosecution. Many petitioners, however, also refused to accept a share of collective guilt and protested that they personally had not committed any offenses. A former SA *Truppführer* and Nazi Party member, asked on what grounds he based his petition, answered simply, "I don't feel guilty." In rejecting this petition, the commissioners noted that "even today he is a complete opponent of democracy."[99] A former SA *Obertruppführer* was pointedly asked, "In Oranienburg you always walked around in a uniform. You are known there. What would the people say if you were now permitted to keep your business license?" The connection between having publicly worn an SA uniform and bearing co-responsibility for Nazism was lost on this petitioner, who answered in his own defense, "But I never did anything to anybody."[100] In a rare case, a petitioner was able to secure approval simply through the conviction with which he stated his innocence.

> *SED:* You were a Nazi. You knew one day you would face denazification. Why haven't you made any effort to secure some defense witnesses?
> *Answer:* If I had been aware of any sort of guilt then I would have

sought out some witnesses . . . I have maintained a pure
conscience and I have brought no crimes upon my head [and] I
was not and am not now aware of guilt on my part.[101]

It is difficult, perhaps impossible, to know for certain if petitioners
were being purposefully evasive or if they truly believed in their innocence. There was definitely a difference between the commissioners'
understanding of guilt and innocence and the understanding of many
petitioners. In some cases it seems as if the two sides were speaking
different languages. The following is drawn from the appearance of a
petitioner before the Provincial Commission. This man, who joined
the NSDAP in 1933, was heavily incriminated because he had served
as a *Blockwart,* an *Ortsgruppenleiter,* and a *Zellenleiter* for the party.

> *VVN:* What would you say and do if Hitler were still in power and
> you had to give evidence that you were a nominal member [of
> the party] while you were still a *Zellenleiter?*
> *Answer:* I don't understand that—I had many good friends who
> were in the SPD and who remained Social Democrats and yet
> they remained my good friends, even though I was in the
> NSDAP.
> *Chairman:* Do you realize that you are implicated in the
> catastrophe?
> *Answer:* I only always strove to help people when I thought that
> things might be going badly for them.
> *Chairman:* So you are not aware of any guilt on your part? Only
> Hitler and his assistants bear any guilt?
> *Answer:* I don't want to say that exactly.[102]

What emerges from the denazification transcripts are two interpretations of the Nazi past. What appeared to "antifascist" commissioners as criminal behavior petitioners saw as nonincriminating. A dentist who claimed that he had always been on the side of the workers
and opposed "the methods of capitalism" was interrupted by the
FDGB representative on the Calau commission: "But that didn't stop
you from leading a battalion in the Volkssturm? That was a gigantic crime!" To which the dentist replied, "I never knew that was a
crime."[103] In this case, the dentist's view of the innocence of his Volkssturm role was actually in keeping with denazification guidelines:
having led a battalion of the Volkssturm could not, in and of itself,
be construed as a "gigantic crime." Something else was going on in

this case, however. For the FDGB representative, himself a committed "antifascist," it was simply inconceivable that one could support the working class, deplore the "methods of capitalism," and yet still agree to lead a Volkssturm battalion. For the dentist, the opposite was apparently the case: he saw no contradiction between his critique of capitalism and his activities in the Volkssturm.

Often the petitioners seemed, like visitors from another culture, truly unaware of what was at stake in the denazification process. A telegraph worker who had joined the SA in 1933, the NSDAP in 1937, and then the NSFK (National Socialist Aviation Corps) was dismissed by the postal service. He appealed this decision to the Provincial Commission.

> *Chairman:* You were in three NS organizations and now appeal the decision of the Oberpostdirektion: On what grounds?
> *Answer:* In the letter I received we were instructed to submit an appeal.
> *Chairman:* You have to bring evidence of antifascist activity. Can you do that?
> *Answer:* No.
> *VVN:* You feel completely guiltless concerning the developments in Germany?
> *Answer:* Yes.[104]

Equally unaware was a meat inspector who had joined the NSDAP in 1933 and was dismissed from his job by a district denazification commission. When asked why he was appealing the decision, he merely replied, "Because I like my job." Asked directly if he was "aware of any sort of guilt" on his part, he stated, "No, not at all."[105] The lack of comprehension on the part of some petitioners could reach astonishing proportions. A former *Blockleiter* from Guben protested to the Provincial Commission that he did not understand how the Guben commission could have revoked his business license.

> *Chairman:* But you do realize that we are implementing Order 201?
> *Answer:* No, I didn't know that.
> *Chairman:* The new denazification order?
> *Answer:* No.
> *Chairman:* Do you ever read the newspaper?
> *Answer:* The Berlin one with the coat of arms.

One can only imagine the commissioners' incredulity in the face of this amazing ignorance: the petition was denied.[106] In another case, which was approved, the Ruppin commission noted of a man who joined the NSDAP in 1929: "[He] gives the impression that he is not capable of understanding the implications of his actions. Revocation of his business license would not serve the interests of anyone."[107]

Only rarely would a petitioner exhibit the level of remorse the commissioners apparently sought. A former postal worker from Wittenberge who joined the NSDAP in 1934 hit the right note with the Provincial Commission.

> *Chairman:* Did you attempt to leave the NSDAP? Or did you ever reflect that you had taken the wrong path?
> *Answer:* To be sure, but there was no longer any turning back.
> *Chairman:* So out of love for your job you continued to finance these crimes [of the Nazi Party]?
> *Answer:* Now I want to make amends for everything.
> *Chairman:* Have you considered how you can now make amends?
> *Answer:* I continue to work faithfully and honestly for myself and my family, for the reconstruction of a new democratic Germany, so that we can all get back on our feet again.

It was noted in approval of this petitioner that "he makes an open and sincere impression."[108]

In order to be effective, statements of remorse had to be given with a certain amount of conviction. Wholly ineffectual was the equivocal admission of a petitioner who joined the Nazi Party in 1932.

> *Chairman:* On what grounds did you join the party in 1932?
> *Answer:* I believed that this was the best party.
> *Chairman:* And what opinion do you have now?
> *Answer:* Everything didn't turn out they way they promised us.
> *Chairman:* Oh, yes, unfortunately everything did turn out as promised! What else do you have for your exculpation?
> *Answer:* Absolutely nothing, I was never politically active.[109]

In another example, a petitioner who had joined the Nazi Party in 1933 failed to grasp the chance to make an admission of remorse when it was handed to him by a Calau commissioner:

> *SED:* You have never given any thought to the measures taken by the Nazis?

Answer: I must admit I haven't.
SED: What was your attitude toward the persecution of the Jews?
Answer: I did not concern myself with it very much.[110]

When it came to justifying one's past behavior, most petitioners had an excuse or an explanation; admissions of remorse were rare, and admissions of actual guilt were almost nonexistent. To hear the average petitioner tell it, no one had mistreated foreign workers or supported the persecution of the Jews, few had joined the Nazi Party out of conviction, and those who had quickly saw their error. The attitude of the general population was likewise unforthcoming; denazification was unpopular, and prosecution witnesses were hard to come by. In light of this situation, the denazification commissioners' task was unenviable. The VVN representative on the Ruppin commission probably spoke for many commissioners when he complained to a petitioner, "You sit here before antifascists, but we have had before this commission only a single case where everything was openly and freely admitted. It is really better if everything is openly and freely admitted, instead of saying, 'We were forced, we were under pressure, etc.'"[111]

In addition to remorse, commissions looked for evidence that former Nazis were taking an active part in reconstruction. Reconstruction encompassed both economics and politics. The term "reconstruction work" *(Aufbauarbeit)* can be broadly defined as including everything from assisting in the clearing of rubble to a shopkeeper's scrambling to reopen a business as quickly as possible after the end of the war. In short, the immediate goal after the end of the war was to return to a semblance of normalcy: petitioners who aided in the attainment of this goal were considered to have made at least partial amends for their past, while those who were judged uncooperative were suspected of still clinging to Nazi beliefs.

The political aspect of reconstruction was no less important than the economic. The commissions looked for evidence that petitioners had broken with their fascist past and had accommodated themselves to the "antifascist" present. A sense of remorse was one indicator of a political change of heart. There were also more concrete manifestations of political transformation; joining a postwar organization such as the FDGB or applying for membership in one of the political parties was looked on with favor by the commissioners. The commissioners also tried to determine what the PGs' attitudes were regarding the question of Germany's territorial and political future.

The ground rules for denazification, continually reiterated by the authorities, were simple: a minority would be classified as activists and punished, but the vast majority were declared nominal and would be given a chance to be reintegrated into society. In most cases, commissions assumed that nominals, having been chastised by their appearance before a commission, would go and sin no more. This public chastisement constituted the ritualistic element of the process. Petitioners were marked, as it were, by their past. Commissions singled these people out and compelled them to appear before an official body that enumerated their errors and passed judgment. Those found to have been activists were given the maximum penalty: they were stripped of the means of their livelihood and left to fend for themselves. Petitioners given conditional approval were shown mercy: they lost their positions but were allowed to continue, in a state of perpetual penance, to earn a living for themselves and their families. The nominals were granted absolution; they were free to reassume their position in society. This last recalls the double meaning attached to denazification during this period: the process not only cleansed society of active fascists but also cleansed those individuals who were granted absolution. In this way, Soviet denazification differed little from the U.S. program, wherein the goal of cleansing became, in Niethammer's term, "fused" with the concept of rehabilitation.[112]

One of the primary tests for reintegration of PGs into society was their willingness to help in the reconstruction. We have already seen, for example, how commissions were instructed to take the postwar activities of doctors and other health care workers into special consideration. Petitioners who could supply concrete evidence that they had willingly committed themselves to economic reconstruction were looked on favorably.[113] As with other types of evidence, the commissions' records often lack detail about what petitioners did to assist reconstruction. Notations such as "Cooperation in the democratic and political construction" or simply "Active in the reconstruction" are common.[114]

Some cases do mention specific activities. One positive indication of a willingness to participate in reconstruction was remaining at one's post immediately following the collapse of the Third Reich. Thus, a druggist was commended because "he had already opened his shop just ten days after the defeat" and a baker because, "immediately after the entrance of the Red Army, he began again to bake bread for the population."[115] In a rare allusion to the widespread rape of German women by Russian soldiers, a gynecologist was given credit for assisting in reconstruction because "he did not leave his clinic for a single hour and saved many women in Rheinsberg during the especially unfortunate state of affairs in Rheinsberg after the entrance of the Red Army."[116]

A few petitioners could not overcome their past affiliations even though they willingly participated in reconstruction, such as the veterinarian who had joined the SS in 1934, and a pharmacist who supplied the population with medicine immediately after the entry of the Red Army into the town, but who had joined the SA and the NSDAP in 1930.[117] Other petitioners had only a weak claim to participation in the reconstruction. Credit for reconstruction work did not extend, for example, to a bar owner who claimed that he was back at his post right after the war ended "continuously busy keeping the community supplied with beer."[118]

A final category of petitioners who were credited with participating in reconstruction were former POWs released from captivity in a western zone who returned to the Soviet zone. This act was seen as compelling exculpation: there are fifteen cases of returned POWs in the data sample, of which fourteen were approved while one was given conditional approval. The commissions' approval of these cases was a tacit recognition of the widespread distaste with which many Germans viewed developments in the Soviet zone. Having been released from captivity in a western zone, these POWs apparently had the option of remaining in the west. The fact that they had voluntarily returned to the Soviet zone was seen as a particularly strong indication that they supported the developments in the east. Whether or not the return of the POWs actually indicated support for the direction taken in the Soviet zone is impossible to determine; it was, of course, only natural that a POW would want to return to his hometown after release from captivity. Regardless, the commissions decided to interpret it as a vote of confidence in the system.

It was difficult for commissioners to determine petitioners' present political attitudes. Needless to say, few would openly admit that they rued the Third Reich's passing or had a negative attitude toward the SED or the Soviets. There was one concrete indicator of political attitude: membership in one of the postwar "antifascist" organizations established in the Soviet zone. Commissions were specifically instructed to consider current membership in such organizations as ex-culpating.[119] We have already seen that former HJ and BDM members could be upbraided by commissioners if they had failed to join a post-war organization. Nevertheless, a paltry number of petitioners in the data sample belonged to these organizations, and there is no correla-tion between membership in an organization and the commissions' decisions. There are 659 denied petitioners in the data sample, 58 (8.8 percent) of whom were in an "antifascist" organization. Surprisingly, the percentages are the same for the other petitions: of the 1,534 ap-proved petitioners, 126 (8.2 percent) were in organizations, as were 45 (9 percent) of the 499 petitioners conditionally approved. These low numbers may reflect the reluctance of petitioners to join an "anti-fascist" organization and also the reluctance of these organizations to accept members with an incriminating past.

Since most petitioners did not belong to an "antifascist" organiza-tion, commissioners had to rely on their interrogations to uncover current political attitudes. One approach was to ask a series of lead-ing questions in the hope that petitioners would slip up and incrimi-nate themselves. Provincial Commission chair Hentschel applied this technique in questioning a man who belonged to five Nazi organiza-tions. After a series of questions regarding the man's activities, Hent-schel observed, "But what a shame it is that this Reich collapsed, isn't it?" To which the unsuspecting petitioner answered, "Yes, indeed." Hentschel pushed further: "It really is rather regrettable." Hentschel's tone must have caught this hapless petitioner off guard, since he once again voiced his agreement. In rejecting the petition, the commission cited the petitioner's responses as concrete evidence that he was still supportive of Nazism.[120]

The majority of commissioners were in the SED, and, while it was not obvious in 1947 that the SED would become the leading party of a separate East German state, SED commissioners certainly wanted a socialist future for Germany. Some commissioners used the interroga-tion process to ferret out potential opponents of the SED. Only in rare cases, however, did the interrogations succeed in uncovering suspect opinions. One example is that of a PG who entered the NSDAP in 1931.

VVN: You joined the party in 1931. Why?
Answer: It was called a workers' party and we are all workers. That's why I joined.

VVN: Why didn't you join one of the other parties? There were others.
Answer: Yes, there were also the socialists.
VVN: Was it because you support the idea of private property?
Answer: What do you mean by that?
VVN: Let's just move on.[121]

In this case, the interrogation uncovered what the Provincial Commission considered an anti-socialist bias and the petition was denied. Similarly, it was noted in the case of a PG who joined the party in 1930, served as a *Blockwart,* and joined the SA in 1932 and held the position of *Scharführer* that "in answer to the question regarding his political affiliations and those of his wife, [he] answered that his wife was in a party, but that he did not know what it was called, the KPD or something like that. He has not yet heard of the unification of the socialist parties. From this answer, the commission determines he has a negative attitude and a complete lack of interest in present political life and the reconstruction.[122]

In many cases, the ritual of denazification required petitioners to give evidence that they were aware of and in agreement with the political system being built in the Soviet zone. This is evident in the Calau commission's interrogations of workers from the Schwarzheide synthetics plant. Consider the following examples of workers who successfully passed the commission's muster. First, a worker who joined the NSDAP in 1940 and belonged to two other National Socialist organizations.

SED: Where do you stand in relationship to the present state?
Answer: I am in agreement with the state.
SED: What do you mean by that?
DFB: Has something changed in the eastern zone?
Chairman: Say something more about this.
Answer: Yes, we have a democracy here.
DFB: What has changed here?
Answer: We have nationalized industries, the large landowners have been expropriated, in addition we have a land reform.
DFB: What is your opinion of that?
Answer: I think it is right, since many farmers have received land from it and that is better for us. We have expropriated the large landowners and they have become powerless . . .

DFB: But tell us, under whose protection have we been able to implement all of these measures?
Answer: Under the protection of the Red Army.[123]

A second example comes from the case of a skilled worker who joined the Nazi Party in 1942.

Chairman: What judgment can you make regarding the present time?
Answer: I started back at work right at the beginning.
Chairman: You should tell me what your attitude is toward the present state.
Answer: Good.
Chairman: Have you attended political meetings?
Answer: I always attend them.
Chairman: What are the differences between the east and west zones?
Answer: The reconstruction is moving forward here in a democratic way.
Chairman: Say it more precisely.
Answer: Production increases month by month.
Chairman: But there are other developments.
Answer: The workers are cared for.[124]

There are numerous examples similar to these. It is important to note that the Calau commission conducted this series of hearings at the synthetics plant in the final month of the denazification process. At this point in time, district commissions were under extraordinary pressure to process the backlog of cases quickly. During this period the Calau commission, which heard more cases during the Order 201 phase than any other district commission, raced through hearings at a breakneck speed, often giving less than five minutes' consideration to each case. In this heated atmosphere it is not surprising that the process took on a perfunctory and almost ritualistic aura.

The ritualistic nature of these interrogations is evident in the manner in which questions were posed. The workers were supposed to have attended political meetings at the plant and to have memorized their lessons. Like a panel of inquisitors, commissioners tested the pupils to determine the extent to which they had studied the new catechism. It is impossible to determine if petitioners actually believed what they said, but it is clear that they knew what they were supposed to say, and when they faltered, they were duly prompted by the commissioners to mouth the expected reply. A current of superficiality runs through many of these interrogations. No matter what their true opinions were, only the most foolish petitioners would have said that they thought expropriation was wrong or that the present political system was a sham. What were commissioners looking for in this ritual? The off chance that a petitioner would voice a genuine opinion and be unmasked as a fascist? Perhaps, but this rarely occurred. The most probable explanation lies in the denazification program itself. There were guidelines, deadlines, and a backlog of cases. In addition, one gets the sense that, particularly in the final months, the whole process had grown as distasteful to the commissioners as it had always been for petitioners. The best that could be made of this situation was to get it over with as soon as possible and to create a written record just in case someone might be held accountable for something in the future.

In addition to eliciting attitudes toward the SED and socialism in general, the commissioners also posed questions regarding the petitioners' attitudes toward the Soviet Union, both as an occupation power and as a model for a future political system. The reasoning behind this line of interrogation was similar to that behind the questions regarding the political system. If Germany was to have a socialist future, then attitudes toward the Soviet Union would reflect attitudes toward the SED and socialism in general. The Soviet Union had, of course, been the target of both Nazi aggression and a vitriolic propaganda campaign. It was reasonable to assume that an unrepentant Nazi would harbor anti-Soviet opinions. In addition, the Soviets as an occupation power suffered from what today would be called a serious public relations problem. The SED was also distrusted by many Germans, in large part owing to the party's close association with the occupation power. Thus, questions regarding attitudes toward the Soviets became part of the denazification ritual. Petitioners usually proved adept at seeing through this transparent line of questioning and came up with satisfactory answers. Naturally, the ultimate goal of most petitioners was to escape punishment, and just as they were unlikely to admit freely an activist Nazi past, they were similarly unlikely to express unfavorable impressions of the Soviets.

Typically, petitioners were directly asked, "What is your opinion of the occupation power and of the Soviet Union?" In the case of a painter who appeared before the Calau commission, the petitioner had learned his catechism well, as evidenced by his answer: "I realize that the Soviet Union only wants to do the best and also wants to promote our economy."[125] This interest in attitudes toward the new political system, the Soviets, and the evolving east-west confrontation came together in the Calau commission's questioning of a book dealer.

> *SED:* What is you attitude toward the Red Army?
> *Answer:* I stated in a public assembly in Senftenberg that we must follow a realistic politics and must be in good standing with the occupation power . . .
> *Chairman:* What is your understanding of "realistic politics"?
> *Answer:* We need to look at things soberly.
> *Chairman:* One could also gather from that, that you are inwardly in opposition to the present situation but out of necessity have adopted this position.
> *Answer:* That is not so. My idea of how to proceed is that the political parties need to unite around a common line. There shouldn't be any east or west orientations, only a German orientation. Germany can get back on its feet only if everyone is united.
> *FDGB:* United according to the proposals of the west or the east?
> *Answer:* I can't say whether or not the Soviet approach is applicable for us. The politics of the west can only bring us harm.[126]

The petition was only conditionally approved, probably owing to his less than enthusiastic opinion of the Soviets, although his disparaging of the west was in line with the answer the commissioners were seeking.

The picture that emerges from this investigation of the decision-making process is complex and not amenable to broad generalizations. That the commissions seriously considered a wide variety of evidence is indicative of the seriousness with which they often approached their task. If the commissions were simply bent on excluding PGs and replacing them with "antifascists," then why would they have engaged in the ritual of the hearing process, and, more to the point, why would they have approved the majority of petitions? The simplest answer, which has been reiterated throughout this study, is that there was no agreed-upon plan, and that commissions tended to judge cases on an individual basis.

The complexity of evidence not only slowed the process but also greatly complicated the task of assigning guilt and granting absolution. Although there were surely some demagogues and time servers on the commissions, many commissioners deserve credit for tackling this thankless task in a fair and thoughtful manner. In the final analysis, the cumulative effect of all of the evidence, combined with the interactions among the commissioners, witnesses, and petitioners on the day of the hearing, may have had a greater effect on the course of denazification than all of the policies handed down by the authorities.

Conclusion

East German historians claimed that denazification in the Soviet zone laid the groundwork for the creation of an "antifascist-democratic" state. On the other side of the Cold War divide, western proponents of the "Stalinization" thesis saw denazification in the east as part of a methodical imposition of a one-party dictatorship. Both of these views shared the assumption that denazification in the Soviet zone was a success. According to the "antifascist-democratic" model, denazification successfully purged the Soviet zone of Nazi influences, while according to the "Stalinization" model, denazification was successfully used to replace opponents of the SED with willing supporters. Both of these models are subject to revision in light of the example of the purge in Brandenburg.

The "Antifascist-Democratic" Model

Although GDR historians did produce worthwhile studies, much of their work on the postwar period, and on the denazification in particular, is destined to be disregarded by future scholars. It was, after all, in studies of the postwar period that the SED's instrumentalization of history was most pronounced, since the history of this period was also the history of the GDR itself. A close examination of denazification in Brandenburg offers little support for the East German interpretation of events.

First, there is the claim that the communist critique of fascism was correct and that it led to the development of an effective denazification. This was not the case: the ideology that informed the Soviet program actually hindered successful implementation of the purge. The most problematic aspects of denazification in the Soviet zone had their roots in the contradictions born of the communist critique of fascism. This includes the conflict between the concepts of collective and individual guilt, the lack of an effective means to differentiate between nominal PGs and Nazi activists, and the confusion surrounding the manner in which nominal PGs could be reintegrated into society. Likewise, the East German claim that leadership of the Soviets and the KPD/SED assured the success of the purge holds little water. The leadership had only weak control over developments, and this weakness was exacerbated by the issuance of contradictory and confusing policies. Finally, there is no support for the argument that the denazification represented an adequate purge of Nazism in the east, since the vast majority of those who fell under the terms of denazification were never touched by the program.

What remains of the "antifascist-democratic" model is the claim that, of all the occupation powers, the Soviets implemented the most successful denazification. The roots of this claim lay in the role that denazification played in the Allies' disputes during the occupation period. Soviet Foreign Minister Molotov, for example, was fond of comparing the total number of people purged in the Soviet zone with similar numbers from the west. East German historians followed suit by deploying detailed accountings of the number of people purged in order to prove the thoroughness of the Soviet program. This argument falters on several grounds. First, as we have seen in the case of Brandenburg, it cannot be assumed that those ordered dismissed from their positions were actually fired. Second, there was inadequate tracking of dismissed workers to prevent their reemployment in similar positions. Finally, there was the widespread use of the reclassification of workers, which in practice resulted in little or no change in many petitioners' occupations. There is sufficient evidence to assume that the government statistics on the number of people purged were inflated, although to what degree is probably impossible to determine. More to the point, the total number of people purged does not obscure the fact that the policy makers themselves were dissatisfied with the results of the program and that they decided to bring denazification to a sudden conclusion because of its perceived failings.

The "Stalinization" Model

The East German interpretation loses much of its explanatory force when tested against the evidence from Brandenburg. The same holds true for the western Stalinization model. As the example of Brandenburg shows, historical interpretations that place denazification in the context of a general Stalinization of the eastern zone are oversimplified. A close look at the transformation of Soviet policy does not reveal a master plan for the imposition of one-party rule, but rather shows a pattern of indecision born of unclear policy goals, faulty lines of communication, and a lack of centralized control. The German political leadership labored under similar constraints, both because of its own ideological and organizational problems and because it was saddled with implementing unclear polices formulated by the Soviets. The same holds for the provincial leadership, which was ultimately responsible for making sense of the often contradictory polices. In short, denazification, which may appear monolithic and single-minded from a distance, is on close examination revealed as a process beset by confusion and contradiction.

In the first place, there were the ideological contradictions that resulted from the communist critique of fascism. An analysis based on historical materialism resulted in a sweeping critique that included the political, social, and cultural development of National Socialism and the Third Reich. At the same time, Leninist tactics demanded action. In short, historical materialism suggested an approach to denazification that was massive in its proportions and unamenable to short-term solutions, while Leninist tactics required a rapid seizure of power. How could a purge rectify this situation? A comparison of the ideas of Ulbricht and Becher outlines the possible solutions. Ulbricht's approach was to use the purge to seize state power. Becher, by contrast, envisioned a long-term transformation of German society and culture. At the beginning, denazification policy attempted to encompass both of these goals. The result was a confusing set of policies that combined calls for differentiation between levels of guilt with a stubborn obsession with the collective guilt of all Germans. This contradiction was never resolved, and in the end, the consolidation of state power became the primary policy goal.

This ultimate privileging of *Realpolitik* over social and cultural transformation was tied to the incompatibility of the purge and reconstruction. At first, the policy makers thought that they could simultaneously conduct a purge and rapidly rebuild the administration and economy. The incompatibility of these twin goals was manifest from the beginning. The idea that a complete political purge was more important than a smoothly functioning administration was short-lived. The same was true for the economy: there were simply too many irreplaceable PGs and not enough well-trained "antifascists." In the end, the contradiction between the purge and reconstruction was solved by ending the purge and concentrating on reconstruction. The swiftness of this transformation is remarkable: at the beginning of denazification, ideological purity was paramount, and yet, less than three years later, Ulbricht observed that consideration of people's past political beliefs was "ancient history," which had no bearing on future socialist construction.

The contradiction between the purge and reconstruction was at the heart of the "problem of the PGs." Was the goal of denazification punishment for past behavior or the reintegration of the PGs into society and reconstruction? At first the desire for retribution held sway. The result was the creation of a "second class" of citizens with limited civil rights. This was an economic and political problem for the SED. Continually threatened with expropriation and other forms of punishment, the PGs withdrew from economic life and, in many cases, fled the Soviet zone. Politically, the pattern of retribution that developed during the first years of the occupation threatened to transform the alienation felt by a large segment of the population into active opposition. Order 201 was to be the solution to these problems. With the release of Order 201, reintegration of the PGs into society took precedence over punishment of past behavior.

Order 201 represented the point at which Soviet denazification policy began to mirror the polices adopted in the western zones, and in the U.S. zone in particular. Developments on the international level propelled this transformation. By mid-1947, Allied unity and cooperation had been shattered. For Germany, this portended a future of division into two states set within competing ideological and political systems. In both the east and the west, denazification became a means of incorporating the Germans into these opposing ideological camps. This is precisely what Niethammer claimed occurred in the U.S. zone: antifascism was replaced by anticommunism and denazification was utilized as a means of bringing closure to the Nazi period in order to rally the west Germans for the Cold War confrontation. Something similar occurred in the Soviet zone. The chief difference is that here the concept of antifascism was not dropped, but instead was transformed into the primary legitimization for incorporating the east Germans into the Soviet struggle against the west. The concept of antifascism remained because of the so-called "fascist restoration" in the west, that is, the claim that German fascism had not been crushed but was alive and well in the west, and that the struggle against fascism would continue, with the German antifascist state in the east at the forefront.

Contradiction also lay at the heart of the denazification commission system that gave decision-making power to local actors. This essentially decentralized system proved impervious to control from above. This not only explains why denazification came to a sudden end in 1948, but also calls into question the idea that the commissions were part of the establishment of communist domination in the eastern zone. The manner in which the commissions considered the evidence in individual cases indicates that they often took their mandate to weigh incriminating and exculpating circumstances seriously. The variety of evidence considered in the process, and the relative weight assigned to different forms of evidence by the commissions, shows that denazification cannot be seen simply as part of a process of Stalinization. Clearly, there are many examples of politically biased decisions taken by the commissions, but there are also as many or more examples that display fairness, compassion, and a sense of justice.

In addition, there are the results of the denazification commission process. The high approval rate of petitions supports the contention that the denazification program became a primary means of reintegrating the PGs into society. It should be recalled, however, that on the policy level, the reintegrative aspect of denazification came to the fore only during the Order 201 phase. Nevertheless, the approval rates were essentially the same—and high—both before and after Order 201. It could be argued that the reintegrative aspects of denazification were first revealed by the commission process and then later adopted by the policy makers.

The system of local commissions was the reason for this development. By placing the decision-making power in the hands of local commissioners, Soviet policy ensured that the purge would be implemented within the matrix of local norms, interpersonal relationships, and shared values and experiences. The commissioners based their decisions on a complex set of variables, which included testimony from witnesses, written evidence, the demeanor of the petitioners, and the commissioners' own perceptions and memories of everyday life during the Nazi period. The variations in the decisions of the individual commissions, the lack of correlation between the political composition of the commissions and their decisions, and the administrative and organizational problems that plagued the process were all by-products of a program that placed decision making in the hands of local actors.

A further point concerns the connection between the occupations of the petitioners and the decisions of the commissions. The evidence from Brandenburg suggests that the connection between one's occupation and the denazification process is not as strong as historians previously assumed. Certain occupational groups were clearly targeted, and different standards were applied to the various groups. Nevertheless, given the complex set of variables considered in each case, it is impossible to regard any one variable as the determining factor in the decisions. The question of occupations also goes to the heart of the Stalinization thesis. The prime example is the treatment of tradespeople and shop owners. The majority of these petitioners were allowed to continue in their lines of work despite their National Socialist backgrounds. If the purge had been a jobs program for "antifascists," one would have expected to see a mass revocation of business licenses and their transfer to supporters of the regime. That this did not occur indicates that the commissions based their decisions on many factors, of which the occupation of the petitioner was only one.

Denazification East and West: A Comparison

Soviet denazification should not be treated as something fundamentally different from what occurred in the western zones. Although there were clear differences in policy, the challenge was the same throughout Germany: to restore a civic and political order in a defeated, destroyed, and occupied country with a shared National Socialist past.

Before the collapse of the East German state, developments during the Soviet occupation period constituted a missing link in historical understanding which prevented comparative analysis of developments between the eastern and western zones. It is now possible to make some initial observations regarding a comparison of eastern and western denazification. This comparative approach also points to a fruitful field for future research: a redirection of historical analysis away from studies of the separate occupation zones and toward a conceptualization of the occupation period as part of postwar German history as a whole. Up to this point, studies of the years 1945–1949 have treated events in the western and eastern zones as two fundamentally different stories. This conceptual east-west divide is a natural result of the division of Germany into two separate countries in 1949. Clearly, beginning in the occupation period, east and west Germany were on two diverging trajectories. Nevertheless, there were aspects of the occupation period that had an effect on all Germans, regardless of which occupation zone they happened to find themselves residing in.

Denazification, or, to put it more broadly, the legacy of Nazi rule and the need to do something about it, was one issue that transcended zonal boundaries during the occupation period. At the beginning, all four occupying powers were in agreement concerning the necessity of a purge of Nazi influences. Early on, the targets of the purge were separated into a small group of war criminals who would be arrested and tried, and a much larger group—potentially numbering in the millions—who would be liable for denazification. By the time of the release of the Allied Control Council's Directive 24 in January 1946, a consensus had formed in favor of the U.S. proposal that the centerpiece of denazification should be the dismissal from their jobs of the bearers of Nazism and militarism.

Although the details of the purge in the four occupation zones differed, there were remarkable similarities in all zones that allow us to consider denazification as a distinct episode in postwar German history, that is, as a historical development that transcended zonal boundaries. As always, the devil is in the details, and the present study has made much of the contention that a clear understanding of how the purge was actually implemented can only be based on a careful examination of events at the local level. We can, however, accept the importance of local developments and still look for the lessons offered by a general overview. Assuming then a macro as opposed to a micro viewpoint, we can discern the outlines of a general picture of postwar denazification on a Germany-wide basis.

In the first place, it was the Allies' critiques of Nazism, and the "German problem" in general, which formed the basis for policy. The western Allies did not share the communist critique of fascism developed before and during the war. There would have been little agreement among western policy makers with Ulbricht's analysis of the German problem or with his goal of creating socialism as a permanent antidote against the reemergence of German fascism. Much of Johannes Becher's analysis, however, would have garnered broad agreement in the west. Becher's version of a *Sonderweg,* or special path of development of German society and political culture, was echoed in western planning for postwar Germany. There was broad agreement among all the Allies that, historically, the path of Germany differed from that of normative development in the west and that the nascent liberalism of the nineteenth century had been smothered in its infancy by antidemocratic conservative elites. The relatively recent historical debates over the usefulness of the *Sonderweg* thesis were not anticipated in Allied planning. Instead, the nefarious influence of Prussian militarism on German political culture, the Germans' alleged inability to practice effective democracy, their xenophobic nationalism, their worship of the state, and their slavish obedience of authority were all components of a conception of Germany and the Germans universally shared by Allied planners. Indeed, a central aspect of the communist critique of Nazism—the connection between conservative elites, big business, and fascism—was also enshrined in the Allies' plans for the "decartelization" of German industry. The best summation of Allied analysis of the German problem circa 1945 were the "Four D's" of the Potsdam Agreement: decartelization, demilitarization, denazification, and democratization.

A second aspect of denazification shared by all the Allies was the mechanics of the purge itself. Here the influence of American planning and the U.S. model for conducting a purge were paramount. Denazification in all four zones shared the following characteristics: an employment-based purge in which the ultimate punishment was dismissal; the use of a questionnaire—the notorious *Fragebogen*—that formed the basis for judging an individual's past; and an increasing reliance on German-staffed denazification commissions whose decisions were ultimately subject to final approval by occupation authorities.

Given their similarities, it is not surprising that the denazification in all four zones suffered from the same set of problems. Developing a reliable means for determining degrees of guilt remained an elusive goal. Likewise, in all zones there was constant friction between the expectations of the occupation authorities and the results of the purge implemented by German-staffed commissions. The fundamental contradiction between the purge and reconstruction was also evident throughout Germany. Thus, one can point to a general pattern in the course of denazification applicable to every zone. First came an initial period of rash dismissals, decreed by the occupation authorities, with the goal of purging the administrative apparatus. Underlying this wave of dismissals was a shared desire for revenge in the wake of the bitter military struggle against the Third Reich. This was followed by a reassessment, a general pulling back from the initial slash-and-burn techniques, and the recognition of the need for a more long-term approach. It was at this point that an understanding of the contradiction between a purge and reconstruction took hold. This was followed by a codification of guidelines for a further purge and, inevitably, the realization that a thorough purge could not be implemented without a prominent role being assigned to the Germans themselves. Lastly, there was the ending of the purge: a steady unraveling of the program, a realization that initial goals were too ambitious and would never be met, and then a messy conclusion accompanied by recrimination, regret, and a general sigh of relief—on the part of both occupiers and occupied—that, for better or worse, the whole ugly business had finally been put to rest.

There was, however, one general difference between the eastern zone and the western zones that had a far-reaching effect on the development of policy: the democratic traditions of the western powers versus the Soviets' lack of similar traditions. One of the hallmarks of democracy is public opinion, the existence of systemic avenues for its articulation, and the expectation that policy makers will take pubic opinion into account. On the democratic side, the western occupation authorities constantly found themselves forced to take domestic public opinion into account, and western occupation policies—including denazification policies—were altered in response. In contrast, public opinion in the Soviet Union had no discernible effect on the development of occupation policy. The absence of a free press and a democratic political system in the Soviet Union left the Soviet occupation authorities free to formulate policy without concern for reaction in the Soviet Union itself.

Likewise, there were no effective avenues for Germans living in the Soviet zone to express negative evaluations of the Soviets' denazification program. At a time when German newspapers in the western zones regularly criticized the failures of denazification, newspapers in the Soviet zone were limited to criticizing the western programs and lauding the Soviet approach. This east-west distinction also marked the conclusion of the denazification programs: the western programs were barraged with negative evaluations, while the Soviets and the SED were able to trumpet their successes without opposition. The influence of democracy and avenues for dissent cannot be overlooked in any comparative evaluation of Soviet and western denazification.

The Historical Significance of Denazification

For all their weaknesses, the "antifascist-democratic" and "Stalinization" interpretive models did give Soviet denazification a historical significance in the context of later developments. In the "antifascist-democratic" model, Soviet denazification was part of the successful creation of East German socialism; in the "Stalinization" model, the same denazification was linked to the implementation of one-party rule in the east. Casting doubt on the usefulness of these interpretive models begs the question of how Soviet denazification fits into the broader context of postwar German history.

On the most general level, Soviet denazification can be understood as part of an attempt by all of the occupation powers to eliminate what were seen as Nazi influences in the German administration, economy, and social structure. The simple fact is that, in the forty years following the foundation of the two states, neither East nor West Germany saw a significant resurgence of National Socialism. This is not to discount the real appearance of so-called "neo-Nazism," but rather to observe that the desire of the Allies to prevent the reemergence of a National Socialist–style dictatorship and a German state that posed a military threat to its neighbors and to world peace was met.

Did denazification rid the German administration of Nazi influences? The answer would be a qualified yes, if denazification is broadly defined as all of the purge activities that occurred between the end of the war and the founding of the two states in 1949. There is no question that, in all zones, the occupation period saw the removal of thousands of former PGs from responsible administrative positions. This does not mean, however, that former Nazis did not continue to hold responsible positions in both East and West Germany. During the Cold War, so-called Brown Books were produced in both states listing former Nazis who continued to hold responsible positions in East and West Germany. Despite the presence of individual former PGs in the administration of both states, it would be incorrect to argue that any significant "re-nazification" occurred in either state. Again, to reiterate, neither East nor West Germany showed tangible evidence that the influence of former PGs in government actually moved the states toward a reintroduction of National Socialism.

In West Germany, for example, the leftist "extraparliamentary opposition" argued that the so-called Grand Coalition, headed by ex-Nazi chancellor Kurt Kiesinger (1966–1969), was evidence of a Nazi-style subversion of the democratic system. The West German electorate's subsequent move toward the left, and the succeeding SPD-led governments of Willy Brandt and Helmut Schmidt, showed leftist fears of "re-nazification" to have been overstated. Indeed, throughout its history as "West" Germany, the FRG proved to be one of the world's most vibrant and stable democracies.

In the case of East Germany, as post-reunification debates about the "totalitarian" nature of the GDR have indicated, superficially at least there were more points of comparison with the Third Reich. Among the most prominent similarities were the one-party state, the presence of ubiquitous secret police forces and their networks of informants, and a ruling political party that controlled social and cultural life. As critics of the neo-totalitarian analyses of the GDR have pointed out, however, such analogies between the GDR and the Third Reich do not hold up under close scrutiny. For example, the model for the SED's one-party state was not the Third Reich but rather the Soviet system and the pattern of rule that emerged in the Warsaw Pact countries. Likewise, although both the Third Reich and the GDR embraced a totalizing ideology as the basis for governance and social organization, there are vast differences between the GDR's brand of Marxism and the Third Reich's racist *Weltanschauung*. Although many charges may be laid at the GDR's doorstep, that of Nazism is certainly invalid.

We can now turn to consideration of one of postwar Germany's main obsessions: "coming to terms" with its National Socialist past and, more to the point of the present study, the connection between this confrontation with the past and Allied denazification. Did denazification represent an adequate "coming to terms" with Germany's National Socialist past? To approach this thorny question, it is important first to clarify what is being asked. It should be stated at the outset that, despite all of the ink which has been spilled during the years of debate over this topic, there is still no consensus concerning what an adequate coming to terms would ultimately involve. One tangible measure, discussed earlier, would be if Germany had shown evidence of backsliding toward a restoration of Nazism and its ways. To date this has not occurred, although some would point with alarm to the appearance of post-reunification neo-Nazism and xenophobia as evidence that the threat still remains.

Another measure would be the extent to which public discourse, both prompted and permitted by the West and East German governments, allowed for a wide-ranging debate, if not a solution, to the question of coming to terms. In his 1997 study of this issue, Jeffrey Herf argues that on balance the West Germans at least facilitated a society-wide debate concerning a reckoning with the past, while the East Germans made the issue effectively taboo.[1] The short answer to why this was so would be democracy: its presence in the west and absence in the east. In the FRG a myriad of questions such as coming to terms with the past were openly debated. Indeed, the entire matter of coming to terms with the past can be seen as a product of the FRG's open democratic system. In East Germany, by contrast, a host of issues, not just the Nazi past, were proscribed by a system obsessed with controlling public debate.

It is at this level of public discourse that the legacy of postwar denazification connects to the problem of coming to terms with the past. In West Germany, historians were free to produce critical analyses of denazification, and the public at large was likewise free to debate the meaning of the Allied program. The result was an impressive body of historical work and the continuing presence of the legacy of denazification in public debate concerning this coming to terms. In East Germany, the production of history was tightly controlled and public debate severely restricted. The result was not only a lack of critical studies of denazification but also a profound silence on all of the issues that revolved around a coming to terms with the past. This comparison can be put in a different way: in West Germany postwar denazification was roundly criticized as inadequate, which meant that the question of coming to terms with the past was still open. In East Germany the Soviet denazification program was lauded as a success, the "antifascist" nature of the state was enshrined, and any further debate was out of the question.

There is another level of the "coming to terms" debate that is more diffuse but nonetheless present. We have seen that denazification, as it developed in the eastern and western zones, increasingly carried with it an exculpatory function. On the individual level, this meant that those who did go through the process were effectively absolved for their past behavior. Those thus absolved could then avoid, if they were so disposed, any further personal confrontation with their own past. On a broader level, the conclusion of the denazification programs meant that the millions of PGs who were never called before a commission could similarly comfort themselves with the thought that their pasts would remain unexamined. This is the sort of blanket exception that Johannes Becher thought could be avoided through a denazification that aimed at both punishing the guilty and bringing about a truly "antifascist" social transformation. All of the denazification programs were concluded far short of such an ambitious goal.

Appendix: Data Sample

In 1947–48, there were thirty-one commissions operating simultaneously in Brandenburg that together processed tens of thousands of cases. It was not possible to research the records of all of these commissions. Four commissions were selected for analysis: the district commissions in Calau, Ostprignitz, and Ruppin, and the Provincial Commission in Potsdam.

The three districts of Calau, Ostprignitz, and Neuruppin represent some of the geographic, economic, and political diversity of Brandenburg. During the occupation period, Calau was the most industrialized district in predominantly rural Brandenburg. *Kreis* Calau is home to the brown coal industry of the Niederlausitz, and the close proximity of this energy source resulted in industrial growth, particularly glass manufacture and textiles. In contrast, the northern district of Ostprignitz represents the agricultural nature of much of Brandenburg. Previously an area with significant large landholdings, Ostprignitz was chosen, in 1945, to be the site of the first symbolic transfer of expropriated land to "new" farmers under the land reform. Politically, however, Ostprignitz was an anomaly: the *Landrat* elected in 1946 was a member of the CDU, only one of two non-SED *Landräte* in the province. Situated immediately to the east of Ostprignitz, the district of Ruppin was in many ways similar, aside from the fact that the *Landrat* was a member of the SED. Ruppin is a particularly attractive district for historical research because the archives of the *Landrat's* office are larger than the archives of other districts in Brandenburg. Table A.1 provides a comparison of the size, population, and population density of the three districts. As shown in the table, the population density of the industrialized Calau district was twice that of the two rural districts. A survey from October 1945 underscores this difference: Calau reported a total of 1,913 industrial, trade, and craft concerns, while Ostprignitz reported 350 and Ruppin 236 (BLHA, Rep. 206, 3064, Bl. 23, 52, 58).

In addition to these three districts, the Provincial Commission was chosen as a check on the regional variations of the districts. Unlike district commissions, which heard only petitions from individuals residing in the district, the Provincial Commission heard petitions from throughout the province. In addition, the Provincial Commission was under the direct control of the Interior Ministry, and its methods of operation closely mirrored the ideal approach to denazification intended by the policy makers in Potsdam.

Methodology

Three types of cases are *not* included in this sample: (1) cases in which it was determined that the individual did not fall under the terms of the denazification; (2) cases in which no decision was reached owing, for example, to a lack of evidence or missing documents; (3) cases in which the record is unclear as to what decision was ultimately reached. It should be noted that the Interior Ministry's statistics do

Table A.1 Area, population, and population density of sample districts (as of 29 October 1946)

District	Total area (in sq. km)	Total population	Population density (per sq. km)
Calau	989.33	130,548	132.0
Ostprignitz	1,786.44	98,673	55.2
Ruppin	1,929.47	124,836	64.7
Landkreise average	1,316.70	104,270	85.6
Province total	26,976.42	2,527,492	93.7

Source: Deutsche Wirtschaftskommission für die sowjetische Besatzungszone Statistisches Zentralamt, *Volks- und Berufszählung vom 29. Oktober 1946* (Berlin: Deutscher Zentralverlag, 1948).

not always tally with the numbers taken from the *Protokolle*. This may be due to adjustments made to the records after they were submitted to the provincial government. All of the data in this sample were taken from the *Protokolle* produced by the commissions on the day of the hearing.

Because of the large number of hearings conducted by the Provincial Commission, only a random selection of records could be included; for the Directive 24 phase, the first fifteen hearings and the last fifteen were chosen. The numbering of the last fifteen varies because often several hearings were conducted simultaneously (in the files these records are labeled 161, 161a, 161b). For the Order 201 phase, only the first eleven records were used; much of the caseload of the Provincial Commission during this period was made up of appeals of cases already decided by the *Kreis* commissions.

For the three *Kreis* commissions, all of the hearings conducted during the Directive 24 phase are included in the sample, with the exception of hearing number 40 of the Ruppin commission, which is missing from the file.

There were many more hearings conducted during the Order 201 phase by the *Kreis* commissions, necessitating a random sampling. For Calau, the first ten hearings and the last eight are used. For Ostprignitz and Ruppin, the first ten hearings and the last ten are used.

Sources

The source material used in the data sample was taken from records at the Brandenburgisches Landeshauptarchiv in Potsdam. The archives of the Interior Ministry (Ministerium des Innern) are catalogued under Rep. 203. These archives are indexed in the *Findbuch* for this repository. Most of the records from the denazification hearings, however, are cataloged separately under Rep. 203, Entnazifizierung. These records are not included in the *Findbuch* and are catalogued separately in a card file *(Kartei)*.

For each hearing, a record *(Protokoll)* was produced giving the names of the commission members who were present, where and when the hearing took place, and the details about each individual case. Since every individual who appeared before a commission was required to file a petition *(Antrag)* for denazification, the individual cases are numbered in the records in the order in which the petitions were presented. In the footnotes of this study, P is used as an abbreviation for the *Protokoll* number, and A is used as an abbreviation for the *Antrag* number. For example, the first petition heard at the first hearing of the Calau commission is cited as BLHA, Rep. 203, Entnazifizierung, 71, P1, A1, 15 January 1947.

Future researchers should note that the protocols often misnumbered the petitions or numbered the petitions in groups. For example, a protocol might note that the next ten petitions were from a particular business firm in the district and these would be numbered 1–10. Then the protocol would note that the following ten petitions were from another business in the district, and these would also be numbered 1–10. In order to avoid confusion, in the footnotes to this study the petitions are numbered in the order in which they were heard, *not* according to the number listed in the records. Thus, to go back to our example, the first petition from the second group of ten petitions is referred to as number 11.

Hearing Records Used in the Data Sample

Provincial Commission, Directive 24 phase: BLHA, Rep. 203, 584, Protokoll 2 (7 January 1947)–Protokoll 15 (14 February 1947); Protokoll 17 (18 February 1947); BLHA, Rep. 203, 584: Protokoll 155 (18 August 1947)–Protokoll 156 (19 August 1947); BLHA, Rep. 203, 594, Protokoll 157 (20 August 1947)–Protokoll 163 (29 August 1947); BLHA, Rep. 203, 596, Protokoll 169 (5 September 1947).

Provincial Commission, Order 201 phase: BLHA, Rep. 203, Entnazifizierung, 647, Protokoll 1 (25 September 1947)–Protokoll 7 (8 October 1947); BLHA, Rep. 203, Entnazifizierung, 648, Protokoll 8 (9 October 1947)–Protokoll 11 (15 October 1947).

Calau Commission, Directive 24 phase: BLHA, Rep. 203, Entnazifizierung, 71, Protokoll 1 (15 January 1947)–Protokoll 12 (13 August 1947).

Calau Commission, Order 201 phase: BLHA, Rep. 203, Entnazifizierung, 798, Protokoll 1 (7 October 1947)–Protokoll 10 (6 November 1947); BLHA, Rep. 203, Entnazifizierung, 801, Protokoll 71 (23 February 1948); Protokoll 83 (3 March 1948)–Protokoll 86 (4 March 1948); Protokoll 88 (6 March 1948)–Protokoll 90 (8 March 1948).

Ostprignitz Commission, Directive 24 phase: BLHA, Rep. 203, Entnazifizierung, 371, Protokoll 2 (20 January 1947)–Protokoll 42 (30 September 1947).

Ostprignitz Commission, Order 201 phase: BLHA, Rep. 203, Entnazifizierung, 1429, Protokoll 1 (7 October 1947)–Protokoll 10 (1 November 1947); BLHA, Rep. 203, Entnazifizierung, 1431, Protokoll 34 (22 December 1947)–Protokoll 43 (5 March 1948).

Ruppin Commission, Directive 24 phase: BLHA, Rep. 203, Entnazifizierung, 431, Protokoll 1 (3 January 1947)–Protokoll 39 (28 July 1947); Protokoll 41 (25 August 1947).

Ruppin Commission, Order 201 phase: BLHA, Rep. 203, Entnazifizierung, 1582, Protokoll 1 (30 September 1947)–Protokoll 10 (28 October 1947); BLHA, Rep. 203, Entnazifizierung, 1583, Protokoll 36 (26 February 1948)–Protokoll 45 (10 March 1948).

Notes

Introduction

1. SAPMO-BA, IV, 2/13, 109, Walter Ulbricht, "Die gegenwärtige Lage und die nächsten Aufgaben," speech before the Interior Ministers' Conference held 31 January–1 February 1947.
2. Figures for the total number of people dismissed range from 408,569 to 520,000. See Helga Welsh, "'Antifaschistisch-demokratische Umwälzung' und politische Säuberung in der sowjetischen Besatzungszone Deutschlands," in Klaus-Dietmar Henke and Hans Woller, eds., *Politische Säuberung in Europa: Die Abrechnung mit Faschismus und Kollaboration nach dem Zweiten Weltkrieg* (Munich: Deutscher Taschenbuch Verlag, 1991), 95. A census of October 1946 put the total population of the Soviet zone at 17.3 million. See Deutsche Wirtschaftskommission für die sowjetische Besatzungszone Statistisches Zentralamt, *Volks- und Berufszählung vom 29. Oktober 1946* (Berlin: Deutscher Zentralverlag, 1948), 1:6.
3. In contrast to the western zones, monetary fines were not levied in the Soviet zone. For an overview of Allied programs, see Clemens Vollnhals, *Entnazifizierung: Politische Säuberung und Rehabilitierung in den vier Besatzungszonen, 1945–1949* (Munich: Deutscher Taschenbuch Verlag, 1991), 7–64.
4. F. Roy Willis, *The French in Germany, 1945–1949* (Stanford: Stanford University Press, 1962) chap. 2.
5. Ibid., 178.
6. Ranier Möhler, *Entnazifizierung in Rheinland-Pfalz und im Saarland unter französischer Besatzung von 1945 bis 1952* (Mainz: v. Hase & Koehler Verlag, 1992), 23–25; Reinhard Grohnert, *Die Entnazifizierung in Baden,*

1945–1949: Kozeptionen und Praxis der "Epuration" am Beispiel eines Landes der französischen Besatzungszone (Stuttgart: W. Kohlhammer Verlag, 1991).

7. Möhler, *Entnazifizierung in Rheinland-Pfalz,* 410.

8. Grohnert, *Die Entnazifizierung in Baden,* 217–218.

9. Nicholas Pronay, "Introduction: 'To Stamp Out the Whole Tradition . . .,'" in Nicholas Pronay and Keith Wilson, eds., *The Political Re-education of Germany and Her Allies after World War II* (London: Croom Helm, 1985), 1.

10. David Welch, "Priming the Pump of German Democracy: British 'Re-education' Policy in Germany after the Second World War," in Ian D. Turner, ed., *British Occupation Policy and the Western Zones, 1945–55* (Oxford: Berg, 1989), 221.

11. Ibid., 237.

12. Ian D. Turner, "Denazification in the British Zone," in Turner, *British Occupation Policy and the Western Zones,* 261.

13. Ibid., 250.

14. In contrast to the traditionally negative assessments of U.S. denazification, see the comments of Hans Woller, "Germany in Transition from Stalingrad (1943) to Currency Reform (1948)," in Michael Ermarth, ed., *America and the Shaping of German Society, 1945–1955* (Providence: Berg, 1993), 34.

15. Pronay, "Introduction," 3.

16. The fullest investigation of American analyses of fascism can be found in Lutz Niethammer, *Die Mitläuferfabrik: Die Entnazifizierung am Beispiel Bayerns* (Berlin: W. Dietz, 1982).

17. Woller, "Germany in Transition," 34.

18. On the post-reunification debate, see Konrad H. Jarausch, ed., *Zwischen Parteilichkeit und Professionalität: Bilanz der Geschichtswissenschaft der DDR* (Berlin: Akademie Verlag, 1991).

19. Hermann Weber, a longtime critic of the East German historical profession, wrote a series of articles criticizing the SED's instrumentalization of history. See Hermann Weber, "Die DDR-Geschichtswissenschaft im Umbruch? Aufgaben der Historiker bei der Bewältigung der stalinistischen Vergangenheit," *Deutschland Archiv* 23 (1990): 1058–70; "Die Stalinismus-Diskussion geht weiter: Widerspruchsvolle 'Aufarbeitung' der Geschichte in der DDR," *Deutschland Archiv* 23 (1990): 1259–66; and "Werden DDR-Geschichtswissenschaft und Marxismus plattgewalzt und ausgemerzt? Die Zeitgeschichtsforschung in der ehemaligen DDR ist noch immer widersprüchlich," *Deutschland Archiv* 24 (1991): 246–257. Former members of the East German historical community have also been critical of their profession. See Heinz Heitzer, "Für eine radikale Erneuerung der Geschichtsschreibung über die DDR," *Zeitschrift für Geschichtswissenschaft* 38 (1990): 498–509. Another East German historian responded directly to Weber's criticisms, arguing that rejection of the Stalinist aspects of GDR

historiography should not lead to a wholesale rejection of Marxist analysis. See Dieter Engelmann, "Vae victis!? Oder: Zur Kritik an der marxistischen Geschichtsschreibung der ehemaligen DDR," *Deutschland Archiv* 24 (1991): 73–78. For a less polemical but still critical view of East German historiography, see Konrad H. Jarausch, "The Failure of East German Antifascism: Some Ironies of History as Politics," *German Studies Review* 14 (1991): 85–102.

20. Norman Naimark, "Politik und Geschichtswissenschaft im osteuropäischen Kontext," in Jarausch, *Zwischen Parteilichkeit und Professionalität*, 135.

21. Institut für Marxismus-Leninismus beim Zentralkomitee der SED, *Geschichte der deutschen Arbeiterbewegung*, 15 vols. (Berlin: Dietz Verlag, 1966–1969).

22. Ibid., 10:55. This analysis was based on the critique of fascism laid down at the Seventh Comintern Congress in 1935. See Gregori Dimitrov, "The Fascist Offensive and the Tasks of the Communist International," *VII Congress of the Communist International: Abridged Stenographic Report of Proceedings* (Moscow: Foreign Languages Publishing House, 1939), 126–127.

23. See, for example, Stefan Doernberg, *Kurze Gesichichte der DDR* (Berlin: Dietz Verlag, 1965), 86–88; Rolf Badstübner, "The Allied Four-Power Administration and Sociopolitical Development in Germany," *German History* 7 (1989): 30–31; Wolfgang Meinicke, "Die Entnazifizierung in der sowjetischen Besatzungszone 1945 bis 1948," *Zeitschrift für Geschichtswissenschaft* 32 (1984): 970.

24. Stefan Doernberg, *Die Geburt eines neuen Deutschland, 1945–1949: Die antifaschistisch-demokratische Umwälzung und die Entstehung der DDR* (Berlin: Rütten & Loening, 1959), 91, 97

25. This interpretation appears in other East German works. See Institut für Marxismus-Leninismus, *Geschichte der Sozialistischen Einheitspartei Deutschlands: Abriß* (Berlin: Dietz Verlag, 1978), 133; Siegfried Thomas, "1945–1949," in Rolf Badstübner et al., *DDR Werden und Wachsen: Zur Geschichte der Deutschen Demokratischen Republik* (Berlin: Dietz Verlag, 1975), 1:108; Karl-Heinz Schöneburg et al., *Errichtung des Arbeiter- und Bauern-Staates der DDR, 1945–1949* (Berlin: Staatsverlag der Deutschen Demokratischen Republik, 1983), 101; Günter Benser, "Konzeption und Praxis der Abrechnung mit dem deutschen Faschismus," *Zeitschrift für Geschichtswissenschaft* 32 (1984): 952.

26. Y. I. Lenin, *State and Revolution* (New York: International Publishers, 1932), 42.

27. Doernberg, *Geburt*, 137. See also Thomas, "1945–1949," 107.

28. Karl Urban, "Die Rolle der staatlichen Organe bei der Entnazifizierung (1945–1948)," *Staat und Recht* 7 (1979): 615–616 (my italics).

29. *Geschichte der SED*, 133.

30. Thomas, "1945–1949," 108.

31. This is the main thesis of Rolf Badstübner, *Restauration in Westdeutschland, 1945–1949* (Berlin: Dietz Verlag, 1965). The renazification-restoration thesis was not confined to East German works. See Ernst-Ulrich Huster et al., *Determinanten der westdeutschen Restauration, 1945–1949* (Frankfurt: Suhrkamp Verlag, 1972); Rolf Steininger, *Deutsche Geschichte, 1945–1961: Darstellung und Dokumente in zwei Bänden* (Frankfurt: Fischer Taschenbuch Verlag, 1983), 1:130–131. See also the reassessment of the renazification concept in Christa Hoffmann, *Stunden Null? Vergangenheitsbewältigung in Deutschland, 1945 und 1989* (Bonn: Bouvier Verlag, 1992), 109–112.

32. Doernberg also argues that, in those areas of the Soviet zone initially occupied by British and American troops, known Nazis were often left in positions of power despite the protests of local Germans. Doernberg, *Geburt,* 93, 96. See also Robert Büchner and Hannelore Freundlich, "Zur Situation in den zeitweilig englisch oder amerikanisch besetzten Gebieten der sowjetischen Besatzungszone (April bis Anfang Juli 1945)," *Beiträge zur Geschichte der Arbeiterbewegung* 6 (1972): 992–1006; Manfred Wille, "Das Ringen der Arbeiterklasse und der anderen Antifaschisten um die Einleitung des Demokratisierungsprozesses in der Provinz Sachsen (April–August 1945)," *Beiträge zur Geschichte der Arbeiterbewegung* 22 (1980): 431–441; Karl-Heinz Gräfe and Helfried Wehner, "Die Hilfe der sowjetischen Militärorgane bei der beginnenden antifaschistisch-demokratischen Umwälzung in Sachsen," *Militärgeschichte* 3 (1985): 219–220.

33. Doernberg, *Geburt,* 96. See also Thomas, "1945–1949," 107; Badstübner, "Four-Power Administration," 29; Meinicke, "Entnazifizierung," 979.

34. Benser, "Konzeptionen und Praxis," 962. In a similar vein, it was argued that the western powers' unwillingness to denazify was a "primary cause of the division of Germany." Urban, "Rolle der staatlichen Organe," 616. See also A. B. Tschernov, "Über die Entnazifizierung Deutschlands," in Bernhard Weißel, ed., *Befreiung und Neubeginn: Zur Stellung des 8. Mai 1945 in der deutschen Geschichte* (Berlin: Akademie-Verlag, 1968), 243.

35. Badstübner, "Allied Four-Power Administration," 33.

36. The terms "orthodox" and "revisionist" have been used previously in this context. See Wilma Albrecht, "Die Entnazifizierung," *Neue Politische Literatur* 24 (1979): 73–84; Turner, "Denazification in the British Zone," 239–267.

37. John D. Montgomery, *Forced to Be Free: The Artificial Revolution in Germany and Japan* (Chicago: University of Chicago Press, 1957); Justus Fürstenau, *Entnazifizierung: Ein Kapitel deutscher Nachkriegspolitik* (Neuwied: Hermann Luchterhand Verlag, 1969), 221–222; Wolfgang Benz, *Von der Besatzungsherrschaft zur Bundesrepublik: Stationen einer Staatsgründung, 1946–1949* (Frankfurt: Fischer Taschenbuch Verlag, 1984), 16; Theodor Eschenburg, *Jahre der Besatzung, 1945–1949* (Stuttgart: Deutsche Verlags-

Anstalt; Wiesbaden: F. A. Brockhaus, 1983), 116; Steininger, *Deutsche Geschichte,* 1:130–131.

38. Niethammer, *Die Mitläuferfabrik,* 24–25.

39. Ibid., 654, 659.

40. Niethammer's focus on the commissions was based on the pathbreaking work of an American historian. See John Gimbel, "American Denazification and German Local Politics, 1945–1949: A Case Study in Marburg," *American Political Science Review* 54 (1960): 83–105. He expanded this analysis to cover additional aspects of the occupation in *A German Community under American Occupation: Marburg, 1945–52* (Stanford: Stanford University Press, 1961).

41. An early attempt to define the focus of *Alltagsgeschichte* can be found in Lutz Niethammer, "Anmerkungen zur Alltagsgeschichte," *Geschichtsdidaktik* 3 (1980): 231–242, reprinted in Klaus Bergmann and Rolf Schörken, eds., *Geschichte im Alltag—-Alltag in der Geschichte* (Düsseldorf: Pädagogischer Verlag Schwann, 1982). See also Lutz Niethammer, "Privat-Wirtschaft: Erinnerungsfragmente einer anderen Umerziehung," in Lutz Niethammer and Alexander Plato, eds., *"Hinterher merkt man, daß es richtig war, daß es schiefgegangen ist": Nachkriegserfahrungen im Ruhrgebiet* (Berlin: Verlag J. H. W. Dietz, 1983), 17–106. Much of the debate on *Alltagsgeschichte* has centered on developing a theoretical and methodological framework for the study of everyday life. See Peter Borscheid, "Plädoyer für eine Geschichte des Alltäglichen," in Peter Borscheid and Hans J. Teutenberg, eds., *Ehe, Liebe, Tod: Zum Wandel der Familie: Der Geschlechts- und Generationsbeziehungen in der Neuzeit* (Münster: F. Coppenrath Verlag, 1983), 1–14; Alf Lüdtke, "Einleitung: Was ist und wer treibt Alltagsgeschichte?" in Alf Lüdtke, ed., *Alltagsgeschichte: Zur Rekonstruktion historischer Erfahrungen und Lebensweisen* (Frankfurt: Campus Verlag, 1989), 9–47. For the role of local and regional studies in *Alltagsgeschichte,* see Heiko Haumann, "Stadt und Land: Bemerkungen zu einem Projekt vergleichender Regionalgeschichte," in Heiko Haumann, ed., *Arbeiteralltag in Stadt und Land* (Berlin: Argument-Verlag, 1982), 147–156.

42. See, for example, Hans Woller, *Gesellschaft und Politik in der amerikanischen Besatzungszone: Die Region Ansbach und Fürth* (Munich: R. Oldenbourg Verlag, 1986); Klaus-Dietmar Henke, *Politische Säuberung unter französischer Besatzung: Die Entnazifizierung in Württemberg-Hohenzollern* (Stuttgart: Deutsche Verlags-Anstalt, 1981); Wolfgang Krüger, *Entnazifiziert! Zur Praxis der politischen Säuberung in Nordrhein-Westfalen* (Wuppertal: Peter Hammer Verlag, 1982); Elmar Ettle, *Die Entnazifizierung in Eichstätt: Probleme der politischen Säuberung nach 1945* (Frankfurt: Peter Lang, 1985).

43. Hermann Weber, *Von der SBZ zur DDR, 1945–1968* (Hannover: Verlag für Literatur und Zeitgeschehen, 1966), 51.

44. Hermann Weber, *DDR: Grundriß der Geschichte* (Hannover: Fackelträger-

Verlag, 1991), 31, 13–15. Weber's defense of the Stalinization model was criticized in Klaus Kellmann, "Deutsche Geschichte nach 1945: Neuerscheinungen vor, während und nach der Auflösung der DDR und der Vereinigung beider deutscher Staaten," *Geschichte in Wissenschaft und Unterricht* 44 (1993): 243–269.

45. Compare, for example, the contemporaneous analysis of Franz Neumann, "Soviet Policy in Germany," *Annals of the American Academy* 263 (May 1949): 165–179, with the study by R. C. Raack, *Stalin's Drive to the West, 1938–1945: The Origins of the Cold War* (Stanford: Stanford University Press, 1995). A noteworthy exception is Christoph Kleßmann, *Die dopplete Staatsgründung: Deutsche Geschichte, 1945–1955* (Göttingen: Vandehoeck and Ruprecht, 1981), which rejects the view that denazification was part of the Stalinization of the eastern zone.

46. Eschenburg, *Jahre der Besatzung,* 119. Another West German survey notes that denazification was "a part of the drastic reform of the entire political, economic, and social system; it was used as an instrument for the replacement of elites" with communists. Benz, *Von der Besatzungsherrschaft zur Bundesrepublik,* 16.

47. Volker Dotterweich, "Die Entnazifizierung," in Josef Becker, Theo Stammen, and Peter Waldmann, eds., *Vorgeschichte der Bundesrepublik Deutschland: Zwischen Kapitulation und Grundgesetz* (Munich: Wilhelm Fink Verlag, 1987), 135. See also Elmer Plischke, "Denazification in Germany: A Political Analysis," in Robert Wolfe, ed., *Americans as Proconsuls: United States Military Government in Germany and Japan, 1944–1952* (Carbondale: Southern Illinois University Press, 1984), 219–220: Lewis J. Edinger, "Post-totalitarian Leadership: Elites in the German Federal Republic," *American Political Science Review* 54 (1960): 78; Neumann, "Soviet Policy," 169; Steininger, *Deutsche Geschichte,* 152.

48. Weber, *Grundriß,* 31–33. Post-reunification historians have produced a growing body of literature on the Soviet camps. See the review by Karl Wilhelm Fricke, "Stalins Archipel GULag in Deutschland," *Deutschland Archiv* 25 (1992): 873–876. For a list of the Soviet camps and their locations, see Georg-Franz Willing, *Umerziehung: Die De-Nationalisierung besiegter Völker im 20. Jahrhundert* (Coburg: Nation Europa-Verlag, 1991), 224–225.

49. Agnes Blänsdorf, "Zur Konfrontation mit der NS-Vergangenheit in der Bundesrepublik, der DDR und in Österreich," *Aus Politik und Zeitgeschichte* 16–17 (1987): 13.

50. Konrad H. Jarausch, "Von Zusammenbruch zur Erneuerung," in Jarausch, *Zwischen Parteilichkeit und Professionalität,* 18–21; Naimark, "Politik und Geschichtswissenschaft," 129–131.

51. Alexander von Plato, "Eine zweite 'Entnazifizierung'? Zur Verarbeitung politischer Umwälzungen in Deutschland, 1945 und 1989," in Ranier Eckert, Alexander von Plato, and Jörn Schütrumpf, eds., *Wendzeiten—*

Zeitenwände: Zur "Entnazifizierung" und "Entstalinizerung" (Hamburg: Ergebnisse Verlag GmbH., 1991), 8. See also Helga Welsh, "Entnazifizierung in der DDR und die 'Wende,'" in Eckert, von Plato, and Schütrumpf, *Wendzeiten—Zeitenwände*, 70.

52. Olaf Groehler, "Antifaschismus—Vom Umgang mit einem Begriff," in Ulrich Herbert and Olaf Groehler, eds., *Zweierlei Bewältigung: Vier Beiträge über den Umgang mit der NS-Vergangenheit in den beiden deutschen Staaten* (Hamburg: Ergebnisse Verlag, 1992), 31; Jarausch, "The Failure of East German Antifascism," 96. See also Frank Trommler, "The Creation of History and the Refusal of the Past in the German Democratic Republic," in Kathy Harms, Lutz R. Reuter, and Volker Dürr, eds., *Coping with the Past: Germany and Austria after 1945* (Madison: University of Wisconsin Press, 1990), 79–93; Antonia Grunenberg, "Antifaschismus—ein deutscher Mythos: Anmerkungen zu einem verdrängten Kapitel der Linken," *Die Zeit* (Hamburg), 26 April 1991, 64; idem, *Antifaschismus—ein deutscher Mythos* (Hamburg: Rowohlt, 1993).

53. Gregor Gysi, "Ideologische, politische und moralische Aspekte der Aufarbeitung," in Gregor Gysi, Uwe-Jens Heuer, and Michael Schumann, eds., *Zweigeteilt: Über den Umgang mit der SED-Vergangenheit* (Hamburg: VSA-Verlag, 1992), 194. See the similar comments in Dan Diner, "On the Ideology of Antifascism," *New German Critique* 67 (Winter 1996): 123.

54. A. James McAdams and John Torpey, "The Political Arsenal of the German Past," *German Politics and Society* 30 (1993): 3.

55. Mary Fulbrook, *Anatomy of a Dictatorship: Inside the GDR, 1949–1989* (New York: Oxford University Press, 1995), 287.

56. Klaus-Dietmar Henke and Hans Woller, "Schaben an einem Gebirge der Schuld: Ein Dauerthema seit dem Zweiten Weltkrieg: Die Aufarbeitung der Vergangenheit," *Süddeutsche Zeitung* (Munich), 7–8 December 1991. Similar observations and reservations concerning denazification as a post-reunification model are made by Renate Meyer-Braun, "Zweimal deutsche Vergangenheit—ein Thesenpapier," in Wiltrud Ulrike Drechsel and Anderas Röpcke, eds., *"Denazification" zur Entnazifizierung in Bremen* (Bremen: Edition Temmen, 1992), 174–181.

57. Hoffmann, *Stunden Null?* 302–310; Horst Möller, "Die Relativität historischer Epochen: Das Jahr 1945 in der Perspektive des Jahres 1989," *Aus Politik und Zeitgeschichte* 18–19 (1995): 3–9.

58. For an overview of the totalitarianism debate, see Eckhard Jesse, "War die DDR totalitär?" *Aus Politik und Zeitgeschichte* 40 (1994): 12–23; idem, "'Vergangenheitsbewältigung' nach totalitärer Herrschaft in Deutschland," *German Studies Review*, Special Issue (1994): 157–171. See also, in the same Special Issue of the *German Studies Review*, Wolfgang-Uwe Friedrich, "Bürokratischer Totalitarismus—zur Typologie des SED-Regimes," 1–22; Wolfgang Bergsdorf, "Politischer Sprachgebrauch und totalitäre Herrschaft," 23–36. On comparing the Nazi regime with the GDR, see Ful-

brook, *Anatomy of a Dictatorship*, 286; Bernd Faulenbach, "Bewahrung der Erinnerung: Bedeutung und Probleme der 'Aufarbeitung' von Vergangenheit heute," in Bernd Faulenbach, Markus Meckel, and Hermann Weber, eds., *Die Partei hatte immer recht—Aufarbeitung von Geschichte und Folgen der SED-Diktatur* (Essen: Klartext Verlag, 1994), 20.

59. The literature on this topic is rapidly growing. See Herbert Obenaus, *NS-Geschichte nach dem Ende der DDR: Eine abgeschlossene Vergangenheit?* (Hannover: Niedersächsischen Landeszentrale für politische Bildung, 1992); Bernd Faulenbach, "Probleme des Umgangs mit der Vergangenheit im vereinten Deutschland: Zur Gegenwartsbedeutung der jügsten Geschichte," in Werner Weidenfeld, ed., *Deutschland: Eine Nation—doppelte Geschichte* (Cologne: Verlag Wissenschaft und Politik, 1993), 175–190; Christa Hoffmann and Eckhard Jesse, "Die 'doppelte Vergangenheitsbewältigung' in Deutschland: Unterschiede und Gemeinsamkeiten," in Weidenfeld, *Deutschland*, 209–234; von Plato, "Eine zweite Entnazifizierung?"; Udo Wengst, "Geschichtswissenschaft und 'Vergangenheitsbewältigung' in Deutschland nach 1945 und nach 1989/90," *Geschichte in Wissenschaft und Unterricht* 4 (1995): 189–205.

60. Eckhard Jesse, "Vergangenheitsbewältigung im Internationalen Vergleich: Die Reaktionen auf den Zusammenbruch des Natinalsozialismus/Faschismus und des Kommunismus," in Peter Eisenmann and Gerhard Hirscher, eds., *Bilanz der zweiten deutschen Diktatur* (Munich: v. Hase & Koehler Verlag, 1993), 19.

61. Peter Steinbach, "Vergangeheitsbewältigung in vergleichender Perspektive: Politische Säuberung, Weidergutmachung, Integration," in Klaus Schroeder, ed., *Geschichte und Transformation des SED-Staates: Beiträge und Analysen* (Berlin: Akademie Verlag, 1994), 395.

62. Claus Leggewie and Horst Meier, "Zum Auftakt ein Schlußstrich? Das Bewältigungswerk 'Vergangenheit Ost' und der Rechtsstaat," in Cora Stephan, ed., *Wir Kollaborateure: Der Westen und die deutschen Vergangenheiten* (Reinbek bei Hamburg: Rowohlt Taschenbuch Verlag, 1992), 51.

1. The Origins of Soviet Denazification Policy

1. Niethammer, *Die Mitläuferfabrik*, 34–52. On the usefulness of Niethammer's methodology in the case of the French zone, see Henke, *Politische Säuberung unter französischer Besatzung*, 9. See also the comments regarding British denazification in Turner, "Denazification in the British Zone," 242.

2. J. V. Stalin, "Concerning the International Situation," in *Works* (Moscow: Foreign Languages Publishing House, 1953), 6:294–295.

3. "Das Programm der kommunistischen Internationale (1928)," in Hermann Weber, ed., *Die Kommunistische Internationale: Ein Dokumentation* (Hannover: Verlag J. H. W. Dietz, 1966), 184–185.

4. "Das EKKI über Faschismus und Sozialdemokratie (1932)," ibid., 259.

5. "Die Faschismus-Theorie der Komintern (1933)," ibid., 281, 279.

6. Arnold Sywottek, *Deutsche Volksdemokratie: Studien zur politischen Konzeption der KPD, 1935–1946* (Düsseldorf: Bertelsmann, 1971), 26–28.

7. Theo Pirker, *Komintern und Faschismus, 1920–1940* (Stuttgart: Deutsche Verlags-Anstalt, 1965), 68.

8. Gregori Dimitrov, "The Fascist Offensive and the Tasks of the Communist International," *VII Congress of the Communist International*, 126–127.

9. Wilhelm Pieck, "Erfahrungen und Lehren der deutschen Parteiarbeit im Zusammenhang mit den Beschlüssen des VII. Weltkongresses der Kommunistischen Internationale," in Klaus Mammach, ed., *Die Brüsseler Konferenz der KPD (3.–15. Oktober 1935)* (Berlin: Dietz Verlag, 1975), 73.

10. Ibid., 76.

11. This was the "Trojan horse" tactic outlined by Dimitrov in his speech at the Seventh Congress of the Comintern. See Walter Ulbricht's 1936 article "Die Taktik des Trojanischen Pferdes," in Hermann Weber, ed., *Der deutsche Kommunismus: Dokumente* (Cologne: Kipenheuer & Witsch, 1963), 410–411.

12. Pieck, "Erfahrungen und Lehren," 113–114.

13. Wilhelm Pieck, "Die gegenwärtige Lage und die Aufgaben der Partei," in Klaus Mannach, ed., *Die Berner Konferenz der KPD (30. Januar–1. Februar 1939)* (Berlin: Dietz Verlag, 1974), 75, 82.

14. Wolfgang Leonhard, *Die Revolution entlässt Ihre Kinder* (Cologne: Kiepenheuer & Witsch, 1955), 77–85.

15. "Erklärung des ZK der KPD zum Abschluss des Nichtangriffspaktes zwischen der Sowjetunion und Deutschland," in Weber, *Der deutsche Kommunismus*, 366.

16. "Molotow zum Stalin-Hitler-Pakt und zum Kreigsausbruch (1939)," in Weber, *Die Kommunistische Internationale*, 319.

17. Wilhem Pieck, "Um was geht es in diesem Krieg?" in Weber, *Der deutsche Kommunismus*, 336.

18. Walter Ulbricht, "Hilferding über den 'Sinn des Krieges,'" ibid., 365–366.

19. Wilhelm Pieck, "Im Sieg der Roten Armee liegt die Rettung des deutschen Volkes," in *Gesammelte Reden und Schriften* (Berlin: Dietz Verlag, 1979), 6:76, 80.

20. Erich Weinert, *Das Nationalkomitee "Freies Deutschland," 1943–1945: Bericht über seine Tätigkeit und seine Auswirkung* (Berlin: Rütten & Loening, 1957), 11.

21. Wilhelm Pieck, "Die Lehren von Stalingrad: Rede in der deutschprachigen Sendung des Moskauer Rundfunks 1. Februar 1943," in Pieck, *Gesammelte Reden und Schriften*, 6:187.

22. On the founding of the NKFD, see Alexander Fischer, *Sowjetische Deutschlandpolitik im Zweiten Weltkrieg, 1941–1945* (Stuttgart: Deutsche Verlags-Anstalt, 1975), 53–59; Sywottek, *Deutsche Volksdemokratie*, 123–147; Karl-Heinz Frieser, *Krieg hinter Stacheldraht: Die deutschen Kriegsge-*

fangenen in der Sowjetunion und das Nationalkomitee "Freies Deutschland" (Mainz: v. Hase & Koehler Verlag, 1981), 63–73; Kai P. Schoenhals, *The Free Germany Movement: A Case of Patriotism or Treason?* (Westport, Conn.: Greenwood Press, 1989).

23. From the NKFD Manifesto, quoted in *Geschichte der deutschen Arbeiterbewegung*, 11:124.

24. From the Central Committee resolution of May 1943, quoted in Schoenhals, *Free Germany Movement*, 26.

25. Fischer, *Sowjetische Deutschlandpolitik, 54–55.*

26. "Manifest des Nationalkomitees Freies Deutschland," in Weber, *Der deutsche Kommunismus*, 390.

27. This was the view of one the leading architects of the NKFD, Erich Weinert, expressed in an article in *Pravda* of 7 August 1943, cited in A. G. Egorova et al., *Internasional′noe sotrudnichestvo KPSS i SEPG: Istoriia i Sovremennost′* (Moscow: Izdatel′stvo Politicheskoi Literaturi, 1987), 120. See also Günter Benser, *Die KPD im Jahre der Befreiung: Vorbereitung und Aufbau der legalen kommunistischen Massenpartei (Jahreswende 1944/1945 bis Herbst 1945)* (Berlin: Dietz Verlag, 1985), 7–8.

28. Fischer, *Sowjetische Deutschlandpolitik*, 103.

29. "Aktionsprogramm des Blockes der kämpferischen Demokratie," in Horst Laschitza, *Kämpferische Demokratie gegen Faschismus: Die programmatische Vorbereitung auf die antifaschistisch-demokratische Umwälzung in Deutschland durch die Parteiführung der KPD* (Berlin: Deutscher Militärverlag, 1969), 199. Niethammer noted in a comparison of the Action Program and U.S. policies that as a blueprint for cleansing the state apparatus, Ackermann's plans read much like a U.S. directive from the same period. Niethammer, *Mitläuferfabrik*, 115.

30. Wilhelm Pieck, "Das Aktionsprogramm der KPD: Rededisposition für eine Lektion an der Parteischule der KPD Nr. 12 in Nagornoje 9. November 1944," in Pieck, *Gesammelte Reden und Schriften*, 6:284–285.

31. Walter Ulbricht, "Thesen über das Wesen des Hitlerfaschismus," in *Zur Geschichte der Deutschen Arbeiterbewegung: Aus Reden und Aufsätzen* (Berlin: Dietz Verlag, 1963), 2:402.

32. Ibid., 403.

33. Ibid., 404.

34. Ibid., 409.

35. Ibid., 411.

36. Ibid., 413–414.

37. Johannes R. Becher, "Zur Frage der politisch-moralischen Vernichtung des 'Faschismus,'" in Peter Erler, Horst Laude, and Manfred Wilke, eds., *"Nach Hitler kommen wir": Dokumente zur Programmatik der Moskauer KPD-Führung 1944/45 für Nachkriegsdeutschland* (Berlin: Akademie Verlag, 1994), 338.

38. Ibid., 339.

39. Ibid., 341.
40. Ibid., 344.
41. Ibid., 345.
42. Ibid., 359.

2. The Purge Begins

1. BLHA, Rep. 206, 3063.
2. For the administrative and social history of this period, see Hans Herzfeld, "Allgemeine Entwicklung und politische Geschichte," in Hans Herzfeld and Gerd Heinrich, eds., *Berlin und die Provinz Brandenburg im 19. und 20. Jahrhundert* (Berlin: Walter de Gruyter & Co., 1968); Kurt Adamy and Kristina Hübener, "Provinz Mark Brandenburg—Gau Kurmark: Eine verwaltungsgeschichtliche Skizze," in Dietrich Eichholtz and Almuth Püschel, eds., *Verfolgung, Alltag, Widerstand: Brandenburg in der NS-Zeit* (Berlin: Verlag Volk & Welt, 1993); Barbara Fait, "(Mark) Brandenburg," in Martin Broszat and Hermann Weber, eds., *SBZ Handbuch: Staatliche Verwaltungen, Parteien, gesellschaftliche Organisationen und ihre Führungskräfte in der Sowjetischen Besatzungszone Deutschlands, 1945–1949* (Munich: R. Oldenbourg Verlag, 1993); Siegfried Schulze, "Der Prozeß der Herausbildung der Provinzialverwaltung Mark Brandenburg und ihre Politik zur Einleitung der antifaschistisch-demokratischen Revolution (Sommer 1945 bis Frühjahr 1946)" (Ph.D. diss., Pädagogischen Hochschule, Potsdam, 1970). On the Niederlausitz, see Frank Förster, *Um Lausitzer Braunkohle, 1849–1945* (Bautzen: VEB Domowina-Verlag, 1990).
3. Provinzialverwaltung Mark Brandenburg, *Ein Jahr Bewährung der Mark Brandenburg: Rückblick und Rechenschaft* (Potsdam: Verlag der Märkischen Volksstimme, 1946), 6. In December 1945 there were 406,000 refugees in Brandenburg, representing 16.4 percent of all refugees in the Soviet zone and 19.5 percent of the total population of the province. See Wolfgang Ribbe, "Das Land Brandenburg in der SBZ/DDR (1945 bis 1952)," in Ingo Materna and Wolfgang Ribbe, eds., *Brandenburgische Geschichte* (Berlin: Akademie Verlag, 1995), 679.
4. On the effects of the war, see Richard Lakowski, "Das Ende der Naziherrschaft in Brandenburg: Mit einer Dokumentation," in Eichholtz and Püschel, *Brandenburg in der NS-Zeit;* Heiger Ostertag, "Vom strategischen Bombenkriegkrieg zum sozialistischen Bildersturm: Die Zerstörung Potsdams 1945 und das Schicksal seiner historischen Gebäude nach dem Kriege," in *Potsdam: Staat, Armee, Residenz* (Berlin: Propylaen, 1993), 487–499; Lorenz Demps, "Die Provinz Brandenburg in der NS-Zeit (1933 bis 1945)," in Materna and Ribbe, *Brandenburgische Geschichte,* 676. Also see the reports of local administrators in BLHA, Rep. 203, 249, "Stenographischer Bericht: Konferenz aller Landräte und Oberbürger-

meister der Mark Brandenburg am 16. und 17. Juli 1945"; the quotation in the text is from this report.

5. BLHA, Rep. 203, 249.

6. The committees were variously referred to as "Antifascist Leagues," "Rebuilding Committees," or, showing the influence of Soviet wartime broadcasts, committees for a "Free Germany." See Günther Benser, "Antifa-Ausschüsse—Staatsorgane—Parteiorganization: Überlegungen zu Ausmaß, Rolle und Grenzen der antifaschistischen Bewegung am Ende des zweiten Weltkriegs," *Zeitschrift für Geschichtswissenschaft* 26 (1978): 785.

7. Grohnert, *Die Entnazifizierung in Baden, 1945–1949*, 33. For the activities of the Antifascist Committees (Antifas) in the U.S. zone, see Niethammer, *Die Mitläuferfabrik*, 126–143. In Franconia, the first measures toward "self-cleansing" were taken not by Antifa Committees but rather by newly appointed German administrators. See Woller, *Gesellschaft und Politik*, 95–111. For Antifa activities in the western zones in general, see Eschenburg, *Jahre der Besatzung*, 105–108.

8. Benser, "Antifa-Ausschüsse, 787.

9. Walter Ulbricht, *Zur Geschichte der neuesten Zeit: Die Niederlage Hitlerdeutschlands und die Schaffung der antifaschistisch-demokratischen Ordnung* (Berlin: Dietz Verlag, 1955), 62; Benser, "Antifa-Ausschüsse", 802. The leading role of the KPD in the Antifa Committees is central to the East German view. See Benser, *Die KPD im Jahre der Befreiung*, 107–116; Thomas, "1945–1949," 15–18.

10. Dietrich Staritz, *Die Grundung der DDR: Von der sowjetischen Besatzungsherrschaft zum sozialistischen Staat*, 2nd ed. (Munich: Deutscher Taschenbuch Verlag, 1987), 97.

11. BLHA-SED, Rep. 330, I/2, 6, Bl. 71. For reports on resistance activity in the closing weeks of the war, see Friedrich Beck et al., *Ausgewählte Dokumente und Materialien zum antifaschistischen Widerstandskampf unter Führung der Kommunistischen Partei Deutschlands in der Provinz Brandenburg, 1939–1945* (Potsdam: Druckerei Märkische Volksstimme, 1985), 2:486–489.

12. BLHA-SED, Rep. 330, I/2, 6, Bl. 63, 6 August 1945.

13. "Richtlinien für die Arbeit der deutschen Antifaschisten in dem von der Roten Armee besetzten deutschen Gebiet," in Laschitza, *Kämpferische Demokratie*, 250–251.

14. SAPMO-BA, I/3/1–2, 114, 7 June 1945. For a similar example from Potsdam, see "Protokoll der gemiensamen Funktionärskonferenz von KPD und SPD in Potsdam am 5. Juli 1945 (Auszüge)," in Beck, *Ausgewählte Dokumente*, 2:531.

15. Kleßmann, *Die doppelte Staatsgründung*, 37–39.

16. Lutz Niethammer, "Zwischen Volksfront und Räten: Die Kommunisten in den Auschüssen," in Lutz Niethammer, Ulrich Borsdorf, and Peter Brandt, eds., *Arbeiterinitiative 1945: Antifaschistische Ausschüsse und Reorganiza-*

tion der Arbeiterbewegung in Deutschland (Wuppertal: Peter Hammer Verlag, 1976), 198.

17. Ulbricht, *Zur Geschichte der neuesten Zeit*, 62–63.

18. Leonhard, *Die Revolution entlässt Ihre Kinder*, 389–390.

19. Naimark, *The Russians in Germany*, 42.

20. Willy Sägebrecht, *Nicht Anboß, sondern Hammer sein: Erinnerungen* (Berlin: Dietz Verlag, 1976), 306.

21. SAPMO-BA, Ulbricht NL, 182, 835, 7 June 1945.

22. The KPD Declaration, dated 11 June 1945, was published in the party's Berlin newspaper, the *Deutsche Volkszeitung*, on 13 June 1945. The Brandenburg section of the party did not have its own paper (*Volkswille*, published in Potsdam) until September 1945. The Declaration has been reprinted in several document collections. The version cited here is from Lothar Berthold and Ernst Diehl, eds., *Revolutionäre deutsche Parteiprogramme: Von Kommunistischen Manifest zum Programm des Sozialismus* (Berlin: Dietz Verlag, 1967), 191–200.

23. Parteihochschule "Karl Marx" beim Zentralkomitee der Sozialistischen Einheitspartei Deutschlands Lehrstuhl Geschichte der SED, *Die SED— führende Kraft der antifaschitisch-demokratischen Umwälzung (1945– 1949)* (Berlin: Dietz Verlag, 1984), 23.

24. *Revolutionäre deutsche Parteiprogramme*, 196. An SPD leader in Berlin recorded the SPD's amazement at the content of the Declaration, noting it was a "communist declaration which was not communist, which moreover was not even socialist." Erich Gniffke, *Jahre mit Ulbricht* (Cologne: Verlag Wissenschaft und Politik, 1966), 27.

25. *Revolutionäre deutsche Parteiprogramme*, 196–198.

26. Wener Bystry, "Genosse Willy Sägebrecht an der Spitze der Bezirksparteiorganisation der Kommunistischen Partei Deutschlands der Provinz Brandenburg im Kampf um die Einheit der Arbeiterklasse (1945–1946)," *Märkische Heimat 5* (1986): 8.

27. Sägebrecht, *Erinnerungen*, 306.

28. For biographical information on Gundelach, see Broszat and Weber, *SBZ Handbuch*, 918.

29. SAPMO-BA, Ulbricht NL, 182, 853, "Parteikonferenz des Kreises Niederbarnim in Bernau am 14.6.45." See also Gundelach's report on the situation in Brandenburg/Havel, ibid., Bl. 56–57.

30. *Revolutionäre deutsche Parteiprogramme*, 191–194.

31. "Den Nazismus ausrotten—aber wie?" *Deutsche Volkszeitung* (Berlin), 13 June 1945, 2.

32. "PG" is the abbreviation for *Parteigenossen*, "party comrades" in the National Socialist Party.

33. "Was tun wir mit den kleinen 'Pgs'?" *Deutsche Volkszeitung* (Berlin), 26 June 1945, 2. See also the follow-up article, "Bis zur Wurzel des Nazismus . . . ," *Deutsche Volkszeitung* (Berlin), 12 July 1945, 1.

34. BLHA-SED, Rep. 330, I/2, 6, Bl. 126, 10 July 1945.
35. Friedrich Ebert, "Wir erfülten unsere historische Aufgabe," in *Vereint sind wir alles: Erinnerungen an die Gründung der SED* (Berlin: Dietz Verlag, 1971), 515.
36. "Einigung aller antifaschistisch-demokratischen Kräfte! Rede in der ersten Zusammenkunft von etwa 200 antifaschisitischen Funktionären im Stadthaus Berlin 12. Juni 1945," in Ulbricht, *Zur Geschichte der deutschen Arbeiterbewegung*, 432–433.
37. BLHA-SED, Rep. 330, I/2, 10, Bl. 25. Belzig continued to be the site of unique developments. By early August, the committee had organized "a few hundred" farmers into a "democratic Framers' League," which a KPD report cited as a model for the rest of Brandenburg. SAPMO-BA, Pieck NL, 36, 684, 9 August 1945, 7.
38. BLHA-SED, Rep. 330, I/2, 10, Bl. 28. The use of the term *nazirein* in this instance echoed the Nazis' use of the term *judenrein* in reference to the deportation and eventual murder of Jews from areas controlled by Germany.
39. SAPMO-BA, Ulbricht NL, 182, 853, Bl. 74–78.
40. From the introduction to the document collection *Freundschaft DDR-UdSSR: Dokumente und Materialien* (Berlin: Dietz Verlag, 1965), 6. See also "Die SMAD: Ihre Rolle bei der Entstehung und Entwicklung revolutionär-demokratischer Staatsorgane," in Schöneburg, *Errichtung des Arbeiter- und Bauernstaates*, 31–40; Fritz Selbmann, "Die sowjetischen Genosssen waren Freunde und Helfer," in *Vereint sind wir alles*, 329–348; Wolfgang Meinicke, "Zur Entnazifizierung in der sowjetischen Besatzungszone unter Berücksichtigung von Aspekten politischer und soziale Veränderungen (1945 bis 1948)" (Ph.D. diss., Humbolt University, Berlin, 1983), 3–4.
41. Naimark, *The Russians in Germany*, 32–36.
42. SAPMO-BA, Ulbricht NL, 182, 853, Bl. 68–73. In a similar instance, a Nazi mayor was allowed to remain in office in exchange for supplying the local Soviet commander with "butter etc.," ibid., Bl. 134–136. See also Ernst Krummel, "Kurier im Auftrag des Zentralkomitees der KPD. 1945," in Beck, *Ausgewählte Dokumente*, 2:550–551.
43. SAPMO-BA, IV, 2/13, 226, 9 June 1947.
44. SAPMO-BA, Pieck NL, 36, 684, 9 August 1945, 8.
45. SAPMO-BA, Ulbricht NL, 182, 853, Bl. 97–98. The crime spree committed by Soviet soldiers is documented in Naimark, *The Russians in Germany*, 32–36, 69–140.
46. BLHA-SED, Rep. 330, I/2, 6, Bl. 91.
47. SAPMO-BA, Pieck NL, 36, 684, 9 August 1945, 9. There are numerous reports concerning this situation. For further examples, see BLHA, Rep. 203, 25, Bl. 31; 64; Ulbricht NL, 182, 853, Bl. 71–73, 101–106.
48. BLHA, Rep. 203, 249.
49. Speech by Walter Ulbricht, ibid. Ulbricht's avoidance of a direct mention of

rape and his reference to stolen bicycles is in line with Naimark's observation that the oft-mentioned example of stolen bicycles during this period was a metaphorical reference to rape. Naimark, *The Russians in Germany,* 136–137.

50. Gniffke, *Jahre mit Ulbricht,* 44; Lucio Caracciolo, "Der Untergang der Sozialdemokratie in der Sowjetischen Besatzungszone," *Vierteljahresheft für Zeitgeschichte* 36 (1988): 290.
51. Gniffke, *Jahre mit Ulbricht,* 35; Leonhard, *Die Revolution entläßt ihre Kinder,* 383.
52. Walter Ulbricht, "Das Aktionsprogramm der KPD in Durchführung: Aus der Rede auf der Groß-Berliner Funktionärkonferenz 12. Oktober 1945," in *Zur Geschichte der deutschen Arbeiterbewegung,* 2:496.
53. BLHA, Rep. 203, 25, Bl. 232, 16 May 1947; Bl. 233, 22 May 1947; Bl. 245–255, 6 August 1947.
54. Broszat and Weber, *SBZ Handbuch,* 866.
55. Schulze, "Der Prozeß der Herausbildung der Provinzialverwaltung Mark Brandenburg," 56; "Erinnerungsbericht des Genossen Bernhard Bechler," in Beck, *Ausgewählte Dokumente,* 2:462–463.
56. The Soviet appointment of Steinhoff was in line with the Soviet policy of placing non-communists at the head of the new provincial governments. See Staritz, *Die Gründung der DDR,* 47.
57. *Verordnungsblatt der Provinzialverwaltung Mark Brandenburg (VOBl.),* 20 October 1945, 1.
58. Biographical information from Broszat and Weber, *SBZ Handbuch,* 932, 1009, 1003.
59. The administrative picture was temporarily complicated by the establishment of four "superior district offices" *(Oberlandratsämter).* These offices were dissolved by order of the SMA in January 1947. See the helpful introductory overview in the index *(Findbuch)* for the archives of these *Oberlandratsämter,* BLHA, Rep. 230. See also Schulze, "Der Prozeß der Herausbildung der Provinzialverwaltung Mark Brandenburg," in general, and in particular his schematic diagram of the provincial administrative structure in the appendix.
60. BLHA, Rep. 203, 249.
61. *VOBl.,* 20 October 1945, 3.
62. BLHA, Rep. 250, LRA Ruppin, 558, 29 July 1945.
63. See also the report concerning Lehnin, where the local Soviet commander blocked all measures against former Nazis because taking such actions might interfere with the harvest. BLHA-SED, Rep. 330, I/2, 10, Bl. 4, 18 August 1945.
64. BLHA, Rep. 250, LRA Ruppin, 558, 20 August 1945.
65. Ibid., 1 September 1945, 1. For a report from a district (Nauen) that met the August deadline, see BLHA, Rep. 203, 332, 24 July 1945.
66. BLHA-SED, Rep. 330, I/2, 6, Bl. 40, 14 August 1945.

67. BLHA-SED, Rep. 330, I/2, 11, Bl. 9, 15 August 1945.
68. BLHA, Rep. 250, LRA Ruppin, 558, 1 September 1945, 2.
69. Steinhoff, "Das Land Brandenburg in der ersten Nachkriegsjahren," 139.
70. BLHA, Rep. 203, 332, 7 August 1945. It is not clear from this report if the "gentleman" *("ein Herr")* in Guben was the *Landrat* or another employee of the local administration.
71. "Gesetz des Landes Thüringen über die Reinigung der öffentlichen Verwaltung von Nazi-Elementen," in *Um ein antifaschistisch-demokratisches Deutschland: Dokumente aus den Jahren 1945–1949* (Berlin: Staatsverlag der Deutschen Demokratischen Republik, 1968), 97–100. On the development of the Thuringia law, see Helga Welsh, *Revolutionärer Wandel auf Befehl? Entnazifizierungs- und Personalpolitik in Thüringen und Sachsen (1945–1948)* (Munich: R. Oldenbourg Verlag, 1989), 43–46; Meinicke, "Zur Entnazifizierung," 9–10.
72. Meinicke, "Zur Entnazifizierung," 11. Meinicke notes that a similar development occurred in Mecklenburg, while Saxony and Saxon-Anhalt issued laws similar to Thuringia's.
73. BLHA, Rep. 203, 330, Bl. 4, 27 August 1945. It is unclear if the district of Potsdam cited in this report was the rural district surrounding the city *(Landkreis)* or the district encompassed by the city itself *(Stadtkreis)*.
74. BLHA, Rep. 203, 330, Bl. 18, 31 August 1945.
75. The KPD's chief of "agitation and propaganda," Fred Oelßner, was at the forefront of the attempt to bring ideological clarity to these issues; see his articles in the *Deutsche Volkszeitung* (Berlin): "Die politisch-moralische Vernichtung des Nazismus," 7 October 1945, 3; "Das reaktionäre Preußentum," 14 October 1945, 3; "Das reaktionäre Preußentum," 21 October 1945, 3; and his postwar remembrances, "Die Anfänge unserer Parteischulung," in *Vereint sind wir alles,* 145–157.
76. SAPMO-BA, I/3/1–2, 114, "Stenographische Niederschrift der Groß-Berliner Funktionärkonfernz im Palast (früher Zirkus Schumann)," 5–6.
77. *Revolutionäre deutsche Parteiprogramme,* 199.
78. SMA Order no. 2, in *Um ein antifascistisch-demokratisches Deutschland,* 54–55. See the analysis of this order in Hermann Weber, *Geschichte der DDR,* 3rd ed. (Munich: Deutscher Taschenbuch Verlag, 1989), 69–71. East German writers regularly pointed out that political activity was first permitted in the Soviet zone, whereas the Americans initially prohibited German political activity. This was especially the case in studies of areas that were initially under U.S. occupation. See Gräfe and Wehner, "Die Hilfe der sowjetischen Militärorgane," 221–222; Wille, "Das Ringen der Arbeiterklasse," 432; Otto Buchwitz, *Brüder in eins nun die Hände* (Berlin: Dietz Verlag, 1956), 13–18.
79. "Kommunique über die Bildung des Blocks der antifaschistisch-demokratischen Parteien," in *Um ein antifaschistisch-demokratisches Deutschland,* 92. See also Manfred Koch, "Der Demokratische Block," in Hermann

Weber, ed., *Parteiensystem zwischen Demokratie und Volksdemokratie: Dokumente und Materialien zum Funktionswandel der Parteien und Massenorgnisationen in der SBZ/DDR, 1945–1950* (Cologne: Verlag Wissenschaft und Politik, 1982), 281–282; the document is also reprinted here, 301–302.

80. SAPMO-BA, Pieck NL, 36, 718, Bl. 99.

81. Several drafts of these guidelines are in the Pieck file, ibid. The 27 July and 3 August drafts are also reprinted in Siegfried Suckut, *Blockpolitik in der SBZ/DDR, 1945–1949* (Cologne: Verlag Wissenschaft und Politik, 1986), 70–74, 76–79. The text of the 3 August guidelines cited here is taken from Suckut, *Blockpolitik*, 76–79.

82. "Strengste Verstrafung der Naziverbrecher," *Deutsche Volkszeitung* (Berlin), 4 November 1945, 1.

83. "The Report on the Tripartite Conference of Berlin (Potsdam), 17 July–2 August 1945," reprinted in Beate Ruhm von Oppen, ed., *Documents on Germany under Occupation, 1945–1954* (London: Oxford University Press, 1955), 42–44.

84. At the same 3 August meeting where the denazification guidelines were approved, it was also decided to hold a public meeting in Berlin to discuss the Potsdam Agreement. The Antifascist Bloc's Declaration produced at this meeting fully supported the provisions of the Potsdam Agreement and the goal of destroying Nazism in Germany. SAPMO-BA, Pieck NL, 36, 718, Bl. 99; "Erklärung des Blocks der antifaschistisch-demokratischen Parteien zu den Beschlüssen der Potsdamer Konferenz," in *Um ein antifascistisch-demokratisches Deutschland*, 119–120.

85. Naimark, *The Russians in Germany*, chap. 1.

86. Ibid., 45–46.

87. *VOBl.*, 30 November 1945, 53. Copies of the circular letter dated 23 October 1945, in BLHA, Rep. 250, LRA Calau/Senftenberg, 221 and BLHA, Rep. 203, 28.

88. BLHA, Rep. 250, LRA Calau/Senftenberg, 221, Bl. 51.

89. Ibid., Bl. 59, Bl. 67.

90. Ibid., Bl. 69–73.

91. Ibid., Bl. 78. Kolessov's answer to this request is penciled in at the bottom of this page by a translator and dated 25 January 1946.

92. Ibid., Bl. 102.

93. Ibid., Bl. 108–109.

94. Ibid., Bl. 118.

95. Ibid., Bl. 119.

96. BLHA, Rep. 250, LRA Ruppin, 637, 28 December 1945.

97. BLHA, Rep. 250, LRA Ruppin, 637.

98. BLHA, Rep. 250, LRA Calau/Senftenberg, 221, 5 February 1946.

99. BLHA, Rep. 230, OLRA Bernau, 15, 18 January 1946.

100. BLHA, Rep. 202A, 39, Bl. 1–4.

101. BLHA, Rep. 250, LRA Beeskow-Storkow, 27, Bl. 18, 24 February 1946.
102. Ibid., Bl. 26.
103. Ibid., Bl. 19.
104. Ibid., Bl. 20.
105. Ibid., Bl. 21.
106. Mayor B. does show up again, two years later, in a report from the *Landrat's* office. By this time he was apparently no longer the mayor but simply held a license to be a glazier in the town. The town's "antifascists" finally got their revenge when three members of the local Antifascist Bloc appeared before a denazification commission and gave incriminating evidence that resulted in the revocation of his business license. BLHA, Rep. 250, LRA Beeskow-Storkow, 343, Bl. 3, 10 March 1948.
107. BLHA, Rep. 250, LRA Ruppin, 558, "Runderlass Nr. 47," 22 February 1946.
108. BLHA, Rep. 250, LRA Ruppin, 558, 24 June 1946.
109. BLHA, Rep. 202A, 39, Bl. 1–4.
110. BLHA, Rep. 203, 421, Bl. 20, 2 July 1946.
111. BLHA, Rep. 250, LRA Ruppin, 558, 15 August 1946.
112. BLHA, Rep. 203, 421, Bl. 29, 12 July 1946.
113. Ibid., Bl. 20, 2 July 1946.
114. BLHA, Rep. 250, LRA Luckenwalde, 211, 16 May 1946; 14 October 1946.
115. SAPMO-BA, IV, 2/13, 7, 13–14 August 1946, 6. For a report on the slowing of dismissals, see BLHA, Rep. 203, 421, Bl. 84–85, 29 October 1946.
116. BLHA, Rep. 203, Entnazifizierung, 8, Bl. 133.
117. Ralf Schäfer, "Die Entnazifizierung von Verwaltung, Justiz und Volksbildung—wichtiger Bestandteil der antifaschistisch-demokratischen Umwälzung: Dargestellt am Land Brandenburg," (Ph.D. diss., Pädigogischen Hochschule Erich Weinert, Magdeburg, 1986), 76.

3. Expropriation, Land Reform, and the PGs

1. "Extracts from the Report on the Tripartite Conference of Berlin (Potsdam)," in von Oppen, *Documents on Germany,* 42–43.
2. SMA Order 42, dated 27 August 1945, *VOBl.,* 1, 20 October 1945, 2.
3. BLHA, Rep. 250, LRA Angermünde, 258, Bl. 1, 1 August 1945; BLHA, Rep. 202G, 150, Bl. 30.
4. SAPMO-BA, Ulbricht NL, 182, 853, Bl. 29, 29 May 1945. A similar registration took place in Beeskow-Storkow. See BLHA, Rep. 250, LRA Beeskow-Storkow, 3357, 11 July 1945.
5. On the attempt to clarify these overlapping registration schemes, see BLHA, Rep. 250, LRA Ruppin, 558, 4 September 1945.
6. BLHA, Rep. 250, LRA Cottbus, 196, Bl. 85–88, 12 October 1945.
7. BLHA, Rep. 250, LRA Cottbus, 196, Bl. 50, 12 January 1946.
8. BLHA, Rep. 250, LRA Ruppin, 68, Bl. 93, 9 June 1945.

9. BLHA-SED, Rep. 330, I/2, 6, Bl. 125, 10 July 1945.

10. BLHA-SED, Rep. 330, I/2, 13, Bl. 5, 3 August 1945.

11. SAPMO-BA, Ulbricht NL, 182, 853, 14 June 1945.

12. BLHA, Rep. 230, OLRA Bernau, 13, 1 November 1945.

13. BLHA, Rep. 206, 3016, Bl. 190.

14. Ibid., Bl. 134, 2.

15. BLHA, Rep. 250, LRA Cottbus, 196, Bl. 51, 10 January 1946.

16. BLHA, Rep. 206, 3016, Bl. 78, 1 February 1946.

17. Ibid., Bl. 10, 25/26 January 1946.

18. Ibid., Bl. 8.

19. Ibid., Bl. 299, 25 July 1946.

20. Monika Stargardt, "Die rechtliche Wirkung von Maßnahmen der Länder der ehemaligen Sowjetischen Besatzungszone Deutschlands zur Enteigung des Aktienvermögens juristischer Personen mit Sitz in der ehemaligen sowjetischen Besatzungszone Deutschlands" (Ph.D. diss., Gesellschaftswissenschaftlichen Fakultät des Wissenschaftlichen Rates der Humblolt-Universität Berlin, 1969), 65.

21. Hans Heitzer, *DDR geschichtlicher Überblick*, 4th rev. ed. (Berlin: Dietz Verlag, 1987), 54.

22. Thomas, "1945–1949," 56, 63.

23. Staritz, *Die Gründung der DDR*, 77; Weber, *Geschichte der DDR*, 110–115; Hans-Georg Merz, "Bodenreform in der SBZ," *Deutschland Archiv* 24 (1991): 1159–66.

24. Kleßmann, *Die doppelte Staatsgründung*, 80–81. Welsh agreed with Kleßmann's approach but nonetheless eschewed studying more than the denazification of the administration. See Welsh, *Revolutionärer Wandel auf Befehl?* 9–10.

25. BLHA-SED, Rep. 330, I/2, 10, Bl. 64, 2, 5 July 1945. A similar decision was taken in Wandlitz. See SAPMO-BA, Ulbricht NL, 183, 853, Bl. 104–106, 22 July 1945. *Landrat* Walter Fenz in Nauen also instituted an expropriation program that targeted PGs who had joined the party before 1935 and "high party functionaries." As far as other PGs were concerned, the decision was made on a case-by-case basis. See Fenz's report in BLHA, Rep. 203, 249, 17 July 1945.

26. BLHA-SED, Rep. 330, I/2, 10, Bl. 29, 8 August 1945, 7.

27. BLHA-SED, Rep. 330, I/2, 6, Bl. 125–126, 10 July 1945. Similar confusion reigned in Fürstenwald/Spree, where the local Soviet commander had declared that all expropriations were to be handled by the courts, while the courts claimed that they had no jurisdiction over such matters. BLHA-SED, Rep. 330, I/2, 12, Bl. 27, 30 August 1945.

28. "Zentrale Regelung der Beschlagnahme der Nazivermögen," *VOBl.*, 20 October 1945. Order dated 16 August 1945.

29. This was due to the fact that the seizures could be construed as violating SMA Order 9 of 21 June 1945, which called for the restarting of industrial

production in the Soviet zone. For a copy of this order, see *Um ein anti-faschistisch-demokratisches Deutschland*, 72–75.

30. "Beschlagnahme von Industriebetrieben," *VOBl.*, 20 October 1945. Order dated 25 August 1945.

31. "Befehl Nr. 124 des Obersten Chefs der Sowjetischen Militäradministration in Deutschland über die Beschlagnahme und die Übernahme einiger Eigentumskategorien," in *Um ein antifaschistisch-demokratisches Deutschland*, 189–192. SMA Order 126, issued 31 October 1945, also called for the confiscations and differed from Order 124 insofar as it required "all German institutions, organizations, firms, concerns, and all private persons" in possession of such property to file a written report with the local German authorities within two weeks. "Befehl Nr. 126 des Obersten Chefs der Sowjetischen Militäradministration in Deutschland zur Konfiskation des Eigentums der nationalsozialistischen Partei, ihrer Organe und der ihr angeschlossenen Organisationen," in *Um ein antifaschistisch-demokratisches Deutschland*, 194–196.

32. BLHA, Rep. 250, LRA Ruppin, 849, 27 November 1945.

33. KA Ruppin, Rat der Stadt Altruppin, I/A/2.1/7, "Protokoll über die Gemeinderatsitzung am 13. Juli 1945 im Rathaus." The constable defended himself before the authorities at the subsequent meeting of the communal council on 20 July 1945; see minutes, ibid.

34. The records of these petitions in the archives of the *Oberlandrat*'s office of Brandenburg/Havel are voluminous, filling three entire files: BLHA, Rep. 230, OLRA Brandenburg/Havel, files 4, 5, and 6.

35. BLHA-SED, Rep. 330, I/2, 10, Bl. 38, 28 August 1945, 3.

36. BLHA, Rep. 212, 409, Bl. 1, 30 November 1945.

37. BLHA, Rep. 250, LRA Ruppin, 637, 12 December 1945.

38. BLHA, Rep. 230, OLRA Brandenburg/Havel, 4, Bl. 14, letter from "Franz K." to "Präsidenten der Provinzialverwaltung," 22 October 1945. Franz K. was one of the people expelled from Breddin; his letter explains what occurred.

39. Ibid., Bl. 19.

40. Ibid., Bl. 20.

41. Ibid., Bl. 2–3.

42. Ibid., Bl. 18.

43. "Enteigung von Nazibesitz," *VOBl.*, 20 February 1946, 56–57. Dated 3 December 1945.

44. "Befehl Nr. 97 des Obersten Chefs der Sowjetischen Militäradministration in Deutschland über die Schaffung einer Deutschen Zentralkommission für Beschlagnahme und Sequestierung mit Ausführungsbestimmen," reprinted, in a slightly abridged version, in *Um ein antifaschistisch-demokratisches Deutschland*, 252–256. An unabridged version of the order can be found in BLHA, Rep. 230, OLRA Bernau, 69, Bl. 24–25.

45. BLHA, Rep. 230, OLRA Bernau, 69, Bl. 21–23, 3 May 1946.

46. Ibid., Bl. 22.
47. BLHA, Rep. 230, OLRA Bernau, 69, Bl. 89–102. Whether those listed as killed by the Red Army died before or after the end of the war is unclear.
48. Ibid., Bl. 6, 2.
49. "Mitteilung über die Übergabe der beschlagnahmten Betriebe der Kreigsverbrecher und aktiven Nationalsozialisten durch die Sowjetische Militäradministration an die Provinzialverwaltung Brandenburg und die Landesverwaltung Thüringen," 8 August 1946, in *Um ein antifaschistischdemokratisches Deutschland,* 318–319. Fait gives slightly different numbers: 1,371 businesses expropriated, but only 532 returned to their previous owners. Fait also notes that by August 1948, the total number of expropriated businesses had increased slightly to 1,428. See Fait, "Brandenburg," 94.
50. "Verordnung zur entschädigungslosen Übergabe von Betrieben und Unternehmungen in die Hand des Volkes," *VOBl.,* 23 August 1946. Dated 5 August 1946.
51. "Befehl Nr. 64 des Obersten Chefs der Sowjetischen Militäradministration in Deutschland zur Beendigung des Sequesterverfahrens," 17 April 1948, in *Um ein antifaschistisch-demokratisches Deutschland,* 620–622.
52. Günter Braun, "Wahlen und Abstimmungen," in Broszat and Weber, *SBZ-Handbuch,* 381–382. See also Helene Fiedler and Traude Köhler, "Dokumente zum Volksentscheid in Sachsen 1946," *Zeitschrift für Geschichtswissenschaft* 34 (1986): 523–533.
53. Friedrich Ebert, "Die nächsten Aufgaben der SED," *Tägliche Rundschau* (Berlin), 29 June 1946, 3.
54. "Verordnung zur entschädigungslosen Übergabe von Betrieben und Unternehmungen in die Hand des Volkes," *VOBl.,* 23 August 1946.
55. Sägebrecht, *Erinnerungen,* 357–358.
56. "Verordnung über die Bodenreform in der Provinz Mark Brandenburg," 6 September 1945, *VOBl.,* 20 October 1946, 8–11.
57. "Grundbesitz der Nazis," 10 October 1945, *VOBl.,* 30 November 1945, 55.
58. BLHA, Rep. 203, 20, Bl. 135–137, 16 September 1945.
59. "Vermessung und Bodenzuteilung," *VOBl.,* 30 November 1945, 54. Order issued 24 September 1945.
60. SAPMO-BA, IV, 2/13, 226. Bechler also reported that, in an attempt to correct some of the "mistakes and hardships" that accompanied the land reform, 108 expropriated landholders who had shown proof of "antifascist" activity were resettled or given positions as agricultural "specialists." Bernhard Bechler, "Provinz Mark Brandenburg im Aufstieg," *Tägliche Rundschau* (Berlin), 13 April 1946, 3.
61. Fait, "Brandenburg," 92. Fait notes that the total numbers for the land reform program are unclear; another tally of the results reported 2,220 expropriated properties totaling 751,115 hectares divided among 72,487 fami-

lies. These lower numbers were cited by Bernhard Bechler, "Einheit—Kampf—Leistung," *Täglicher Rundschau* (Berlin), 1 January 1946, 3.

62. Bernhard Bechler, "Zur Durchführung der Bodenreform und der Aufgaben der Gegenseitigen Bauernhilfe," in Provinzausschuß der Gegenseitigen Bauernhilfe Mark Brandenburg, *Parlament der Bauern: Erster Provinz-Kongress der Gegenseitigen Bauernhilfe der Mark Brandenburg am 16. und 17. März 1946 in Potsdam* (Potsdam: Verlag Märkische Volksstimme, n.d. [1946]), 26–27. The Mutual Assistance Committees were established to oversee the disbursement of livestock, agricultural machinery, seed, and fertilizer to the beneficiaries of the land reform program. See "Ausführungsverordnung Nr. 6 zur Durchführung der Bodenreform über die Bildung der 'Ausschüsse der gegenseitigen Bauernhilfe,'" 17 October 1945, *VOBl.*, 15 November 1945, 32–33, and Brandenburg Industry and Agriculture Minister Heinrich Rau's description of the committees' duties in *Aus eigener Kraft: Wirtschaftsplan 1946 für die Landwirtschaft der Mark Brandenburg* (Potsdam: Verlag "Der Märker", n.d. [1946]), 26–28. For an overview of the political role of the committees, see Dietrich Staritz, "Vereinigung der gegenseitigen Bauernhilfe (VdgB)," in Broszat and Weber, *SBZ-Handbuch*, 760–766.

63. "Bauernstimmen von den großen brandenburgischen Bauernkonferenzen," *Volkswille* (Potsdam), 13 October 1945, 4.

64. SAPMO-BA, I/2/5, 40, Bl. 162–163, 19/20 November 1945. Sägebrecht's figures regarding the number of settlers refer to the entire Soviet zone, not just Brandenburg.

65. "Befehl Nr. 2 des Obersten Chefs der Sowjetischen Militäradministration in Deutschland über die Zulassung antifaschistischer Parteien und Organisationen," 10 June 1946, in *Um ein antifaschistisch-demokratisches Deutschland*, 54–55. The formation of the SED was seen by both eastern and western historians as a crucial turning point in the political history of the Soviet zone. For many West German historians, the amalgamation of the parties was a "forced unification" that gave the communists, and thus the Soviets, ultimate control over what was to become the dominant party in the GDR. This viewpoint was succinctly presented in Reiner Pommerin, "Die Zwangsvereinigung von KPD und SPD zur SED: Eine britische Analyse vom April 1946," *Vierteljahresheft für Zeitgeschichte* 36 (1988): 319–338. East German historians rejected this viewpoint. For a good comparison with the Pommerin article, see Hans-Joachim Krusch, "Zur Gründung der SED in April 1946: Die Vereinigung von KPD und SED in den Bezirken," *Zeitschrift für Geschichtswissenschaft* 34 (1986): 195–209. For the formation of the SED in Brandenburg, there are currently only monographs by East German historians. Two noteworthy studies are Karl Urban, *Die Vereinigung von KPD und SPD in der Provinz Brandenburg* (Potsdam: SED-Bezirkleitung Potsdam, Kommission zur Erforschung der Geschichte der örtlichen Arbeiterbewegung, 1976); Rena Wilhelm, *Die SED—führende*

Kraft des antifaschistisch-demokratischen Neuaufbaus im Land Branden-burg, April 1946 bis Mitte 1948 (Potsdam: SED-Bezirkleitung Potsdam, Kommission zur Erforschung der Geschichte der örtlichen Arbeiter-bewegung, 1988). For an analysis of the Brandenburg SED's political pro-gram during the occupation, see Elke Warning, "Die Politik der SED zur Entwicklung der Staatsorgane—unter besonderer Berücksichtigung der Volksvertretungen—der Provinz Mark Brandenburg bzw. des Landes Brandenburg zu Interessenvertretungen des werktätigen Volkes (1946 bis Oktober 1949)" (Ph.D. diss., Institute für Marxismus-Leninismus beim Zentralkommitee der Sozialistischen Einheitspartei Deutschlands, Berlin, 1982).

66. Braun, "Wahlen und Abstimmungen," 384.
67. For the communal elections, see "Wahlordnung für die Gemeindewahlen in der sowjetischen Besatzungszone Deutschlands," *VOBl.*, 26 July 1946, 180. For the provincial and *Kreis* elections, see "Wahlordnung für die Landtags- und Kreistagswahlen in der sowjetischen Besatzungszone Deutschlands," *VOBl.*, 7 October 1946, 323. These two statutes employ al-most identical wording in the relevant sections regarding the voting rights of PGs. The only substantial difference between the two statutes is that the law governing the communal elections excluded all former members of the National Socialist Workers' Party, whereas the second law added a phrase excluding members of other National Socialist organizations as well.
68. Otto Grotewohl, "Über die Bedeutung der Gemeindewahlen," *Tägliche Rundschau* (Berlin), 28 June 1946, 4.
69. BLHA, Rep. 250, LRA Beeskow-Storkow, 244.
70. On provincial government plans, see Heinrich Rau, "Die Rolle der Gegen-seitigen Bauernhilfe bei der Frühjahrbestellung: Rede auf dem Ersten Provinz-Kongreß der Gegenseitigen Bauernhilfe der Mark Brandenburg, 16 März 1946," reprinted in idem, *Für die Arbeiter-und-Bauern-Macht: Aus-gewählte Reden und Aufsätze, 1922–1961* (Berlin: Dietz Verlag, 1984), 170–171.
71. BLHA, Rep. 250, LRA Angermünde, 252, 29 August 1946.
72. Ibid., 27 August 1946.
73. On the prohibition of telephone and radios, see BLHA, Rep. 230, OLRA Brandenburg/Havel, 6, Bl. 7, 24 November 1945; BLHA, Rep. 203, 20, 2 October 1945; "Wozu brauchen Nazis Radioapparate?" *Volkswille* (Pots-dam), 28 February 1946. On the control of bank accounts, see BLHA, Rep. 203, 21, Bl. 425, 9 March 1946. For the suspension of welfare and pension benefits, see BLHA, Rep. 250, LRA Ostprignitz, 50, Bl. 78, *Nach-richtenblatt des Landratsamte des Kreises Ostprignitz*, 19 October 1945; BLHA, Rep. 250, LRA Ostprignitz, 51, Bl. 98, "Btr. Auszahlung von Pensionen," in *Nachrichtenblatt des Landratsamte des Kreises Ostprignitz*, 26 July 1946.
74. BLHA-SED, Rep. 330, I/2, 11, Bl. 29–30, 30 September 1945.

75. BLHA-SED, Rep. 330, I/3, 165, letter from the KPD Ortsgruppe Brück, 14 January 1946, and reply from the KPD Kreisleitung Zauch-Belzig, 26 January 1946. The view expressed in this instance by the KPD leadership was more an expression of deference to the wishes of the Soviet commander than a reflection of KPD policy regarding forcing PGs to attend meetings. Compare, for example, the positive report in the Brandenburg KPD's newspaper of a "special assembly" of 450 PGs in Eichwalde who were shown an atrocity film, *Stadt und Land, Volkswille* (Potsdam), 9 December 1945, 8.
76. BLHA, Rep. 250, LRA Cottbus, 196, Bl. 85–88, 12 October 1945.
77. BLHA-SED, Rep. 330, I/2, 15, Bl. 58, 14 January 1946.
78. BLHA-SED, Rep. 330, I/3, 108, Bl. 32, 19 January 1946.
79. "Der antifaschistisch-demokratische Block und die Rolle der Sozialistischen Einheitspartei Deutschlands: Aus dem Referat auf der 1. Funktionärkonferenz der SED, Provinzialverband Mark Brandenburg, Potsdam, 2 Juni 1946," in Friedrich Ebert, *Einheit der Arbeiterklasse—Unterpfand des Sieges: Ausgewählte Reden und Aufsätze* (Berlin: Dietz Verlag, 1959), 44.
80. Hans Teubner, "Der Kampf gegen die Nazis," *Deutsche Volkszeitung* (Berlin), 11 November 1945, 1.
81. "Willhelm Pieck an die Gratulanten" (speech on the occasion of his seventieth birthday), *Deutsche Volkszeitung* (Berlin), 5 January 1946, 3.
82. M. K. [probably Max Keilson, editor in chief], "Was wird aus den Nazis?" *Deutsche Volkszeitung* (Berlin), 31 January 1946, 1.
83. "Aus der Rede Otto Grotewohls auf der Sitzung des Parteivorstandes der SED vom 18. bis 20. Juni," in Ruth-Kristin Rößler, ed., *Die Entnazifizierungspolitik der KPD/SED 1945–1948: Dokumente und Materialen* (Goldbach: Keip Verlag, 1994), 88–93. Grotewohl's views regarding the PGs became the SED's official line in the period leading up to the elections. See "SED und nominelle Pgs," 20 June 1946, in *Dokumente der Sozialistischen Einheitspartei Deutschlands* (Berlin: Dietz Verlag, 1952), 1:52–53; Fred Oelssner, "Unser Kampf gegen den Faschismus: Unsere Stellungnahme zu den nominellen Pgs," *Neues Deutschland* (Berlin), 13 August 1946, 2; "Die kleinen Pgs," *Neues Deutschland* (Berlin), 19 October 1946, 2.

4. The Denazification Experiment

1. Directive 24 was published in the *Official Gazette of the Control Council for Germany*, no. 5, 31 March 1946, 98–115. On its implementation in Berlin, see LA Berlin, OMGBS 4/17–1/2, Allied Komandantura Berlin, "Establishment of Denazification Commissions and Appeal Procedure," 26 February 1946.
2. "Richtlinien für die Entnazifizierung," *Tägliche Rundschau* (Berlin), 12 March 1946, 5–6.
3. "Sitzungsprotokoll des Landesblockausschusses der antifaschistisch-demokratischen Parteien Brandenburgs," 17 April 1946, reprinted in Fritz

Reinert, ed., *Protokolle des Landesblockausschusses der antifaschistisch-demokratischen Parteien Brandenburgs, 1945–1950* (Weimar: Verlag Hermann Böhlaus, 1994), 42.

4. BLHA, Rep. 250, LRA Beeskow-Storkow, 26, Bl. 114, letter from the Antifascist Bloc to "Rechtsanwalt und Notar Dr. K," 31 July 1946. For Dr. K.'s letter, see ibid., Bl. 115, 9 July 1946. See also the similar request, ibid., Bl. 112, 1 August 1946, and the letter from the *Oberlandrat* in Bernau to all *Kreis* leaders regarding the status of Directive 24, ibid., Bl. 130, 13 July 1946.

5. *Der Sprach-Brockhaus: Deutsches Bildwörterbuch für Jedermann,* 5th ed. (Leipzig: F. A. Brockhaus, 1949), 167.

6. For critical reports on denazification commissions in western sectors of Berlin, see "Entnazifizierung am laufenden Band," *Tägliche Rundschau* (Berlin), 31 July 1946, 6; "Entnazifizierungskommissionen," *Tägliche Rundschau* (Berlin), 22 August 1946, 1–2; "Schein-Entnazifizierung in Tempelhof," *Tägliche Rundschau* (Berlin), 24 August 1946, 6. For reports on the inefficacy of the western commissions, see "Die Entnazifizierung in Bayern," *Neues Deutschland* (Berlin), 4 July 1946, 2; "Wie wird die Entnazifizierung in den Westzonen durchgeführt?" *Tägliche Rundschau* (Berlin), 14 August 1946, 3; "Entnazifizierung in der Kreise," *Neues Deutschland* (Berlin), 6 November 1946, 1; "Die politische Reinigung," *Neues Deutschland* (Berlin), 10 November 1946, 1; "Die Komödie der 'Entnazifizierung,'" *Tägliche Rundschau* (Berlin), 10 November 1946, 1–2; "Entnazifizierungsgroteske," *Neues Deutschland* (Berlin), 8 January 1947, 1.

7. W. P. [Wilhelm Pieck?], "Entnazifizierung," *Tägliche Rundschau* (Berlin), 16 March 1946, 1–2; Hilde Benjamin, "Keine Hemmung bei der Entnazifizierung," *Tägliche Rundschau* (Berlin), 4 June 1946, 5.

8. Wilhelm Pieck, "Wir brauchen die Einheit Deutschlands," speech before an SED meeting in Cottbus, 13 September 1946, BLHA, Rep. 250, LRA Cottbus, 198, Bl. 438, 4. Hans Schlange-Schöningen, a Weimar conservative and former member of the second Brüning government, was the head of the food distribution administration in the British zone.

9. Directive 24, 98.

10. LA Berlin, OMGBS, 4/38–3/40, "Report Concerning Denazification Commissions in the Russian Sector," 17 January 1947.

11. Ibid., 102–115.

12. BLHA, Rep. 203, 421, Bl. 105–106, "Protokoll Nr. 18: Über die Besprechung der Personal-Referenten der Provinzialverwaltung Mark Brandenburg," 12 December 1946.

13. BLHA, Rep. 203, Entnazifizierung, 72, letter from "Leiter der Verwaltung der SMA der Provinz Brandenburg." The letter is undated but is attached to documents from January 1947.

14. BLHA, 203, 617, Bl. 82–83, 6 February 1947.

15. Bernhard Bechler, "Letzter Abschnitt der Entnazifizierung und Ent-

militarisierung in der Provinz Mark Brandenburg," in Provinzialverwaltung Mark Brandenburg, *Direktive 24: Entfernung von Nationalsozialisten und Personen, die den Bestrebungen der Alliierten feindlich gegenüber stehen, aus Ämtern und verantwortlichen Stellungen* (Potsdam: Märkische Druck- und Verlags-GmbH., [1947]), 3; 5.

16. BLHA, Rep. 203, 629, Bl. 174, 3 April 1947.

17. StA. Brandenburg/Havel, 202, 27, 18 December 1946.

18. BLHA, Rep. 203, Entnazifizierung, 15, Protokoll 1, 23 December 1946.

19. "Durchführung der Direktive Nr. 24 des Alliierten Kontrollrates (Runderlaß Nr. 0004/I)," *VOBl.*, 6 March 1947, 69–70. A copy of the circular letter as sent to the local authorities can be found in BLHA, Rep. 203, Entnazifizierung, 72.

20. Ibid.

21. Ibid.

22. BLHA, Rep. 203, Entnazifizierung, 72, 9 January 1947. This memo can also be found in BLHA, Rep. 250, LRA Luckau, 556.

23. BLHA, Rep. 203, 421, Bl. 115, "Protokoll Nr. 20 über die Besprechung der Personal-Referenten der Provinzialverwaltung Mark Brandenburg," 14 January 1947.

24. BLHA, Rep. 203, Entnazifizierung, 72, "Runderlass Nr. 11/I," 20 January 1947. An even shorter deadline of 10 February 1947 was set for the denazification of the police. BLHA, Rep. 250, LRA Ruppin, 543, Bl. 35, "Rundschreiben Nr. 7/IX," 14 January 1947. For an example of the establishment of unauthorized denazification commissions, see the report from the commune of Schmellwitz (*Kreis* Cottbus), where four village commissions were established in February 1947. BLHA, Rep. 250, LRA Cottbus, 197, Bl. 299, 6 March 1947.

25. BLHA, Rep. 203, Entnazifizierung, 72, "Runderlass Nr. 18/I," 7 February 1947.

26. BLHA, Rep. 250, LRA Luckau, 556, 30 January, 20 February 1947. The situation in Spremberg was similar. The chair of the denazification commission sent a circular letter to district mayors complaining of their misunderstanding of the "political necessity" of the program and their failure to submit reports. BLHA, Rep. 250, LRA Spremberg, 173, 10 February 1947.

27. BLHA, Rep. 250, LRA Ruppin, 543, Bl. 38, "Resulution der Betriebsgruppe der SED beim Landratsamt des Kreises Ruppin," 3 January 1947.

28. BLHA-SED, Rep. 332, L/IV/2/12, 825, Bl. 3, 30 January 1947.

29. On the tensions between KPD and SPD members and the formation of the SED, see Naimark, *The Russians in Germany,* 275–317; Henry Krisch, *German Politics under Soviet Occupation* (New York: Columbia University Press, 1974); Norbert Mattedi, *Gründung und Entwicklung der Parteien in der sowjetischen Besatzungszone Deutschlands, 1945–1949* (Bonn: Bundesministerium für Gesamtdeutsche Fragen, 1966); Albrecht Kaden, *Einheit oder Freiheit? Die Widergründung der SPD 1945/6* (Berlin: Verlag

J. H. W. Dietz, 1964). For a discussion of the roots of the SPD-KPD tensions, see Andreas Dorpalen, "SPD und KPD in der Endphase der Weimarer Republik," *Vierteljahrshefte für Zeitgeschichte* 31 (1983): 75–107.

30. BLHA, Rep. 203, 311, Bl. 585, 7 March 1947.

31. Ibid., Bl. 582–583, 26 March 1947.

32. BLHA, Rep. 203, 631, Bl. 86.

33. See, for example, the letter from the mayor of Beeskow to the district denazification commission complaining of personnel shortages owing to Directive 24. BLHA, Rep. 203, 629, Bl. 118, 7 February 1947.

34. BLHA-SED, Rep. 332, L/IV/2/3, 23, Bl. 30, "Protokoll der Sekretariatsstizung," 17 February 1947. Economics Minister Rau made similar observations. See BLHA-SED, Rep. 332, L/IV/2/3, 23, Bl. 43, "Protokoll der Sekretariatsstizung," 24 February 1947. See also the SED Central Committee report, SAPMO-BA, IV, 2/13, 4, "Bericht über den Stand der Entnazifizierung der Wirtschaft und Verwaltung der Industrie und des Handwerks der Mark Brandenburg von 30 Januar 1947," 18 February 1947.

35. N. Orlow, "Was heißt Entnazifizierung?" *Tägliche Rundschau* (Berlin), 13 February 1947, 1.

36. "Schreiben des Blocks der antifaschistisch-demokratischen Parteien an die Sowjetische Militäradministration in Deutschland betreffend den Erlaß von Durchfürhungsbestimmungen zur Kontrollratsdirektive Nr. 24," in *Um ein antifaschistisch-demokratisches Deutschland,* 385.

37. Wilhelm Pieck, "Der Sinn der Entnazifizierung," *Neues Deutschland* (Berlin), 21 February 1947, 2. This article was also published in the SED's Brandenburg newspaper, *Märkische Volksstimme* (Potsdam), 25 February 1947, 1–2. See also the follow-up article on the new policy, "Keine schematische Durchführung der Direktive 24," *Märkische Volksstimme* (Potsdam), 26 February 1947, 2.

38. BLHA, Rep. 203, 630, Bl. 50, 24 February 1947.

39. Ibid., Bl. 48, 24 March 1947.

40. BLHA, Rep. 250, LRA Ostprignitz, 59, Bl. 205–206, speech delivered 27 February 1947. Document dated 7 March 1947.

41. BLHA, Rep. 203, Entnazifizierung, 72, "Runderlass Nr. 26/I," 4 March 1947.

42. BLHA, Rep. 203, 630, Bl. 97, 10 April 1947.

43. BLHA, Rep. 250, LRA Cottbus, 195, Bl. 70, 21 April 1947.

44. "Noch einmal: die kleinen Pgs," *Märkische Volksstimme* (Potsdam), 5 March 1947, 1; "Zur Frage der kleinen Pgs: Keine Diskiminierung der Kleinen!" *Märkische Volksstimme* (Potsdam), 14 March 1947, 2. See also a follow-up article, "Zur Frage der kleinen Pgs: Gerichtsverfahren zur Rehabilitierung?" *Märkische Volksstimme* (Potsdam), 15–16 March 1947, 2.

45. Bernhard Bechler, "Noch einmal: Entnazifizierung," *Märkische Volksstimme* (Potsdam), 19–20 April 1947, 1–2.

46. The idea of registering all former PGs was rejected by the interior ministers

of the Soviet zone on 1 June 1947. See SAPMO-BA, IV, 2/13, 109, "Protokoll der Konferenz der Innenminister der sowjetischen Zone," 3.

47. Alfred Grosser, *Germany in Our Time: A Political History of the Postwar Years,* trans. Paul Stephenson (New York: Praeger Publishers, 1971), 65.

48. Lucius D. Clay, *Decision in Germany* (New York: Doubleday & Company, 1950), 150, 152.

49. "Denazification and Democratization of Germany: Statement Made at the Sitting of the Council of Foreign Ministers, March 13, 1947," in V. M. Molotov, *Problems of Foreign Policy: Speeches and Statements, April 1945–November 1948* (Moscow: Foreign Languages Publishing House, 1949), 350–352.

50. Ibid., 351–352.

51. That the Soviets hoped to make the most of denazification at the Moscow meeting is evident in an order from the Brandenburg Interior Ministry two months before the conference was convened. In reference to denazification of the administration, it was noted that "the action should be completed before the beginning of the Moscow conference." BLHA, Rep. 250, LRA Luckau, 556, 13 January 1947.

52. "Aus der Rede Wilhelm Piecks auf der Sitzung des Parteivorstandes der SED am 21/22. Mai 1947," in Rößler, *Entnazifizierungspolitik,* 139.

53. "Aus der Rede von Walter Ulbricht auf der Sitzung der Innenminister vom 1. Juni 1947," ibid., 145.

54. "Order 201: Directives for the Execution of Control Council Directives Nos. 24 and 38 on Denazification," in von Oppen, *Documents,* 234–235. In Brandenburg, Order 201 was published in the SED newspaper *Märkische Volksstimme* (Potsdam), 18 August 1947, 1, and in *VOBl.,* October 1947, 185–186.

55. BLHA, Rep. 203, Entnazifizierung, 1, "Runderlaß 46/I," 27 August 1947, 4.

56. "Ausführungsbestimmung Nr. 2," published in the official handbook for the implementation of Order 201, Provinzialverwaltung Mark Brandenburg, *Befehl Nr. 201 des Obersten Chefs der Sowjetischen Militärverwaltung und Ausführungsbestimmungen 1–3, Direktiven 24 und 38 des Kontrollrats und die zugehörigen Runderlasse der Landesregierung Brandenburg* (Potsdam: Landesregierung Brandenburg Minister des Innern, [1947]), 8. A copy of the *Handbuch* is in BLHA, Rep. 203, 583.

57. BLHA, Rep. 203, Entnazifizierung, 1, "Runderlaß Nr. 46/I," 27 August 1947.

58. BA Potsdam, DVdI, Bestand 7, 69, Bl. 7, "Verfahrensordnung für die Entnazifizierungskommissionen gemäss Ausführungsbestimmungen (AB) Nr. 2 zum Befehl Nr. 201 des Obersten Chefs der SMAD."

59. BLHA, Rep. 250, LRA Spremberg, 97, 23 August 1947.

60. Paul Hentschel had been a member, along with Bechler, of the NKFD while a POW in the Soviet Union. After the war he was the head of the Interior

Ministry's Department of Administration of Personnel Questions. Hentschel was also the chairman of the provincial denazification commission in Potsdam. Biographical information from Broszat and Weber, *SBZ Handbuch*, 928.

61. BLHA, Rep. 250, LRA Calau/Senftenberg, 57, Bl. 1–2, 27 September 1947.

62. SAPMO-BA, Fechner NL, 101, 19, Zentralsekretairat Ulbricht-Fechner, "Einheitliche Durchführung von Massnahmen auf Grund des Befehls Nr. 201," 27 August 1947.

63. "Passives Wahlrecht auch für nominelle Pgs," *Neues Deutschland* (Berlin), 17 August 1947, 1.

64. "Ein Beschluß von weittragender Bedeutung," *Märkische Volksstimme* (Potsdam), 18 August 1947, 1.

65. "Ein Befehl von historischer Bedeutung," *Tägliche Rundschau* (Berlin), 17 August 1947, 1.

66. SAPMO-BA, Fechner NL, 101, 19, Zentralsekretairat Ulbricht-Fechner, "Einheitliche Durchführung von Massnahmen auf Grund des Befehls Nr. 201," 27 August 1947.

67. BLHA, Rep. 212, 500, Bl. 3, "Kurzer Vermerk über der Zonenkonferenz am 29.8.1947 bei der Deutsche Justizverwaltung in Berlin über der Durchführung der Befehl 201 der SMAiD."

68. "Was bedeutet der Befehl 201? Grundsätzliche Ausführungen des brandenburgischen Innenministers dazu," *Märkische Volksstimme* (Potsdam), 28 August 1947, 1.

69. BLHA, Rep. 250, LRA Lebus/Seelow, 53, Bl. 28, 29 August 1947.

70. Ibid., Bl. 31, 1 September 1947.

71. Ibid., Bl. 33, 1 September 1947.

72. BA Potsdam, DVdI, Bestand 7, 368, Bl. 41, Landeskriminalpolizeiamt Potsdam, "Tätigkeitsbericht August 1947," 8 September 1947.

73. BLHA, Rep. 202A, 39, 5 August 1947.

74. BLHA, Rep. 250, LRA Ruppin, 76, 13 September 1947.

75. Ibid., 12 November 1947.

76. BLHA, Rep. 250, LRA Cottbus, 197, Bl. 330, 9 October 1947.

77. Ibid., Bl. 287, 20 September 1947.

78. All quotations are from BLHA, Rep. 203, Entnazifizierung, 8, "Stimmen aus der Bevölkerung zum Befehl 201," 8 October 1947. Sokolovsky was the commander of the SMA beginning in the spring of 1946; he replaced the original commander, Zhukov, who was demoted in a "shake-up" of the SMA in early 1946. See Naimark, *The Russians in Germany*, 24.

79. BLHA, Rep. 203, 421, Bl. 207, "Protokoll Nr. 38 über die Besprechung der Personal-Referenten der Provinzialverwaltung Mark Brandenburg," 30 September 1947, 13–16.

80. [Bernhard] Bechler, "Es geht um die weitere Demokratisierung. An die Bevölkerung des Landes Brandenburg," *Märkische Volksstimme* (Potsdam), 4/5 October 1947, 1.

81. BLHA, Rep. 250, LRA Beeskow-Storkow, 344, Bl. 111–112, 8 October 1947.
82. KA Ruppin (Neuruppin), *Ruppiner Kreisblatt,* no. 24, 11 December 1947; no. 25, 18 December 1947; no. 26, 25 December 1947; no. 1, 1 January 1948; no. 6, 29 January 1947; no. 12, 11 March 1947.
83. BLHA, Rep. 250, LRA Angermünde, 262, Bl. 388, hearing, 4 November 1947; Bl. 448, hearing, 2 December 1947.
84. BLHA, Rep. 250, LRA Luckau, 556, "An die Bevölkerung des Kreises Luckau," *Luckauer Kreisblatt,* 28 November 1947, 1.
85. SAPMO-BA, IV/2/13, 103, "Innerministerkonferenz am 12 Oktober 1947 in Rehfelde/Sachsen," 7. Ulbricht's speech is a separate document in this file and has its own page numbers. At this same meeting, Erich Mielke, head of the zonal Interior Ministry (Deutsche Verwaltung des Innern, or DVdI), favorably noted Bechler's recently published call for public support of denazification as an example that should be followed in the other provinces. For Mielke's remarks, see ibid., p. 4 of the Protocol.
86. BA Potsdam, DVdI, Bestand 7, 81, Bl. 34–36.
87. BLHA, Rep. 203, Entnazifizierung, 1, 12 November 1947.
88. Wilhelm Koenen, "Die Demokratie von Innen sichern," *Märkische Volksstimme* (Potsdam), 3 September 1947, 1–2; "Über die Stellung der nominellen Pgs," *Märkische Volksstimme* (Potsdam), 6–7 September 1947, 1; "Was wird aus den ehemaligen Pgs?" *Märkische Volksstimme* (Potsdam), 19 September 1947, 1.
89. BLHA-SED, Rep. 332, L/IV/2, 3, Bl. 232, 19 December 1947.
90. BA Potsdam, DVdI, Bestand 7, 432, 13.
91. "Alle Kräfte für die Friedensarbeit: Der Demokratische Frauenbund des Landes Brandenburg zum Befehl 201," *Märkische Volksstimme* (Potsdam), 29 August 1947, 2.
92. "Aufruf betreffs Durchführung des Befehls 201," in Reinert, *Protokolle des Landesblockausschusses,* 171.
93. BLHA, Rep. 250, LRA Calau/Senftenberg, 223, "Um Schuld und Sühne der ehemaligen Pgs. (Die Durchführung des Befehls 201 des Marschalls Sokolowski)."
94. BLHA, Rep. 250, LRA Cottbus, 197, Bl. 330, 9 October 1947.
95. BA Potsdam, DVdI, Bestand 7, 432, 15 October 1947.
96. Ibid.
97. BLHA, Rep. 203, Entnazifizierung, 644, 4, 27 October 1947.
98. SAPMO-BA, IV 2/13, 4, "Über den Stand der Durchführung des Befehl 201," 31 October 1947, 13.
99. Ibid., "Besprechung über den Befehl 201 und damit verbundenen Aufgaben der Partei vom 30. Oktober 1947," 1.
100. Ibid., 2. Mielke based his charge that SED members paid bribes to assist Nazis on an incident in Brandenburg, where an SED member offered a 2,000 mark bribe to police to secure the release of a man arrested for mis-

treating forced laborers during the Nazi period. For details on this case, see SAPMO-BA, IV 2/13, 4, "Über den Stand der Durchführung des Befehl 201," 31 October 1947, 5.

101. BA Potsdam, DVdI, Bestand 7, 435, Bl. 8, "Zum Bericht über die Dienstfahrten im Lande Brandenburg," 5 November 1947.

102. BA Potsdam, DVdI, Bestand 7, 432, 8, 2 December 1947. This view was echoed in a 6 December 1947 report from the Landeskriminalpolizeiamt in Potsdam. BA Potsdam, DVdI, Bestand 7, 368, Bl. 145. Similar criticism of the mass organizations and the lack of interest among the population was made at a 2 January 1948 meeting of representatives of the denazification commissions in Brandenburg. See BA Potsdam, DVdI, Bestand 7, 435, "Protokoll über die Arbeitsbesprechung der Vertreter des 'Buros 201' der Entnazifizierungskommission des Landes Brandenburg in Potsdam am 2. Januar 1948," 4. This criticism was reiterated in a report for Ulbricht on Order 201 of 24 January 1948. See SAPMO-BA, Ulbricht NL, 182, 1197, 1.

103. BA Potsdam, DVdI, Bestand 7, 432, Bl. 42, "Protokoll der Tagung über den Befehl 201 am 22. Dezember 1947 mit dem stellvertr. Innenministern und den Leitern der Landesuntersuchungsorgane (K5)." The Brandenburg Interior Ministry issued an order for all denazification commissions to end their work by 15 December 1947. See BLHA, Rep. 203, 583, Bl. 22, "Rundverfügung Nr. 3," 18 November 1947. A subsequent order of 8 December 1947 extended the deadline to 15 January 1948. BLHA, Rep. 203, Entnazifizierung, 1, "Rundverfügung Nr. 4."

104. BA Potsdam, DVdI, Bestand 7, 432, "Protokoll der Tagung über den Befehl 201 am 22. Dezember 1947 mit dem stellvertr. Innenministern und den Leitern der Landesuntersuchungsorgane (K5)."

105. BLHA, Rep. 203, Entnazifizierung, 1, "Runderlass Nr. 61/I," 12 January 1948. A week before this circular letter was released, Hentschel laid the groundwork for the new program. He ordered the department heads of the provincial administration to forward to the district denazification commissions the names and personal *Fragebogen* of all employees dismissed on "political grounds" before 31 December 1946—i.e., before the beginning of the formal denazification. BLHA, Rep. 203, Entnazifizierung, 645, Bl. 209–213, 6–7 January 1948.

106. BA Potsdam, DVdI, Bestand 7, 432, 1–2.

107. Ibid., 10–11.

108. SAPMO-BA, IV/2/13, 4, "Auswertung die Tätigkeit der Entnazifizierungskommissionen seit dem Erlass des Befehls 201," 7 April 1948, 5.

109. Ulbricht's speech, "Die gegenwärtige Lage und die nächsten Aufgaben," is included in the protocol of the "Innenminister Konferenz am 31. Januar und 1. Februar 1948 in Altenstein, Thüringen," SAPMO-BA, IV/2/13, 109, 17. Ulbricht's speech is a separate document in this file with its own page numbers. The transcript is dated 4 February 1948.

110. Ibid., 19.
111. Ibid.
112. BA Potsdam, DVdI, Bestand 7, 434, Bl. 412, "Bericht über den Besuch beim Vertreter des Innenministers von Brandenburg, Herrn Hentschel am 6.2.1948."
113. Ibid., Bl. 412–413. See also BLHA, Rep. 203, Entnazifizierung, 1, "Rund-verfügung Nr. 5," 17 February 1948; "Rundverfügung Nr. 6," 6 March 1948.
114. BLHA, Rep. 203, Entnazifizierung, 1, "Rundverfügung Nr. 7," 12 March 1948.
115. BA Potsdam, DVdI, Bestand 7, 425, Bl. 10.
116. For the text of Order 35, see *Um ein antifaschistisch-demokratisches Deutschland,* 588–590.
117. BLHA, Rep. 203, 632, Bl. 82, 24 August 1949.
118. On the general crisis of apathy, defeatism, and hopelessness among many rank-and-file SED members in 1947, see Naimark, *The Russians in Germany,* 294–298.

5. The Denazification Commissions and the Purge

1. SAPMO-BA, Fechner NL, 101, 19, 27 August 1947.
2. BLHA, Rep. 203, 583, "Ausführungsbestimmungen Nr. 2," in *Befehl Nr. 201 und Ausführungsbestimmungen,* 3.
3. BLHA, Rep. 203, Entnazifizierung, 1, "Runderlaß Nr. 46/I," 27 August 1947, 2. See the request by the VVN for inclusion on the commissions. BLHA, Rep. 203, Entnazifizierung, 645, 62, Bl. 1, 1 August 1947.
4. BLHA, Rep. 203, 583, "Ausführungsbestimmungen Nr. 2," in *Befehl Nr. 201 und Ausführungsbestimmungen,* 3.
5. SAPMO-BA, IV, 2/13, 4, 25 February 1948.
6. BA Potsdam, DVdI, Bestand 7, 431, Teil I, Bl. 63–70. The SED held 67 per-cent of the seats in Brandenburg and had even greater control in the other four provinces of the Soviet zone: in Mecklenburg, 74 percent of the com-mission members were SED; in Sachsen-Anhalt, 70 percent; in Thuringia, 71 percent; and in Saxony, 69 percent.
7. SAPMO-BA, IV, 2/13, 4, 25 October 1947.
8. Ibid., 31 October 1947, 18–19.
9. BA Potsdam, DVdI, Bestand 7, 432, Bl. 104, 3 November 1947. Bechler later alerted the SMA to the number of PGs in the Forst LDP and noted that the head of LDP in the city was also a member of the provincial assembly known for his "aggressive and reactionary politics." BLHA, Rep. 203, 25, 10 November 1947. The situation in Forst led to a broader discussion within the Brandenburg Antifascist Bloc about allowing the political parties to recruit nominal PGs as members. The CDU and LDP came out strongly in favor of allowing PGs to join political parties, while the SED maintained

that this question should be put off until denazification was completed. Eventually it was determined that the parties could decide which PGs were permitted to join, but that these decisions could be overturned by the Antifascist Bloc. Reinert, *Protokolle des Landesblockausschusses*, "Sitzungsprotokoll Nr. 30," 28 October 1947, 176–177; "Sitzungsprotokoll Nr. 32," 28 November 1947, 181–183; "Sitzungsprotokoll Nr. 33," 19 December 1947, 183–185.

10. SAPMO-BA, Ulbricht NL, 182, 1197, Bl. 208, 24 January 1948.

11. BA Potsdam, DVdI, Bestand 7, 422, Bl. 32, 29 January 1948.

12. BLHA, Rep. 203, Entnazifizierung, 645, Bl. 290, 14 January 1948.

13. BLHA, Rep. 203, 630, Bl. 175, 23 March 1947.

14. BLHA, Rep. 203, 631, Bl. 53.

15. Tens of thousands of these *Fragebogen* are still stored in the Interior Ministry archive (BLHA, Rep. 203, Entnazifizierung) in Potsdam. These archives are closed to researchers under the terms of the federal Law for the Protection of Personal Data (Datenschutzgesetz). A blank copy of the *Fragebogen* used in Brandenburg during the Order 201 phase can be found in BA Potsdam, DVdI, Bestand 7, 433, Bl. 141–143.

16. BLHA, Rep. 203, 421, Bl. 209, 30 September 1947.

17. BLHA, Rep. 250, LRA Guben, 115, 18 October 1947.

18. BLHA, Rep. 250, LRA Beeskow-Storkow, 344, Bl. 3.

19. On the role of K5 in the creation of the secret police, see Naimark, *The Russians in Germany*, chap. 7.

20. Bechler, "Letzter Abschnitt der Entnazifizierung und Entmilitarisierung in der Provinz Mark Brandenburg," 5.

21. BLHA, Rep. 203, 617, 20 August 1947, 2.

22. BLHA, Rep. 203, Entnazifizierung, 1, "Runderlass Nr. 61/I," 12 January 1948.

23. BLHA, Rep. 203, Entnazifizierung, 644, Bl. 61, 10 February 1948.

24. BLHA, Rep. 203, Entnazifizierung, 8, Bl. 178–179, 3 March 1948.

25. BLHA, Rep. 203, 617, Bl. 143, 5 June 1947.

26. BLHA, Rep. 203, 631, Bl. 117, 14 July 1947.

27. SAPMO-BA, IV, 2/13, 4, 18 February 1947.

28. BLHA, Rep. 203, 629, Bl. 58, 22 November 1947; BA Potsdam, DVdI, Bestand 7, 432, Bl. 138, 2 December 1947; BA Potsdam, DVdI, Bestand 7, 422, Bl. 31, 29 January 1948; BLHA, Rep. 203, 412, Bl. 190, 5 June 1947.

29. BA Potsdam, DVdI, Bestand 7, 435, Bl. 31–32, 2 January 1948.

30. SAPMO-BA, IV, 2/13, 4, 28 April 1947, 4.

31. Ibid., 30 May 1947.

32. SAPMO-BA, Ulbricht NL, 182, 1197, Bl. 124, 4 August 1947.

33. BLHA, Rep. 203, 617, Bl. 4–12, 23 June 1947.

34. SAPMO-BA, Fechner NL, 101, 19, 27 August 1947.

35. BA Potsdam, DVdI, Bestand 7, 69, Bl. 11, "Verfahrensordnung für die

Entnazifizierungskommissionen gemäss Ausführungsbestimmungen (AB) Nr. 2 zum Befehl Nr. 201 des Obersten Chefs der SMAD."

36. BA Potsdam, DVdI, Bestand 7, 69, Bl. 110–113, 22 November 1947; SAPMO-BA, IV, 2/13, 109, 12 October 1947, 6.

37. BLHA, Rep. 203, Entnazifizierung, 72, Bl. 11, 19 September 1947.

38. SAPMO-BA, IV, 2/13, 109, 12 October 1947, 6.

39. BA Potsdam, DVdI, Bestand 7, 423, Bl. 47, 13 November 1947.

40. Ibid., Bl. 54, 10 December 1947.

41. SAPMO-BA, IV, 2/13, 4, 31 October 1947, 20.

42. BA Potsdam, DVdI, Bestand 7, 435, Bl. 1, 3 November 1947.

43. BLHA, Rep. 250, LRA Beeskow-Storkow, 344, Bl. 70, 18 November 1947.

44. Ibid., Bl. 31, 2 January 1948.

45. BA Potsdam, Bestand 7, DVdI, 432, Bl. 101–105.

46. Ibid., Bl. 38, 10 January 1948.

47. BLHA, Rep. 202A, 39, Bl. 154, 5 August 1948.

48. Naimark, *The Russians in Germany,* 284–289.

49. SAPMO-BA, IV, 2/13, 109, 1 June 1947, 14–15.

50. SAPMO-BA, Ulbricht NL, 182, 1197, 12 February 1948. This circular letter, "Rundverfügung Nr. 1," was eventually released on 21 February 1948. See the copy in BA Potsdam, DVdI, Bestand 7, 421, Bl. 118–120.

51. For example, see BLHA, Rep. 203, Entnazifizierung, 8, Bl. 178–181, 3 March 1947; BLHA, Rep. 203, 617, Bl. 43–45, 5 June 1947, and Bl. 16–42, 20 August 1947; BLHA, Rep. 203, Entnazifizierung, 8, Bl. 107–108, 4 September 1947.

52. For example, see BLHA, Rep. 250, LRA Prenzlau, 991, 10 October 1947; BLHA, Rep. 250, LRA Lübben, 151, Bl. 125, 11 October 1947.

53. BLHA, Rep. 203, 600.

54. The Calau commission was apparently the first to suffer a visit from the provincial commissioners. The commission in Forst was similarly singled out in June 1947. BLHA, Rep. 203, 617, Bl. 144, 5 June 1947.

55. BLHA, Rep. 203, Entnazifizierung, 72, letter from *Landrat* Calau to *Oberleutnant* Feodorow, Senftenberg, 26 April 1947; see also the *Fragebogen* of Bernhard Gonschorowski, dated May 1947, and Heinrich Schapp, dated 1 March 1947. The personnel file contains no information on two commission members: Johannes Krestan, representative of the SED, and Oskar Behnke of the FDGB. Krestan and Behnke took part in only the first two hearings; in early 1947 Krestan became mayor of Werchow, and Behnke assumed the same post in the city of Calau.

56. Freter's *Lebenslauf,* dated 8 August 1947, BLHA, Rep. 203, Entnazifizierung, 797.

57. BLHA-SED, Rep. 332, L/VI/2, 3, 23, Bl. 13, 15 January 1947.

58. Wollny's *Lebenslauf,* dated 8 August 1947, BLHA, Rep. 203, Entnazifizierung, 797.

59. Harnau's *Fragebogen*, 27 February 1947, BLHA, Rep. 203, Entnazifizierung, 72.

60. Schapp's *Fragebogen*, 1 March 1947, ibid.

61. Krause's *Fragebogen*, 27 February 1947, ibid.

62. The NSKOV was an organization for "war victims." "All officials at any time" of this organization fell under Article 10 of Directive 24. Why Roblick was permitted to serve despite this background is unclear. The RdK was a pro-natalist group founded in 1923 and subsequently taken over by the Nazis. See Jill Stephenson, *The Nazi Organization of Women* (London: Croom Helm, 1981), 60–61. The RdK did not fall under the terms of Directive 24.

63. Roblick's *Fragebogen*, 28 February 1947, BLHA, Rep. 203, Entnazifizierung, 72.

64. For Figura, see BLHA, Rep. 203, Entnazifizierung, 72, letter from *Landrat Kreis* Calau to *Oberleutnant* Feodorow, 26 April 1947. For Gonschorowski, see his *Fragebogen*, May 1947, BLHA, Rep. 203, Entnazifizierung, 72.

65. BLHA, Rep. 203, Entnazifizierung, 71. The total number of cases heard by the commission was 254, of which 28 were delayed for the purpose of collecting more evidence but never reappeared in the *Protokolle*. The disappearance of these cases does not preclude the possibility that they were reexamined under Order 201, which took effect in September 1947. A further 8 cases were dismissed because the individuals did not fall under the terms of Directive 24. One case was forwarded to the Provincial Commission for final decision. Subtracting these cases from the total leaves 217 decisions.

66. This discussion is based on BLHA, Rep. 203, Entnazifizierung, 19, Protokoll 78a, 24 April 1947.

67. BLHA, Rep. 203, Entnazifizierung, 71, P1, A19, 15 January 1947. For more information on the system of citation used for hearing records in this study, see the Appendix.

68. Calau was the site of stiff resistance against the approaching Red Army on 19 April 1945. See Max Pilop, *Die Befreiung der Lausitz: Militärhistorischer Abriß der Kämpfe im Jahre 1945,* 3rd ed. (Bautzen: Domowina Verlag, 1990), 174–178, and the memoirs of a Red Army tank commander who took part in the battle for Calau, A. P. Riazanskii, *V ogne Tankovykh Srazhenii* (Moscow: Nauka, 1975), 175–176. Neither source mentions a role played by the local Volkssturm. For a chronology of the fighting in *Kreis* Calau, see Sekretariats der Kreisleitung Calau der SED, *Die Befreiung des Kreises Calau von Faschismus: Ergebnisse eines Forschungsvorhabens der Abteilung Volksbildung beim Rat des Kreises Calau und der Kreisleitung Calau der FDJ zum 40. Jahrestag des Sieges und der Befreiung* (Calau: Sekretariats der Kreisleitung der SED, [1985]). This publication notes the stiff resistance put up in defense of Calau by regular army troops and the SS but also notes that "in most places the Volkssturm offered no resistance and disbanded." *Die Befreiung des Kreises Calau,* 11.

69. The pastor's memory would appear to be correct in this instance; the Red Army had occupied the town center by 1:30 on the afternoon of 19 April. See Pilop, *Die Befreiung der Lausitz*, 176; *Die Befreiung des Kreises Calau*, 11.

70. BLHA, Rep. 203, Entnazifizierung, 71, P1, A3, 15 January 1947.

71. Working for the SD could be construed as either punishment or reward depending on circumstances and the SD informer's classification. See Robert Gellately, *The Gestapo and German Society: Enforcing Racial Policy* (Oxford: Clarendon Press, 1990), 61–68.

72. BLHA, Rep. 203, Entnazifizierung, 71, P1, A16, 15 January 1947.

73. SAPMO-BA, IV, 2/13, 4, 25 February 1948.

74. Ibid., 7 April 1948.

6. *The Demographics of Denazification*

1. "Directive 24," 98, 104, 113.

2. "Einstellung ehemaliger Angehöriger der HJ," *VOBl.*, 19 January 1946, 25. Order dated 16 December 1945. Members of the HJ who were "transferred" to the SS were excluded from this order.

3. Similar youth amnesties were put into force in the other occupation zones. For the U.S. and British zones, see Fürstenau, *Entnazifizierung*, 59, 130; for the French zone, see Vollnhals, *Entnazifizierung*, 41.

4. Landtag der Mark Brandenburg, "Stenographischer Bericht, 6. Sitzung," 1 February 1947, in *Akten und Verhandlungen des Landtags der Mark Brandenburg, 1946–1952* (Frankfurt: Keip Verlag: 1992), 71.

5. Ibid., 72.

6. "Gesetz betreffend die staatsbürgerliche Behandlung der nach dem 1. Januar 1919 geborenen Personen, die nicht mehr als nur nominelle Mitglieder der ehemaligen NSDAP oder einer ihrer Gliederungen waren," *VOBl.*, 21 March 1947, 86.

7. "Runderlaß Nr. 29/I," 14 April 1947, *VOBl.* Circular letter dated 22 May 1947, 173.

8. BLHA, Rep. 250, LRA Luckau, 556, 13 January 1947.

9. BLHA, Rep. 250, LRA Lübben, 150, Bl. 91, 28 January 1947.

10. BLHA, Rep. 250, LRA Luckau, 556, 4 February 1947.

11. BLHA, Rep. 203, 632, Bl. 320, 27 February 1947.

12. BLHA, Rep. 203, 584, P10, A3, 6 February 1947.

13. BLHA, Rep. 203, 584, P5, A14, 21 January 1947. Beginning in 1935, quotas were established for the number of HJ members who could join the SA, but SA membership remained voluntary. See Mathilde Jamin, "Zur Rolle der SA im nationalsozialistischen Herrschaftssystem," in Gerhard Hirschfeld and Lothar Kettenacker, eds,. *Der Führerstaat, Mythos und Realität: Studien zur Struktur und Politik des Dritten Reiches* (Stuttgart: Klett-Cotta, 1981), 339–360.

14. BLHA, Rep. 203, 584, P5, A13, 21 January 1947.
15. Ibid., P11, A3, 7 February 1947.
16. BLHA, Rep. 203, Entnazifizierung, 431, P10, A2, 6 February 1947.
17. BLHA, Rep. 203, 584, P4, A1, 14 January 1947.
18. Ibid., P7, A30, 28 January 1947.
19. Ibid., P13, A20, 12 February 1947.
20. How BDM members could have been automatically transferred to the NSDAP is unclear. At age eighteen BDM members were eligible to apply for party membership, but membership was apparently not automatic. See Dagmar Reese, "Bund Deutscher Mädel—Zur Geschichte der weiblichen deutshchen Jugend im Dritten Reich," in Frauengruppe Faschismusforschung, eds., *Mutterkreuz und Arbeitsbuch: Zur Geschichte der Frauen in der Weimarer Republik und im Nationalsozialismus* (Frankfurt: Fischer Taschenbuch Verlag, 1981), 186–187; Arno Klönne, *Jugend im Dritten Reich: Die Hitler-Jugend und ihre Gegner* (Düsseldorf: Eugen Diedrichs Verlag, 1982), 46; Michael H. Kater, *The Nazi Party: A Social Profile of Members and Leaders, 1919–1945* (Cambridge, Mass.: Harvard University Press, 1983), 152. One historian notes that BDM members were transferred to either the NSF or the NS-Frauenwerk at age twenty-one, but makes no mention of forced membership in the party. See Ute Frevert, *Women in German History: From Emancipation to Sexual Liberation* (New York: Berg, 1990), 243. On NSF and NSDAP dual membership, see Stephenson, *The Nazi Organization of Women*, 148–150.
21. BLHA, Rep. 203, 584, P11, A3, 7 February 1947; BLHA, Rep. 203, Entnazifizierung, 431, P10, A1, 6 February 1947.
22. BLHA, Rep. 203, Entnazifizierung, 431, P4, A22–A23, 16 January 1947.
23. BLHA, Rep. 203, 584, P11, A8, 7 February 1947.
24. Ibid., P11, A10, 7 February 1947.
25. Ibid., P12, A28, 11 February 1947.
26. Gerhard Rempel, *Hitler's Children: The Hitler Youth and the SS* (Chapel Hill: University of North Carolina Press, 1989), 25; Klönne, *Jugend im Dritten Reich*, 46–47; Martin Broszat, *Der Staat Hitlers*, 4th ed. (Munich: Deutscher Taschenbuch Verlag, 1974), 380–381.
27. BLHA, Rep. 203, 584, P6, A11, 24 January 1947.
28. Ibid., P12, A26, 11 February 1947.
29. On the reluctance of women to join the NSDAP, see Kater, *Nazi Party*, 148.
30. For Nazi attitudes toward women in the workplace, see David Schoenbaum, *Hitler's Social Revolution* (New York: Doubleday, 1966), chap. 6.
31. See the analysis of the status of women and the continuities between the Nazi period and the Soviet occupation in Ina Merkel, "Leitbilder und Lebensweisen von Frauen in der DDR," in Hartmut Kaelble, Jürgen Kocka, and Hartmut Zwahr, eds., *Sozialgeschichte der DDR* (Stuttgart: Klett Cotta, 1994), 362–365.
32. BLHA, Rep. 203, Entnazifizierung, 1583, P41, A11, 5 March 1948.

33. BLHA, Rep. 203, Entnazifizierung, 431, P8, A3, 30 January 1947.
34. Ibid., P25, A4, 21 April 1947.
35. BLHA, Rep. 203, Entnazifizierung, 798, P3, A1, 14 October 1947.
36. BLHA, Rep. 203, 584, P15, A14, 14 February 1947.
37. BLHA, Rep. 203, Entnazifizierung, 798, P6, A5, 25 October 1947.
38. BLHA, Rep. 203, Entnazifizierung, 1429. P8, A1, 29 October 1947.
39. Ibid., P8, A10, 29 October 1947.
40. BLHA, Rep. 203, Entnazifizierung, 798, P7, A5, 28 October 1947.
41. BLHA, Rep. 203, Entnazifizierung, 371, P9, A5, 19 February 1947.
42. BLHA, Rep. 203, 584, P13, A31, 12 February 1947.
43. BLHA, Rep. 203, Entnazifizierung, 798, P10, A1, 6 November 1947.
44. BLHA, Rep. 203, Entnazifizierung, 371, P21, A5, 15 April 1947.
45. BLHA, Rep. 203, Entnazifizierung, 644, Bl. 4, 27 October 1947.
46. The head of the Brandenburg criminal police, for example, complained that there were no controls in place for the granting of interzonal passports to PGs. BA Potsdam, Bestand 7, 368, Bl. 41, 8 September 1947.
47. BA Potsdam, DVdI, Bestand 7, 434, Bl. 412, 6 February 1948.
48. BLHA, Rep. 203, Entnazifizierung, 72, "Ausführungsbestimmung zum ordnungsgemässen Geschäftsgang bezug Runderlass Nr. 0004/I," 9 December 1946.
49. BLHA, Rep. 203, 584, P3, A7, 10 January 1947.
50. "Ausführungsbestimmung Nr. 2," *VOBl.*, 9 October 1947, 187.
51. BLHA, Rep. 203, Entnazifizierung, 1, "Runderlaß 46/I," 27 August 1947, 3. There were a number of points in Directive 24 not covered in Paragraph 7. See BA Potsdam, DVdI, Bestand 7, 422, Bl. 147. Mielke admitted this at an Interior Ministers' conference at the end of 1947: "Must all of those who fall under Directive 24 be brought before a [denazification commission]? All [who] have something to do with Implementation Decree number 2. Directive 24 has been somewhat limited [*begrenzt*] through Order 201." BA Potsdam, DVdI, Bestand 7, 432, Bl. 58, 22 December 1947.
52. BLHA, Rep. 203, Entnazifizierung, 645, Bl. 249, 10 February 1948.
53. BA Potsdam, DVdI, Bestand 7, 69, "Verfahrensordnung," 2–3.
54. BLHA, Rep. 203, Entnazifizierung, 72, "Rundverfügung Nr. 1," 19 August 1947, 4.
55. Typhus, diphtheria, and sexually transmitted diseases were particularly rampant during this period. See Provinzialverwaltung Mark Brandenburg, *Ein Jahr Bewährung*, 44–45.
56. Ibid., 43–44.
57. BLHA, Rep. 203, Entnazifizierung, 371, P27, A1, 4 May 1947.
58. BLHA, Rep. 250, LRA Prenzlau, 31, 31 March 1947.
59. BLHA, Rep. 203, 617, 20 August 1947, 19.
60. BLHA-SED, Rep. 332, L/IV/2/12, 825, Bl. 2, 17 October 1947.
61. BA Potsdam, DVdI, Bestand 7, 435, Bl. 2, 3 November 1947.
62. SAPMO-BA, IV, 2/13, 4, 31 October 1947, 14.
63. BA Potsdam, DVdI, Bestand 7, 434, Bl. 386–388, 20 December 1947.

64. Ibid., Bl. 391–392, 16 January 1948.
65. Ibid., Bl. 412, 6 February 1948.
66. BLHA, Rep. 203, Entnazifizierung, 371, P10, A5, 21 February 1947.
67. Ibid., P33, A13, 6 June 1947.
68. For an East German analysis of the role of teachers in the "antifascist-democratic transformation" of the Soviet zone, see Karl-Heinz Günther and Gottfried Uhlig, *Geschichte der Schule in der Deutschen Demokratischen Republik, 1945–1971* (Berlin: Volk und Wissen, 1974).
69. BA Potsdam, DR-2, 1332, Bl. 90, 29 March 1946.
70. "Befehl Nr. 40 des Obersten Chefs der Sowjetischen Militäradministration in Deutschland über die Vorbereitung der Schulen auf den Schulbetrieb," 25 August 1945, in *Um ein antifaschistisch-demokratisches Deutschland*, 128–130.
71. BLHA, Rep. 203, 21, 8 January 1946.
72. BLHA, Rep. 205A, 346, Bl. 2.
73. BLHA, Rep. 205A, 217, Bl. 1, Bl. 3. There was no report submitted from *Landkreis* Cottbus for its high schools. Not included in these figures are five PGs employed in the fifteen *Hilfsschulen* (schools for special education) in Brandenburg; these five PGs represented 9 percent of the *Hilfsschulen* teachers. Ibid., Bl. 2.
74. BA Potsdam, DR-2, 943, 19 December 1946.
75. BLHA, Rep. 203, 617, 20 August 1947, 19.
76. See the remembrances of the first chief of the Brandenburg Education Ministry, Fritz Rücker, "Neue Schule, neue Lehrer—ein neuer Geist in Potsdam," in *Die Ersten Jahre: Erinnerungen an den Beginn der revolutionären Umgestaltung* (Berlin: Dietz Verlag, 1979), 303–319. The SED was concerned not only with purging the teaching corps of PGs but also with replacing the dismissed teachers with SED members. A report given at the second provincial SED conference at the end of August 1947 noted with satisfaction that 38 percent of all teachers were members of the SED. SAPMO-BA, IV, 2/13, 6, 11.
77. BLHA, Rep. 250, LRA Spremberg, 173, 23 January 1947.
78. BLHA, Rep. 203, 421, Bl. 146, 25 February 1947.
79. Ibid., Bl. 161, 18 March 1947.
80. BLHA, Rep. 205A, 104, Bl. 55, 15 August 1947.
81. BLHA, Rep. 203, Entnazifizierung, 1429, P5, A1, 21 October 1947.
82. BA Potsdam, DVdI, Bestand 7, 435, Bl. 2, 3 November 1947.
83. BLHA, Rep. 203, Entnazifizierung, 1, 11 November 1947.
84. BLHA, Rep. 203, 629, 13 November 1947.
85. BLHA, Rep. 205A, 460, Bl. 342–343, 1 February 1947.
86. BLHA, Rep. 203, Entnazifizierung, 1582, P9, A1, 23 October 1947.
87. BLHA, Rep. 203, 584, P4, A3, 14 January 1947.
88. BLHA, Rep. 203, Entnazifizierung, 72, "Runderlass Nr. 11/I," 20 January 1947, 2.
89. BLHA, Rep. 203, 584, P5, A6, 21 January 1947.

90. BLHA, Rep. 203, 629, Bl. 118, 7 February 1947.

91. BLHA, Rep. 203, Entnazifizierung, 431, P4, A29, 16 January 1947.

92. Ibid., P11, A5–A6, 10 February 1947.

93. Ibid., P12, A10 (approved), A9 (dismissed), 13 February 1947.

94. For the Ruppin *Landrat*, see BLHA, Rep. 203, 584, P7, A1, 28 January 1947. For Bechler's membership in the Nazi Party, see Broszat and Weber, *SBZ Handbuch*, 866; Ribbe, "Das Land Brandenburg in der SBZ/DDR," 692. See also the remembrances of Bechler's ex-wife, who recalled that he had been an outspoken supporter of National Socialism before the war, "the only National Socialist in the family." Margret Bechler, *Warten auf Antwort: Ein deutsches Schicksal,* rev. ed. (Frankfurt: Ulstein, 1990), 15. This aspect of Bechler's past is not included in the short biography published by the provincial government in 1947, *Handbuch des Landtages des Landes Brandenburg* (Potsdam: Märkische Druck- und Verlags-GMBH., 1947), 114. Schäfer, in his dissertation on the denazification in Brandenburg, also overlooked this aspect of Bechler's past and claimed that the interior minister was "without party" during the Nazi period. Schäfer, "Die Entnazifizierung," 44.

95. BLHA, Rep. 203, Entnazifizierung, 72, "Runderlass Nr. 18/I," 7 February 1947.

96. BLHA, Rep. 250, LRA Lübben, 151, Bl. 48, 17 March 1948.

97. BLHA, Rep. 250, LRA Ruppin, 543, Bl. 87, 23 March 1948.

98. BLHA, Rep. 203, Entnazifizierung, 371, P14, A2, 7 March 1947.

99. BLHA, Rep. 203, Entnazifizierung, 71, P4, A4, 26 February 1947.

100. BLHA, Rep. 203, 584, P4, A6, 14 January 1947.

101. Ibid., P15, A14, 14 February 1947. The spring flooding of the Oder eventually reached catastrophic proportions in 1947.

102. BLHA, Rep. 203, Entnazifizierung, 431, P38, A4, 21 July 1947.

103. BLHA, Rep. 203, Entnazifizierung, 72, "Runderlass Nr. 18/I," 7 February 1947, 4.

104. Ibid., "Runderlass Nr. 11/I," 20 January 1947, 3.

105. Ibid., "Runderlass Nr. 18/I," 7 February 1947, 3. This exemption for manual laborers was continued during the Order 201 phase. BLHA, Rep. 203, Entnazifizierung, 72, "Rundverfügung Nr. 1," 19 August 1947, 2.

106. BA Potsdam, DVdI, Bestand 7, 432, Bl. 55, 22 December 1947.

107. BLHA, Rep. 203, Entnazifizierung, 1, "Runderlass Nr. 61/I," 12 January 1948, 2–3.

108. BLHA, Rep. 203, Entnazifizierung, 431, P7, A4, A5, A6, A7, and A8, 29 January 1947.

109. Ibid., P3, A17–A34, 13 January 1947.

110. The Reichsbahndirektion, Oberpostdirektion, and Zentralverwaltung der Brennstoffindustrie were ordered to dissolve their commissions on 28 August 1947. BLHA, Rep. 203, Entnazifizierung, 645, Bl. 39, 47, 49.

111. After several extensions, the dissolution of the Directive 24 commissions

was finally set for 15 January 1948. BLHA, Rep. 203, Entnazifizierung, 1, "Rundverfügung Nr. 4," 8 December 1947.

112. BLHA, Rep. 203, 630, Bl. 275, 5 November 1947.
113. BLHA, Rep. 250, LRA Calau/Senftenberg, 223, 17 November 1947.
114. BLHA, Rep. 203, Entnazifizierung, 645, Bl. 199, 4 December 1947.
115. BLHA, Rep. 203, Entnazifizierung, 1, 11 November 1947.
116. BA Potsdam, DVdI, Bestand 7, 423, Bl. 46, 13 November 1947.
117. BA Potsdam, DVdI, Bestand 7, 432, Bl. 182, 31 January 1948.
118. BLHA, Rep. 203, 632, Bl. 310, 24 November 1947.
119. BLHA, Rep. 203, Entnazifizierung, 645, Bl. 56, 5 September 1947.
120. SAPMO-BA, IV, 2/13, 226, 3 October 1947, 1.
121. Walter Ulbricht "Die gegenwärtige Lage und die nächsten Aufgaben," SAPMO-BA, IV, 2/13, 109, 19.
122. SAPMO-BA, Ulbricht NL, 182, 1197, 25 August 1947.
123. BLHA, Rep. 203, 631, Bl. 228, 9 June 1947.
124. BA Potsdam, DVdI, Bestand 7, 432, Bl. 34, 4 November 1947; 435, Bl. 35, 2 January 1947.
125. BLHA, Rep. 203, Entnazifizierung, 1, 11 November 1947.
126. BLHA, Rep. 203, 632, 12 December 1947.
127. BA Potsdam, DVdI, Bestand 7, 432, Bl. 59, 22 December 1947.
128. BLHA, Rep. 203, Entnazifizierung, 1583, P44, A9 and A14, 9 March 1948.
129. Ibid., P39, A18, 3 March 1948.

7. The Varieties of Guilt and Innocence

1. Shelia Fitzpatrick, *Stalin's Peasants: Resistance and Survival in the Russian Village after Collectivization* (New York: Oxford University Press, 1994), 299.
2. In the data sample, the Calau commission noted the impression made by petitioners in five cases, the Ostprignitz commission in twenty-one cases, and the Ruppin commission in twenty-three.
3. BLHA, Rep. 203, 584, P8, A33, 4 February 1947.
4. Ibid., P10, A5, 6 February 1947; P17, A31, 18 February 1947.
5. BLHA, Rep. 203, 594, P155, A4, 18 August 1947; 584, P156, A14, 19 August 1947.
6. BLHA, Rep. 203, 594, P163, A11, 29 August 1947.
7. BLHA, Rep. 203, 584, P15, A4, 14 February 1947.
8. BLHA, Rep. 203, Entnazifizierung, 647, P7, A6, 8 October 1947.
9. BLHA, Rep. 203, 584, P8, A9, 4 February 1947.
10. Ibid., P156, A15, 18 August 1947; P14, A5, 13 February 1947.
11. Ibid., P156, A11, 19 August 1947.
12. BLHA, Rep. 203, 584, P10, A13, 6 February 1947.
13. BLHA, Rep. 203, Entnazifizierung, 648, P8, A2, 9 October 1947.
14. BLHA, Rep. 203, 584, P3, 10 January 1947; BLHA, Rep. 203, Entnazi-

fizierung, 72, "Rundverfügung Nr. 1," 19 August 1947, 3; "Runderlaß Nr. 0004/I," 9 December 1946, 5; BLHA, Rep. 203, Entnazifizierung, 1, "Runderlaß Nr. 46/I," 27 August 1947, 6.

15. BLHA, Rep. 250, LRA Ruppin, 76, 13 September 1947.

16. BLHA, Rep. 250, LRA Calau/Senftenberg, 223, 25 October 1947. For a copy of the poster announcing this hearing, see ibid., 28 October 1947.

17. BA Potsdam, DVdI, Bestand 7, 432, Bl. 108, 3 November 1947. The Provincial Commission traveled to the factory at Soviet urging. Hentschel reported that he was in contact with the Soviet commander in Schwarzheide regarding the factory and that there had been many foreign workers and Soviet POWs at the plant who had been "bestially mistreated and even murdered" during the war. BA Potsdam, DVdI, Bestand 7, 432, Bl. 8, 5 November 1947.

18. BA Potsdam, DVdI, Bestand 7, 432, Bl. 136, 2 December 1947.

19. Ibid., Bl. 284, 6 December 1947.

20. SAPMO-BA, Ulbricht NL, 182, 1197, Bl. 209–210, 24 January 1948.

21. BA Potsdam, DVdI, Bestand 7, 432, Bl. 182 and 186, 31 January 1948.

22. BLHA, Rep. 250, LRA Guben, 113, Bl. 246, 7 April 1948.

23. BLHA, Rep. 203, Entnazifizierung, 371, P13, A10, 1 March 1947.

24. Ibid., A11.

25. BLHA, Rep. 203, 594, P161c, A20, 27 August 1947.

26. On the role of the Antifascist Committees during the occupation period, see Koch, "Der Demokratische Block," 281–292.

27. These "certificates of unobjectionability" were somewhat analogous to the so-called *Persilscheine* used in the U.S. zone. The chief difference was that the *Unbedenklichkeitsbescheinigungen* in the Soviet zone were issued by the Antifascist Committees and sometimes by the political parties. In the U.S. zone there were no comparable Antifascist Committees, and the term *Persilscheine* was used to refer to statements of support, which came not only from political parties but also from acquaintances of the accused. In Brandenburg such statements of support were referred to as "character references" *(Leumundszeugnisse)* and usually did not carry the "official" weight of a certificate issued by an Antifascist Committee. For the role of the *Persilscheine* in the U.S. zone, see Niethammer, *Mitläuferfabrik,* 613–617.

28. KA Ostprignitz, Stadtverwaltung Neustadt, SN3.

29. BLHA, Rep. 203, 630, Bl. 183, 25 January 1947; Bl. 182, 31 January 1947. See also BLHA, Rep. 203, 632, Bl. 251, 5 February 1947.

30. BLHA, Rep. 250, LRA Beeskow-Storkow, 27, Bl. 1, "Richtlinien für die Arbeit in den Antifaschistischen Ausschüssen der Mark Brandenburg."

31. BLHA, Rep. 203, Entnazifizierung, 71, P5, A33, 6 March 1947. For other examples, see, in the same hearing, A36, A38, and A43.

32. KA Ostprignitz, Stadtverwaltung Neustadt, SN3, 7 May 1947.

33. Ibid., 10 August 1946 and 13 October 1947.

34. BLHA, Rep. 203, Entnazifizierung, 647, P3, A2, 30 September 1947.

35. BLHA, Rep. 203, 584, P15, A3, 14 February 1947.

36. Siegfried Suckut, *Die Betriebsrätebewegung in der Sowjetisch Besetzten Zone Deutschlands (1945–1948)* (Frankfurt: Haag & Herchen, 1982), 126–127.

37. "Law No. 22: Works Councils," *Official Gazette of the Control Council for Germany,* no. 6, 30 April 1946, 134.

38. SAPMO-BA, Ulbricht NL, 182, 1197, Bl. 181, "Rundschreiben 61/47," 19 September 1947.

39. BLHA, Rep. 203, Entnazifizierung, 431, P8, A6–A20, 30 January 1947.

40. Ibid., A21–A30. The rejected petition is A30.

41. Ibid., A22.

42. BLHA, Rep. 203, Entnazifizierung, 71, P4, A29–A34, 26 February 1947.

43. BLHA, Rep. 203, 584, P3, A1–A2, 10 January 1946.

44. BLHA, Rep. 203, Entnazifizierung, 71, P1, A19, 15 January 1947. This is the same petitioner whose approval was later overturned by the visiting Provincial Commission. See chapter 6.

45. BLHA, Rep. 203, Entnazifizierung, 71, P5, A12, 6 March 1947.

46. Ibid., A17.

47. The NSV (Nationalsozialistische Volkswohlfahrt) was a party organization for the welfare of party members and their families.

48. BLHA, Rep. 203, Entnazifizierung, 71, P11, A18, 13 August 1947.

49. Ibid., P5, A31, 6 March 1947.

50. Ibid., P9, A18, 10 May 1947. Alfred Rosenberg was a leading theorist of National Socialism. His book outlining his racist theories was first published in 1930.

51. BLHA, Rep. 203, 594, P5, A25, 21 January 1947; P161, A9, 27 August 1947.

52. BLHA, Rep. 203, 584, P2, A1, 7 January 1947; P7, A28, 28 January 1947.

53. BLHA, Rep. 203, 594, P163, A16, 29 August 1947.

54. Ibid., P157a, A5, 20 August 1947.

55. BLHA, Rep. 203, Entnazifizierung, 798, P8, A3, 29 October 1947.

56. BLHA, Rep. 203, 584, P2, A10, 7 January 1947. For other unsubstantiated claims of "antifascist" activity, see BLHA, Rep. 203, 584, P6, A2, 24 January 1947; P7, A29, 28 January 1947; P8, A16, 4 February 1947; P13, A21, 12 February 1947; P14, A17 and A25, 13 February 1947.

57. BLHA, Rep. 203, 584, P8, A6, 4 February 1947; P9, A2, 5 February 1947; P12, A2, 11 February 1947; P14, A23 (claim of leaving the SA); P15, A3, 14 February 1947; P156, A2 and A3, 19 August 1947.

58. On the Soviet "special camps" and the activities of the Soviet secret police, see Karl Wilhelm Fricke, *Politik und Justiz in der DDR: Zur Geschichte der politischen Verfolgung, 1945–1968: Bericht und Dokumentation* (Cologne: Verlag Wissenschaft und Politik, 1979), 55–149; Uwe Greve, *Lager des Grauens: Sowjetische KZs in der DDR nach 1945* (Kiel: Arndt Verlag, 1990); Naimark, *The Russians in Germany,* 376–390.

59. Lutz Prieß und Peter Erler, "Sowjetische Speziallager in der SBZ/DDR 1945

bis 1950," in Günter Agde, ed., *Sachsenhausen bei Berlin: Speziallager Nr. 7, 1945–1950* (Berlin: Aufbau Taschenbuch Verlag, 1994), 20.

60. [Bernhard] Bechler, "Es geht um die weitere Demokratisierung: An die Bevölkerung des Landes Brandenburg," *Märkische Volksstimme* (Potsdam), 4/5 October 1947, 1.

61. BLHA, Rep. 203, 810, Bl. 544, 6 October 1947.

62. SAPMO-BA, IV, 2/13, 4, 31 October 1947, 5.

63. BLHA, Rep. 250, LRA Guben, 113, Bl. 39, received by the denazification commission on 29 January 1948.

64. BLHA, Rep. 203, Entnazifizierung, 371, P4, A1, 30 January 1947; P20, A3, 1 April 1947; BLHA, Rep. 203, Entnazifizierung, 431, P28, A3, 5 May 1947.

65. BLHA, Rep. 203, Entnazifizierung, 1583, P44, A6, 9 March 1948; P45, A7, 10 March 1948.

66. Ibid., P45, A8, 10 March 1948.

67. Ibid., P41, A2, 5 March 1948.

8. Responses to the Nazi Period and the PGs in the New Germany

1. Peter Hoffmann, *German Resistance to Hitler* (Cambridge, Mass.: Harvard University Press, 1988), 61, 55.

2. For an overview of resistance studies, see Leonidas E. Hill, "Towards a New History of German Resistance to Hitler," *Central European History* 14 (1981): 396–399; Klaus-Jürgen Müller and Hans Mommsen, "Der deutsche Widerstand gegen das NS-Regime: Zur Historiographie des Widerstandes," in Klaus-Jürgen Müller, ed., *Die deutsche Widerstand, 1933– 1945* (Paderborn: Verlag Ferdinand Schöningh, 1986), 13–21; Gerhard Paul, "Die Widerspenstige 'Volksgemeinschaft': Dissens und Verweigerung im Dritten Reich," in Peter Steinbach and Johannes Tuchel, eds., *Widerstand gegen den Nationalsozialismus* (Berlin: Akademie Verlag, 1994), 395–410.

3. Detlev Peukert, *Inside Nazi Germany: Conformity, Opposition, and Racism in Everyday Life*, trans. Richard Deveson (New Haven: Yale University Press, 1987).

4. Klemens von Klemperer, *German Resistance against Hitler: The Search for Allies Abroad, 1938–1945* (New York: Oxford University Press, 1992), 13 n. 11.

5. All three petitioners had been imprisoned in a concentration camp. BLHA, Rep. 203, 584, P9, A5, 5 February 1947; BLHA, Rep. 203, Entnazifizierung, 647, P5, A14, 2 October 1947; BLHA, Rep. 203, Entnazifizierung, 1583, P38, A9, 1 March 1948.

6. These include one petitioner who was not a member of a resistance group but who "demonstrated through concrete evidence that he . . . performed substantial illegal work against the NSDAP" (BLHA, Rep. 203, 584, P7,

A2, 28 January 1947) and two others of whom it was simply noted that they had taken part in "antifascist activity." BLHA, Rep. 203, Entnazifizierung, 648, P11, A9, 15 October 1947; BLHA, Rep. 203, Entnazifizierung, 371, P21, A6, 15 April 1947.

7. BLHA, Rep. 203, 584, P3, A1–A2, 10 January 1947; P2, A14, 7 January 1947; P7, A5, 28 January 1947; BLHA, Rep. 203, Entnazifizierung, 1583, P41, A29, 5 March 1948.

8. BLHA, Rep. 203, Entnazifizierung, 648, P8, A13, 9 October 1947.

9. BLHA, Rep. 203, 584, P13, A30, 12 February 1947; BLHA, Rep. 203, Entnazifizierung, 1431, P37, A4, 8 January 1948.

10. BLHA, Rep. 203, 594, P157a, A7, 20 August 1947. For the other member of the Confessing Church whose petition was denied, see BLHA, Rep. 203, 584, P3, A11, 10 January 1947.

11. BLHA, Rep. 203, Entnazifizierung, 371, P21, A8, 15 April 1947; BLHA, Rep. 203, Entnazifizierung, 1431, P42, A6, 2 March 1948. The *Ortsgruppenleiter* stood at the top of the Nazi organization of local communities, and their power was considerable, particularly in rural areas. See Kater, *Nazi Party*, 222–223; Peter Diehl-Thiele, *Partei und Staat im Dritten Reich: Untersuchungen zum Verhältnis von NSDAP und allgemeiner innerer Staatsverwaltung, 1933–1945* (Munich: Verlag C. H. Beck, 1969), 163–165.

12. BLHA, Rep. 203, Entnazifizierung, 431, P15, A4, 3 March 1947; BLHA, Rep. 203, 594, P155, A6, 18 August 1947.

13. BLHA, Rep. 203, Entnazifizierung, 431, P21, A9, 31 March 1947. On the role of the *Blockleiter* in the Nazi system, see Dietrich Orlow, *The History of the Nazi Party: 1933–1945* (Pittsburgh: University of Pittsburgh Press, 1973), 173–174; Diehl-Thiele, *Partei und Staat im Dritten Reich*, 166.

14. BLHA, Rep. 203, 584, P13, A4, 12 February 1947.

15. BLHA, Rep. 203, Entnazifizierung, 431, P23, A27, 12 April 1947. In a similar case, another dairy owner in the district joined the party in 1933 "because he feared retribution" after he had fired an employee who was an SA member. BLHA, Rep. 203, Entnazifizierung, 431, P25, A1, 21 April 1947.

16. BLHA, Rep. 203, 584, P13, A34, 12 February 1947.

17. BLHA, Rep. 203, Entnazifizierung, 798, P9, A4, 4 November 1947.

18. BLHA, Rep. 203, Entnazifizierung, 371, P10, A2, 21 February 1947.

19. Ian Kershaw, *The "Hitler Myth": Image and Reality in the Third Reich* (Oxford: Oxford University Press, 1987).

20. BLHA, Rep. 203, Entnazifizierung, 431, P12, A14, 13 February 1947.

21. Ibid., P14, A6, 24 February 1947. The year 1943 witnessed a sharp escalation of Allied bombing raids and a parallel rise in discontent among the Germans living in targeted areas. Earl R. Beck, *Under the Bombs: The German Home Front, 1942–1945* (Lexington: University Press of Kentucky, 1986), 57–83.

22. BLHA, Rep. 203, 594, P161b, A4, 27 August 1947.

23. Jeremy Noakes, "Social Outcasts in the Third Reich," in Richard Bessel, ed., *Life in the Third Reich* (New York: Oxford University Press, 1987), 83–96.

24. Michael Burleigh and Wolfgang Wippermann, *The Racial State: Germany, 1933–1945* (New York: Cambridge University Press, 1991).

25. There were 7,616 Jews living in Brandenburg in 1936, representing 0.55 percent of the total population. Frankfurt/Oder, with 568 Jews, had the largest Jewish population of any city in the province. The systematic deportation of Jews from Brandenburg began in April 1942. Demps, "Die Provinz Brandenburg in der NS-Zeit," 625, 656.

26. BLHA, Rep. 203, 584, P2, A12, 7 January 1947.

27. BLHA, Rep. 203, 584, P3, A5, 10 January 1947, and P15, A23, 14 February 1947; BLHA, Rep. 203, 594, P156, A6, 19 August 1947; BLHA, Rep. 203, Entnazifizierung, 647, P1, A3, 25 September 1947, and P3, A1, 30 September 1947; BLHA, Rep. 203, Entnazifizierung, 371, P3, A1, 28 January 1947; P12, A1, 28 February 1947; P14, A9, 7 March 1947; P16, A5, 11 March 1947; and P21, A6, 15 April 1947.

28. BLHA, Rep. 203, 584, P9, A11, 5 February 1947; BLHA, Rep. 203, Entnazifizierung, 71, P12, A2, 13 August 1947; BLHA, Rep. 203, 594, P158, A15, 21 August 1947; BLHA, Rep. 203, Entnazifizierung, 431, P29, A5, 12 May 1947. On the boycotts and "aryanization" of Jewish businesses in Brandenburg, see Irene Diekmann, "Boykott—Entrechtung—Progrom—Deportation: Die "Arisierung" jüdischen Eigentums während der NS-Diktatur: Untersucht und Dargestellt an Beispielen aus der Provinz Mark Brandenburg," in Eichholtz, *Verfolgung, Alltag, Widerstand,* 207–229.

29. BLHA, Rep. 203, 596, P169, A19, 5 September 1947.

30. BLHA, Rep. 203, Entnazifizierung, 431, P24, A8, 14 April 1947. For an example of a petitioner married to a "half-Jew," see BLHA, Rep. 203, 584, P11, A5, 7 February 1947. There are three examples of protection of Jewish sons-in-law: BLHA, Rep. 203, 584, P8, A1, 4 February 1947; BLHA, Rep. 203, Entnazifizierung, 1582, P8, A8, 21 October 1947; BLHA, Rep. 203, Entnazifizierung, 1583, P45, A15, 10 March 1948; and one example of protection of a sister-in-law: BLHA, Rep. 203, Entnazifizierung, 1583, P42, A27, 6 March 1948.

31. BLHA, Rep. 203, Entnazifizierung, 647, P6, A9, 7 October 1947.

32. As of March 1943 there were 262,348 foreign laborers working in Brandenburg. Demps, "Brandenburg in der NS-Zeit," 659.

33. Burleigh and Wippermann, *The Racial State,* 298.

34. Beck, *Under the Bombs,* 96–97; Jill Stephenson, "Triangle: Foreign Workers, German Civilians, and the Nazi Regime: War and Society in Württemberg, 1939–45," *German Studies Review* 15 (1992): 344–345.

35. Burleigh and Wippermann argue that the "indifference" many Germans showed toward the mistreatment of the foreign workers "is indicative both of the degree to which the regime's racism intersected with prejudices in the

population as a whole, and of how far racism became part of everyday life."
Burleigh and Wippermann, *The Racial State,* 262.

36. BLHA, Rep. 203, Entnazifizierung, 647, P7, A3, 8 October 1947.

37. See, for example, BLHA, Rep. 203, 584, A15, P23, 14 February 1947;
BLHA, Rep. 203, 594, P160, A12, 26 August 1947; BLHA, Rep. 203,
Entnazifizierung, 431, P21, A3, 31 March 1947.

38. BLHA, Rep. 203, Entnazifizierung, 71, P2, A24, 30 January 1947. As we
saw in Chapter 6, Calau commission members frequently knew the petitioners who appeared before them. In this case, the CDU representative
Krause also happened to own a tobacco shop, and he testified to the petitioner's purchase of large quantities of cigarettes for distribution to the Russians. For another example of help given to Russian POWs, see BLHA,
Rep. 203, Entnazifizierung, 371, P31, A7, 30 March 1947.

39. BLHA, Rep. 203, Entnazifizierung, 371, P25, A5, 25 April 1947.

40. BLHA, Rep. 203, Entnazifizierung, 810, P85, A14, 4 March 1948; BLHA,
Rep. 203, Entnazifizierung, 371, P27, A7, 4 May 1947.

41. BLHA, Rep. 203, 594, P158, A5, 21 August 1947; BLHA, Rep. 203, Entnazifizierung, 371, P14, A8, 7 March 1947; BLHA, Rep. 203, 594, P163,
A11, 29 August 1947. See also the case of a doctor who aided individuals
who had been beaten by the SA (BLHA, Rep. 203, Entnazifizierung, 371,
P30, A6, 23 May 1947) and the case of a grocer who provisioned "KPD
people and concentration camp inmates" (BLHA, Rep. 203, Entnazifizierung, 1429, P8, A7, 29 October 1947).

42. BLHA, Rep. 203, Entnazifizierung, 371, P36, A1, 24 June 1947.

43. BLHA, Rep. 203, 594, P159, A5, 22 August 1947.

44. Orlow, *The History of the Nazi Party,* 473. See also Franz W. Seidler,
Deutscher Volkssturm: Das letzte Aufgebot 1944/45 (Munich: F. A. Herbig,
1989). For a sometimes humorous account of one man's involvement with a
ragtag Volkssturm unit in Brandenburg, see Peter Bloch, *Zwischen Hoffnung und Resignation: Als CDU Politiker in Brandenburg, 1945–1950*
(Cologne: Verlag Wissenschaft und Politik, 1986), chaps. 1 and 2.

45. For unspecified acts of sabotage, see BLHA, Rep. 203, Entnazifizierung,
371, P14, A9, 7 March 1947; for obstructing the taking up of arms as the
Red Army approached, see BLHA, Rep. 203, Entnazifizierung, 1582, P9,
A1, 23 October 1947; for preventing destruction of bridges, BLHA, Rep.
203, Entnazifizierung, 1583, P43, A15, 8 March 1948. In addition to those
in the Volkssturm, members of the military could gain exculpation by showing evidence that they had been punished for "subversion of the military effort [*Zersetzung der Wehrkraft*]." BLHA, Rep. 203, Entnazifizierung, 431,
P20, A5, 24 March 1947, and P21, A2, 31 March 1947.

46. BLHA, Rep. 203, 584, P7, A1, 28 January 1947.

47. Ibid., P12, A1, 11 February 1947.

48. BLHA, Rep. 203, Entnazifizierung, 647, P2, A4, 26 September 1947. For
other petitioners who were also rejected because they could not remember

the particulars of foreign broadcasts, see BLHA, Rep. 203, Entnazifizierung, 647, P4, A13, 1 October 1947, and P6, A8, 7 October 1947; BLHA, Rep. 203, Entnazifizierung, 648, P9, A1, 10 October 1947. One petitioner who correctly identified the call sign of London Radio had his petition approved. BLHA, Rep. 203, Entnazifizierung, 647, P7, A2, 8 October 1947.

49. BLHA, Rep. 203, 584, P13, A29, 1 February 1947.
50. BLHA, Rep. 203, Entnazifizierung, 647, P4, A1, 1 October 1947.
51. BLHA, Rep. 203, 594, P161b, A7, 27 August 1947; BLHA, Rep. 203, 596, P169, A23, 5 September 1947.
52. BLHA, Rep. 203, Entnazifizierung, 71, P2, A9, 30 January 1947; BLHA, Rep. 203, Entnazifizierung, 431, P9, A4, 3 February 1947.
53. BLHA, Rep. 203, 584, P14, A3, 13 February 1947.
54. BLHA, Rep. 203, Entnazifizierung, 371, P9, A2, 19 February 1947. For other examples of successful pleas of inner migration, see BLHA, Rep. 203, Entnazifizierung, 371, P24, A2, 22 April 1947, and P38, A3, 11 July 1947; BLHA, Rep. 203, Entnazifizierung, 1429, P7, A2, 28 October 1947, and P9, A4, 31 October 1947; BLHA, Rep. 203, Entnazifizierung, 1431, P39, A4, 19 February 1948; BLHA, Rep. 203, Entnazifizierung, 431, P23, A14, 12 April 1947, and P25, A10, 21 April 1947.
55. BLHA, Rep. 203, 594, P161b, A6, 27 August 1947.
56. BLHA, Rep. 203, 584, P15, A9, 14 February 1947.
57. BLHA, Rep. 203, Entnazifizierung, 798, P2, A2, 10 October 1947.
58. Niethammer, *Mitläuferfabrik,* 609, 611.
59. BLHA, Rep. 203, 584, P15, A4, 14 February 1947.
60. BLHA, Rep. 203, Entnazifizierung, 431, P21, A10, 31 March 1947. Four additional cases, all approved, mention "fellow traveler" status as exoneration: BLHA, Rep. 203, Entnazifizierung, 431, P1, A4, 3 January 1947; BLHA, Rep. 203, Entnazifizierung, 1582, P1, A6, 30 September 1947, and P4, A13, 7 October 1947; BLHA, Rep. 203, Entnazifizierung, 371, P37, A6, 1 July 1947; BLHA, Rep. 203, Entnazifizierung, 1429, P3, A1, 14 October 1947.
61. BLHA, Rep. 203, Entnazifizierung, 644, Bl. 29, 23 September 1947.
62. Peukert, *Inside Nazi Germany,* 73; Kater, *Nazi Party,* 73, 158.
63. BLHA, Rep. 250, LRA Beeskow-Storkow, 344, Bl. 70, 18 November 1947.
64. BLHA, Rep. 203, 584, P5, A11, 21 January 1947; BLHA, Rep. 203, Entnazifizierung, 431, P6, A1, 23 January 1947, and P22, A4, 3 April 1947.
65. Kater noted that, especially during the war years, a PG "who took his membership seriously . . . had to conform to a pattern of behaviour that required ever greater service to the party as the war progressed. In return he could not expect to receive much, apart from an honorary party citation that did not even include a medal for his lapel." Kater, *Nazi Party,* 159.
66. BLHA, Rep. 203, 584, P17, A34, 18 February 1947.
67. BLHA, Rep. 203, 594, P159, A9, 22 August 1947; BLHA, Rep. 203, Entnazifizierung, 647, P7, A2, 8 October 1947.

68. See, for example, the cases of five nurses from Neuruppin who appeared before the Provincial Commission. BLHA, Rep. 203, 594, P157, A11–A16, 20 August 1947. In Pritzwalk (*Kreis* Ostprignitz) all nurses were apparently forced to join the NSDAP in 1935. See BLHA, Rep. 203, Entnazifizierung, 371, P35, A10, 13 June 1947.
69. BLHA, Rep. 203, Entnazifizierung, 431, P21, A4, 31 March 1947.
70. BLHA, Rep. 203, Entnazifizierung, 1429, P8, A10, 29 October 1947.
71. BLHA, Rep. 203, Entnazifizierung, 371, P14, A2, 7 March 1947.
72. BLHA, Rep. 203, Entnazifizierung, 1431, P36, A8.
73. Ibid., P35, A6, 23 December 1947.
74. Ibid., P34, A2–A3, 22 December 1947.
75. BLHA, Rep. 203, Entnazifizierung, 1583, P42, A15, 6 March 1948. The *Ortsbauernführer* was the rural equivalent of the *Blockwart*, charged with implementing Nazi agricultural policy and enforcing political conformity. See J. E. Farquharson, *The Plough and the Swastika: The NSDAP and Agriculture in Germany, 1928–1945* (London: Sage Publications, 1976), 71–73, 210.
76. In the data sample there are eighteen cases of compulsory transfer from the BDM to the NSDAP, eight of transfer from the HJ to the NSDAP, and fourteen from the SA to the NSDAP. According to SA regulations, party membership was mandatory, but there is evidence that this regulation was only laxly followed. In the period between 1933 and 1934, when the NSDAP had closed its membership rolls, the SA was actually "massively" recruiting new members. It has been estimated that, by 1934, only one quarter of SA members were also in the NSDAP. See Conan Fischer, *Stormtroopers: A Social, Economic, and Ideological Analysis, 1929–35* (London: George Allen and Unwin, 1983), 19.
77. Orlow, *History of the Nazi Party: 1933–1945,* 202.
78. BLHA, Rep. 203, Entnazifizierung, 647, P5, A15, 2 October 1947; BLHA, Rep. 203, Entnazifizierung, 648, P9, A2, 10 October 1947.
79. BLHA, Rep. 203, Entnazifizierung, 431, P13, A12–A17, 20 February 1947; P14, A7–A19, 24 February 1947.
80. BLHA, Rep. 203, Entnazifizierung, 371, P11, A2, 27 February 1947. The Nazis, beginning in 1933, instituted a scheme to reduce unemployment in the ranks of the SA as well as in the SS and Stahlhelm. See Fischer, *Stormtroopers,* 87.
81. BLHA, Rep. 203, Entnazifizierung, 1583, P38, A12, 1 March 1948.
82. BLHA, Rep. 203, Entnazifizierung, 371, P33, A13, 6 June 1947.
83. BLHA, Rep. 203, Entnazifizierung, 431, P25, A6, 21 April 1947.
84. Ibid., P22, A5, 3 April 1947.
85. "Directive 24," 144.
86. See, for example, BLHA, Rep. 203, 584, P7, A4, 28 January 1947; BLHA, Rep. 203, Entnazifizierung, 431, P21, A10, 31 March 1947; P36, A6, 30 June 1947; P38, A4, 21 July 1947; P41, A6, 25 August 1947.

87. For example, see BLHA, Rep. 203, 584, P8, A16, 4 February 1947; BLHA, Rep. 203, Entnazifizierung, 647, P3, A5, 30 September 1947; BLHA, Rep. 203, Entnazifizierung, 431, P28, A4, 5 May 1947, and P39, A7, 28 July 1947.

88. BLHA, Rep. 203, Entnazifizierung, 1429, P6, A2, 22 October 1947.

89. For examples of successful claims of pressure from a *Landrat,* see BLHA, Rep. 203, Entnazifizierung, 371, P19, A3, 28 March 1947; P25, A1, 25 April 1947; P28, A3, 5 May 1947. For *Ortsgruppenleiter,* see BLHA, Rep. 203, Entnazifizierung, 371, P12, A2, 28 February 1947. In Laaske (*Kreis* Ostprignitz), the *Ortsgruppenleiter* was known to have been "extraordinarily active and aggressive against people who did not belong to the party." BLHA, Rep. 203, Entnazifizierung, 371, P35, A3. In another case, a petitioner was doubly pressured by an *Ortsbauernführer* and an *Ortsgruppenleiter.* BLHA, Rep. 203, Entnazifizierung, 371, P16, A1, 11 March 1947.

90. BLHA, Rep. 203, Entnazifizierung, 371, P38, A5, 11 July 1947.

91. Ibid., P29, A3, 12 May 1947.

92. BLHA, Rep. 203, Entnazifizierung, 648, P11, A5, 15 October 1947.

93. BLHA, Rep. 203, Entnazifizierung, 1429, P10, A3, 1 November 1947.

94. Ibid., P3, A1, 14 October 1947.

95. Ibid., A2.

96. BLHA, Rep. 203, Entnazifizierung, 798, P6, A3, 25 October 1947.

97. Ibid., P7, A1, 28 October 1947.

98. Ibid., P3, A1, 14 October 1947.

99. BLHA, Rep. 203, Entnazifizierung, 647, P2, A7, 26 September 1947.

100. Ibid., P3, A11, 30 September 1947.

101. BLHA, Rep. 203, Entnazifizierung, 798, P1, A1, 7 October 1947.

102. BLHA, Rep. 203, Entnazifizierung, 648, P8, A4, 9 October 1947.

103. BLHA, Rep. 203, Entnazifizierung, 798, P7, A5, 28 October 1947.

104. BLHA, Rep. 203, Entnazifizierung, 648, P9, A6, 10 October 1947.

105. Ibid., P10, A8, 14 October 1947.

106. Ibid., P8, A3, 9 October 1947.

107. BLHA, Rep. 203, Entnazifizierung, 431, P22, A6, 3 April 1947.

108. BLHA, Rep. 203, Entnazifizierung, 647, P4, A8, 1 October 1947.

109. BLHA, Rep. 203, Entnazifizierung, 647, P3, A17, 30 September 1947.

110. BLHA, Rep. 203, Entnazifizierung, 798, P4, A1, 17 October 1947.

111. BLHA, Rep. 203, Entnazifizierung, 1582, P9, A1, 23 October 1947.

112. Niethammer, *Mitläuferfabrik,* 653.

113. Of 122 cases in the data sample, 92 (75.4 percent) were approved, 23 (18.9 percent) were given conditional approval, 7 were denied. Ten cases cite a lack of participation in reconstruction as incrimination: 7 were denied, 2 approved, 1 conditionally approved.

114. BLHA, Rep. 203, 594, P156, A9, 19 August 1947; P159, A3, 22 August 1947.

115. BLHA, Rep. 203, 596, P169, A25, 5 September 1947; BLHA, Rep. 203, Entnazifizierung, 431, P21, A8, 31 March 1947.
116. BLHA, Rep. 203, Entnazifizierung, 431, P24, A10, 14 April 1947.
117. BLHA, Rep. 203, Entnazifizierung, 431, P41, A1, 25 August 1947; P15, A12, 3 March 1947.
118. BLHA, Rep. 203, Entnazifizierung, 647, P5, A4, 2 October 1947.
119. See Bechler's opening remarks at a Provincial Commission hearing. BLHA, Rep. 203, 584, P5, 21 January 1947.
120. BLHA, Rep. 203, Entnazifizierung, 647, P4, A10, 1 October 1947.
121. BLHA, Rep. 203, Entnazifizierung, 648, P8, A10, 9 October 1947.
122. BLHA, Rep. 203, Entnazifizierung, 431, P21, A7, 31 March 1947.
123. BLHA, Rep. 203, Entnazifizierung, 801, P71, A1, 23 February 1948.
124. Ibid., A14.
125. BLHA, Rep. 203, Entnazifizierung, 798, P6, A5, 25 October 1947.
126. Ibid., P5, A1, 20 October 1947.

Conclusion

1. Jeffrey Herf, *Divided Memory: The Nazi Past in the Two Germanys* (Cambridge, Mass.: Harvard University Press, 1997).

Sources

Archival Sources

Berlin Landesarchiv (LA Berlin):
  United States Office of Military Government Berlin Sector (OMGBS): 4/17–
  1/2; 4/38–3/40.

Brandenburgisches Landeshauptarchiv, Potsdam (BLHA):
  Rep. 202A, Büro des Ministerpräsidenten: 39.
  Rep. 202G, Amt für Imformation: 150.
  Rep. 203, Ministerium für Inneres: 20; 21; 25; 28; 249; 311; 330; 332; 412;
    421; 583; 584; 594; 596; 600; 617; 629; 630; 631; 632; 810.
  Rep. 203, Entnazifizierung, Ministerium für Inneres: 1; 8; 15; 19; 71; 72; 371;
    431; 644; 645; 647; 648; 797; 798; 1429; 1431; 1582; 1583.
  Rep. 205A, Ministerium für Volksbildung: 104; 217; 346; 460.
  Rep. 206, Wirtschaftsministerium: 3016; 3063.
  Rep. 212, Minisertium der Justiz: 409; 500.
  Rep. 230, Oberlandratsämter (OLRA):
    OLRA Brandenburg/Havel: 4; 5; 6.
    OLRA Bernau: 13; 15; 69.
  Rep. 250, Landratsämter (LRA):
    LRA Angermünde: 252; 258; 262.
    LRA Beeskow-Storkow: 26; 27; 244; 343; 344; 3357.
    LRA Calau/Senftenberg: 57; 221; 223.
    LRA Cottbus: 195; 196; 197; 198.
    LRA Guben: 113; 115.
    LRA Lebus/Seelow: 53.
    LRA Lübben: 150; 151.

LRA Luckau: 556.
LRA Luckenwalde: 211.
LRA Ostprignitz: 50; 51; 59.
LRA Prenzlau: 31; 991.
LRA Ruppin: 68; 76; 543; 558; 637; 849.
LRA Spremberg: 97; 173.
Rep. 330, KPD Bezirksleitung, (BLHA-SED): I/2: 6; 10; 11; 12; 13; 15; I/3: 108; 165.
Rep. 332, SED Landesvorstand Brandenburg, (BLHA-SED): L/IV/2: 3, 23; 12, 825.

Bundesarchiv Potsdam, (BA-Potsdam):
Deutsche Zentralverwaltung für Volksbildung, DR2: 943; 1332.
Deutsche Verwaltung des Innern (DVdI): Bestand 7: 69; 81; 368; 421; 422; 423; 425; 431; 432; 433; 434; 435.

Kreisarchiv Ostprignitz, Kyritz (KA Ostprignitz): Stadtverwaltung Neustadt, SN3.

Kreisarchiv Ruppin, Neuruppin (KA Ruppin): Rat der Stadt Altruppin, I/A/2.1/7.

Stadtarchiv Brandenburg/Havel, (StA. Brandenburg/ Havel): 202, 27.

Stiftung Archiv der Parteien und Massorganizationen der DDR, Berlin, (SAPMO-BA):
Historisches Archiv der KPD, Bezirk Berlin-Brandenburg, Lausitz-Grenzmark: I/3/1–2: 114.
Historisches Archiv der KPD (Politbüro): I, 2/5: 40.
Zentralkomitee der SED, Abteilung Staat und Recht: IV, 2/13: 4; 6; 7; 109; 103; 226.
Max Fechner Nachlaß, (NL), 101: 19.
Wilhelm Pieck Nachlaß, (NL), 36: 684; 718.
Walter Ulbricht Nachlaß, (NL), 182: 853; 1197.

Government Publications

Allied Control Council. *Official Gazette of the Control Council for Germany.* Berlin: Berliner Kulturbuch-Vertrieb, 1946.
Landtag. der Mark Brandenburg. *Handbuch des Landtages des Landes Brandenburg.* Potsdam: Märkische Druck- und Verlags-GMBH., 1947.
———. *Akten und Verhandlungen des Landtags der Mark Brandenburg, 1946–1952.* Frankfurt: Keip Verlag: 1992.
Luckau Landratsamt (Luckau), *Luckauer Kreisblatt*, 1947.
Provinzialverwaltung Mark Brandenburg. *Ein Jahr Bewährung der Mark Brandenburg: Rückblick und Rechenschaft.* Potsdam: Verlag der Märkischen Volksstimme, 1946.

————*Direktive 24: Entfernung von Nationalsozialisten und Personen, die den Bestrebungen der Alliierten feindlich gegenüber stehen, aus Ämtern und verantwortlichen Stellungen.* Potsdam: Märkische Druck- und Verlags-GmbH., [1947].

————*Befehl Nr. 201 des Obersten Chefs der Sowjetischen Militärverwaltung und Ausführungsbestimmungen 1–3, Direktiven 24 und 38 des Kontrollrats und die zugehörigen Runderlasse der Landesregierung Brandenburg.* Potsdam: Landesregierung Brandenburg Minister des Innern, [1947].

————*Verordnungsblatt der Provinzialverwaltung Mark Brandenburg (VOBl.),* 1945–1948.

Ostprignitz Landratsamt (Kyritz). *Nachrichtenblatt des Landratsamte des Kreises Ostprignitz,* 1945–1946.

Provinzausschuß der Gegenseitigen Bauernhilfe Mark Brandenburg. *Parlament der Bauern: Erster Provinz-Kongress der Gegenseitigen Bauernhilfe der Mark Brandenburg am 16. und 17. März 1946 in Potsdam.* Potsdam: Verlag Märkische Volksstimme, [1946].

Ruppin Landratsamt (Neuruppin). *Ruppiner Kreisblatt,* 1947–48.

Newspapers

Deutsche Volkszeitung (Berlin), 1945–46.
Märkische Volksstimme (Potsdam), 1947–48.
Neues Deutschland (Berlin), 1946–1948.
Tägliche Rundschau (Berlin), 1946–1948.
Volkswille (Potsdam), 1945–46.

Published Primary Sources and Document Collections

Bechler, Margret. *Warten auf Antwort: Ein deutsches Schicksal.* Rev. ed. Frankfurt: Ulstein, 1990.

Beck, Friedrich et al., eds. *Ausgewählte Dokumente und Materialien zum antifaschistischen Widerstandskampf unter Führung der Kommunistischen Partei Deutschlands in der Provinz Brandenburg, 1939–1945.* Part II. Potsdam: Druckerei Märkische Volksstimme, 1985.

Berthold, Lothar, and Ernst Diehl, eds. *Revolutionäre deutsche Parteiprogramme: Von Kommunistischen Manifest zum Programm des Sozialismus.* Berlin: Dietz Verlag, 1967.

Bloch, Peter. *Zwischen Hoffnung und Resignation: Als CDU Politiker in Brandenburg, 1945–1950.* Cologne: Verlag Wissenschaft und Politik, 1986.

Buchwitz, Otto. *Brüder in eins nun die Hände.* Berlin: Dietz Verlag, 1956.

Clay, Lucius D. *Decision in Germany.* New York: Doubleday, 1950.

Communist International. *VII Congress of the Communist International: Abridged Stenographic Report of Proceedings.* Moscow: Foreign Languages Publishing House, 1939.

Deutsche Wirtschaftskommission für die sowjetische Besatzungszone, Statistisches Zentralamt. *Volks-und Berufszählung vom 29. Oktober 1946.* Berlin: Deutscher Zentralverlag, 1948.

Dokumente der Sozialistischen Einheitspartei Deutschlands. Berlin: Deitz Verlag, 1952.

Ebert, Friedrich. *Einheit der Arbeiterklasse—Unterpfand des Sieges: Ausgewählte Reden und Aufsätze.* Berlin: Dietz Verlag, 1959.

———"Wir erfülten unsere historische Aufgabe." In *Vereint sind wir alles: Erinnerungen an die Gründung der SED,* 509–524. Berlin: Dietz Verlag, 1971.

Erler, Peter, Horst Laude, and Manfred Wilke, eds. *"Nach Hitler kommen wir": Dokumente zur Programmatik der Moskauer KPD-Führung 1944/45 für Nachkriegsdeutschland.* Berlin: Akademie Verlag, 1994.

Freundschaft DDR-UdSSR: Dokumente und Materialien. Berlin: Dietz Verlag, 1965.

Gniffke, Erich. *Jahre mit Ulbricht.* Cologne: Verlag Wissenschaft und Politik, 1966.

Lenin, V. I. *State and Revolution.* New York: International Publishers, 1932.

Leonhard, Wolfgang. *Die Revolution entlässt Ihre Kinder.* Cologne: Verlag Kiepenheuer & Witsch, 1955.

Mammach, Klaus, ed. *Die Berner Konferenz der KPD (30. Januar–1.Februar 1939).* Berlin: Dietz Verlag, 1974.

———*Die Brüsseler Konferenz der KPD (3.–15. Oktober 1935).* Berlin: Dietz Verlag, 1975.

Molotov, V. M. *Problems of Foreign Policy: Speeches and Statements, April 1945–November 1948.* Moscow: Foreign Languages Publishing House, 1949.

Pieck, Wilhelm. *Gesammelte Reden und Schriften,* Vol. 6. Berlin: Dietz Verlag, 1979.

Rau, Heinrich. *Aus eigener Kraft: Wirtschaftsplan 1946 für die Landwirtschaft der Mark Brandenburg.* Potsdam: Verlag "Der Märker," [1946].

———*Für die Arbeiter- und Bauern-Macht: Ausgewählte Reden und Aufsätze, 1922–1961.* Berlin: Dietz Verlag, 1984.

Reinert, Fritz, ed. *Protokolle des Landesblockausschusses der antifaschistisch-demokratischen Parteien Brandenburgs, 1945–1950.* Weimar: Verlag Hermann Böhlaus, 1994.

Riazanskii, A. P. *Vogne Tankovykh Srazhenii.* Moscow: Nauka, 1975.

Rößler, Ruth-Kristin, ed. *Die Entnazifizierungspolitik der KPD/SED, 1945–1948: Dokumente und Materialen.* Goldbach: Keip Verlag, 1994.

Rücker, Fritz. "Neue Schule, neue Lehrer—ein neuer Geist in Potsdam." In *Die Ersten Jahre: Erinnerungen an den Beginn der revolutionären Umgestaltung,* 303–319. Berlin: Dietz Verlag, 1979.

Ruhm von Oppen, Beate, ed. *Documents on Germany under Occupation, 1945–1954.* London: Oxford University Press, 1955.

Sägebrecht, Willy. *Nicht Anboß, sondern Hammer sein: Erinnerungen.* Berlin: Dietz Verlag, 1976.

Selbmann, Fritz. "Die sowjetischen Genosssen waren Freunde und Helfer." In *Vereint sind wir alles: Erinnerungen an die Gründung der SED*, 329–348. Berlin: Dietz Verlag, 1971.

Sozialistische Einheitspartei Deutschlands. *Dokumente der Sozialistischen Einheitspartei Deutschlands.* Vol. 2. Berlin: Dietz Verlag, 1952.

Stalin, J. V. *Works.* Vol. 6. Moscow: Foreign Languages Publishing House, 1953.

Steinhoff, Karl. "Das Land Brandenburg in den ersten Nachkriegsjahren." *Märkische Heimat* 3 (1959): 138–145.

Ulbricht, Walter. *Zur Geschichte der neuesten Zeit: Die Niederlage Hitlerdeutschlands und die Schaffung der antifaschistisch-demokratischen Ordnung.* Berlin: Dietz Verlag, 1955.

————*Zur Geschichte der Deutschen Arbeiterbewegung: Aus Reden und Aufsätzen.* Berlin: Dietz Verlag, 1963.

Um ein antifaschististisch-demokratisches Deutschland: Dokumente aus den Jahren 1945–1949. Berlin: Staatsverlag der Deutschen Demokratischen Republik, 1968.

Weber, Hermann, ed. *Der deutsche Kommunismus: Dokumente.* Cologne: Kipenheuer & Witsch, 1963.

————ed. *Die Kommunistische Internationale: Ein Dokumentation.* Hannover: Verlag J. H. W. Dietz, 1966.

Weinert, Erich. *Das Nationalkomitee "Freies Deutschland," 1943–1945: Bericht über seine Tätigkeit und seine Auswirkung.* Berlin: Rütten & Loening, 1957.

Index